2/15/17

To
Kathy
Blessings on your
Journey
Mekennoch.

MANDALA-365

A DAILY WORKBOOK OF HOLISTIC HEALING

DR. M. P. KHAN, MD/NMD

BALBOA.
PRESS
A DIVISION OF HAY HOUSE

Balboa Press books may be ordered through booksellers or by contacting:

Balboa Press
A Division of Hay House
1663 Liberty Drive
Bloomington, IN 47403
www.balboapress.com
1 (877) 407-4847

Because of the dynamic nature of the Internet, any web addresses or links contained in this book may have changed since publication and may no longer be valid. The views expressed in this work are solely those of the author and do not necessarily reflect the views of the publisher, and the publisher hereby disclaims any responsibility for them.

The author of this book does not dispense medical advice or prescribe the use of any technique as a form of treatment for physical, emotional, or medical problems without the advice of a physician, either directly or indirectly. The intent of the author is only to offer information of a general nature to help you in your quest for emotional and spiritual well-being. In the event you use any of the information in this book for yourself, which is your constitutional right, the author and the publisher assume no responsibility for your actions.

Any people depicted in stock imagery provided by Thinkstock are models, and such images are being used for illustrative purposes only.
Certain stock imagery © Thinkstock.

Print information available on the last page.

ISBN: 978-1-5043-6618-2 (sc)
ISBN: 978-1-5043-6620-5 (hc)
ISBN: 978-1-5043-6619-9 (e)

Balboa Press rev. date: 11/01/2016

Dedicated to all my teachers and my patients.
They taught me the lessons I needed to learn.

DISCLAIMER FOR *"MANDALA-365/ A DAY BOOK FOR HOLISTIC HEALING."*

* All material published in print or digital format is protected by U.S. copyright laws and is available only to subscribers of MANDALA-365 and cannot be reproduced or shared in paper, digital, cyber or audio-visual format without express permission from the author.

** All materials published in "MANDALA-365" are for information purposes only and not a substitute for advice from a health professional. All information is screened for accuracy but because of the nature of complimentary/alternative medicine with new research emerging constantly, some of the data may be outdated or inaccurate at time of publication. The publishers/author of MANDALA-365 will make every effort to update data, on an ongoing basis.

*** All supplements in MANDALA-365 are referenced to 'Douglas Labs: HVL.' This manufacturer of supplements has been carefully selected (and I use them personally) because of their use by my patients for the last fifteen years with good efficacy and safety. I have given careful consideration to their quality and GMP (Good Manufacturing Practices) and can recommend their products without any reservations for support in various health related issues.

Although there are several reputable companies manufacturing high quality supplements, it is not logistically possible for me to review all the products that you may be using form these providers. Instead I will suggest products for your particular health concerns from the Douglas Labs catalogue and will leave the decision for their use (or other comparable products) to you. I hold no stock or a direct financial interest in this company.

If you wish to order their products, follow the below steps:

1) Look up the specific product that I have recommended on their web site at *www.douglaslabs.com*. Call the toll free number below.

Be sure to check out the science behind their products and the research references.

2) Call toll free week days 1-(877) 666-6408 to establish an account and identify yourself as a patient/student of Dr M. P. Khan. You cannot establish an account on the web so this is a crucial step! Also Douglas Labs does not sell directly to the general public.

3) Give a reference number of 2138203 and place your order. Make sure you ask for a 10% discount and a flat shipping fee. Most orders are fulfilled in 2 working days but some popular products may be on back order and delayed in their delivery.

4) If you have any specific concerns about a supplement, ask to speak with their onsite product specialists. I have found them very helpful in assisting clients through the sometimes confusing maze of ingredients and their uses that are found in supplements.

Foreword

There is good news *and* not so good news. The good news is that most of us can expect a much longer life expectancy than the thousands of generations that preceded us. The not so good news is that more modern humans than ever, confront a growing burden of chronic, complex disease. *It has been said that we live too short and we die too long.* No one can deny the exploding epidemic of obesity, diabetes, hypertension, heart disease, cancer, autoimmunity, autism, depression, anxiety, substance abuse and addiction, etc. These epidemics have exploded right before our eyes over the last two generations while at the same time more money has been spent on attempting to keep the fire under control. One out of two American adults is confronting at least one (and many with multiple) chronic complex disease. Modern medicine has lengthened life expectancy with chronic disease and all too often, the quality of life suffers profoundly. So common is the trajectory of a diminished quality of life that it is natural to assume that getting old means slowing down, hurting more, having less energy, taking more medications and waving goodbye to a quality of life that seems available only to the young.

Mark Twain once said, "It's not what we don't know that gets us into trouble. It's *what we know that ain't so*". We are in the midst of a knowledge revolution. Our current systems of education, governance and policy, and public health- medical guidelines are not nimble enough to translate the rapid shifts in our understanding of who we are as modern humans and how we function within the complex relationships with our natural world. This explosion of knowledge is revealing many challenges to *"what we know that ain't so"*. Effective self-care requires having the courage to question and challenge long-held beliefs that may not be serving you well. Noteworthy examples of *"things we know that ain't so."* include:

- *I can't do anything about the genes I have inherited.* The burgeoning field of epigenetics suggests we are not prisoners of our DNA. Our genes indeed form a powerful blueprint but it is our lifestyle that ultimately influences how our genes express themselves. If a parent (or other family members) had a chronic disease e.g. depression, diabetes or cancer, it does not mean you are destined for the same. As important, if you have a diagnosis shared by a parent or grandparent, it does not mean you are stuck with it. Lifestyle can trump that which you may have inherited. Wow!

- *Germs are bad!* The human microbiome refers to the thousand-plus species of bacteria that reside with, on and inside us. Germs, universally viewed as health threats, can powerfully promote human health when these complex ecosystems on our skin, in our mouths and in our guts are in balance and harmony with the hosts they inhabit. The balance and diversity of this ecosystem drives health and disease and is entirely under the influence of lifestyle. Who would have thought?

- *If I consume fewer calories than I burn I will successfully lose weight and keep it off.* As it turns out, eating less and exercising more i.e. burning more calories than consuming, worthy as it may seem is a message that is both ineffective and impossible to sustain. The knowledge of the "new medicine" suggests that what matters most is the quality of our calories not the quantity. In this radical shift, caloric content means little if the food is whole and unprocessed. The shift here is not eating to lose weight but eating to be healthy. The weight piece will follow.

- *Low-fat is good for me*: Most low-fat nutrition is very high in refined and processed carbohydrates e.g. grain-based flour, sugar, etc. that has done more to fuel our current epidemic of obesity and chronic complex disease than it has helped. Eating much more quality fat from less toxic sources e.g. grass fed butter, beef, eggs, bacon, ghee, avocados, nuts, fatty fish, extra virgin olive and coconut oils, etc. For most, more fat from quality sources will dramatically improve health. Say what?

These are just a few examples that remind us to take inventory of what is working in our lives and what isn't. Effective self-care is as much about unlearning as it is learning. We know that lifestyle contributes to at least 75% of all health issues we confront! From that perspective, all care is ultimately, self-care. We all need good doctors and public health systems to support our health and well-being. However at the end of the day, healthy living does not happen at doctor's offices. It does not happen at hospitals or in ambulatory surgery centers. The road to healthy living in its final analysis, is paved by the choices we make each and every moment i.e., how we eat; how we move, how we sleep; how we interpret and respond to stress in our lives; how much meaning we cultivate in our work, love and play; how we manage our exposure to environmental toxins; how socially connected we are; how we navigate the minefields of conflict, etc. These are dimensions of our lives that speak to our genes and to our microbiome in a manner that will produce health or undermine health. Ultimately, we can choose to *engage* our lives or to *endure* our lives.

In *Mandala-365/A Daily Workbook of Holistic Healing*, Dr. Mehernosh Khan, a wise and experienced primary care provider, poet, and holistic healer with a remarkable lifetime of commitment to helping others, reminds us that what was once old is new again. Dr. Khan understands the root causes that interfere with one's capacity to thrive and addresses them in an enlightened mosaic of cutting edge science, ancient wisdom, and entertaining anecdotes. He has truly crafted an engaging and pragmatic roadmap for anyone seeking more traction in his or her lives.

The accessible and bite-size portions he has created make the journey less overwhelming. While reading Mandala-365 it is impossible not to imagine you are walking with Dr. Khan in a very personal way. One cannot help but feel you are a close friend, the beneficiary of a lifetime of accumulated wisdom. Each day, week and month introduces beautifully woven pearls of wisdom from the fields of nutrition, mindfulness, exercise physiology, social psychology, the arts, and community-connection. The journey you are about to embark on will truly be a holistic one. Mind, Body, Spirit, and Community are the prism through which this remarkable guide has been translated.

The project of self-care is a serious commitment. In this "new medicine" you become the healer of you. It requires an ongoing commitment to learning and unlearning. It requires the awareness to test cause and effect. We sometimes refer to the N=1. Unlike most published medical research that examines groups of people, this journey requires your willingness to change or add something to your life and to witness the consequence.

You are biologically unique! With your doctor you become a co-investigator. This is not about right or wrong. No place for judgement here. Dr. Khan reminds us that the wisdom we need is alive and well in each of us. The most powerful interventions in our lives are "low tech" and more accessible than we realize. Our challenge as modern humans is to transcend the distractions of our lives in order to more fully connect to that wisdom. This can only happen if we pay more full attention to who we are, with love, compassion and empathy. Mandala-365/A Daily Workbook of Holistic Healing will help show you the way! This could not have come at a better time.

Mark C. Pettus MD

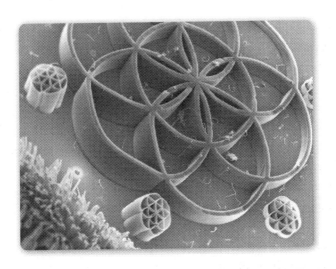

Introduction

In a very real sense, each of us is a mandala. Some of us have intricate patterns and colors reflecting the complex experiences of our lives. Some of us are clean arcs of existence with minimalist designs and subtle colors. And every possible combination in between, each as unique as our individual DNA; which strangely on electron microscopy in cross-section looks like a mandala!

But unlike our DNA, our mandalas are constantly shifting shapes and colors as we make our choices as to the best way to live our lives. All designs of the mandala have a border, the interface we have with each other and the material world. And each mandala has a center, the singularity, where the trinity of Mind, Body and Spirit integrates and unites with the divine self.

My medical school in India (established almost 150 years ago by the British) had a crest with the Latin words inscribed below:

"MENS SANO EN CORPORO SANO"

Which is loosely translated as "A Healthy Mind in a Healthy Body." To that I would also add "SPIRITOS SANO" or "Healthy Spirit." This trifecta of a fully integrated Mind, Body and Spirit will be the Holy Grail of the future of medicine as expressed by the "Integrated Model" of practice that this entire book is dedicated to!

MANDALA-365 is also a journey of transformation and like most journeys it is unique in its sights and sounds. To misquote Forrest Gump of movie fame, "it is like a box of chocolates!" You never know what each day will bring into your consciousness. And like any collection of this nature, some of the chocolates may not be to your liking. But someday, when you least expect it, the information or the lesson of that day could be useful to you. So try to *keep an open mind* about this and chew on the wisdom-candy for another day. And as someone cracked after this much used cliché: *"But don't let your brains fall out!"*

I have tried to share, not only what I have learned about medicine over thirty-five years of practice, but also what lessons that living has revealed to me; lessons that have not always been pleasant. But it is fire that tempers steel! In that sense, this collection of parables, poetry and practical approaches to using alternative medicine approaches, is in some ways autobiographical. This book came into fruition on the urging of several of my patients who were also my teachers. They have educated me about human nature, and the incredible power of the mind to hurt and heal, more than any text book of medicine ever could. This book is dedicated to them. I thank you!

And this is also a "Work-Book" with the emphasis on that four letter word, 'WORK." All transformation requires an effort on our part. So this is not a program that will change your life in "Seven Easy Steps" or "A 21 Day Program" to an enlightened way of living! In fact, this "WORK" could take the rest of your living days and this book may be just a starting point in realizing your true potential. Remember, we are all perfect but we are also 'works' in progress. In the end, you and this effort, will be worth it!

Following most days of revelation, is an exercise that you may want to complete. I have sometimes spread out a single topic over several days so as to avoid cramming it into a single day. This helps to breakdown an intense or complicate subject matter into bite sized segments. The intent is to open you up to the unbound possibilities of who you could be. The journey towards optimal health is not just a combination of taking the right supplements or some obscure yoga pose; in the final analysis it is the journey that defines our humanity. As you read the pages, try to relish and reflect on the process and not the destination.

Because the destination is an illusion; it is really a starting point for yet another journey.

NAMASTE

Mehernosh P Khan MD/NMD

FYI: **'Chairman Moo'** is my alter ego as Editor of my medical school weekly and bears no relation to that Chinese revolutionary and author of a famed red book! The above image is a representation of a scanning electron image of a cross-section of DNA.

A special thanks to Tony Segal, friend and neighbor for his exhaustive and constructive pre-publication review of this book.

JANUARY

WHY A DAY BOOK?

"The longest journey begins with a single step."
—Anon

It is the first day of a New Year. I just finished reading a book of spiritual teachings by Mark Nepo (*The Book of Awakening: Having the Life you Want by Being Present to the Life You Have*).Written in a daybook form, it has a certain synchronicity. Initially I had planned to have a text book approach to various topics in the area of a holistic and integrated approach to health care. Several issues made me reconsider:

One: There already existed several worthy tomes on the subject. And the end result would be a dry and hefty volume of facts which would sit quietly on some shelf. I wanted this book to be a friend and companion. Something you could read on your smart phone or tablet on the bus or at home and share with your friends and fellow passengers!

Two: The subject matter was very fluid with research data touted as scientific gospel only to be later overturned as false heresy. Someone once wisely quipped *"Ten years after you graduate from medical school, you will realize that one-third of what you learnt is now found to be untrue. Only then, you didn't know what that one-third was!"*

Three: I would be presenting myself as an authority in an area of medicine that is in its infancy and promises to grow into a valid and meaningful system of not only health care in a physical sense, but also in broader terms, a way to live a life, fully integrating our spiritual and emotional beings. We are all muddling through the difficult work of merging our inner and outer lives. Besides there are enough New Age Gurus out there filling the airwaves and print media with the *idea du jour*. Resveratrol anyone? **We are each on a journey in finding our own unique inner healer.** I wanted this book to be a gentle guide, a map with several paths, and with the full understanding of what the term "holistic" means if that was to be our final destination.

These three objections prompted me to write this book in the form of a daily work book composed of good advice based on the ***best science available (for now anyway) towards our physical well-being; parables that help us make sense of the chaos of the human condition; and finally of the power of poetry and great literature to nourish our spirit.*** After all, we are fellow travelers on this path and who knows what strange wonders and great beauty awaits us!

And finally the healing journey requires some *work* on your part, hence the sub-title. A process that will have its own rewards as the days and months go by. Moving towards the final goal of finding your inner healer, each day of information is mostly followed by an exercise that is to be completed. And this part will not always be easy as it will require accessing some deep (and sometimes dark) corners of your soul.

WHY A DAY BOOK?

Record three goals that you would like to achieve at the end of the year. Make them reasonable and modest. Even the ascent of Mount Everest needed several base camps.

In my goals towards physical well-being I would like to:

Get rid back pam
Holister foods - suplements
+ exerk
Cont relat + sleep well

Towards evolving in my emotional growth I would like to:

Seize the day - don't say no to chances +
have to be z oekes   Try sping no
                                      commelments
MY core - Strong - worthy
Find love - get out there

For the growth of my spiritual life I would like to:

Have more faith + hope
Be kinder - not Critical words
Know am not responsility for others

MAKE COPIES/PRINTOUTS OF THIS PAGE AND POST IT ON YOUR REFRIGERATOR AND ON A PROMINENT LOCATION AT WORK.

January 3

SPIRITUALITY IS A NO-NO

*"We are spiritual beings having
a human experience."*

—Anon

I am convinced that a lot of emotional dysfunction that I see walking through my office doors is a result of a kind of spiritual bankruptcy. I do not sit in judgment. I have seen this in my personal life and with disastrous consequences; to myself and to those who were close to me. When we lose our moral compass, who knows onto what shore our boat will end up on! As healers, realizing its importance, we should feel comfortable asking about our patient's spiritual beliefs and accept them regardless of our personal biases. And as a patient, no matter what your religious disposition is, be able to share them with your healers as part of the healing process.

This poem (or prayer) came to me one afternoon. Since then I have shared it with many of my colleagues and patients. It is an aspiration, not an absolute.

A HEALER'S PRAYER:

*As this day begins,
Guide my heart, hands and mind.
Let my heart be full of compassion;
Let my hands be sure and steady;
Let my mind be calm and clear.*

*If the privilege of knowledge makes me arrogant;
If the wealth of experience makes me callous;
Help me remember that I am the emissary of the Ultimate Physician,
Blessed with the gift of healing,
Shared with all that seek it.*

DR. M. P. KHAN, MD/NMD

And as this day ends,
If all my science and will cannot conquer death,
Help me understand the inevitability of living.
Let me then transcend my role as healer,
And share the pain and glory of our common humanity.

MK/2008

* Spirituality as defined by our personal relationship to a higher power as a result of our life experiences vs. religious teachings and dogma.

SPIRITUALITY IS A NO-NO

As a healer or an individual seeking healing, at this time of your life what are your spiritual beliefs? How have they changed over time? How do they fit with your religious upbringing?

_____

_____

_____

_____

_____

_____

_____

_____

_____

_____

Do your spiritual/religious beliefs help or hinder the healing process? How?

_____

_____

_____

_____

_____

_____

_____

_____

_____

_____

January 5

A SECOND OPINION!

"The patient should be the center of the medical universe."
—Osler

I have a cartoon placed in a small corner of where patients check in. It shows a young man perched on the exam table holding a sheaf of printouts from a dubious website confronting a visibly alarmed doctor. The caption reads:

"I already know what my problem is Doc! I just want a second opinion!"

Hidden between the chuckles that this little vignette elicits there is a dilemma. Do we challenge the patient with our hard earned facts and debunk all, but what the current state of knowledge and medical research advises us is the standard of care? Or do we validate or at least acknowledge that the patient may have their own set of beliefs? That buried in all those printouts and half-truths, there may be gleanings of information that may help in understanding the unique dysfunction of that unique individual before us.

All medical interactions are basically a dialogue between a *person* who needs healing and a *person* who is perceived to have the knowledge to provide that healing. This basic tenet is true from the shaman with his ancient chants and magical herbs and potions to the super-sub-specialist adorned with the full power of the high tech tools of modern medicine. The key word is PERSON and the only real separation between the patient and the physician/shaman is *knowledge*.

This is not to denigrate the years of training and self-discipline needed to achieve this knowledge. It is when this knowledge is attached to ego that it becomes a form of hubris. Instead of a free flowing spring that nourishes healing, it is frozen into dogma. There is no more dialogue, only a pedantic monologue. But this paradigm has already shifted! Gone are the days of the authoritarian parent figure with sage advice about losing weight and to quit smoking as he/she subtly flicks the ashes of a Camel cigarette and adjusts his/her ample behind on the exam stool. No longer a passive bystander; today's patient is fully armed with information garnered from the media, the internet and medical advice from five other friends as to what his/her medical condition is.

And they expect us to walk the walk, not just talk the talk.

In other words: *Are we as physicians/ shamans/healers prepared to accept patients as our partners in the healing process and to use our mutual knowledge base as a scaffold, integrating the hard science of medicine with the common and yet different healing journey of the individual? And are we prepared to accept our own crucial, and sometimes difficult, journey of healing?*

January 6

A SECOND OPINION!

As a physician/shaman how would you answer the above question?

_____
_____
_____
_____
_____
_____
_____

As a patient, what is your experience when you have expressed interest in a healing partnership?

_____
_____
_____
_____
_____
_____
_____

As a patient or a physician, how would you overcome the barriers that block a healing partnership?

_____
_____
_____
_____
_____
_____
_____

TO 'D-3' OR NOT TO 'D-3'?

"Let the sunshine in, let the sunshine in"
—*"Hair,"* the musical.

Looking out on my dreary snow covered backyard and another 6 inches predicted, Vitamin D, also known as the 'sunshine' vitamin, is an appropriate reminder that the brightness of summer and the overhead equatorial sun are where our ancestors started their great migrations to the northern climes. A stark contrast to the weak winter sun, low in the January sky, most of its ultra violet light absorbed by the ozone layer. It is the magic of special organelles in the skin and UV light that manufactures Vitamin D, which is not a vitamin at all. It is really a hormone (like Insulin) and under the right conditions the body makes almost 10,000 units in about 10 minutes of exposure to direct summer sun or about the time you take for a leisurely walk to the mailbox and back. The other sources of this vitamin are foods such as fatty fish, (especially wild salmon) dairy and eggs.

The limiting factors to production by the skin are pigmentation and UV light. The darker your skin, the less the production of Vitamin D as the melanin in the skin blocks UV light. Also the higher the latitude you live in, the less UV light gets through, also decreasing its production. The use of sunscreen with a high SPF (Sun Protective Factor) has the same effect. With the bogey man of skin cancer, it is no longer advisable to get prolonged and direct exposure to sunlight. As a result there is an almost endemic deficiency of Vitamin D.

As physicians we should be offering our patients a blood test to check these levels and most labs charge around $20-$30 for a basic 25-OH Vitamin D level ordered as a total Vitamin D level. Most insurance plans cover this test with the right diagnostic codes. It is not necessary to get the complete panel.

DR. M. P. KHAN, MD/NMD

Over the last year I did a study which can be easily replicated if you practice in the northern latitudes. I started checking Vitamin D levels on most of my adult patients in my practice. There was almost a universal insufficiency with most levels in the low 20's range (a deficiency is a level below 20: normal range 30-100) independent of the time of year. The lowest level I have seen recently is '4' in an African American working the night shift!

As a result, at least in this geographical area, I recommend supplementation with 5000 units/day of D3 in the winter months (Nov-March) and 3000/units/day the rest of the year with measurements every 6 months to a year apart till the level reaches into the 50's. I recommend the D3 form also known as cholecalciferol. It is very inexpensive and averages about 1-2 cents per 1000 unit dose and a lot cheaper than a winter getaway to the sunny Bahamas. And even if you are one of the docs who believe that vitamins are a lot of hokum, this one is a keeper. Try the dose of 3000-5000 units of D3 for yourself on a daily basis. One of its benefits is its mood elevating effect (the winter blahs!) and it also boosts the immune system.

TO 'D' OR NOT TO 'D'

Ask your physician about ordering a baseline test to be included as part of your routine chemistry tests before cranking up your intake of Vitamin D3 in the form of supplements. There are certain medical conditions (kidney stones, sarcoidosis, some diseases of the kidney) that may require careful monitoring of Vitamin D levels or even complete avoidance.

What is your baseline Total Vitamin D level?

_____

What is your level after Vitamin D supplementation for a 3-6 month period?

_____

How do you feel physically and emotionally after a 3-6 month period of Vitamin D supplementation?

_____

_____

_____

_____

_____

What is your average daily Vitamin D intake from your food sources?

_____

_____

_____

_____

January 9

JUST CAN'T LOSE THOSE
10 POUNDS, DOC!

"Make Food your Medicine and
Medicine your Food."

—**Hippocrates**

A Zen master gave a willow branch to two of his students. Their job was to bend the branch into a perfect circle.

One of the students was overly zealous to please the master and started bending the willow branch impatiently. To his dismay, the branch snapped and he vehemently declared to the Zen master that this was impossible and was very angry that he was assigned this task.

The other student was more patient. Every day he bent the willow branch just a little. As the months went by, he never mentioned the task to anyone. And one day as they were gathered around the Zen master, he presented with a flourish, the willow branch bent into a perfect circle.

Every day in my practice I see patients who want to make positive changes in their lifestyles and especially with weight loss. True to the above parable, there is a tendency to bend the willow branch too quickly. There is this great effort to exercise frequently, dramatically cut down on calories and read up on and follow whatever diet craze that is currently popular. And human nature, being what it is, those efforts fizzles out after a few weeks. After all how much grapefruit or watermelon can you possibly eat? And all you dream about is apple pie and French fries if you get my drift. The branch is broken and this is followed by the inevitable guilt followed by the feeling; *why even bother.* Before we get to the specifics of what foods etc. we need to really look at the behavior of eating if we are to succeed with weight loss.

So let me give you the 4 Golden Rules about changing behavior, ANY behavior.

First: Believe you can do it! Remember the time you were in great shape!

Second: Make a very small change. Take the stairs instead of the elevator at work. Drink one less can of pop. You get the picture!

Third: Be consistent with that change. Studies show that it takes between 3-6 months to make that behavior a part of your lifestyle. So be 'patient.'

Fourth: If you slip up it's not the end of the world. Learn from it and get back on the saddle. Before you could ride a bike, there were the inevitable falls and scrapes!

Over the next few days I plan to lay out some suggestions for healthy eating patterns that are entirely focused on lifestyle changes. So put those miserable bathroom scales away and get ready to have some fun with your food.

JUST CAN'T LOSE THOSE
10 POUNDS, DOC!

When was the last time you felt really good about yourself?

_____

What was it that felt good? Be very specific.

_____
_____
_____
_____

What small change/changes would you like to make? Again be specific and at the same time be realistic.

_____
_____
_____
_____

What plans do you have to sustain this change over the next 3-6 months?

_____
_____
_____
_____

What strategy do you have in the event of a slip up? How do you plan to get back on track?

_____
_____
_____
_____

MANGA LIKE A CRO-MAGNON

"My soul is dark with stormy riot, directly
traceable to this diet."
—Samuel Hoffenstein

Repeat this mantra after me; *"Diets don't work."* One more time, *"Diets don't work."* The large number of diets and weight loss programs that are out there speaks to that; a JAMA study on various diet programs showed that one of the few weight loss programs that *maintained* weight loss at the end of one year was Weight Watchers. Almost all other commercial weight loss programs failed to do so. As a result we have a billion dollar weight loss industry which is designed to fail so it can generate the next billion dollars. So the next time you want to buy a book on some diet making the rounds on daytime TV, *don't*. Put it back on the shelf.

Over the next few months, I will outline some suggestions to help you with your quest. I would suggest you take each recommendation and try to implement it in your daily life. The focus is more on changing the pattern of eating rather than numbers of pounds lost, with the goal of making meaningful and sustainable lifetime changes.

#1: Eat like your great grandparents.

Kerin O'Dea, a research physiologist, took ten Australian Aborigines with Metabolic Syndrome (high blood pressure, diabetes, high cholesterol and obesity) living in an urban setting and returned them to their Hunter Gatherer ways.

Within 7 weeks most of their abnormal labs normalized. Just to prove that this was not a fluke she repeated this experiment in Native Americans and native Hawaiians with similar results. Would it not be nice if we could all do that? Unfortunately we would have to give up our day jobs and besides we don't have the skills to live in the bush.

More likely we would be the main course!

At the time of writing of this book, there are several books published on the Paleo-Diet. So let's take a look at the Paleolithic diet of this guy or gal about 40,000 years ago: The typical items on the menu had:

No food additives.
Half the fat.
Twice the calcium (no milk in the diet)
One-sixth the salt.
Three times the potassium.
Four times the Vitamin C.
Six times the fiber and Higher B vitamins and Minerals.

January 12

MANGA LIKE A CRO-MAGNON

Sounds like a real healthy way of eating. And without the knowledge of the mysterious Food Pyramid and without the benefit of any Neanderthal diet gurus. They just ate what they found naturally occurring in their environment. Of course all this changed with the advent of agriculture and farming.

How to manga like a Cro-Magnon!

The next time you go to a grocery store, get in touch with your inner cave-man! If you were a hunter gatherer, make a list of what groceries you would buy/gather for your next meal? (Fire was already invented! Plastic wrap was not!)

Hint: All these items are in the periphery of the store. And NO; chocolate chip cookies don't grow on trees.

_____

_____

_____

_____

_____

_____

_____

_____

_____

_____

_____

_____

_____

_____

_____

_____

DR. M. P. KHAN, MD/NMD

I AM NOT A VITAMIN (D), REALLY!

"To all my little Hulkamaniacs, say your prayers, take your vitamins and you will never go wrong."
—Hulk Hogan

It seems that everybody is talking about Vitamin D. No other form of supplementation has stirred up this much excitement and controversy. I cannot pick up a journal or a popular magazine without mention of some research article touting the wonders of this Vitamin. In the entry of January 4th, I briefly mentioned the need for checking levels and adequate supplementation. You may have noticed that the amount I recommended far exceeded the RDA (400-800 units) or required daily allowance. Keep in mind that this is the amount needed to prevent problems with calcium deposition in the bones or 'Rickets;' a nutritional deficiency that most physicians have heard of but will never see in their lifetime. Instead Vitamin D is proving to be a Super-Star in a wide spectrum of conditions besides its role in the more well known in the prevention of osteoporosis.

Recent data from the Long Island Breast Cancer Study Project, which studied 1,026 women with breast cancer matched to a control group of 1,075. Women who had blood levels of 40ng/ml had 40% lower odds of breast cancer versus those with levels of 20ng/ml or lower. And these results were consistent for estrogen receptor negative and positive cancers. A similar conclusion was reached by a much larger and well known study, the Woman's Health Initiative Health Report which showed a 20% reduction in breast cancer incidence in women who took more than the RDA of 400 units daily. A 2007 study concluded that levels over 50 ng/ml decreased the odds of breast cancer by 50%. All this from a Vitamin supplement that is free (sunshine) or costs around 10 cents a day for a 5000 international units tablet!

There is also increasing evidence that higher levels of Vitamin D decrease the risk of *recurrence* of breast cancer in women, a study published in the Journal of Clinical Oncology, 2009. A similar observation was made in the Long Island study.

So is more Vitamin D better? Large amounts of Vitamin D can cause significant problems such as kidney stone, bone demineralization, and irregular heartbeats. For that to occur, blood levels would have to reach 150 ng/ml. Studies supplementing with 10,000 units of Vitamin D for up to 5 months showed no signs of toxic levels. However I would not recommend this dosing.

So how much Vitamin D should an adult supplement with? The answer as previously mentioned are 3000 IU (summer)-5000 IU (winter) units a day with levels checked every 6 months so as to get blood levels around 50ng/ml .If initial levels are in the low 20's you can boost up the levels quickly by starting on 10,000 units daily for 14 days and then with the above maintenance dose of 5000 IU daily. I prefer the single 5000 unit dose tabs/gel-caps for convenience.

DR. M. P. KHAN, MD/NMD

I AM NOT A VITAMIN (D), REALLY!

What is the perception of your overall emotional and physical health, with a 10 being the best and 1 being the worst? Where do you stand? What changes would you like to see? Do you see a worsening of your mood in the shorter days of winter?

_____

_____

_____

_____

_____

_____

Supplement with Vitamin D as per the above recommendations for the next 4 weeks. Do you notice a difference in your overall health? Where are you on the scale now? What changes have you seen?

_____

_____

_____

Supplement with Vitamin D as per the above recommendations for the next 8 weeks. At this point it is a good idea to get a total Vitamin D level done. Do you notice a difference in your overall health? Where are you on the scale? Compared to 12 weeks ago when you started supplementation, how do you feel emotionally and physically?

_____

_____

_____

_____

_____

_____

THIS IS A LONG WINTER

"Winter must be cold for those with
no warm memories."
—Movie: *"An Affair to Remember."*

One of the traditions of a New Year's Day is that of poems that Karen and I write. Someday I plan to write homages for the rest of the seasons to complete the set. Soon, very soon, it will be spring!

SOLSTICE (winter):

When men's exhalations steam and turn hoary,
I am the scarlet dawn intruding on the frost blue skies of morning.
The howling wind, a troubadour, heralds my arrival
As I grip your world in my icy embrace.
A conjurer of light bereft of warmth and silence bereft of peace
I put to slumber the child-like dreams of summer.

I beckon you from warm beds to reluctant labor.
Wary steps struggle, greetings of sharp cracks on slicked paths
Adrift with the virginal kisses of deep winter drifts,
A foolish endeavor, for hunger is my handmaiden.
Look! I have frozen the turn of the worm and the robin's cry
And ransacked once sylvan fields of grains that gave life succor.

But despair not, the nights grow shorter.
For I am also the laughter of a child's first snowflake,
The crackle of friendship around evening fires,
A desperate yearning of the crocus for the spring.
And in my passage understand the seasons of heaven and earth
And why all life must die to be born once more.

MK/New Year's Day/07

DR. M. P. KHAN, MD/NMD

January 16

THIS IS A LONG WINTER

Describe a winter scene or memory, a good one or an unpleasant one. Connect to your inner poet (or not) as you write. If you live in a climate devoid of snow, download a winter scene and imagine yourself in it.

_____

_____

_____

_____

_____

_____

_____

_____

_____

_____

_____

_____

_____

_____

_____

_____

_____

_____

January 17

DON'T BE SO S.A.D.

"Lucky man who has known only physical pain.
Someday that will end.
Unlucky man who knows the pain of mental anguish.
That may last a lifetime."

—Chairman Moo

Recently we were visiting friends of ours. The conversation turned to the seemingly interminable winter months and the inevitable 'cabin fever.' N was convinced that she had Seasonal Affective Disorder and it seems an appropriate topic for today.

Two seasonal patterns of SAD have been described: the fall-onset SAD which has the more atypical symptoms of depression as noted below and the summer-onset SAD which has more typical symptoms of depression. The fall-onset type, also known as "winter depression," is more commonly seen and major depressive episodes begin in late fall to early winter and get better during the summer months.

It is characterized by:

1) Increased rather than decreased sleep patterns (hibernation mode).
2) Increased appetite with carbohydrate craving.
3) Weight gain.
4) Irritability, short tempered.
5) Difficulties with interaction with others (especially sensitive to being rejected)

It is more common in women with a peak age of 23 years. Naturally there is a higher incidence in the more northern latitudes. There are several theories of why S.A.D. happens, the common denominator being the effect of the lack of sunlight on brain chemistry. There is some research regarding the decreased production of melatonin and serotonin as a result of less light entering the eyes. There may be a poorly understood connection between the optic nerves, the pineal gland and the hypothalamus coupled with disturbances in the Circadian rhythm which may account for this.

The obvious treatment for this is exposure to light. I prefer a full spectrum light source. Light therapy is initiated with a commercially available 10,000-lux box. The eyes should remain open but staring directly into the light source, is not advised. Treatment is started with one, 15 minute session per day, gradually increasing the session's duration to 30 to 45 minutes twice a day, with a maximum of 90 minutes depending upon the response.

Before therapy with bupropion or other SSRI type drugs, I would recommend 5-Hydroxy Tryptophan, 50-100 mg at bed time.

DON'T BE SO S.A.D.

Some TIPS for S.A.D.

An easy and cheap way of increasing the light exposure in the winter months is to replace the bulb of your desk lamp with a full spectrum bulb. Try to spend at least an hour in front of these light sources. The light does not have to directly shine on the eyes. Another alternative is to get a plant grow lamp bulb. I have one above my office desk. Also replace some of your fluorescent tube lamps with grow light tubes. I would recommend these changes even if you do not have SAD and live in a climate with short daylight hours in the winter months!

Increase your outdoor activities, especially on those rare sunny winter days. Go for a walk or build a snow man with your kids. If you plan to spend a lot of time outdoors on snowy days, be careful. The amount of UV may actually be very high because of reflection of the snow and can damage your eyes so sun glasses that block UV are critical.

Establish a regular sleep pattern. Try to go to bed and get up at the same time, even on weekends. Don't stay up watching the local news. It will just add to your depression anyway! Try to get at least 7-9 hours of sleep.

Get your Vitamin D levels checked and supplement as per the previous suggestion at a dose of 3000 iu to 5000 iu of Vitamin D3 to get serum levels between 45-55 ng/ml. Check levels again after 4-6 weeks of supplementation.

DR. M. P. KHAN, MD/NMD

HERBAL TEA-TIME (PART 1)

"The word 'drugs' is derived from the Dutch translation of dried plants or herbs"

—Anon

*The below encounter and the persona of Mrs. Smith, though fictional, is a composite of a typical patient and actual questions asked at visits.

It was a busy day and Mrs. Fields*, a new patient to our practice, was the last one on the schedule. My nurse Sally, after taking a brief history and checking her pulse and blood pressure emerged from the exam room. *"You're going to be in there for a while"* she murmured, as she whisked past me. With some trepidation, I entered the exam room and made my introduction.

"Hi, I am Mrs. Olga Fields" she announced brightly *"and boy do I have some questions for you"* at which point she emptied a large shopping bag of colored plastic bottles on the exam table, whipped out a sheaf of pages from her purse, and adjusted her bifocals.

I emerged almost a half hour later, exhausted but impressed by the scope of questions that we had covered during the visit. The encounter* went something like this:

Dr. Khan, I have just started taking all these herbs and vitamins because I want to take better care of my health. It's not that I don't trust my doctor! I am getting older and all my friends are taking them and they told me to try some. I'll admit I got carried away. Honestly I think it's another fad until something else comes along!

The one thing I can assure you Mrs. Fields is that herbs and supplements are not a passing fad. The statistics speak for themselves. In the year 2000 it was estimated that 70% of adults had used herbs for their medicinal benefits and spent almost 5 billion dollars annually on herbs and other food supplements. The main

reason for their use was to take charge of their own health. And 66% of adults surveyed felt herbs could be as effective as pharmaceutical drugs! In the year 2015, it's close to 80% or higher.

Herbs have been used for their medicinal benefits in mainstream American medicine since the 1890s and were introduced mainly by German Naturopaths from the Old World. What was interesting were the similarities between Native American herbs and those introduced from Europe! Many of the native herbs (black cohosh used in menopause) were used by the early settlers and are still in use today. Surprisingly many of the currently fashionable herbs like Echinacea were on the American Formulary up to and including the early 1950s. They fell out of favor with the introduction of pharmaceutical drugs of which a large number, are plant based. Digitalis (Foxglove) and some anticancer drugs (Taxol from the Yew tree) are good examples.

DR. M. P. KHAN, MD/NMD

HERBAL TEA-TIME (PART 1)

Here are some resources for Mrs. Fields that I recommended:
Suggested reading:

> <u>The Green Pharmacy</u> by James Duke
> <u>Herbal Remedies for Dummies</u> by Christopher Hobbs
> <u>The Honest Herbal</u> by Varro Tyler
> <u>The Commission E Monographs</u>

Suggested Web sites:

> <u>www.herbs.org</u>
> <u>www.herbalgram.org</u>
> <u>www.consumerlab.com</u>
> <u>www.drugfacts.com</u>

HERBAL TEA-TIME (PART-2)

"Caveat emptor OR Customer beware. Read the label."
—Chairman Moo

No history of herbal use can be complete without mention of the Shaker community. Established in 1799 as a commercial venture, they gathered and cultivated 248 varieties of herbs. Renowned for their quality, they were sold and distributed worldwide .You and I (if you live in the Berkshires) actually live very close to a once vibrant Shaker community (Hancock Shaker Village). If you get a chance, visit a Shaker farm. Some of them still have an extensive herb gardens and offer classes in their medicinal use.

That makes me feel a little better doctor. But it seems that everybody is selling them. I bought most of my herbs from my neighbor's daughter. I am not sure I need half of these. Can't believe what I paid for them. Maybe you can help me out with what I need and what I don't?

Certainly! If you could leave a list of the herbs and supplements you are taking I can review them and give you a call later. There are two major problems with herb and supplements used in the US. Until 1994 herbs were regulated by the FDA (Food and Drug Administration). Congress passed the DHEA (Dietary Health and Education Act) in 1994 under which Medicinal Herbs are regulated as food supplements and not regulated as strictly as pharmaceuticals are.

This opened up a real Pandora's Box. The responsibility for safety and labeling was up to the manufacturer. One could potentially package and market an herb from the basement of your home!! A recent laboratory analysis of over 200 Ginseng preparations showed the correct amount of the active ingredient in only 30 products. *In fact about 25 had no active ingredient at all!*

The second major problem is the claims made by shady manufacturers. The FDA has very strict guidelines about advertising. A manufacturer of Glucosamine (which is on your list) is allowed to claim that it helps support joint health but cannot claim that it cures arthritis. It also encourages inappropriate use of supplements. A recent news article found a high incidence of heat stroke related deaths in college football players. Many of them had used Ephedra, (an herbal stimulant found in many "natural diet/energy" pills and drinks) before the game with disastrous consequences. Ephedra or Ma Huang also known as 'herbal speed' acts like adrenaline, and in some instances can be fatal.

HERBAL TEA-TIME (PART-2)

Make a list of common herbs and plants found in your kitchen and from your garden. Check out the above web sites to research one or two medicinal uses of these common herbs mentioned below.

GARLIC _____
_____

TURMERIC _____
_____

CINNAMON _____
_____

GINGER _____
_____

CHILI-PEPPER _____
_____

ECHINACEA _____
_____

PEPERMINT _____
_____

BASIL _____
_____

January 23

HERBAL TEA TIME (PART-3)

"Words you will <u>never</u> hear in a medical emergency "Is there an herbalist in the house?"
—Chairman Moo

Mrs. Field's again:

I had no idea it was this complicated. And dangerous! You also have a list of the prescription drugs that I am taking. And do I have Ephedra as an ingredient in the diet pill I picked up at the nutrition store? Now that you tell me that all herbs are drugs, is it safe to take them with my regular pills?

The interactions between herbs and pharmaceutical drugs can be complicated* and subtle. In fact 31% of herbal users use it with prescription drugs or over the counter drugs. Some herbs enhance the effect of a drug while others oppose it. The Ephedra in your diet pill will work against the high blood pressure pill that I see you are taking regularly. Although it is too complex to cover all the possible interactions between herbs and drugs, I am going to give you a few broad guidelines. And stop the diet pill right away.

* Tell your doctor, nurse or other health professional about ALL the herbs and vitamins you are on.

* If you are on Coumadin (warfarin) it is best to avoid all herbs because Coumadin interacts with almost everything (including broccoli). Ask your doctor for some of the newer drugs which work like Coumadin such as Xarelto or Pradaxa which eliminate the need for frequent blood tests and may not interact with herbal supplements.

* Do not take any drug or herb with grapefruit juice. There is a component in grapefruit juice which increases the absorption

of the drug (this effect can last for 72 hours) and can cause high blood levels of the drug.

* Stop taking herbs and vitamins at least a week before surgery. Some vitamins and herbs can thin the blood and can cause bleeding.

* It is best to avoid immune stimulating herbs such as Echinacea if you are on drugs to suppress the immune system (prednisone). Also avoid them if you are pregnant or breast feeding although (*Mrs. Fields chuckles*) I am sure there is nothing for you to worry about.

DR. M. P. KHAN, MD/NMD

HERBAL TEA TIME (PART-3)

Good God, doctor! I am done with those days. I know you are kidding me. Thanks a lot. I will look forward to hearing from you about the different herbs I am on. By the way do you like oatmeal raisin cookies? I will bake them for you at the next visit. They go well with ginger tea!

Oh, by the way Doc, and what should I be looking for so I can get a good quality product?

Ask the lab if they meet all or some of the below criteria.

- **NSF International GMP Registration**
- **ISO 9001 manufacturing certification**
- **Health Canada, European Union GMP Certified**
- **Written Standard Operating Procedures (SOPs) to comply with current Good Manufacturing Practices (c GMP) ensuring consistent quality**
- **ISO 17025 accreditation of in-house laboratories performing Chemical, Physical, And Microbial testing**
- **Finished products that meet and often exceed United States Pharmacopeia (USP30) specifications**
- **Certificates of Analysis available**
- **VCP (Vendor Certification Program) to ensure raw material quality**
- **Compliance with the Public Health Security and Bioterrorism Preparedness and Response Act of 2002**

*** Douglas Labs meet and exceed these criteria. I recommend their products without reservation. Check them out at*

www.douglaslabs.com

January 25

HERBAL TEA TIME (PART-4)

"It gets curiouser and curiouser."
—Alice in Wonderland / **Lewis Carroll.**

Mrs. Fields returns for her follow up visit. She now has a smaller plastic bag of supplements and is very pleased that she is not taking all those "pills."

Good morning, Doctor Khan. Could not believe the amount of money I was spending. My neighbor keeps pestering me to buy the product line that she says has worked miracles for her diabetes and her arthritis.
It's called _____.

Good morning to you too. Unfortunately, Mrs. Fields, I have not heard of this company. They may very well have an excellent product line. It would be a good idea to research their manufacturing practices. Remember *Caveat emptor;* **it's Latin for** *buyer beware.*

But doctor, surely they would not be in business if they were not reputable!

There is a plethora of manufacturers out there selling herbal supplements and while a few of them are reputable, most of them peddle inferior quality products, sometimes with very little or no active ingredients. Remember that herbs are drugs and have a physiological effect on the body. It's like buying aspirin. Suppose you need 81mg of aspirin to prevent a heart attack but the tablet had only 21mg. You would get pretty mad about this and demand a refund besides the fact that it would have no therapeutic action. This truth in marketing does not apply to herbal supplements. Since herbs are marketed as a food there is no requirement to ensure that the right amount of the active ingredient of the herb is present.

DR. M. P. KHAN, MD/NMD

So what should I do, doctor. She seems like a nice woman. And the clerk at the local nutrition store tells me otherwise. I am so confused!

This is confusing even for professionals. When a pharmaceutical drug is marketed, there is the assumption that the drug is manufactured with strict quality control and the dosage mentioned is what is in the drug. Even then, there have been several situations where the oversight was lacking and the drugs had to be pulled from the shelves. So what is one supposed to do? I would suggest that physicians and consumers research a few manufacturers and once you find one, stick with it! Don't be afraid to pick up the phone and ask questions. A reputable company usually has well trained professionals who will be happy to answer your questions. And it is a good learning experience to boot!

January 26

HERBAL TEA TIME (PART-4)

Caveat emptor. That would be a good place to start. Meanwhile I did bring all the herbs and supplements I am taking! And I am going to tell all the folks in my Bingo club how sweet you are to go to all that trouble!

Make a list of all the supplements and herbal products that you are currently taking. Make sure that <u>you list the actual products in the supplement and not just list the proprietary name</u> of the product. There are hundreds of brand names and may not make sense to the physician or healer reviewing your list. Better still take the actual bottles with you.

Take your list to a physician or healer trained in herbal medicine for review. Ask their help to remove supplements that are duplicates or harmful from your list. Make copious notes so as to make your visit more meaningful.

_____

_____

_____

_____

_____

_____

_____

_____

_____

_____

_____

_____

_____

_____

DR. M. P. KHAN, MD/NMD

THOSE PESKY POUNDS

"We never repent of having eaten too little."
—Thomas Jefferson

True to her word, Mrs. Fields has spread the word to her Bingo Club. As a result, Mr. Adiposa makes an appointment to see me. True to his name, he is a heavy set individual who confides in me that he is sweet on Mrs. Fields. He is concerned that she call him 'Chubs" and would like *"to lose those pesky pounds"* He promptly empties a shoebox of weight loss supplements and wants my advice on them as well as any "diet" I can start him on. After a review of some of the various colored bottles, this is my advice.

Mr. Adiposa, I would strongly advise you to return most of these supplements. And in the future stay away from products with *ma huang* (which is the Chinese name for ephedra or ephedrine, a powerful cardiac stimulant) The FDA has announced a ban on all products containing Ephedra which to date has been related in 81 deaths. Also avoid products with guarana and caffeine which are also stimulants. One of my patients, a 32 yr. old truck driver took an ephedra product called "truck drivers helper" to stay awake on long hauls and ended up in the local Emergency room with a myocardial infarction. (Heart attack)

Another popular supplement is *Chromium*. Although it does regulate blood sugar and I recommend it to patients with diabetes and hypoglycemia (100 mcg daily) it has no role in weight loss.

Chitin fiber **made from crab shells can absorb fat in the food and is certainly harmless. A recent Polish study used 1500 mg of chitosan 3 times a day before meals along with a 1000 calorie/day diet over 6months. The study group lost 30lbs vs. 20lbs for the placebo group. Watch for loose stools and avoid if you are allergic to fish and shrimp.**

Also take a vitamin supplement (fiber blocks absorption of D, E, A and K: the fat soluble vitamins). Interestingly Chitosan is used in combat and is applied directly to coagulate bleeding wounds!

A popular replacement for ephedra because of the impending ban is *Garcinia cambogia*. Used widely in India in Ayurvedic medicine as a treatment for worms, it also suppresses the appetite by increasing products called ketones which suppress the hunger center. To date trials with Garcinia have resulted in controversial findings and no definite studies have shown any benefit over placebo.

THOSE PESKY POUNDS

Here is some homework for you, Mr. Adiposa!

Make a list of all the "Diets" you may have tried in the past:

_____

_____

_____

_____

_____

_____

_____

_____

What were the reasons why these diets failed? Be specific.

_____

_____

_____

_____

_____

_____

What emotion (for example; boredom, depression, stress, frustration) made you gain the weight back again? Once again be specific.

_____

_____

_____

What other behaviors can you replace the eating behavior in the future when dealing with the above emotion?

_____

_____

_____

January 29

THOSE PESKY POUNDS

*"Very often it not __what__ you eat but __why__
you eat make one chubby."*

—Chairman Moo

I have saved the star of weight loss supplements for last and that is *green tea*. Patients were given green tea extracts (250 mg with 25% catechins) for 3 months with an average weight loss of about 5%. Green tea works by blocking fat absorption from the gut and increasing thermos-genesis or the metabolism rate of the body *without affecting the heart rate or blood pressure* because of substances called catechins. One approach would be to drink 3 cups (6oz) of green tea daily but watch for caffeine at 30 mg per cup.

To address the last part of your question, it is best to avoid any diet which has the word "diet" in it because all diets only have a 5% success rate at end of one year. The problem is not carbs but the wrong kind of carbs, the white sugar and white flour variety. Americans already have the highest incidence of kidney failure in the world because of the high protein diet that we already eat and a diet that advises bacon three times a day cannot be heart healthy. Instead, focus on the long term to make changes in your lifestyle. I want you to complete the work sheet of January 10 and place it in a prominent place. "Diets" fail because the behavior of eating has not changed.

If you eat when stressed out, especially if you crave sweets, you may be trying to increase serotonin levels; which is what carbs do. The only problem is that the effect does not last long and you start craving sweet foods and refined flour products again. Also your blood sugar goes on a roller coaster ride which can actually result in insulin resistance (diabetes) and subsequent obesity; exactly the opposite of losing weight and inches. One suggestion is to start

5-Htp at 50-100 mg at bedtime. This restores serotonin level (5-Htp is a raw material used in the production of serotonin) and also results in weight loss.

Exercise at 30 minutes a day of an aerobic exercise (a brisk walk in the neighborhood) five days a week is ideal. Remember that exercise is *not* a good way to lose weight. One donut would require a walk at four miles per hour for 40 minutes to burn off. It is however a good way to maintain weight and a sense of well-being.

January 30

EAT REAL FOOD

*"If you eat to live or live to eat, make damn sure you eat
darn GOOD food".*

—**Chairman Moo**

*OK Doc, I get the picture. Can you give me some practical suggestions so I can
lose some of this flab?*

**Remember Eating Suggestion #1. Well here is a handout for
Eating Suggestion #2. And by the way, no more Mrs. Fields cookies!**

#2. Eat real food, preferably organic and local.

Eat whole foods. Of course is a chicken raised in a factory farm and
fed corn, hormones and antibiotics considered a whole food? Fresh or
frozen whole foods are a good start followed by canned. Also buy food
that is locally grown, spoils easily (and therefore fresh) and mostly found
in the periphery of a supermarket.

As far as ingredients of packaged or frozen food:

*If you can't pronounce it don't eat it
OR If there are more than five (ingredients), it isn't alive.*

Isn't organic food more expensive?

A common complaint about organic food is that it is relatively more
expensive. And how much do you spend on your cable bill? Food from
the Dirty Dozen list had an average of ten pesticide exposures a day vs.
two from the clean list. Use it the next time you shop so you can make
intelligent and money saving food choices.(See below) Good food is not
cheap and as the jingle goes "You are worth it!."

DR. M. P. KHAN, MD/NMD

Why Should I Care About Pesticides?

The growing consensus among scientists is that small doses of pesticides and other chemicals can cause lasting damage to human health, especially during fetal development and early childhood. Scientists now know enough about the long-term consequences of ingesting these powerful chemicals to advise that we minimize our consumption of pesticides.

What's the Difference?

EWG research has found that people who eat the 12 most contaminated fruits and vegetables consume an average of 10 pesticides a day. Those who eat the 15 least contaminated conventionally-grown fruits and vegetables ingest fewer than 2 pesticides daily. The Guide helps consumers make informed choices to lower their dietary pesticide load.

January 31

EAT REAL FOOD

Will Washing and Peeling Help?

Nearly all the studies used to create these lists assume that people rinse or peel fresh produce. Rinsing reduces but does not eliminate pesticides. Peeling helps, but valuable nutrients often go down the drain with the skin. The best approach: eat a varied diet, rinse all produce and buy organic when possible.

How Was This Guide Developed?

Environmental Working Group analysts have developed the Guide based on data from nearly 87,000 tests for pesticide residues in produce conducted between 2000 and 2007 and collected by the U.S. Department of Agriculture and the U.S. Food and Drug Administration. You can find a detailed description of the criteria EWG (ewg.org) used to develop these rankings and the complete list of fruits and vegetables tested at a dedicated website, www.foodnews.org.

BELOW IS A LIST OF "THE DIRTY DOZEN" (actually FIFTEEN FOODS) THAT SHOULD PREFRABLY BE ORGANIC) AND "THE CLEAN FIFTEEN" FOODS THAT CAN BE NON-ORGANIC. USE THIS GUIDE THENEXT TIME YOU GO SHOPPING!!

DIRTY FIFTEEN: (I HAVE ADDED THREE MORE)

PEACH, APPLE, BELL PEPPER, CELERY, NECTARINE, STRAWBERRY, CHERRIES, KALE, LETUCE, GRAPES, CARROTS, PEAR, (MINE) COFFEE, CHOCOLATE, TEA.

CLEAN FIFTEEN:

ONION, AVOCADO, SWEETCORN, PINEAPPLE, MANGO, ASPARAGUS, SWEET PEAS, KIWI, CABBAGE, EGGPLANT, PAPAYA, WATERMELON, BROCCOLI, TOMATO, SWEET POTATO.

FEBRUARY

1-Feb	THE KINDNESS OF STRANGER! The parable of the scorpion.
2-Feb	THE KINDNESS OF STRANGERS! And how did it change your life?
3-Feb	TO FORGIVE DIVINE! Move, Fly, Dive.
4-Feb	TO FORGIVE DIVINE! Forgiving the Unforgivable.
5-Feb	THE WINTER ITCHIES! A holistic approach to dry skin.
6-Feb	THE WINTER ITCHIES! A super yummy oatmeal cookie recipe.
7-Feb	VITAL VITAMINS! The ' vhich' & 'vhat' of vitamins.
8-Feb	VITAL VITAMINS! Reviewing your Vitamins.
9-Feb	THE BATTLE OF THE VITAMINS! 'Vhich' vitamin to choose?
10-Feb	AND THE 'VINNER' IS? By a knockout punch.
11-Feb	WHAT IS Co-Q 10 ANYWAY? Ubiquitous ubiquinone.
12-Feb	HAPPY BELATED BITHDAY M.L.K. The man and a poem "FOR MLK"
13-Feb	HAPPY BELATED BITHDAY M.L.K. An iconic speech "I have a dream."
14-Feb	A DAY OF VALENTINES .Mushy Alert, a poem "LAST DANCE."
15-Feb	A DAY OF VALENTINES. And a mushy exercise; or not!
16-Feb	THEOBROMA CACOA ANYONE? The Mysteries of Chocolate.
17-Feb	THEOBROMA CACOA ANYONE? Check out this website!
18-Feb	AN ESSENTIAL QUESTION! The alpha of omega-3 fatty acids.
19-Feb	AN ESSENTIAL QUESTION! The mercury content of omega-3 fatty acids.
20-Feb	A FISHY ANSWER? Some medical uses of omega-3 fatty acids.
21-Feb	A FISHY ANSWER? Buying and using omega-3 fatty acids.
22-Feb	MORE FISHY ANSWERS. In dementia and depression.
23-Feb	MORE FISHY ANSWERS. And a great recipe for salmon.
24-Feb	A COUPLE OF D-LIGHTFUL USES. And medical uses of Vitamin D.
25-Feb	A COUPLE OF D-LIGHTFUL USES. Making the case for high dose D.
26-Feb	YUMMY YOGURT. Singing the praises of yogurt. Eating Suggestion #4.
27-Feb	YUMMIER YOGURT. And more praises.
28-Feb	MORE YUMMIER YOGURT. A Super No Excuse Smoothie.
29-Feb	A LEAP OF FAITH.

DR. M. P. KHAN, MD/NMD

THE KINDNESS OF STRANGERS

"Have you had a kindness shown? Pass it on;
T'was not given for thee alone, Pass it on;
Let it travel down the years,
Let it wipe another's tears.
Pass it on."

—Rev. Henry Burton

A holy man is camped out in the desert. Outside his tent, he finds a scorpion at the bottom of his bucket, struggling to get out. He promptly helps the scorpion climb out of the bucket. Just as promptly, the scorpion stings him, the intense pain bringing tears to his eyes.

The next day when he wakes up he finds the same scorpion, at the bottom of his bucket, struggling and trying to climb the smooth sides, but to no avail. And once again the holy man helps the scorpion out, who once again painfully stings him.

The day after that the story repeats itself. The scorpion, his curiosity aroused asks the holy man "You foolish man! Why do you keep rescuing me? I will always sting you. This is what scorpions do. I will always repay your kindness with a sting!"

To this the holy man replied "Sting! Yes that's what scorpions do. That is their nature. Kindness, that's what I do. That is my nature!"

The above parable repeats itself in my life and maybe even yours. How do we keep connected to our inherent kindness when life keeps pulling us away from it? It's so easy to lash out at a perceived injustice done to us. Understandably, it is a very primal reaction; because it threatens the survival of our ego. To react to that "sting" with kindness is a profound and conscious act. An act that elevates us spiritually in its response. It means that we understand the inherent nature of the "scorpion." It is the first flowering of compassion.

Another manifestation of kindness is what we do for others every day, the random actions of kindness without anticipation of rewards or returns.

It is a language that is universally understood. It can be simple such as holding the door open for somebody whose hands are full of packages to providing volunteer help in an earthquake zone. It all adds up, like a bank account of our humanity. Our lives would be impoverished without the acts of kindness done for others and that others have done for us.

February 2

THE KINDNESS OF STRANGERS

Make a list of the acts of kindness you have done to others over the years.

_____

_____

_____

_____

_____

_____

_____

Make a list of the acts of kindness that others have done for you.

_____

_____

_____

_____

_____

_____

_____

How has it changed your life?

_____

_____

_____

_____

_____

_____

_____

TO FORGIVE, DIVINE

"If I cannot forgive myself for all the blunders
That I have made over the years,
Then how can I proceed?
How can I ever dream perfection-dreams?
Move, I must, forward.
Fly, I must, upward.
Dive, I must, inward,
To be once more what I truly am And shall forever
remain."

—Sri Chinmoy

Sometimes we can forgive others much more easily. To forgive ourselves of our own misdeeds and imperfections is so much harder. The above poem by Sri Chinmoy eloquently urges us to do so. If we have to find our *divine* nature, then we have to forgive the *fallible* human nature of ourselves and others. Otherwise we will never climb out of the trap that our guilt, and our perceived morality, has provided for us.

I wrote this poem several years ago for someone I once loved. In the hope that it would help heal her past and maybe, herself! It mirrors the sentiment of the above poem by Sri Chinmoy. Reading it today, it is a reminder for me to begin each day as a clean slate, to live in this moment, free from the regrets of the past. It is my sincere hope that it can do the same for you. Move. Fly. Dive. But first forgive yourself. And others!

Remember: *It's never too late to have a happy childhood!*

SOMEDAY:

Someday we have to forgive ourselves,

Someday we will have to absolve our children and our parents.

For in the relentless cycle of our lives,

Genius and madness; passion and compassion; love and indifference;

Are creatures of our imagination, the burdens of our past.

And joy trapped in the wings of our hearts, awaits unfettered flight.

Liberated from the prisons of our guilt, we shed the chains of painful memories,

And with childish innocence, dance to the face of the sun.

MK/1994

February 4

TO FORGIVE, DIVINE

Is there an event in your life that is unforgivable in yourself?

_____
_____
_____
_____
_____
_____
_____

Is there event in your life that is unforgivable in others?

_____
_____
_____
_____
_____
_____
_____

Can you find it in yourself to forgive that event? How do you plan to do so?

_____
_____
_____
_____
_____
_____
_____

DR. M. P. KHAN, MD/NMD

THE WINTER ITCHIES

"Happiness is having a scratch for every itch."
—**Ogden Nash**

In my office, the parade of illnesses is very seasonal. Winter is usually heralded by complaints of dry itchy skin and nose bleeds along with the usual suspects of runny noses and influenza. Our skin is the largest organ in the body and performs multiple functions. The outer layer called the epidermis is constantly being shed as new cells from the dermis or inner layer are being formed. The skin also produces oil like substances from sebaceous glands, which help in the hydration of the skin. Aging, tobacco smoke and UV light damage (sunlight, tanning beds) can inhibit the ability of the skin to perform its functions. So here are some suggestions to be nice to your skin.

Most of us cut down our water intake this time of the year, although because of the dry air this time of the year, we may be having a higher fluid loss form the skin and not realize it. Although there are several guidelines as to how much water one should drink, one approach is to check for any coloring in the urine, especially in the evening. It should be the color of water, that is: colorless. This is generally a sign of adequate fluid intake.

The other problem is the soap we use for our daily needs. Most of the popular soaps have detergents in them which can strip the skin of its natural oils. This impairs the ability of the skin to control the loss of moisture. Switch to a soap which has oatmeal in it. Oatmeal is an emollient and has anti-inflammatory properties. It is generally available as soap in a liquid form, preferably fragrance free. It may take some getting used to because of its slimy feel when first used on the skin. I use an oatmeal based soap year around. Another alternative is to add colloidal oatmeal to bath water and soak in it for 10 minutes. This is available commercially. A more economical approach is to take two cups of unflavored oats. Place in a blender and run until you get a fine powder. Add one cup of baking soda to the oats. This makes enough for a single use.

I also recommend a hydrating agent to be applied topically twice a day. Although several commercially available lotions are available, they have a boat load of chemicals in them. All lotions are a combination of oil and water. The water hydrates the skin and the oil locks the water in. A cheaper and cleaner alternative is to use almond oil or olive oil on wet skin, especially after a bath or shower. A tablespoon of the oil generally provides enough coverage for the entire body.

Winter also means that the environment you live and work in is extremely dry. A nebulizer or a cold mist vaporizer can help considerably, especially in the bedroom. Also increase the daily intake of omega-3 fatty acids. (3000 mg of fish oil capsules daily).

THE WINTER ITCHIES

Another creative way to use oat meal, and a delicious snack on a cold winter day!

(Hot Chocolate optional)

Dr. K's Super Yummy Oatmeal Cookies:

- *1 cup quick cooking oats*
- *1 cup all-purpose flour*
- *1/2 cup dry unsweetened shredded coconut*
- *1 /2 cup chopped raw almonds or walnuts or cashews or a little of all.*
- *1 /2 cup raisins or dried cranberries*
- *1 /2 to 1 cup brown sugar (depending on your sweet tooth) or Stevia equivalent.*
- *2 tablespoons of candied ginger, chopped up*
- *1 1/2 teaspoons baking soda*
- *2 tablespoons boiling water*
- *1/2 cup butter or Earth Balance (if you are vegan)*
- *1 tablespoon maple syrup or agave nectar*

DIRECTIONS:

Preheat oven to 350 degrees F.

Grease 2 baking sheets. Mix quick oats, flour, coconut, nuts, brown sugar, and ginger in a bowl.
Dissolve the baking soda in boiling water. In a small saucepan, melt the butter, and stir in the maple syrup to combine. Pour in the dissolved baking soda, and pour the mixture into the dry ingredients. Stir lightly

until just combined; drop by rounded tablespoon about 2 inches apart onto the prepared baking sheets.

Bake in the preheated oven at 375 F until the cookies are golden brown, 10 to 15 minutes. Cool for 10 minutes.

And save some for your friends!!

DR. M. P. KHAN, MD/NMD

VITAL VITAMINS

"The Best Vitamin for making friends....B-1"

Every once in a while I get asked the "million dollar" question *"What is the best vitamin to take and do I really need them?* I dread answering this question because the answer is simple yet complicated. As regards to the second part of the question, there is considerable controversy regarding the use of vitamins as a supplement. For example beta-carotene in high doses in smokers actually increases the risk of lung cancer and vitamins in children under three years of age can increase the risk of allergies. So here goes.

A JAMA article (2002 June quoting Drs. Fletcher and Fairfield of Harvard's Department of Ambulatory Care cited "sub optimal intake of some vitamins, above levels causing classic deficiency, is a risk factor for chronic diseases and common in the general population, especially in the elderly." Noting the widespread deficiencies in the American diet (folic acid, B6, B12, A, E, D) and the relation between chronic diseases, they feel that "it appears prudent for all adults to take vitamin supplements." Currently, about 40% of adults in the US take some forms of vitamins.

In spite of mounting evidence of nutritional deficiencies in the average diet (if you have a perfect diet stop reading this article and give me a call, you could make the cover of Newsweek) some of my physician colleagues consider this "expensive urine." The real question is the role of large doses (ortho molecular) of vitamins as a supplement. None of us will see a case of Scurvy or Beriberi in our lifetime as we all get the Required Daily Allowance. But the RDA's are not enough if we have to use vitamins as antioxidants in soaking up the free radicals which cause the damage leading to degenerative diseases such as cataracts, Alzheimer's disease and heart disease. For example the 400 mcg allowance for folic acid falls short of the 500-1000 mcg requirement to reduce levels of homocysteine and indirectly reduce the ravages of Alzheimer's disease.

With a plethora of manufacturers of vitamins, the first part of the above question is just as difficult. Lyle McWilliams, a biochemist and former member of Canada's Parliament published a landmark study; *The Comparative Guide to Nutritional Supplements* (www.comparativeguide.com) which compared 500 commercial vitamins to see what brands reached the standard for optimal daily preventive nutrition. Douglas Labs UP X (DL formula 20911) was in the top 10 list. Some well-known consumer brands including the more popular mega and single daily dose vitamins scored very poorly. I recommend 4 daily of the UP X (instead of the suggested 8) if you have a relatively healthy diet.

February 8

VITAL VITAMINS

WARNING!!A Consumer Lab (www.consumerlab.com) test of 24 off-the-shelf products to see if the product contained the amount stated on the label failed 14 out of the 24 products tested. Avoid high doses of vitamin A (do not exceed 15000 units daily) because of toxicity. Patients on chemotherapy need to advise their physician as some vitamins can interfere with some of the drugs used such as methotrexate.

So what does the multivitamin you take look like?

List the type and amount of the vitamins and minerals (PER SERVING) of the Vitamin Supplement that you are taking. It is usually located in small print on the back of the container. Or you can skip this step which will be repeated on February 9:

_____

_____

_____

_____

_____

_____

_____

_____

_____

_____

_____

_____

_____

_____

_____

_____

THE BATTLE OF THE VITAMINS

"Definition: *WIKIPEDIA- A vitamin_is an organic compound required by an organism as a vital nutrient in limited amounts. An organic chemical compound (or related set of compounds) is called a vitamin when it cannot be synthesized in sufficient quantities by an organism, and must be obtained from the diet.* (Which is why Vitamin D is really not a vitamin, but a hormone made by the skin in the presence of sunlight)."

Below is a list of the constituents of a popular once a day vitamin supplement. Even though it says 100% of the RDA, this amount may not be enough to prevent or help chronic disease states. More on ortho molecular (higher than Required Daily Allowance) doses of vitamins in the future.

Each Tablet Contains	% Daily Value
Vitamin A 3500 IU (29% as Beta-Carotene)	70%
Vitamin C 60 mg	100%
Vitamin D 400 IU	100%
Vitamin E 30 IU	100%
Vitamin K 25 mcg	31%
Thiamin 1.5 mg	100%
Riboflavin 1.7 mg	100%
Niacin 20 mg	100%
Vitamin B_6 2 mg	100%
Folic Acid 400 mcg	100%
Vitamin B_{12} 6 mcg	100%

Biotin 30 mcg	10%
Pantothenic Acid 10 mg	100%
Calcium 200 mg	20%
Iron 18 mg	100%
Phosphorus 20 mg	2%
Iodine 150 mcg	100%
Magnesium 50 mg	13%
Zinc 11 mg	73%
Selenium 55 mcg	79%
Copper 0.5 mg	25%
Manganese 2.3 mg	115%
Chromium 35 mcg	29%
Molybdenum 45 mcg	60%
Chloride 72 mg	2%
Potassium 80 mg	2%
Boron 75 mcg	*
Nickel 5 mcg	*
Silicon 2 mg	*
Tin 10 mcg	*
Vanadium 10 mcg	*

* Daily Value not established.

Most single tablet multivitamins have percentages and constituents similar to the above with slight variations.

AND THE VINNER IS.......

This is compared to another product that I had talked about yesterday. Even at four a day, the levels of vitamins and minerals (UP X- Douglas Labs) is superior to the previous product and costs a little more than a dollar a day or a third the price of a caramel latte at your favorite caffeine establishment.

Eight Tablets Contain: (At Four a day, it is ½ the Amount)

Vitamin A .... 15,000 I.U. (33% as Vitamin A Palmitate [5,000IU]/67%

[10,000 IU] as Natural Beta-Carotene) from D. Salina with full spectrum carotenoids**)

Vitamin C .... 700 mg. (as Ascorbic Acid/Ascorbyl Palmitate/

Calcium and Magnesium Ascorbate complex)

Vitamin D-3 .... 1,000 I.U.

Vitamin E .... 400 I.U. (natural, as d-alpha tocopherol plus mixed tocopherols)

Thiamine .... 100 mg.

Riboflavin .... 50 mg.

Niacin/Niacinamide .... 190 mg.

Niacin/Niacinamide .... 95 mg.

Vitamin B-6 .... 100 mg. (as Pyridoxine HCl/ Pyridoxal-5-Phosphate Complex)

Folate .... 800 mcg. (As L-methyl folate, Metafolin®)

Vitamin B-12 .... 250 mcg. (As methyl cobalamin)

Biotin .... 300 mcg.

Pantothenic Acid	500 mg. (as d-Calcium Pantothenate)
Calcium	100 mg. (as Calcium Citrate/ Ascorbate Complex)
Iodine (from kelp)	200 mcg.
Magnesium	100 mg. (as Magnesium Aspartate/ Ascorbate Complex)
Zinc	25 mg. (as Zinc Amino Acid Chelate)
Selenium	200 mcg. (As Selenium Krebs*/Kelp complex)
Copper	2 mg. (as Copper Amino Acid Chelate)
Manganese	10 mg. (as Manganese Aspartate Complex)
Chromium	200 mcg.
Molybdenum	100 mcg.
Potassium	99 mg. (as Potassium Aspartate Complex)
Lutein (natural)	6 mg.
Lycopene (natural)	6 mg.
Zeaxanthin	1 mg.
Inositol	100 mg.
Trace Elements	approx. 100 mcg. (From Sea Vegetation)
Choline	60 mg. (from 150 mg Choline Citrate/Bitartrate)
PABA	50 mg. (para-amino benzoic acid)
Boron	1.5 mg. (as Boron Aspartate/Citrate complex)
Vanadium	50 mcg.(as Vanadium Krebs*)
L-Cysteine/N-Acetyl L-Cysteine	150 mg.
Betaine	114 mg.(from 150 mg Betaine HCl)

Bromelain (2,000 GDU/g) .... 50 mg.

Glutamic Acid .... 20 mg.(from 25 mg Glutamic Acid HCl)

L-Methionine .... 12.5 mg.

Rose Hips .... 100 mg.

Lemon Bioflavonoids .... 100 mg.

Red Wine Proanthocyanidins/Pine

Bark Extract ....50 mg.

Hesperidin ....35 mg.

Rutin ....25 mg.

Fruits and Herbs Proprietary Organic Fruit

Vegetable Blend ....700 mg.

Garlic ....100 mg. (bulb, Pure-Gar®, odorless)

Cauliflower (entire plant) ....100 mg.

Spirulina ....100 mg.

Chlorella (broken cell wall) ....100 mg.

Green Papaya Extract ....100 mg.(fruit)

Blackberry (Fruit) ....80 mg.

Celery powder (leaf) ....70 mg.

Black radish powder (root) ....70 mg.

Apricot powder (fruit) ....70 mg.

Green Tea Extract (leaf) ....50 mg.

Apple Pectin (fruit) ....50 mg.

Compare the amount of the vitamins and mineral in the multi vitamin supplement that you are on next to the above ingredients based on the exercise from the previous day.

Notice the presence of lutein (eyes) and lycopene (anti-cancer) along with the presence of essential amino acids and vegetable extracts.

DR. M. P. KHAN, MD/NMD

WHAT IS CO Q-10 ANYWAY?

"Definition: A coenzyme is an organic non-protein molecule, frequently a phosphorylated derivative of a water-soluble vitamin, that binds with the protein molecule (Apo-enzyme) to form the active enzyme (Holo-enzyme)."

Coenzyme Q10 is also known as ubiquinone and is an antioxidant. Japan is one of the only sources of mass production of this supplement because of patents. It is similar in structure to vitamin E and Vitamin K but is not classified as a vitamin. It plays an essential role in energy production in the cell at the mitochondria level and when deficient can cause the cell to function less efficiently.

In Europe it is one of the first line treatments for CHF. Studies have shown that patients with advanced CHF have a Co-Q10 deficiency compared to healthy patients. Using echocardiograms, 651 patient were followed for one year using Co-Q10 vs. placebo in a random double blind study (Morisco, Molecular Aspects Med 1994;15:S287-294) At the end of the study they found a significant decrease in the number of hospitalizations.(23%-CoQ10 vs.37%-placebo) This rate was comparable to patients treated with pharmaceutical drugs.

The other class of patients that benefit from CoQ10 are patients on statin class of (simvastatin, pravastatin) drugs. These drugs compete with CoQ10 and if this level is low can cause the classic side effects of statins such as muscle and liver damage. When statins are used for lowering lipids (overprescribed in the U.S.) it is generally a good idea to recommend a daily dose of 100-300 mg of CoQ-10 at the same time

CoQ10 is also useful in patients after an acute myocardial infarction (heart attack). In a recent random double blind study the incidence of all heart related events at the end of one year was 24.6% in the CoQ10 group vs. 45% in the placebo group. (Singh- Molecular Cell Biochem2003; 246:75-82). CoQ10 is now being studied in high (1200 mg/day) concentrations in the treatment of Parkinson's disease.

I would recommend a dose of 100mg to 300mg. a day in the oral wafer form (Douglas Labs CoQ10-MLT catalogue # 98555 although several other forms of CoQ10 are also available) as this gives good absorption from the lining of the mouth. At this dose there are no side effects. Since they are similar to Vitamin K it can make Coumadin less effective. The best approach is to buy products from a reputable manufacturer.

HAPPY BELATED BIRTHDAY-M.L.K.

January 17th was his birthday. Although this should have been placed in the appropriate month, it does not truly matter as this tribute could have been placed on any day of the year. His message is timeless!!

I wrote this poem as a dedication to this great soul whose life was tragically cut short at the young age of 39. And yet he had a profound impact on my life.

For M. L. K.:

Once they were Kings and Queens
In the dream that was Africa.
A Mother who dreamed of braiding her daughter's hair
Preparing her beauty for a joyous marriage to come.
A Father who dreamed of sons hunting the Wildebeest
On the plains of the Serengeti, the spear's arc in its fatal flight.
A Husband who dreamed of love songs under a full moon,
The home fire beckoning him to her tender breasts.
A Woman who dreamed of her man's strengthened loins,
Their union and the children she would someday bear.

And they awoke from that dream into a nightmare,
Shackled, deep in the putrid bowels of slave ships.
Sold like so much cattle to the plantations of the South,
The Master's whip scarred and crushed them into slavery.
This is how inhumanity justifies its cruelty,
Manifests a noxious stink in the cesspool of our shameful history.

Then there was another King in another time,
Who in recent memory also had a dream.
For Mothers who would someday see their daughters
Grow up to be Doctors and Deans of great Universities.

For Fathers who would see their sons realize a singular vision
In a future of Presidents and Statesmen in high offices.
For Husbands who would fearlessly embrace their wives,
Far from hunger and shame, in the shelter of their homes.
For Women who loved deep and lusted for their men,
And birthed healthy children into a bright free world.
Once they were Kings and Queens,
In the dream that was America.

MPK/2013

February 13

HAPPY BELATED BIRTHDAY-M.L.K.

"Darkness cannot drive out darkness; only light can do that.

Hate cannot drive out hate; only love can do that.

Hate multiplies hate, violence multiplies violence, and toughness multiplies toughness in a descending spiral of destruction....

The chain reaction of evil—Hate begetting hate,

Wars producing more wars—must be broken, or we shall be plunged into the dark abyss of annihilation."

—**Martin Luther King, Jr.,** *Strength to Love*, **1963.**

In every century there are men whose message is universal. It crosses boundaries of race. MLK was such a man. He held up a mirror to our conscience and his words will echo wherever there is inequality and oppression.

Take the time today to reflect on his words. What meaning do they have for you?

_____

_____

_____

_____

_____

_____

Sometimes words can be very powerful and truly mightier than the sword. Check out the iconic speech he gave in Washington DC. It starts out as "I have a dream....."

What do these words mean to you as an American?

_____

_____

_____

A DAY OF VALENTINES

"Be certain in the religion of Love there are
no believers or unbelievers. Love embraces all."

—Rumi

This poem, written in the style of Rumi is positively mushy and is my Valentine's Day wish for my wife. I read this poem on our wedding day, almost fifteen years ago. I hope it can embrace her, not just today, but always. It is titled:

LAST DANCE:

In the bitter-sweet anguish of restless nights,
You waltz through the fabric of my dreams.
An ephemeral gossamer creation,
Which disappears with the morning sun, leaving only faint memories.
Awake, if not for your vision, 1 would be blind.

In every breath 1 feel your love, fragrant as a jasmine flower,

Its essence permeating my soul.

In your eyes, I have found my peace.
In your arms, my home,
In your laughter, my song,
In your warm skin, my eternity!

Life is a dance, the world our ballroom.

Give me your passionate tangos and the slow embrace of a waltz.
As the evening fades, keep me gentle and close.
This song will never end.
Save the last dance for me!

MK/4/02

February 15

A DAY OF VALENTINES

Write down the names of some of the people that you would like to send Valentine Day wishes to.

_____

_____

_____

_____

Now makeup some of the mushiest and craziest Valentine Day wishes that you would like to send to the people in the list.

_____

_____

_____

_____

_____

_____

_____

_____

February 16

THEOBROMA CACOA; ANYONE?

"Researchers have discovered that chocolate produces some of the same reactions in the brain as marijuana. The researchers also discovered other similarities between the two but can't remember what they are."

—**Matt Lauer**

It's the day after V-Day and scattered around your home or work space are the inevitable boxes of chocolate, calling you to try one more as you try just as hard to resist it. But before you toss them in the garbage, remember the words of Henry Ford who when asked what colors of the Model-T he would make, replied "You can have any color of car you want, as long as it is black!" And this goes for chocolate too "as long as it is dark!" This, by definition is greater than 70% of cocoa content (the rest is sugar and fat). Less than that and you lose the benefits of chocolate and you also add those pesky calories.

The active ingredients of chocolate can affect brain chemistry in several ways. Chocolate is high in tryptophan which is the raw material of serotonin, a mood elevator. Another effect is the release of endorphins which also causes the release of dopamine, the brains 'feel good" chemical. But the more interesting action of chocolate is due to a neuro peptide called anandamide (anand = joy; *Sanskrit*) which binds with the same receptors as the active chemical in marijuana; (see Matt Lauer's quote) THC or Tetra Hydro Cannabinol! But before somebody makes chocolate an illegal drug, one would have to consume several pounds of chocolate daily to have any significant impact (get high in other words) on brain chemistry.

Chocolate also has compounds called flavonoids. They are in the category of phytochemicals which have been extensively investigated for their antioxidant capacities. Flavonoids appear to exert their protective effects on the heart and circulation by defending against oxidation, improving endothelial function, reducing the tendency of blood to clot by improving platelet function and decreasing blood pressure and reducing the risk of heart disease. (More on cocoa flavonoids in September). Research, suggests that cocoa has a greater weight to flavonoid ratio than teas and red wine. Organic cocoa has a higher amount of the flavonoids as compare to the non-organic variety of cocoa. Also the process of making cocoa powder greatly reduces the content of flavonoids.

Endothelial (it is the thin layer of cells that line the inside of blood vessels) dysfunction appears to play a key role in the pathogenesis of atherosclerosis, coronary artery disease, diabetes mellitus and high blood pressure. The flavonoids in cocoa also increase circulation by activating the nitric oxide system. This results in the dilation of the blood vessels and lowers the blood pressure. Flavonoids also appear to decrease the tendency for blood to clot, by reducing platelet stickiness (like aspirin). Chocolate is also a very rich source of magnesium, a mineral responsible for muscle relaxation and lowering blood pressure. Magnesium is generally deficient in most Standard American Diets or SAD. A craving for chocolate may be actually be the body's signal for a magnesium deficiency.

February 17

THEOBROMA CACOA; ANYONE?

Some of my favorite Dark Chocolate varieties are:

*Green & Black's Organic Bittersweet Dark Chocolate Bar

*Pacari Organic Raw 100% Cacao

*Plantation Menavana Madagascar 72% Cocoa.

* 'Theo' brand of dark chocolate.

Check out: www.chocolate.com and add a piece of this super food to your daily diet.

As if you needed any more convincing about the research data, tell your doctor about this or better still share a piece of your favorite Dark with him.

Chocolate is also an ingredient of Mole Sauce and is used extensively in Mexican cooking. An excellent but lengthy recipe for preparation of Mole Sauce is found on the link below.

http://allrecipes.com/Recipe/Mole-Sauce/Detail.aspx?evt19=1

Also watch the movie starring Johnny Depp titled "Chocolat." Hint; Good movie for V-Day.

February 18

AN ESSENTIAL QUESTION

"Three ounces of salmon has 35 times more omega-3s than three ounces of beef. As a dietitian, I tell people to eat fish for omega-3s and eat beef for other nutrients, like B vitamins, zinc and iron."

—Mary Young

So what's the big deal on the omega-3 fatty acids? A very timely question and interestingly enough the USDA is going to add the EFA to the food pyramid. Essential Fatty Acids are a broad class of fatty acids of which omega 3 is one of them. They are 'Essential' because the body cannot make them and must get it from a food source. Flax seed and flax seed oil, Canola oil, walnuts and deep ocean fish such as tuna and salmon are a good source of omega- 3 EFA. All other vegetable oils are high in omega-6 and animal fats are high in omega-9.

Briefly the body converts these eventually into hormone like products called prostaglandins. Omega 3 end up as E3 (anti-inflammatory) which lower cholesterol, raise the HDL or good cholesterol, reduce inflammation and make platelets less sticky and prevents clots in the arteries. On the other hand omega 6 and 9 end up as E1 and E2 prostaglandins (pro-inflammatory) which have the reverse effect of the E3 and hence are bad for you Further research has now proven that deficiencies of the EFA are linked to heart problems as well as diseases as diverse as MS, psoriasis, eczema and slow healing of wounds!

Recently a blood test has been designed to measure Red blood cell omega 3 levels. A recent AMA article (1995, 274) showed a 90 % reduction in fatal cardiac arrest when the omega 3 blood levels increased from 3% to 9% by an ongoing regimen of omega-3 supplementation. Final clinical conclusions are still pending but the preliminary data is very impressive. 16 oz. of tuna or salmon a week would provide adequate daily levels.

If eating fish is not your thing consider one salmon oil capsule (1000 mg. per capsule) **or** one tablespoon (15ml) of flax seed oil **or** two tablespoons of flax seed on a *daily* basis. Although salmon oil is the best source of omega-3, watch for mercury levels. It is best to buy salmon oil from a reliable source. (I get mine from Douglas Labs: brand named QUELL; Nordic Naturals is another source). Equally important is to reduce the amount of saturated fats (watch the burgers and fries) in the diet as these are high in omega-6 and can counteract the effects of the omega-3. People who are allergic to fish should avoid salmon/fish oil capsules. Vegans can use algae based omega-3 EFA.

February 19

AN ESSENTIAL QUESTION

The mercury level in sea food is of real concern. One way is to avoid fish which is high in mercury. A good resource is <u>www.monterybayaquarium.org</u> where you can download a shopping/eating guide for your geographical area and at the same time avoid buying fish that could be overharvested. They also have a handy guide you can print and carry.

List the safe sea food choices in your area using the guide. (See September for a safe sea food guide for MA)

_____

_____

_____

_____

_____

_____

_____

_____

Try to eat up to 12 oz. of seafood (preferably wild caught) a week (8 oz. in pregnancy) using the above guide. Fatty fish is also a great source of Vitamin D. A great resource for wild caught fish and other goodies along with great recipes and credible information about the benefits of sea food although it does have a commercial bias. <u>www.vitalchoice.com</u>

February 20

A FISHY ANSWER

"A number of previous studies have linked lower levels of omega-3 to clinically significant conditions such as major depressive disorder, bipolar disorder, schizophrenia, substance abuse and ADD."

—**Sarah Conklin**

Which brings me to the importance of omega-3 intake in the diet.

And another eating suggestion.

<u>*# 3: Eat like an Eskimo, or go fishing! Cut down on red meat, pork and chicken.*</u>

Cardiovascular Disease: Fatty fish it's where it's at. Deep fried frozen fish sticks are a no-no. I encourage the intake of real fish on a regular basis. If mercury intake is of concern, check out the **www.seafoodwatch.org** for safe fish for your geographic region. The smaller the better (sardines) and wild caught fish is preferred over farmed fish. If you have to eat meat try wild game such as venison and Amish/farm raised chicken or grass fed beef. Add lentils and beans to the diet. A study by Hu et al .postulated that eating 12 oz. of fatty fish (wild caught salmon, halibut, shrimp and lobster,) a week may prevent 100,000 sudden cardiac deaths annually, plus a good source of vitamin D. Farm raised salmon has low levels of omega-3 as salmon in their natural habitat get omega-3 in the wild downstream of the food chain (from krill, who in turn get it from algae). If you are a vegan, watercress is a good food source of omega-3.

Besides the health benefits in preventing sudden cardiac death, there are several ways that omega-3 fatty acids can be used in disease states.

DR. M. P. KHAN, MD/NMD

Rheumatoid arthritis: Although plant based omega-3 such as those found in flax seed oil and walnuts (alpha-linolenic acid or ALA) have an anti-inflammatory effect, they are essentially converted to EPA and DHA or fish based omega-3 by the body. They are three to five times more effective than the plant based fatty acids (ALA) in reducing inflammation. A recent study (James MJ, Cleland LG. Dietary n-3 **EFA** and therapy for rheumatoid arthritis. *Semin Arthritis Rheum* 1997; 27:85-97.) showed a mark decrease in joint pain after 12 weeks of therapy with EPA/DHA. There was also a reduction in the use of NSAIDS (Ibuprofen, Naproxen) in the study group vs the placebo. The studies used around 4 grams of EPA and around 2 grams of DHA. To get to those doses, it is necessary to take 4 capsules of 1000 mg of fish oil three times a day. More concentrated pharmaceutical preparations of omega-3 are available but are not indicated for RA.

A FISHY ANSWER

One way to find out if omega-3 supplementation is helpful in RA or the more common osteoarthritis is to keep a daily calendar of morning pain and stiffness over the next three months using a 0-5 scale. 0=Minimal Pain/Stiffness UPTO 5=Maximal Pain/Stiffness

Use 4 capsules of 1000 mg fish-oil (OR two of *QUELL) three times a day. There are minimal side effects to therapy with loose stools and fishy belches leading the list. One way to counter this is to take store the bottle in the freezer and take the capsules in the frozen form. Also start slowly adding one capsule a week to your regimen. They can slightly elevate the LDL cholesterol but this is outweighed by their cardio protective effects and also by lowering triglycerides.

Conjunctiva sicca or Dry Eye Syndrome: Another therapeutic use of fish-oil is in the 'dry eye syndrome' also known as 'conjunctiva sicca'. Use 2 capsules of fish oil (OR one of QUELL) three times a day.

IMPORTANT: Continue therapy daily for at least 6-12weeks before you see results!!

Because of the high doses required, it is essential that the fish-oil capsules be free from mercury products and pesticides. Usually the cheap discount brands of fish-oil are suspect and are best avoided. A good resource is to check the brand out at www.consumerlab.com or use more reliable manufacturers such as www.douglaslabs.com or www.nordicnaturals. com. When larger doses of fish-oil are needed for therapeutic purposes, I recommend Douglas Labs QUELL line of omega-3. Below is an excerpt from a handout that I provide to my patients.

QUELL (OMEGA-3/ FISH OIL); FORMULA # 200981;

"*Supercritical fluid extraction uses CO2 (carbon dioxide) instead of oxygen to gently extract the fatty acids, which also protects them from microorganisms that can't survive without oxygen. No chemical preservatives, solvents, or undesirable compounds are found in QÜELL Fish Oils. Many fish oils contain only about 30% omega-3 fatty acids, of which roughly 18% is EPA and 12% DHA. The remaining 70% is a varying mixture of other components. These other components may include cholesterol, omega-6 fatty acids, saturated fatty acids, oxidation products and contaminants. Highly concentrated fish oil, like QÜELL, provide at least 75% active ingredients, leaving less room for nonessential compounds.*"

MORE FISHY ANSWERS

"He that takes medicine and neglects diet, wastes the skill of the physician."

—Chinese Proverb

My patients always ask me where I buy my fish from. One of the places I recommend is www.vitalchoice.com as mentioned in a previous workbook. The fish is Alaskan wild caught, and comes flash frozen and vacuum packed so when it is defrosted, it as close to fresh as humanly possible. Although it is a little pricy, I use one to two pieces of fish (around 20 oz.) a week and supplement my protein intake with, eggs, lentils and veggies for the rest of the week. A cheaper source of omega-3(and relatively free of mercury) are canned sardines and herring.

Neuro-cognitive disease states: In continuing on the uses of omega-3 in disease states, there are some good studies emerging in their use in neurological dysfunction as well as improving IQ and cognition in non-disease states. In fact there has been proven or equivocal evidence that omega-3 EFA are helpful in conditions as diverse as *Alzheimer's* disease to *Attention Deficit Disorder.* Omega-3 EFA is a primary component of brain membrane phospholipids and source of fuel for brain function. In fact about 30% of the brain's composition is omega-3 fatty acids. There is some thinking that these more flexible and anti-inflammatory fatty acids help the neuro-transmitters like serotonin and dopamine to function more efficiently.

A recent study was done measuring omega-3 EFA levels in patients with Alzheimer's disease. Their levels were only 60-70% when compared to age matched controls. A recent study by the Chicago Health and Aging project found 60% decrease in long term risk of AD with two 8 oz. serving/week (16 oz.) consumption of fish. This would be the same as supplementing with 2000 mg of fish oil on a daily basis. I would recommend that all of us, young and old, supplement or eat at least 16 oz. of a fatty fish once a week on a regular basis.

A study conducted in Rotterdam (Tiemeier H, van Tuijl HR, Hofman A, Kiliaan AJ, Breteler MM: concluded that plasma fatty acid composition is inversely related to *depression* in the elderly: the Rotterdam study. Am J Clin Nutr 2003; 78:40–46) screened 3,884 subjects older than 60 years of age for symptoms of *major depression*. The study yielded 264 with depressive symptoms and they were compared to 461 randomly selected subjects. The subjects with depression had a significantly lower concentration of omega-3 and a high ratio of omega-6 to omega-3. Also countries such as Japan with high fish consumption (150lbs. a year per person) had a lower incidence of *seasonal affective disorder.*

February 23

MORE FISHY ANSWERS

<u>*Recipe for Pan Seared Salmon:*</u>

Start with a fresh or thawed flash frozen filet of salmon or halibut filet about an inch thick three inches wide and six inches long. You will need:

* 1 Tbsp. coconut or any high temperature oil.
* 2 cloves garlic thinly sliced.
* Prepared fish Rub. (Try Tokyo rub or any other commercial rub but my favorite is Penang Curry rub made by The Teeny Tiny Spice Co. of Vermont: www.TeenyTinySpice.com)
* Fresh ground black pepper to taste.

Heat the oil in a cast iron pan or any heavy pan for even heat distribution on high heat. When the oil is hot, add garlic and pepper.

Meanwhile pat the fish on both sides with the rub and place gently in the oil. Cover with a lid to prevent splatter. Cook on high for a minute on each side.

Then turn the stove OFF and keep the pan covered. Do not remove the fish from the pan. Let the fish finish cooking for the next three to five minutes. This is the secret to not overcooking the fish so that it is moist and flaky when you serve it.

Place on plate, garnish with lemon slices and serve.

DR. M. P. KHAN, MD/NMD

A COUPLE OF 'D' LIGHTFUL USES

"May flowers always line your path and sunshine light your day.
May songbirds serenade you every step along the way.
May a rainbow run beside you in a sky that's always blue.
And may happiness fill your heart each day your whole life through."
–Irish Blessing

The morning sun filtering through my window once again turns my thoughts to spring and green expanses of grass. But that vision is almost another six weeks away and meanwhile there is the retinue of patients with runny noses and unstoppable coughs and pesky sore throats marching into my exam rooms. And you thought I was done with Vitamin D!

Many human tissues including muscle, bone and cells in the bone marrow which are cells responsible for immune function have Vitamin D Receptors or VDR and this vitamin/hormone binds to these receptors and produce profound physiological effects. Vitamin D is a powerful modulator of the immune system. As a result Vitamin D has a direct effect on the immune system and specifically on upper respiratory infections (URI) caused by viruses and bacteria. In fact there is evidence that the increased incidence of URI in the winter months is due to a Vitamin D deficiency.

Various studies have a direct correlation between Vitamin D levels and viral URI with 40 being the cutoff. The groups below this level had a significant number of URI's and the lower the level, the more frequent the URI. (Arch Internal Medicine 2009; 169: 384-390)

Another Canadian study in children younger than two found that Vitamin D may be more effective in bacterial infections than in viral infections. Another study in children younger than five years of age found that children admitted to the ICU had Total Vitamin D levels in the 20's as compared to children not admitted to the ICU (level in the 30's). There could be some confounders in this study. I would recommend supplementation in this age group at a minimum of 1000 iu. of Vitamin D on a daily basis. (The RDA is 400 international units/daily)

At the other end of the spectrum, Vitamin D deficiency in the elderly can lead to frequent fall. There are VDR in the muscles as well and especially the large muscle groups such as the flexor muscles of the hip. A low vitamin D level leads to poor muscle tone. A recent study showed 30% less falls in a nursing home population when their vitamin D levels were raised into the 40 plus range as compared to a control population. As physicians, it would be a good idea to add a Vitamin D level the next time you order labs work, especially for home bound or nursing home patients!

DR. M. P. KHAN, MD/NMD

A COUPLE OF 'D' LIGHTFUL USES

On an average it takes 1000 iu. of D-3 daily over a three month period to raise the level by10 ng/ml. As discussed previously, when levels are very low I advise 2 x 5000 iu. (International units) capsules of D-3 for 2 weeks and then one 5000 iu. capsule daily indefinitely. Check levels of 'total D' in three months. You can lower your dosage of D-3 in the summer months to 3000 iu. daily but this gets confusing. I personally take 5000 iu. on a daily basis year round.

Another strategy is to start on 50,000 units of Vitamin D-3 <u>once a week</u> and check levels in three months. This dosage form is covered by most insurance plans as a prescription but can lead to problems if not administered properly, and I prefer the daily form.

February 26

YUMMY YOGURT

"I opened-up a yogurt, underneath the lid it said, 'Please try again.' because they were having a contest that I was unaware of. I thought maybe I opened the yogurt wrong. Or maybe The Yummy Yogurt Co. was trying to inspire me...
'Come on Mitchell, don't give up!'
After I finished the contents, the bottom
of the container read:
"Fruit on the bottom, hope on top".

—**Mitch Hedberg**

Another eating suggestion and a very important one. *Really!*

 # 4: Eat yogurt (or any other source of pro-biotic*) on a consistent basis or about 4-6 oz. For 3-5 days/wk. (more on probiotics later).

*Other sources of probiotics are culture (pardon the pun) dependent

Korea=Kimchee; Germany=sauerkraut; Middle East=Kefir. (More on the incredible healing power of pro-biotics in September)

At the risk of sounding gross, the typical bowel movement is made up of a large amount of bacteria (40% of the total mass). There are 100x more bacteria in your gut then cells in the human body. And 80%of your immune system cells are in the gut. Probiotics are critical for efficient functioning of the immune system. They have an increasing role in the reduction of symptoms of Irritable Bowel Syndrome or IBS, and to prevent Antibiotic Associated Diarrhea and to prevent infection with a nasty bug called Clostridium difficile which is usually seen with long term antibiotic therapy

Probiotics are essentially the good bacteria and yeast, which keep the population of bad bacteria and harmful yeast organisms under control,

DR. M. P. KHAN, MD/NMD

thus keeping the bowels healthy. These good bacteria have a very low population in the stomach (0 and upto10 to the power of 3 or 10,000) and in the stool up to 10 to the power of 12 (10 trillion). The common bacteria that are beneficial are Lactobacillus and Bifidobacterium which keep the bad bacteria such as Pseudomonas and Clostridia under control. But they also play a very important role in the complex environment of the gut in regulating the immune system. And in the modulation of neuro transmitters.

February 27

YUMMIER YOGURT

This above effect is achieved by modulating the Immune system. This may be its most important function. It stimulates the Immune system in healthy individuals and down regulates in hypersensitive individuals by affecting Immune globulins A and G. The average child gets eleven upper respiratory infections a year and between two and three ear infections a year. In one recent study children given active cultures of lactobacillus had a 17% reduction in colds and ear infection and dental cavities as compared to controls. Also I would definitely crank up probiotic intake if your child is on any antibiotics and give the probiotics at least one hour after or before administration of antibiotics. This effect may also be useful in Crohn's disease and ulcerative colitis where the immune system is up regulated.

I routinely advise my patients to take 4 oz. of yogurt with active cultures on a daily basis, especially if they are on an antibiotic. In fact diarrhea associated with antibiotics tripled in the population not on probiotics. A common cause of hospital and nursing home diarrhea is a bacterium called Clostridium difficile which usually follows after long term use of antibiotics and which is paradoxically treated with another antibiotic. Supplementation with probiotics is critical if a cure is to occur. Also in resistant cases of C Diff. infections after several courses of antibiotics have failed, fecal material (good bacteria plus probiotics) from a healthy individual is transplanted into the diseased individuals with remarkable cure rates.

It also helps reduce the risk of food allergies. This is a function of IgA (one of the immune proteins secreted by the gut), as reaction to food antigens which cross the natural barrier of the gut. I recommend high doses of probiotics in patients with skin condition such as eczema and also to avoid cow milk (lactose) based products. Infants who ate yogurt consistently had lower incidence of eczema or atopic dermatitis especially if they were testing positive on skin tests.

If all of the above reasons don't convince you to add yogurt (frozen yogurt has no active cultures) or other fermented foods as part of a healthy diet, probiotics are also available in capsule form. I recommend this form only when I want to increase the pro-biotic levels quickly and I suggest that the capsule contents mixed in with the yogurt.

One common concern I hear is of lactose intolerance. The lactose load of yogurt is very low or absent as the probiotic bacteria use it as a food source and the intolerance is load dependent. Of course if you have a true milk allergy, then I would only use the capsule form.

Whenever I prescribe antibiotics to my patients, I ask them to start eating 4-6 oz. of yogurt or kefir on a regular basis and also to eat them two hours after they take the antibiotic and to continue the yogurt or kefir for one to two more weeks after they have completed the course of antibiotics.

Every once in a while I will hear patients tell me they have a real aversion to yogurt because of its consistency. I suggest a smoothie, recipe to follow. The banana adds flavor and is also a pre biotic.

February 28

MORE YUMMIER YOGURT

<u>*Dr K's Super No Excuse Smoothie:*</u>

4-6 oz. of vanilla yogurt (Stonyfield Farms Organic or Side Hill Farms) or plain kefir.

4-6 oz. of Chocolate or Plain Milk or Plain/Vanilla/Chocolate Soy Milk-All Organic

1 Ripe Banana.

2 Tablespoons of walnuts.

½ cup Mixed Berries (Cascadian Farms Frozen) or fresh raspberries, blueberries and strawberries.

Place all in blender and run until smooth and enjoy. Yields 2 -8 oz. portions.

Some other benefits of probiotics are:

1) *Aids in the digestion of proteins and fiber and keep gas production down. There is a condition called dysbiosis which is bacterial overgrowth which contributes to this problem. More on that later.*
2) *Reduce the activity of enzymes, which change pre-cancer compounds to cancer compounds and increase the activity of the body's natural killer cells.*
3) *Neutralizes toxins from common molds that we may accidentally ingest.*
4) *May help constipation by increasing the moisture content. Yogurt also has a fiber called Inulin which is a soluble fiber like oat meal.*

DR. M. P. KHAN, MD/NMD

Check out the website www.stonyfieldfarms.com for a great education in the blessings of yogurt. Also lots of recipes that use yogurt. Definitely one of the foods I would like to have if stranded on a desert island.

CAUTION: If you use ANY dairy products I would recommend that they be organic.

A LEAP OF FAITH

Celebrate this day. This a bonus for you!

Go for a walk. Meet up with some friends and go out for a cup of coffee. Go to a movie. Listen to rock'n'roll or classical music. Go dancing. Play a drum. Kiss someone you love. Call and connect with your family. Be kind to a stranger. Cook a great meal to share with your neighbors.

This day comes once every four years; so what are you waiting for?

DR. M. P. KHAN, MD/NMD

MARCH

1-Mar	DOWN WITH THE 6, UP WITH THE THREE! (PART-1)Omega-3, 6 & a recipe.
2-Mar	DOWN WITH THE 6, UP WITH THE THREE! (PART-1) Bouillabaisse Anyone?
3-Mar	RIDERS IN THE SKY. Jim Morrison and the Doors and 'Sanctuary.'
4-Mar	RIDERS IN THE SKY. The Vietnam War and the end of innocence.
5-Mar	A LITTLE NIGHT MUSIC! A homage to Mozart and a poem.
6-Mar	A LITTLE NIGHT MUSIC! Tickets to a ' Passion Play; ACT III'.
7-Mar	DOWN WITH THE 6, UP WITH THE THREE! (PT-2).O-3 medical indications.
8-Mar	DOWN WITH THE 6, UP WITH THE THREE! (PT-2). Research on Omega-3.
9-Mar	MY ACHING SWOLLEN LEGS! All about bad circulation and poor veins.
10-Mar	MY ACHING SWOLLEN LEGS! And a couple of herbal remedies.
11-Mar	I HAVE THE BLUES (BERRIES) Eating Suggestion # Four.
12-Mar	I HAVE THE BLUES (BERRIES). Free radicals and Nitric Oxide.
13-Mar	THE SUFI SUFFICETH. Two parables. In, and Out of, the box.
14-Mar	THE SUFI SUFFICETH. Dealing with Anger and Problems.
15-Mar	TERRIFIC TURMERIC (PART-1). Introducing Curcumin longa.
16-Mar	TERRIFIC TURMERIC (PART-1) and a recipe follows.
17-Mar	TERRIFIC TURMERIC (PART-2) .Use in chronic disease states.
18-Mar	TERRIFIC TURMERIC (PART-2) and another recipe follows.
19-Mar	KUNG HII FATT CHOI. The Year of the Horse and three Koans.
20-Mar	KUNG HII FATT CHOI. Dissolving the Koans.
21-Mar	GOTTA GO-AGAIN! About the prostate and urinary frequency.
22-Mar	GOTTA GO-AGAIN! Prostatism; What is your symptom score?
23-Mar	AND WHAT WAS THAT -AGAIN! Supplements for senior moments.
24-Mar	AND WHAT WAS THAT -AGAIN! A quick test for dementia.
25-Mar	NIRVANA DAY. 'Happiness' and the smile of the Buddha.
26-Mar	NIRVANA DAY. And wishing you many more days of peace.
27-Mar	LOVE (OR SOMETHING LIKE IT). "When Love Leaves."
28-Mar	LOVE (OR SOMETHING LIKE IT).You've lost that loving feeling.
29-Mar	FELIS DOMESTIC-US. All about a rose bush and a cat named Athena
30-Mar	FELIS DOMESTIC-US. Our favorite cat and feline foods and products.
31-Mar	A KRAZY KAT POEM. Enjoy ' The Fearless Cats' and all together now.

DR. M. P. KHAN, MD/NMD

DOWN WITH 6, UP WITH 3 (PART-1)

"Eat Omega-3, your heart will feel free. Eat Omega-6, your heart will sorry be."

—Chairman Moo

I just received my shipment of wild caught salmon and halibut and I am already making a mental note (and drooling a little) of the ingredients I will need to make Bouillabaisse or the more mundanely named "Fish Soup." A quick and easy recipe follows!

This brings me to the issue of omega-3 and omega-6 EFA or the "omega imbalance." Most of my patients that I see are already on some form of fish oil on a daily basis. The problem is that the ratio of Omega-3 to Omega- 6 EFA in the Standard American Diet or SAD is 1 to 30. Remember the Cro-Magnon diet. It was 1 to 4. In effect we are eating almost seven times more Omega-6 than our ancestors did in the form of vegetable oils, processed foods, and corn fattened animal products. In fact the more omega-6 we eat the more omega-3 we need to keep the ratio down. The American Heart association, in spite of the data of the below study, has not addressed this issue and mostly advises our diet to be low in saturated fat.

A landmark study called the Lyon study done in France, compared a large number of individuals eating the AHA advised diet low in saturated fat (butter, lard, whole milk dairy products) but <u>high</u> in Omega-6 *and compared it with* the Mediterranean Diet which is *high* in Omega-3(from fatty fish and dark greens) and *low* in Omega-6 (which is mostly derived from olive oil). At the end of the 12 month study, they found a *70% reduction in mortality from cardiac causes as well as cancer* in the Mediterranean Diet group.

Vegetable oils like Olive oil and Canola have 10% and 20% respectively of a fatty acid called Linoleic acid or LA while safflower oil may have up to 75% of LA. This LA is converted to Arachidonic Acid or AA, a vital part of the cell membrane especially in nerve tissue.

A high level of LA, however increases the AA which is inflammatory in nature, and plays an important role in the inflammation cascade.

More significantly however, LA also interferes with the conversion of plant based Omega-3 called Alpha Linolenic Acid or ALA found in flax seed, dark greens and walnuts to the EPA and DHA, the Omega-3 molecules that your body need for various functions (they are also the fatty acids found in fish oil and fatty fish).

And if all this is very confusing, just remember to use olive (not EXTRA VIRGIN OLIVE OIL or EVOO) oil and canola oil if used for deep frying. (Although you can use EVOO for stir-frying.) Eat plenty of wild caught fatty fish, (farm raised fish are usually grain fed and are subsequently much lower in Omega-3) dark leafy vegetables and a daily handful of tree nuts and peanuts.

DOWN WITH 6, UP WITH 3 (PART-1)

<u>*Dr. K's Super Fast but Great Tasting Recipe for Sort of Bouillabaisse:*</u>

6 oz. Salmon, cut up in ½ inch cubes
6 oz. Halibut, (can sub with cod) cup in ½ inch cubes.
6-8 large prawns or 12-16 shrimp.
1 small onion, sliced thinly.
4 cloves of garlic, sliced thinly.
3x8 oz. cans of preferably organic (not condensed)
1) Tomato Soup, 2) Clam Chowder, 3)Corn chowder

2 Cups Greens: baby Spinach or Kale or Swiss chard.
¼ cup Olive oil.
1 cup Tomato Sauce. (Bottled pasta sauce will do)
½ cup White Wine.
1 cup Vegetable broth.
Fresh ground pepper, Salt to taste.

Heat olive oil on low flame and fry onions and garlic till soft. Add fresh ground pepper and then add the 3 cans of soup, the tomato sauce and the fish and shrimp. Add the vegetable broth so you get a slightly thinned consistency.

Let this simmer on low heat for about 10 minutes. Add the wine and the greens. Add salt to taste. Simmer for another 10 minutes and then serve. Makes 6-8 servings of a delicious soup high in Omega-3, Lycopene, (tomato) and Allicin (garlic, onions).

PS: To make this vegetarian (so sorry, French Purists) eliminate the sea food and the clam chowder. Sub with a can of Minestrone soup and use extra firm tofu cut in ½ inch cubes.

March 3

RIDERS IN THE SKY

"Better to burn than to fade away."
—Neil Young

Last month we celebrated the 41ˢᵗ Anniversary of the Paris Peace Accord of 1973 which ended the war in Vietnam and the U.S.A. involvement in it. It was an event that polarized a generation and put an end to a very contentious era of American history. I was living in Mumbai (Bombay) at that time but the protests to end the war and the horror of the conflict were widely reported in the news. That a country would actually allow its citizens to question the morality of a war was amazing. In my country of origin, India, any organized protest to a nationally sanctioned conflict would most likely have led to imprisonment or worse. This homage to an equally controversial icon of those times, Jim Morrison, was penned many years later.

His death as well as his life intrigues me. At the time of his death he was 27 years old; the third in the trinity of Hendrix, and Joplin. Their credo "' *Better to burn than to fade away"* was sadly a mantra of their times. Monsieur Morrison is buried at the Pere Lachaise cemetery; appropriately home to a large number of feral cats. How did this phallic symbol of his generation, the" Electric Shaman", the crotch grabbing avatar of acid rock end up in a graffiti covered tomb in Paris? Maybe in this "City of Lights" he finally found his "Sanctuary!"

SANCTUARY:

Jim, you should have perished in a poet's grave,
Buried in some Elysian field of unspoken dreams.
Where night divides the day
And wild horses trample the wet earth,
Loamed by worms into your resting place.

Instead, you rot in a gray concrete tomb in Gay Paree!
Why Jim? "Parlez vous francais? Un petit fours, s'il vous plait!
Sycophants all, they leave you cut flowers
and pray for your futile soul.

But you were beyond redemption.
For your life and your words
harnessed the dark phantoms of our nightmares.
Jim, there was no sanctuary from the riders in the sky,
Heavy with the thunder-clouds of Vietnam.
No sanctuary from the lightning that followed you.

But hey! You probably rocked them in Hades. And hailed the Devil;
"COME ON BABY, LIGHT MY FIRE!
MPK/2002

March 4

RIDERS IN THE SKY

If you were a Boomer and lived in that era, what are your thoughts on Vietnam almost 40 years later? How did it change you?

Very young men sent to kill others, many killed for no reason, war should be stopped

Country fighting for end to war. Support for troups.

If you were not a Boomer, look up the Vietnam War. It was a fascinating and also a defining period. America and Americans were never the same afterwards. Check out www.pbs.org/wgbh/amex/vietnam

What are your thoughts on the current conflicts in Iraq and Afghanistan that the U.S. is embroiled in?

Bottom line is always money, if middle east didn't have oil, war would end.

isis is huge threat to US

Don't trust trump, can't believe people voted him in..

DR. M. P. KHAN, MD/NMD

March 5

A LITTLE NIGHT MUSIC

"Neither a lofty degree of intelligence nor imagination nor both together go to the making of genius. Love, love, love, that is the soul of genius."

—W.A. Mozart

Oops! I did it again. I forgot Mozart's Birthday. On the other hand I can be forgiven. Listen to Mozart any day of the year and it is a celebration, a rebirth. He was born on January 27th 1756 and died on December 5th 1791 at the young age of thirty-five. Born in Salzburg, Austria, he was a child prodigy and gave his first public performance at age six and amazingly, he could play multiple instruments by that time. His father, Leopold Mozart, also a renowned musician and composer, was a stern but loving taskmaster. His sister, Maria Anna, nicknamed 'Nanner' was equally talented but once she reached marriageable age, she was prohibited from performing in public as was the custom at that age.

In 1783, Wolfgang Amadeus Mozart became enthralled with the work of Johannes Sebastian Bach and Handel and this, in turn, resulted in several compositions in the Baroque style and influenced much of his later compositions, such as passages in the opera *Die Zauberflote* (The Magic Flute). During this time, Mozart met Joseph Haydn and the two composers became close friends and often performed together in concerts.

Any clues that I have to his genius cannot be found in the written word. The really amazing aspect of his music was that he transcribed the music directly onto paper and without revision. So sure was he of his passion. And he was probably the most prolific of all western composers in that his collected works require over a hundred and fifty CD's!

As I write this, I am listening to the Symphony No. 41 in C Major ("Jupiter"), K. 551. Its beauty makes my heart soar. The poem that follows was not written specifically for him. Actually it was a reflection of a difficult yet interesting time of my life. Mozart, if history is to be believed, had a tumultuous life and so this one is dedicated to him and the glorious music that he made. The poem is part of a larger piece titled 'Passion Play'

Happy Birthday M! Hope you like it?

PS: "The Magic Flute" is a good introduction to opera and to his genius!

DR. M. P. KHAN, MD/NMD

March 6

A LITTLE NIGHT MUSIC

<u>PASSION PLAY: Act III:</u>

Passion; a serpent. Multi-hued creature of our desires.
Once in Eden it was lucent, a vision of pristine clarity.
Slowly we color its albino with this life's frailty,
Pursuing its nascent form, in its embrace we mire.

Hungry for its venomous kiss, any price I would pay.
Two punctures rapture my skin, such bliss, I feel no pain.
Convulsing my placid dreams, her toxins race through my veins.
Tao and rhythm dissolving, chaos and cacophony hold sway.

The cross is heavy, my thirst unquenched by tenderness or lust.
That crimson apple is smooth and seductive, its core, pure white.
But in its flesh dwells the worm, with this knowledge I take a bite;
"The inferno awaits" in dulcet tones the reptile hisses, "Choose you must!"

Yet once this Dark Angel my parched throat did slake,
Was it in God's passion, and not love, that my universe was made?

MK/2007

March 7

DOWN WITH 6, UP WITH 3 (PART-2)

"OMEGA; Noun: Symbol ω, ω the 24ᵗʰ letter of the Greek alphabet.

Adjective: Of or characterizing a chemical group or position at the end of a molecular chain, such as omega-oxidation."

You should really try the Easy Bouillabaisse recipe. Actually "omega" is the last letter in the Greek alphabet. And yet its designation in the end chain of a fatty acid makes it a star in the science of nutrition. The more I research these fatty acids, especially omega-3, and its imbalance with its cousin omega-6; I keep discovering more of its importance in the optimal functioning of the miracle that is the human body!

Depression/Mood Disorders: A Committee on Research on Psychiatric Treatments of the American Psychiatric Association (APA) appointed eleven prominent experts in the field to an Omega-3 Fatty Acids Subcommittee, for the purpose of reviewing the evidence. Three areas were looked at. A Meta-analysis of randomized controlled trials was done. (Meta-analyses use statistical methods to pool and analyze the results of multiple clinical trials.) A population study was also done that compared people's consumption of omega-3s with rates of depression and related mood disorders along with clinical studies that compared tissue levels of omega-3s with people's psychiatric health.

The study concluded that that people who consume higher amounts of omega-3 EFA's, particularly the "marine" omega-3s from fish (EPA and DHA) had a reduced risk of depression, bipolar disorder (manic-depression), and related mood disorders.

(Freeman MP, Hibbeln JR, Wisner KL, Davis JM, Mischoulon D, Peet M, Keck PE Jr, Marangell LB, Richardson AJ, Lake J, Stoll AL. Omega-3 fatty acids:

DR. M. P. KHAN, MD/NMD

evidence basis for treatment and future research in psychiatry. J Clin Psychiatry. 2006 Dec; 67(12):1954-67.

Colon Cancer: In one meta-analysis, when fish consumption was at least seven times monthly, the relative risk improved and became more significant. Furthermore, the authors estimate that each additional time per week that fish is consumed, or for each additional 100 g (1.5 oz.) of fish eaten per week, there is a 3% or 4% lower risk of colorectal cancer, In addition, fish is known to contain selenium, vitamin D, and taurine, all of which have some anti-neoplastic activity. The overall cancer-protective effect of fish, therefore, could be a synergy of effects from the omega-3 EFA and the other micronutrients.

(Norat T, et al. Meat, fish, and colorectal cancer risk: The European Prospective Investigation into Cancer and Nutrition. J Natl Cancer Inst 2005; 97:906-916.

Wu S, et al. Fish consumption and colorectal cancer risk in humans: A systematic review and meta-analysis. Am J Med 2012; 125:551-)

DOWN WITH 6, UP WITH 3 (PART-2)

Congestive Heart Failure: or CHF. A trial was conducted by scientists from Italy's University of Brescia and Chicago's Northwestern University. 133 heart failure patients were recruited. They were already receiving standard drug therapy e.g., beta blockers and were divided randomly into two groups: A test group took 2 grams of omega-3-rich fish oil daily, while the other control group took identical placebo capsules.

At the end of 12 months they compared pumping capacity in the participants using 2D-echocardiography and stress testing.

The omega-3 group showed key advantages over the placebo group in 5 critical areas of cardiac function.

1) Pumping capacity in the left ventricle increased by 10.4 percent, in contrast to a five percent decline in the placebo group.
2) Peak VO2 – (the maximum amount of oxygen your heart can provide to your muscles during sustained exercise) increased by 6.2 percent, in contrast to a 4.5 percent decline in the placebo group.
3) Exercise duration increased by 7.5 percent, in contrast to a 4.8 percent decline in the placebo group.
4) Their average score on the New York Heart Association's CHF-severity scale decreased from 1.88 to 1.61 (good), but increased from 1.83 to 2.14 in the placebo group.
5) Hospitalizations related to CHF occurred in six percent of the fish oil group, versus 30 percent of the placebo group.

(Lau DH, Psaltis PJ, Carbone A, Kelly DJ, Mackenzie L, Worthington M, Metcalf RG, Kuklik P, Nelson AJ, Zhang Y, Wong CX, Brooks AG, Saint DA, James MJ, Edwards J, Young GD, Worthley SG, Sanders P. Atrial Protective Effects of n-3

Polyunsaturated Fatty Acids: A Long Term Study in Ovine Chronic Heart Failure. Heart Rhythm. 2010 Dec 7. [Epub ahead of print]

Nodari S, Triggiani M, Campia U, Manerba A, Milesi GO, Cesana BM, Gheorghiade M, Dei Cas L. Effects of n-3 Polyunsaturated Fatty Acids on Left Ventricular Function and Functional Capacity in Patients With Dilated Cardiomyopathy. J Am Coll Cardiol. 2010 Dec 29. [Epub ahead of print])

Once again, if you are already not on them, start 2 x 1000mg capsules of fish oil daily (or one QUELL) and decrease the omega-6 based food in your diet. The defense rests!

MY ACHING SWOLLEN LEGS!

*"I told the doctor I broke my leg in two places. He told me
to quit going to those places."*

—Henry Youngman

A common complaint that I hear in the office is that of legs swelling and aching at the end of the day. There is the inevitable request for water pills and the concern for having "heart failure?" Although congestive heart failure can cause these symptoms, it is usually associated with shortness of breath and a history of having heart problems and can be readily diagnosed with appropriate tests.

More likely, this is a common condition known as "dependent edema." It is usually the result of poor venous circulation; or in popular terms" bad veins." It affects 10% of men and 20% of women. It may or may not be associated with varicose veins. As it progresses it can cause discoloration and ulcers especially on the inside of the lower legs. People whose jobs involve standing for long periods of time and women who have had multiple pregnancies are more prone. Usually the swelling is down in the morning when you awake and worsens in the evening. This is unique to humans because of gravity and our erect posture. Of course if we lived on the moon or walked on all fours, this wouldn't be a problem. Diuretics or "water pills" are not helpful besides causing dehydration and have side effects on the electrolytes. Leg elevation (heel higher than hips), compression stockings and walking can be useful in prevention. Another infrequent cause of swelling around the ankles is inadequate intake of protein in the diet. This can usually be diagnosed by a blood test measuring the "prealbumin" level which is low and can be corrected by increasing protein intake in the diet

The other condition that can cause leg pain is poor arterial circulation and can cause pain with walking:" intermittent claudication" especially in the calves. This is seen in chronic smokers, diabetics and with hardening

DR. M. P. KHAN, MD/NMD

of the arteries: arteriosclerosis. This can also be a sign of coronary artery disease. Stopping smoking, controlling the diabetes and cholesterol are important steps in prevention. There is also a condition called "pseudo-claudication" which is seen in with spinal stenosis, or narrowing of the spinal cord in the lower (lumbar) part of the spine. This mostly causes pain in the upper thighs when walking and feels better with rest and when bending forward or resting. To date there is no medical treatment for it and usually requires surgical decompression of the spine which sometimes relieves the symptoms.

Arterial and Venous Doppler studies, which are relatively non-invasive tests, can be good screening tools for further testing. Other test can involve an arteriogram where dye is injected into the arteries. A CT scan of the lumbar spine can usually pick up stenosis.

March 10

MY ACHING SWOLLEN LEGS!

A Couple of Herbal remedies:

For vein problems, I recommend Horse Chestnut, (Brand name: Venastat) which is also used in the treatment for varicose veins and hemorrhoids. No pharmaceutical equivalent exists. The active ingredient is escin and this inhibits enzymes that cause leakage in the veins. A study using 150mg of escin daily caused significant reduction in leg volumes over a two week period and this effect persisted over a 6-week period after treatment. Another German study documented a 60% reduction in pain and discomfort within a week. In trials the side effects were low at 1% and safety has not been established in pregnancy.

Another treatment is the topical application of witch hazel (the name has nothing to do with the occult. It is old English 'wiche' for plant or bendable) which is commercially available at your local drug store. Use it topically at bedtime and on awakening.

For arterial circulation, pharmaceutical drugs do exist. In the herbal family, however Gingko biloba may be useful and they work by inhibiting platelets and blood cell stickiness. . A Standard product should contain 24% gingkosides and 6% lactones and is used at 120mg. /day. Gingko increases production of nitric oxide and this causes the arteries to open up. Check out the DL preparations of gingko. A JAMA article (2000; 108; 276-81) reported that gingko increased the walking distance by 33meters as compared to placebo. Patients who take anticoagulants such as Coumadin (warfarin) or on anti-seizure drugs should have their drug levels checked before taking gingko.

DR. M. P. KHAN, MD/NMD

And Walking:

Walk on a level surface and with a stopwatch, note the time elapsed before you start having calf and leg pain.

Rest.

Start walking again and gradually over weeks and months, you will increase the time before you start having leg pain. This is because as muscle oxygen demand increases, there is improved collateral circulation.

March 11

I HAVE THE BLUES (BERRY)

"You ought to have seen what I saw on my way
to the village, through Mortenson's pasture to-day:
Blueberries as big as the end of your thumb,
real sky-blue, and heavy, and ready to drum
in the cavernous pail of the first one to come!
And all ripe together, not some of them green
and some of them ripe! You ought to have seen!"
—**"Blueberries" by Robert Frost**

Which brings me to another eating suggestion!

4: Eat lots of fresh fruits, especially berries (organic).

One would hope that the blueberries that Mr. Frost picked were organic. Fresh blue berries this time of the year (winter) are usually from South America and can be heavily sprayed with pesticides including DDT. This is why I would recommend Instant Quick Frozen organic blueberries (Cascadian Farms). Or buy them fresh seasonally and freeze them in Ziploc bags for later use.

Blueberries are excellent sources of phytochemicals that are believed to have significant biological activity. The objective of this study was to determine whether incorporation of blueberries into food products affects their phenolic content or antioxidant and anti-proliferation (prevents cancer cells from multiplying) activity. Several blueberry fruit–containing products including fresh, individually quick frozen (IQF), freeze-dried, spray-dried, heat-dried, cooked, juice concentrate, pie filling, and jam were fractionated to remove sugars and isolate groups of phytochemicals based on solubility. For both cultivated and wild berries, fresh and IQF berries had the highest total phenols, antioxidant activity, and anti-proliferation activity. Whole freeze-dried wild blueberries also retained significant

DR. M. P. KHAN, MD/NMD

anti-proliferative activity and ranked close to the activities recorded for fresh and IQF whole fruit.

Of course other berries such as blackberries, mulberries and raspberries are also high in phenolic activity and work well in various recipes. Once again, they are heavily sprayed with pesticides and so go for fresh and organic.

In summary, the closer the product is to the natural fruit, the better is its nutritious value. Also, now there are processed food products on the market which claim to have blueberry like substances with pretty colored pictures of blueberries on the packaging but have no real fruit at all. *Read the packaging!*

March 12

I HAVE THE BLUES (BERRY)

I would like to expand on the above terminology. Polyphenols are chemicals produced by plants or *Phytochemicals* which help the plant fight off insects and fungal infections; in other words improve the immune functions of the plant. When plants including blueberries are cultivated by using pesticides, the plants markedly reduce or lose their ability to make these polyphenols which is one more reason to eat organic food.

These polyphenols play a vital role in body functions as anti-oxidants by turning on gene switches that prime anti-oxidants in the body soaking up the free radicals. They also produce nitric oxide (NO) which helps the blood vessels dilate. This is exactly what a nitroglycerine tablet does for patients with angina. They are also an excellent and delicious source of soluble fiber besides their above virtues.

Del Bo' C, Kristo AS, Kalea AZ, Ciappellano S, Riso P, Porrini M, Klimis-Zacas D. The temporal effect of a wild blueberry (Vaccinium angustifolium)-enriched diet on vasomotor tone in the Sprague-Dawley rat. Nutr Metab Cardiovasc Dis. 2010 Aug 14.

Remember that Smoothie recipe. Try it again, this time with blueberries.

You can also add blueberries to a Buckwheat Pancake Mix for a delicious Sunday Morning breakfast.

I have three blueberry bushes in my garden. Can't wait for summer, that is, if the birds don't beat me to it!

March 13

THE SUFI SUFFICETH

"The Wound is the place where the Light enters you."
—Rumi

*There was once a small boy who banged a drum all day and loved every moment
of it. He would not be quiet, no matter what anyone else said or did. Various people,
who called themselves wise men, were called in by neighbors and asked to do something
about this troublesome child.*

*The first wise man told the boy that, if he continued to make so much noise it would
perforate his eardrums. This reasoning was too advanced for the child. The second told
him that drum beating was a sacred activity and should be carried out only on special
occasions. The third offered the neighbors plugs for their ears; the fourth gave the boy a
book to read to distract him; the fifth gave the neighbors books that described a method
of controlling anger through biofeedback; the sixth gave the boy meditation exercises to
calm him down and explained that all reality was illusion.*

Each of these remedies worked for a short while, but not for very long.

*Eventually, a Sufi came along. He looked at the situation, handed the boy a
hammer and chisel, and said, "I wonder what is INSIDE the drum?"*

This little parable is an interesting lesson in simplicity; of thinking
outside the box (or drum). This story has several layers and reflects
the wisdom of a mystic branch of Islam called Sufism. In the popular
archetype, Sufis are portrayed as men with tall hats who whirl around in
spiritual ecstasy. In reality, it celebrates the direct relationship that man
has to God without the intermediate trappings and rituals of religious
dogma. Their whirling dance is an inner expression of their joy and a
kind of meditation. Its appeal, like the Zen branch of Buddhism, is that it
embraces a simple yet beautiful approach to life. But whereas Zen (more
about that later) is the path of mindfulness and meditation, Sufism is the
path of joy and loving affirmation. Although a definite polarity exists,

each path is valid in our spiritual development. And the parable that follows teaches us that we learn best from the difficulties in our lives.

A Sufi is asked to describe the qualities of his teacher. The Sufi explains that his teacher wrote beautiful poetry, and inspired him with his self-sacrifice and his service to his fellow man. His questioner readily approves of these qualities. But he is puzzled when the Sufi rebukes him:

Then he proceeds to list the qualities which he admires in his teacher. "My teacher made me irritated, which caused me to examine my irritation, to trace its source. My teacher made me angry, so that I could feel and transform my anger.

My teacher intentionally provoked vicious attacks upon himself, in order to bring the failings of both his students and critics to light, allowing them to be seen for what they really were"

Steve kind, helped others about + beyond. helped vulnerable, those in great need. He did seem interested when he talked to me on phone "How is everyone..." Call me if you want to do something — if I can't — Call again.

Founders day — came over.

Very sad — wife very sick for many years — took care of her, how cont. take care of others.

Stay at bottom of ladder.

Don't analyze

DR. M. P. KHAN, MD/NMD

March 14

THE SUFI SUFFICETH

There are valuable lessons in the above two parables! We all have had problems that we cannot seem to solve. Here is a profound truth and I believe it is attributed to Einstein.

"You cannot solve a problem by asking the same question that created the problem in the first place."

Which sounds incredibly obvious. Yet most of us keep beating our heads against a difficult situation instead of thinking outside the box.

Write down a problem that is really troubling you. Come up with a novel or creative way to get around the problem (not through it) which can have a positive resolution.

PS: Hint; keep your ego aside!!

> Face the fear, I deserve to dance, don't stop going because of him. He was unclear - a bit rude. It didn't work out last year - get back in - dance - focus on dancing which is what my intentions were. Not my problem - don't know what makes him tick

Life's travails are our ultimate teachers. Much as we like the "good" times, it is the tumultuous times that teach us compassion and kindness and which connect us to the common thread of our humanity. And the next time that someone or something rubs you the wrong way, they may be holding up a mirror that reflects our own failings!

Write down an incident or an act by an individual that really made you angry. Could you see the cause of the anger in yourself?

> Eileen aloof i helping Betty. Eileen mad because I didn't ask her to move in i me. I helped her in other way. I had to pull myself up - She wasn't there for me.

TERRIFIC TURMERIC (PART-1)

*"Each spice has a special day to it. For turmeric it is
Sunday, when light drips fat and butter-colored into the
bins to be soaked up glowing, when you pray to the nine
planets for love and luck."*
—Chitra Banerjee Divakaruni

Curcuma longa or turmeric and the powder made from the dried out root
was highly valued by early Asian civilizations and is still an important
ingredient in the complex of spices used in Indian cooking. Curcuma is a
perennial herb indigenous to Southeast Asia (Tamil Nadu) and belongs to
the Zingiberaceae family. (Ginger) Of the genus *Curcuma*, two plants, *C.
longa* and *C. xanthorrhiza* have medicinal properties but most of the research
has been done the *longa* species. Because of its golden color, it is symbolic
of sunlight. In Ayurveda medicine, turmeric has the quality of *pita* (fire/
yellow) or *gauri* (brilliant). Because of its antimicrobial and antioxidant
properties, it is used to preserve foods and prevented spoiling. In Western
cuisine, turmeric is used as a preservative in the pickling process, and as a
dye to color fabric and as a natural food coloring. Extracts from turmeric,
have been used in Ayurvedic medicine for more than 2,000 years for a
wide variety of unrelated medical conditions from parasitic intestinal
infections and skin cancer to liver disease and externally as a poultice. In
TCM, (Traditional Chinese Medicine) it is better known as Jianghuang,
and has been used for dyspepsia, liver disease, and hyperlipidemia. It is
listed in the Chinese Materia Medica. In herbal medicine it is a super-star
and is used in various conditions because of its anti-inflammatory and
ant-bacterial properties.

*Dyspepsia:*NThis is a condition associated with flatulence, burping and
right upper quadrant pain generally due to stasis of bile. Several random
control studies have demonstrated relief of these symptoms. It is also known

as NUD or Non-Ulcer Dyspepsia. One study done in Thailand reported the effect of turmeric powder compared with a combination anti-flatulence product containing ginger, capsaicin, and cascara with placebo. One hundred sixteen patients with clinically diagnosed dyspepsia were randomized to take 500 mg turmeric powder orally four times a day in capsule form for seven days. 53% of placebo patients were "improved or cured" compared to 83% of those assigned to the anti-flatulence product and 87% of those in the turmeric group (P < 0.008 for either drug vs. placebo).

High doses of turmeric can cause gastric ulcers and should be avoided if a gastric ulcer is suspected. As it stimulates bile production, it is best to rule out gall stones (pain under the right ribs) by an ultrasound, as it could trigger a gall bladder attack The recommended dose for dyspepsia is one capsule of 300 mg. of turmeric, standardized to 95% curcuminoids twice a day before lunch and dinner, for four to six weeks. (DL Turmeric Max V)

March 16

TERRIFIC TURMERIC (PART-1)

*And here is a recipe if you would rather use the aromatic qualities of
this wonder herb. It is a common recipe used in Indian cooking and
may not be for everyone. But part of the healing process is to be open to
new experiences! So give it a try.*

*LEMON RASAM: Rasam, a thin, lemony soup made with toor dal
(lentils), a type of split pea, is served as a starter in South Indian
households. Purchase toor dal in Indian grocery stores and online, or
look for gold lentils in natural food stores.*

- *⅔ Cup dry toor dal (split pigeon peas). Soak dal in water overnight.*
- *1 Tbs. grated fresh ginger (from 1-inch piece)*
- *2 serrano chilies, stemmed, seeded, and minced(or any green chilies*
- *1 14.5-oz. can plum tomatoes, drained and diced*
- *¾ tsp. salt*
- *2 tsp. ghee or vegetable oil*
- *1 tsp. brown mustard seeds (optional)*
- *½ tsp. asafetida powder (optional)*
- *1 red Kashmiri chili (dried red Indian chili), or any hot dried
  red chili, halved*
- *½ tsp. ground cumin*
- *½ tsp. ground black pepper*
- *¼ cup lemon juice*
- *Chopped cilantro, for garnish*
- *¼ tsp. ground turmeric*

1. *Combine toor dal with 4 cups water and turmeric in medium
   saucepan. Bring to a boil over medium heat. Reduce heat to
   medium-low, partially cover, and simmer 45 minutes, or until
   toor dal is soft. Transfer to blender or food processor, and blend
   until smooth. Measure, and return to saucepan.*

2. *Stir in ginger, serrano chilies, tomatoes, and salt, and bring to a boil over medium heat. Reduce heat to medium-low, and simmer 5 minutes to marry flavors, stirring occasionally.*

3. *Meanwhile, heat ghee or vegetable oil in skillet over medium heat. Add mustard seeds; asafetida powder; red Chile; curry leaves, if using; cumin; and pepper. Cover and heat 1 to 2 minutes, or until mustard seeds begin to pop. Pour into soup. Remove soup from heat, and stir in lemon juice. Season with salt and pepper, if desired. Serve garnished with chopped cilantro.*

March 17

TERRIFIC TURMERIC (PART-2)

"If to eating turmeric there is a point, it's that it will really help your joints."

—Chairman Moo

Rheumatoid Arthritis: Rheumatoid Arthritis or RA is an autoimmune disease which classically affects the small joints of the hands and feet (mostly the more proximal joints) and over a period of time actually eats away at the cartilage causing deformities and loss of function. In a previous day we discussed the role of omega-3 in the relief of symptoms. Turmeric extract is another supplement that can be used with fish oil with some pretty impressive results.

In a randomized study published *Phytotherapy Research*, 45 patients with an established diagnosis of RA were randomized into three groups. One received curcumin-500mg (the active ingredient of turmeric), the second received diclofenac sodium 50mg (an NSAID like ibuprofen) and the third received a combination of above.

End points were reduction in the Disease Activity Score or DAS-28. Although all groups showed a statistical change in the DAS score, the curcumin group showed the greatest change in the DAS score. Moreover the curcumin treatment group had no adverse side effects! Although the weakness of the study is in the small numbers and it has not been easily duplicated, it may be a useful adjunct in the treatment of RA and may be useful in preventing flare-ups.

Also a 2004 study in the journal *Oncogene* found that curcumin was an effective alternative to the drugs aspirin, indomethacin, naproxen and celecoxib in exerting anti-inflammatory effects in animal studies. Once again, more research needs to be done before this can be extrapolated to human models.

DR. M. P. KHAN, MD/NMD

Diabetes mellitus: Although still in the research phase, a 2009 study in the journal *Biochemistry and Biophysical Research Community* showed the potential of curcumin in the treatment of Type-2 Diabetes. (more natural remedies for DM-2 to follow) Its action is very similar to a commonly used drug called metformin. This drug activates an enzyme called AMPK in the liver which suppresses new production of glucose by the liver. Curcumin in the form of tetra hydro curcuminoid is 500-100,000 time more potent than metformin; molecule for molecule, and is one more reason to add turmeric to your diet.

Atherosclerosis: Before hardening of the arteries can occur, there is a breakdown of the lining of the artery called 'endothelial dysfunction.' One of the actions of Atorvastatin or Lipitor is to reduce this endothelial dysfunction and thus slow down the process of atherosclerosis. It was found that a standardized dose of turmeric compared favorably to Lipitor in reducing endothelial dysfunction although it did not significantly lower cholesterol when compared to the statin drug.

STAY TUNED FOR MORE USES OF THIS AMAZING HERB!!

March 18

TERRIFIC TURMERIC (PART-2)

THAI CURRY NOODLES: This recipe uses ingredients commonly used in many Thai recipes. An increasing number of grocery stores carry Thai curry paste and cilantro (coriander).

- *2 tsp. vegetable oil*
- *2 large shallots, chopped (1 cup) or 1 large onion*
- *¼ cup finely chopped cilantro stems, plus ¼ cup chopped cilantro leaves, for garnish*
- *2 Tbs. yellow or red Thai curry paste*
- *1 tsp. curry powder(optional)*
- *1 tsp. ground turmeric*
- *1 15-oz. can light coconut milk*
- *¾ cup low-sodium vegetable broth*
- *2 tsp. light brown sugar*
- *1 12-oz. pkg. firm tofu, drained and cut into ½-inch cubes*
- *5 oz. dry fettuccine*
- *5 cups broccoli florets*
- *6 lime wedges, for garnish*

1. *Heat oil in medium pot over medium-high heat. Sauté shallots in oil for 2 minutes. Add cilantro stems, curry paste, curry powder, and turmeric; cook 1 minute. Stir in coconut milk, broth, and brown sugar, and bring to a simmer. Reduce heat to medium, and cook 5 minutes, then stir in tofu. Simmer 10 minutes.*
2. *Cook fettuccine in large pot of boiling salted water according to package directions. Add broccoli to pot for last 2 minutes of cooking time. Drain, and add to tofu, the curry mixture. Mix well, and serve with lime wedges and chopped cilantro.*

KUNG HII FATT CHOI

"Congratulations and be Prosperous" is the loose translation of this traditional greeting for the Chinese New Year, the Year of the Horse when this day was born. The celebrations last for 15 days and is known as "The Spring Festival" even though it occurs in winter because of the disparity between the Chinese and Western method of computing the seasons. And not too long ago, the date of the Chinese New Year also coincided with the designated birthday of the Maitrya Bodhisattva or the Buddha-to-be.

Whereas Sufism tries to decipher the mysteries of the universe through parables and dance, it is the Koan that typifies the teachings of Zen Buddhism. Koans are essentially riddles that help us connect to our divine nature by forcing us to think outside the narrow confines of what our mind perceives as reality. Once again, outside the box! They cannot be solved, only dissolved!

The three Koans that follow can be difficult and frustrating if they are to be answered in a logical manner. Maybe the answer lies in the question, like an intellectual Mobius strip.

THREE KOANS: *1*

Am I the sea, my crest foaming eternally, on the shifting sands of a distant seashore/

Or am I a grain of sand lost in the desert of reality, craving the infinite depth of a divine ocean?

2

Am I the night providing simple solace to a lonely scimitar moon? Or am I the moon brightly intruding on the solitude of the velvet darkness?

3

Am I the flower, its promiscuous petals wantonly open to every passing bee?
Or am I the bee, stinger ready, devouring nectar in a frenzy of broken blossoms?

MK/1992

KUNG HII FATT CHOI

What does each of these Koan mean to you?

The Sea Koan:

_____
_____
_____
_____
_____
_____
_____
_____

The Moon Koan:

_____
_____
_____
_____
_____
_____
_____
_____

The Bee Koan:

_____
_____
_____
_____
_____
_____
_____
_____

March 21

GOTTA GO- AGAIN!

"A new medical study reports that men who eat ten pizzas a week are less likely to develop prostate problems at age 50. That's because they are usually dead by age 40."

—Jay Leno

OK guys. One of these days we are all going to get there. If we live long enough, we eventually have the problem of getting up frequently at night to urinate. Before your significant other thinks it's funny and suggests adult diapers, maybe it's time to make an appointment for a very common problem known as BPH or Benign Prostate Hypertrophy.

Of course you may have an infection of the bladder or kidneys. This is easily treatable after an analysis of the urine. If this is not the case, you have a common male problem due to enlargement of the prostate gland. This is a walnut sized gland that sits at the base of the bladder and when enlarged can cause the symptoms you have been experiencing along with difficulty starting urination and a weak stream. This symptom complex is called 'prostatism.' An index for prostatism exists (See Below) which can score how severe the problem is. A Digital Rectal Exam (DRE) and a (PSA) Prostate Specific Antigen level can confirm if you have Benign Prostatic Hyperplasia (BPH). Be warned though; there is considerable controversy in the medical literature of the benefits of screening for PSA and it is not recommended after age 75. Your physician can guide you in this matter.

One of the popular therapies (in Europe the therapy of first choice) is Saw Palmetto Extract (SPE) and is one of the top selling herbs in the US. SPE was once on the National Formulary and was dropped (thanks Big Pharma! Herbs can't be patented!!). It's mechanism of action is the presence of a fatty acid; *sitosterol*, which inhibits the enzyme *5-alpha reductase*. This enzyme converts *testosterone* to *dihydrotestosterone* which causes the prostate tissue to grow.

DR. M. P. KHAN, MD/NMD

A recent study on 85 men receiving SPE at 160 mg 2/day showed significant improvement in flow rate of urine and symptoms as compared to placebo over a six month period. Currently the NIH is conducting a 6 year study with 3100 men. Although a pharmaceutical drug works in the same way, (Finasteride) SPE does not cause any sexual dysfunction and does not affect the PSA level. (Finasteride will ½ the PSA level so you will have to double the PSA reading the lab gets to get the actual level). No drug interactions exist and it is dosed at 160mg, 2 x day and it is sometimes compounded with stinging nettle and pumpkin seeds.

I would recommend (DL# 82044) Uro-Pro x 2 daily which has 160 mg of SPE along with Zinc and Pygeum and pumpkin seed or plain SPE, (DL # 83910) also 2 daily. Symptom improvement should occur at 12 to 24 weeks. SPE can be combined with drugs such as Flomax.

GOTTA GO -AGAIN!

American Urological Association Urinary Symptom Score (USS) or International Prostate Symptom Score (IPSS)

Questions to be answered: Not at all=0; Less than1 time in 5=1; Less than half the time=2; About half the time=3; More than half the time=4; Almost always =5

(Circle one number on each line)

---

1. Over the past month, how often have you had a sensation of not emptying your bladder completely after you finished urinating?
0 1 2 3 4 5

2. Over the past month, how often have you had to urinate again less than 2 hours after you finished urinating?
0 1 2 3 4 5

3. Over the past month, how often have you found you stopped and started again several times when you urinated?
0 1 2 3 4 5

4. Over the past month, how often have you found it difficult to postpone urination?
0 1 2 3 4 5

5. Over the past month, how often have you had a weak urinary stream?
0 1 2 3 4 5

6. Over the past month, how often have you had to push or strain to begin urination?
0 1 2 3 4 5

---

7. Over the past month, how many times did you most typically get up to urinate from the time you went to bed at night until the time you got up in the morning?

0 1 2 3 4 5

Sum of circled numbers (AUA symptom score): TOTAL _____

0 to 7: *Mild symptoms;* **8 to 19**: *Moderate symptoms;* **20 to 35**: *Severe symptoms*

What is your PSA level? _____*What is your Symptom Score* _____*What is your Symptom Score after a 24 week trial of SPE (Saw Palmetto)?* _____

March 23

AND WHAT WAS THAT-AGAIN!

"He that will not apply new remedies must expect new evils; for time is the greatest innovator."
—Francis Bacon

Sometimes I like to recommend multiple herbal/vitamin/mineral supplementations in specific disease states. Although, I like to use discreet supplements over combination products, I will occasionally use them for convenience sake and/or financial reasons. Below are some of the supplements and vitamins I recommend for early stages of memory impairment and dementia which is a more global loss in multiple intellectual functions.

1) *Gingko:* This was reviewed previously. The active ingredients are glycosides and terpenoids. They act as antioxidant and decreases platelet activity. Also may increase cerebral circulation and acetylcholine receptor sites Use 50:1 extract (GBE) at a dose of 2 x 60 mg daily in patients age 45-90 years to improve cognitive function for 52 weeks. Short-term use has shown no significant improvement from placebo in moderate AD. Its real role may be in prevention of dementia. Currently there is a $15 million study ongoing to see if gingko can prevent Alzheimer's. No significant side effects but watch with Coumadin, aspirin and NSAID (ibuprofen) because of increased risk of bleeding.

2) *Huperizine:* Isolated from Huperisia serrata, a Chinese herb, it is a potent acetylcholine esterase inhibitor and works like Aricept without side effects. Extensive and well controlled studies have been done in China. It also acts as antioxidant. Dosage is 100 mcg to 200mcg daily and is available as Cerebra in US. Also found in Douglas Labs product Cogni-Flex. Currently in trial but an early 8 week trial showed mark improvement in all dementia

parameters. Mild side effects and no known drug interactions although caution with cholinergic and anticholinergic drugs.

3) *C & E vitamins (food sourced):* The Rotterdam study showed that foods high in vitamin C and E and flavonoids (but not supplements) along with a low fat diet, showed after a 10 yr. follow-up, a reduced risk of AD in 5395 participants with an average age of 55yrs. Similar results were noted with the Rush University study. High doses of natural Vitamin E 2000 iu/daily (natural has alpha and gamma tocopherol) did delay the progression of AD although this is controversial and I would not recommend this.

4) *Phosphatidylserine: (PS):* Foods such as fish and soy are high in PS. PS is also manufactured by the body and increases glucose uptake and use by the brain. Available as a food supplement, it has been shown in doses of 300 mg a day to improve memory and depressive symptoms in 12-24 week controlled studies. No adverse effects but avoid use with heparin. Use soy based PS and not bovine (animal based) because of safety concerns. A combination product called Cogni-flex (combines 1, 2, and 4) is available from Douglas Labs.

Other useful herbs may be Rosemary, Sage, and Gotukola. No studies available at this time but strong traditional use and rich in lecithin and choline. And remember to add omega-3 and Vitamin D!

AND WHAT WAS THAT-AGAIN!

Here is a quick and easy test for detecting early dementia.

Step 1. *Remember three unrelated words, such as "ball," "dog," and "window."*

Step 2. *Draw a simple clock set to 10 minutes after eleven o'clock (11:10). A correct response is drawing of a circle with the numbers placed in approximately the correct positions, with the hands pointing to the 11 and 2.*

Step 3. *Recall the three words from Step 1. One point is given for each item that is recalled correctly.*

If Step 2 and Step 3 are completed without any difficulty, dementia is very unlikely. If there is any concern in completion of any of the above steps, a medical consultation is advised.

Several more detailed tests are available such as the Folstein or MMSE (Mini Mental Status Exam) and the more comprehensive MATTIS test which is usually administered by a neuro- psychologist.

March 25

NIRVANA DAY

"Yes, there is Nirvana; it is in leading your sheep to a green pasture, and in putting your child to sleep, and in writing the last line of your poem."
—Kahlil Gibran

Somewhere on the calendar there is actually a day of the week designated Nirvana Day. It was inevitable that when a Seattle grunge band goes by that name that someone would try to make it a Hall Mark moment. Maybe Gibran captured it best. Maybe Nirvana is to be at peace with the simple pleasures of life, those small instances which make us smile. Look at a statue of the Buddha. In his repose he is always smiling. Like he has found the answer to our suffering and is telling us *"Forget all those philosophies and metaphysical arguments. For every theory and dogma, there is an opposite and contradictory explanation. Find what you love and merge with it. The path to happiness is that simple."* In my younger years I explored the concept of happiness (and Nirvana) in the poem that follows. Excuse the naïveté! It is titled, what else:

HAPPINESS:

Is happiness a bed of flowers?
A cool breeze, a sweet nap;
Romantic notions of mushy valentines?
Will the promises of love wilt with the heat of time
And leave a bitter after taste of fickle euphoria?

It seems that my life is an endless road of travails.
The desert of monotony surrounds me,
Dissonance beats down, hot with brazen intensity.
This thirsty traveler longs
For the cool springs of compassion.

Happiness is the elusive prey I seek.
Wraith like, it twists and turns,
Defies the mighty hunter's guns.
Yet comes eagerly to the gentle call
Of the Brahmin with sugared hand.

I want to live with fiery passion,
Of life pulsating with each heartbeat,
Throbbing in the echo chambers of eternity,
Each systole circulating the very essence of creation,
As I vibrate in harmony with the Universe.
This place, this life, is my Nirvana!

MK/72

DR. M. P. KHAN, MD/NMD

NIRVANA DAY

What is your version of Nirvana?

_____
_____
_____
_____
_____
_____
_____

Describe the last time you felt completely at peace with yourself.

_____
_____
_____
_____
_____
_____
_____

List three simple pleasures that bring you joy or inner peace.

_____
_____
_____
_____
_____
_____
_____

March 27

LOVE (OR SOMETHING LIKE IT)

*"All you need is love. But a little chocolate now and then
doesn't hurt."*

—**Charles M. Schulz**

One of my co-workers is still very upset that she did not receive the
traditional chocolate and flowers from her significant other on Valentine's
Day. Boy is that SO in the dog house; it's almost six weeks since that
holiday! Her feelings resonate with the times when we have been rejected
in love. And the inevitable blues. Been there and done that. And to add
further indignity to that loving feeling, science tells us, we could be
victims of our brain chemistry going awry.

I recently read in a popular magazine that the sensation of love is due
to a bunch of molecules, dopamine I think, going amok in our brain and
that chocolate (see February-14) does pretty much the same thing! And
eventually these chemicals cool down in a couple of years. And then the
arguments about whose turn it is to do the dishes? This poem reflects on
how love and I have parted company in different ways in different times.
It probably explains why I am addicted to chocolate! Especially:

WHEN LOVE LEAVES:

When love leaves,
Is it a stocking foot burglar,
A dark demon of moonless nights
Creeping down stairs, stepping over the one that creaks;
A stealth cat hauling the booty of broken promises
And fencing them for pennies on lonely streets?
When love leaves,
Is it a Harlequin dancer,
Blue-gold diamond and silk scarves twirling
Over gilded carousels of gloating wooden horses?

DR. M. P. KHAN, MD/NMD

A raucous Mardi gras of bare bosomed jubilation;
Pride will summon a rain of tears on this parade!

When love leaves,
Is it a white-vested Norse goddess?
Harbinger of a desolate winter,
An icicle clad ghost hiding
In her folds a carnal stiletto
Fresh with the gore of ripped-open hearts!

When love leaves, why weep, was it ever ours to keep?
When love leaves, why grieve, was it ever ours to give?

MK/5/2000

LOVE (OR SOMETHING LIKE IT)

What were your feelings the last time you were unlucky in love? It is better to have loved and lost than to have never loved at all although it is better to win at it. But we all have been there.

Rejection - never love,
first dance partner who
"was" practicing" with me - h
was aloof, asked me out then
ignored me - I ended it

OCD thoughts as to
" what in the hell happened"

Week after Maggie did -
reminder of losses in my life
Stopped dancing Cheryl's classes

How did you get over those feelings?

Social worker
power positive thinking
options
back to dance class
with or without him Then

CORE PRAYERS

Hope of meeting someone
first . Still working on it

DR. M. P. KHAN, MD/NMD

FELIS DOMESTIC-US

"In order to keep a true perspective of one's importance, everyone should have a dog that will worship him and a cat that will ignore him."

—Anon.

If you are not a cat person, skip this page. On second thought, read it anyway. Loving cats is like an act of faith. The connection can't be explained rationally. Once they get their claws into you, you are hooked for life. So today is dedicated to all you cat people (or not) and to one cat in particular. Her name was Athena.

She came into our life on a fall afternoon. We had seen an ad in a local newspaper about a breeder who had to move to a smaller place and was looking for a home for some of her young kittens. After a thorough vetting by the breeder of our situation, she stopped by and handed us a young cat. She advised us that it was a blue point Egyptian Mau. All we saw was outrageous ears, large green eyes and a heart to match. Pretty soon she had our older cats, (a male and female, Odin and Hanna; Norwegian Forest cat or Wedgies as they our known in cat circles which as of this date have passed on to the great litter box in the sky)) going bonkers with her antics. This cat defied gravity as she systematically explored every cupboard top and other impossible situations.

At night she would generally curl up near my pillow and then make her way on to my outstretched hand. There she would plunk herself down and purr herself to sleep. Very quickly, she became an essential part of our lives, like food and air. Contrary to the popular archetype of the aloof and self-centered feline, Athena was almost dog like in her devotion, as she followed us around from room to room.

But the backyard was a different story. Many a mole saw those large green eyes as the last thing they would remember. Mau's are the fastest cats in the world of domestics. They have an extra skin flap between their hind legs which helps them stretch out at a full run. This made her pretty much impossible to catch, unless she wanted to be caught. And she found creative ways to escape by going under and over our so called "cat proof fence". After several of those instances, Karen decided to walk her on a leash in the yard. Amazingly, she still could snag an occasional mole while attached to the leash!

Athena is now buried in the backyard of our home in Monroeville, PA in a small grave next to the raspberry bushes. Karen planted a rose bush over her grave. She was only 5 years old. Later we found out that this breed is prone to cardiac hypertrophy or thickening of the heart muscle. She had a large blood clot travel into her lungs from the heart and despite heroic and urgent efforts from a local veterinarian; she passed on to Cat Valhalla. All this was several years ago but her unbounded spirit still haunts me and I miss her.

FELIS DOMESTIC-US

The list that follows was put together by Karen. They are products and services that we use on our cats. We have no financial connections to any of them.

SOURCES OF INFORMATION, PRODUCTS AND CAT FOOD:

1. Critter Oil: *(Natural Flea Control) (put on animals collar, for cats use release collar) Naturals for Animals, 514-37'' St North, St. Petersburg, FL 33713-7516 727-327-2356*

2. *2. Lumino brand Diatomaceous Earth (Food Grade) for natural flea and tick control*

LuminoWellness.com

3. Forti Flora *by Purina, A combination of Probiotics and Vitamins. Important for gut health and if your pet is on any anti-biotic.*

4. Pet Guard Inc. *Yeast and Garlic Powder: (Natural Flea Control) Orange Park, Fl. 32073 800-874-3231 Organic food/ supplements Food found at East End Coop*

5. Berkshire Organics; Guido's and Chez Petz: *These stores carry most of the below mentioned products.*

6. Petzlife tooth paste: www.Petzlife.com *888-334-0096. 888-474-7387 Prevents and cures red gum line/ tartar. It works!*

7. Dental Wipes *by Petco, useful in the daily cleaning of teeth and gums.*

8. Books on Pet Health:
    a. <u>Natural Healing for Dogs and Cats</u> by Diane Stein; The Crossing Press Inc. Herbs, Acupressure, nutrition, psychic healing, homeopathy, flower essences and muscle testing.
    b. <u>Four Paws Five Directions</u> by Cheryl Schwartz DVM Celestial Arts Publishing
    c. <u>Complete Guide to Natural Health for Cats and Dogs</u> Rodale Press

9. Sources for toxic house or garden plants:
    a. Books for Veterinarians: Penn State Book Store, or Ebay. <u>Small Animal Toxicology</u> by Gfeller, Publisher: Mosby or <u>A Guide to Plant Poisoning of Animals of North America</u> by Anthony Knight
    b. <u>Poison Control Toll numbers animals specifically 1-900-680-0000,</u>

10. <u>"Joints"</u> made by Pet Superfood is an organic blend of supplements with hyaluronic acid and chondroitin and various dried mushroom extracts.

11. Recommended Cat Food:
    a. Newman's Own Premium Cat Food (Wet and Dry/Organic)
    b. Organix by Castor and Pollox. (Dry/Organic)
    c. Wellness-Core (Food Grade/Wet and Dry)
    d. Pet Guard (Food Grade/Wet Food)

A KRAZY KAT POEM

THE FEARLESS CATS (of Massachusetts):

(Verse in italic to be read all together)
Just to be clear;
We are not scaredy cats from Pawtucket,
We are fearless cats from Massachusetts.

And on moonless night we warn ya,
With our endless caterwauling (we are actually plotting),
How to sneak up from behind and really get ya.

We are stealth cats,
Fat cats,
Slick cats,
Scat cats

Just to be clear;
We are not scaredy cats from Pawtucket,
We are fearless cats from Massachusetts.

Our purring rubbing ways are designed to fool ya,
In the day as we doze away the hours (not really),
We are actually dreaming up ways to nail ya.
We are cool cats,
Bad cats,
Fab cats,
Alley cats.

Just to be clear;
We are not scaredy cats from Pawtucket,
We are fearless cats from Massachusetts.

Feed us Fancy Feast, Purina. Yecch!
Would rather eat a fur ball, I tell ya,
It's no secret little birdies and
other small critters we like to munch on,
But a secret no self-respecting cat will confess;
we really do love ya.

Just to be clear;
We are not scaredy cats from Pawtucket,
We are fearless cats from Massachusetts.

MK 10/13

DR. M. P. KHAN, MD/NMD

APRIL

1-Apr	ORANGE YOU A FOOL. An absurd clever poem.
2-Apr	ORANGE YOU A FOOL. And your favorite AF day prank?
3-Apr	TRANSITIONS' TO A BETTER LIFE. The Permaculture Movement
4-Apr	TRANSITIONS' TO A BETTER LIFE. Permaculture; some resources.
5-Apr	DERMATOLOGICAL HERBAL (PART-1) Topical; oral preparations
6-Apr	DERMATOLOGICAL HERBAL (PART-2) Common skin conditions.
7-Apr	CATASTROPHIC COSMETICS (PART-1) All the dangerous skin stuff.
8-Apr	CATASTROPHIC COSMETICS. (PART-1) Check out the ones you use.
9-Apr	CATASTROPHIC COSMETICS (PART-2) And still more dangerous skin stuff.
10-Apr	CATASTROPHIC COSMETICS (PART-2) And Some more homework.
11-Apr	THE POETRY OF SKIN. The medical to the metaphysical.
12-Apr	THE POETRY OF SKIN. Some 'mindful touching.
13-Apr	SUCROSE=GLUCOSE+FRUCTOSE. Sorting the sweet stuff.
14-Apr	SUCROSE=GLUCOSE+FRUCTOSE.HFCS in your pantry.
15-Apr	CHILDWISH. A poem about fatherhood.
16-Apr	CHILDWISH. Childhood memories, good or bad!
17-Apr	AN ABUNDANCE OF ATTENTION. Really a deficit?
18-Apr	AN ABUNDANCE OF ATTENTION. A quick test for ADD.
19-Apr	ADHD. MMMM! WHAT WAS THAT? This is personal.
20-Apr	ADHD. MMMM! WHAT WAS THAT? Helpful herbs & supplements.
21-Apr	ADHD.....MMMM! WHAT WAS THAT, AGAIN? The upside of it
22-Apr	ADHD.....MMMM! WHAT WAS THAT, AGAIN? Looking for the positive.
23-Apr	REMEMBERING ALOIS ALZHEIMER. The pathology dementia.
24-Apr	REMEMBERING ALOIS ALZHEIMER. And a poem in his memory.
25-Apr	EAT THIS, NOT THAT. Eating Suggestions # 5 and false assumptions.
26-Apr	EAT THIS, NOT THAT. More false assumptions about food.
27-Apr	HERBAL TEA TIME (PART V) Herbs to help prevent the big C.
28-Apr	HERBAL TEA TIME (PART V) Cancer screening guidelines.
29-Apr	HERBAL TEA TIME (PART VI) Herbs to help the heart.
30-Apr	HERBAL TEA TIME (PART VI) More herbs to help the heart.

DR. M. P. KHAN, MD/NMD

April 1

ORANGE YOU A FOOL

"This is the day upon which we are reminded of what we are on the other three hundred and sixty-four."
—Mark Twain

The first day of April is traditionally a day when we can play pranks on unsuspecting people and get away with it. Its tradition is generally attributed to Chaucer's Canterbury Tales where the fox plays a trick on the vain cock on the 32nd day of March or April 1. It gives us a chance to admit to ourselves that, at one time or another in our lives we have acted foolishly. And yet we have survived to tell the tale. A reminder not to take ourselves too seriously!

The poem that follows was part of a writing project using the word 'orange' and is the silliest (and foolish) poem I have written to date. The difficulty lies in using that word in every line, to keep the rhyming, and yet making sense of the poem. For example in the above title, *"ORANGE YOU"* is phonetically the same as *"AREN'T YOU."*

O IS FOR ORANGE:

*My poem on that color **orange** could be quite conventional,*
*Oh puke! "The setting sun was like an **orange** ball"*
*Don't be **borange**, give me poetic license, a little you all,*
*And my musing on that hue could be quite **oranginal**.*

*Late again, my **clockwork-orange** demised that morning,*
*My day was starting quite **disorangised** it appeared.*
*A quick breakfast (**orangic** of course) and a beer,*
*Kissed my **orang-putah*** wife, I really have to get going.*

Shifting my Ferrari (guess the color) through **orange** of gears,
Orange county (CA) traffic as usual, was quite a mess.
Pedal to the metal, I was **ovaranging** 90, I confess,
When a **deoranged** driver crashed into my rear.

Hark, can it be? I hear herald **orangels** sing!
My wife made funeral **orangements** at my behest.
And now finally I can lay this very **orang**e poem to rest,
And no flowers please, lots of **OJ**,
We'll make it a happening.

MK/04

* Indonesian for 'woman'

DR. M. P. KHAN, MD/NMD

April 2

ORANGE YOU A FOOL

These are some of my favorite April Fool's Day pranks.

In 1996, Taco Bell took out a full-page advertisement in The New York Times announcing that they had purchased the Liberty Bell and renamed it the "Taco Liberty Bell". And the White House fueled the rumor that The Lincoln Memorial was purchased by the Ford Motor Company and renamed The Lincoln Mercury Memorial!

In 1998, Burger King ran an ad saying that people could get a Whopper for left-handed people. The condiments were designed to drip out of the right side. Not only did customers order the new left handed burgers, but some specifically requested the "old" right-handed ones.

And my personal favorite hoax: A BBC television program, 'Panorama,' ran a show in 1957, showing Swiss farmers harvesting spaghetti from trees. They had claimed that the troublesome pest, the spaghetti weevil, had been eradicated and as a result the spaghetti harvest was thriving once again. A large number of people contacted the BBC wanting to know how to cultivate their own spaghetti trees.

Based on your own experiences, which is you favorite AF day prank?

_____

_____

_____

_____

_____

_____

_____

_____

April 3

'TRANSITONS' TO A BETTER LIFE

"Be the change you want to see in the world."
—Mahatma Gandhi

This was a while ago when we were living in Pennsylvania, Karen and I were invited to a meeting of "Sustainable Monroeville" at the local library. One of our pet peeves has been the lack of the ability of local businesses to recycle plastics and glass. Our goal at this meeting was to convince them that doing so was good for them and the planet! Dinner was pot luck, but the food you brought had to be of local origin. Much to our surprise there must have been around forty individuals ranging from college students with ecology majors to a council woman of the local municipality and a couple of business types from the city. It seems that we all had a different agenda but with a common theme; to live in harmony with the environment in a sustainable way. The energy in the room was palpable.

After we had all introduced ourselves, there was a lot of discussion about Transition Training. Apparently the movement started in the U.K. as a result of the austerity measures of the World War II and has since blossomed into a worldwide movement. Some of the basic principles of the training are:

* Explore ways of increasing community resilience.

* Learn to describe the challenges of Peak Oil (the worldwide consumption of oil is more than we are pumping out), climate change and economic instability in ways that bring people together and inspire action.

* Receive tools for community outreach, education and creating shared vision.

* Learn ways to work with obstacles that prevent communities from responding to the challenges.

* Learn how to facilitate community collaboration-support existing activities and expanding the number and diversity of people involved.

* Meet others in your region who share your concerns and want to transition to greater security and stability. Become part of a rapidly growing positive, inspirational, global movement.

April 4

'TRANSITONS' TO A BETTER LIFE

And before you dismiss this as idealistic and" who has time for this" ask yourself if you can afford not to be involved. The change or "transition" is not going to happen by some government legislation but by small scale grassroots movements. Unless we all pitch in and do our part, individually and collectively, the clock for our species may be running out.

One of the basic tenets of the transition movement is the concept of "permaculture" which is a fusion word for "permanent agriculture." Its chief guru is Bruce Charles 'Bill' Mollison; a researcher, author, scientist, teacher and naturalist. The Wikipedia definition of Permaculture "is an integrated system of design that encompasses not only agriculture, horticulture, architecture and ecology, but also economic systems, land access strategies and legal systems for businesses and communities."

Here is some reading material on the Transition Movement and Permaculture

- *The Transition Handbook: from oil dependency to local resilience - by Rob Hopkins*
- *The Transition Timeline: for a local, resilient future - by Shaun Chamberlin*
- *Local Food: how to make it happen in your community - by Tamzin Pinkerton and Rob Hopkins*
- *Local Money: how to make it happen in your community - by Peter North*
- *Local Sustainable Homes: how to make them happen in your community - by Chris Bird*
- *Local Communities and Local Councils: working together to make things happen - by Alexis Rowell*
- *Bell, Graham. The Permaculture Way. 1ˢᵗ edition, Thorsons, (1992), ISBN 0-7225-2568-0, 2ⁿᵈ edition Permanent Publications (UK) (2004), ISBN 1-85623-028-7.*

- *Bell, Graham. The Permaculture Garden. Permanent Publications (UK) (2004), ISBN 1-85623-027-9.*
- *Burnett, Graham. Permaculture: A Beginner's Guide. Spiralseed (UK).*
- *Fern, Ken. Plants for a Future. [Permanent Publications] (UK) (1997). ISBN 1-85623-011-2. Google Books link.*
- *Fukuoka, Masanobu. "The One Straw Revolution." Rodale Books (US). Holistic Agriculture Library*
- *Holmgren, David. Permaculture: "Principles and Pathways beyond Sustainability." Holmgren Design Services (Australia).*
- *Holmgren, David. "Update 49: Retrofitting the suburbs for sustainability". CSIRO Sustainability Network*
- *Hart, Robert. "Forest Gardening". Green Books (UK) ISBN 1-900322-02-1.*

April 5

DERMATOLOGICAL HERBAL (PART-1)

"Cultivate poverty like a garden herb.
Things do not change, we change.
Sell your clothes and keep your thoughts."
                         —Henry David Thoreau

I am often asked about natural approaches to skin conditions. I would divide these into two broad classes. 1) Internal or supplements taken *orally* and 2) Those applied *topically*.

ORAL:

General: Almost all skin conditions respond to high doses of omega-3 fatty acids and I would recommend 3000-6000 mg of fish oil on a regular basis. Specific conditions that respond are eczema and psoriasis.

Warts. Thuja in homeopathic proportions is good for warts although the exact mechanism is not known.

Herpes Simplex. Recurrent cold sores and genital herpes respond well to an immune booster like 'Phyto-shield' which is a proprietary blend (Douglas Labs) of Echinacea and other immune boosters as prophylaxis. Also oral L-Lysine at a dose of 500 mg twice a day could help in prevention of outbreaks.

Acne. Vitex or Agnes castus taken orally is shown to be effective against premenstrual acne at 400 mg a day. (DL# 77301). An oral extract of Neem Oil (Ayurvedic preparation) is also helpful in reducing acne.

TOPICAL:

Acne: A dilute solution of witch hazel twice daily acts as an astringent. Fruit acids such as glycolic work as exfoliate agents but higher concentrations

DR. M. P. KHAN, MD/NMD

can be irritating. A 5 % gel of tea tree oil works just as well as some commercial preparations. Tea tree oil comes from Australia only so beware of knock-offs. I advise against long term use as it could be sensitizing.

Wounds and burns: Topical Aloe Vera gel is excellent for reducing the pain after an injury but be careful not to use the powder (which is a laxative). The gel produces a substance which increases the circulation and inactivates pain producing agents. Magnesium lactate in the gel also reduces the itching by reducing histamine release. Calendula also known as marigold in topical form is a good treatment for boils, rashes, and herpes zoster lesions (shingles) and in superficial burns. It is widely used as a treatment for diaper rash. The tincture can also be used as a gargle for sore throats.

April 6

DERMATOLOGICAL HERBAL (PART-2)

Herpes simplex: Mellissa is a lemon scented member of the mint family and is available as "balm". Applied topically 5 times a day does cut down on the healing time. You will also smell nice at the same time. Shingles and post herpetic neuralgia respond well to topical licorice or hibiscus.

Fungal infections: 10% tea tree oil cream is effective against skin fungus infection and the straight oil (undiluted) is more effective than pharmaceutical or OTC agents, on Tinea or ring worm. Wash off any topical application after 6-8 hours. Toe nail fungus (onychomycosis) responds well to topical 100% tea tree oil over a six month period and has a cure rate comparable to pharmaceutical agents. Avoid tea tree oil in open areas of skin.

Chronic Coughing: Though not strictly skin, the back of the throat or pharyngeal mucosa is actually a variation of skin and responds well to topical agents. I often recommend straight honey, around a teaspoon every 4 hours for a cough due to post nasal drainage. Although studies have been done with buckwheat honey, in my experience any kind of honey works just as well. Diabetics should be cautious because of the glucose load though a teaspoon of honey has around 30 calories. In one study, 130 children aged 2-17 with runny nose and cough were randomized to receive nightly doses of buckwheat honey, artificial honey-flavored cough medicine (dextromethorphan), or no treatment.

Buckwheat Honey was found to be the most helpful in reducing nighttime cough and improving sleep in children with upper respiratory infection. Improvement was seen in all of the groups, children receiving honey had the fewest episodes of nocturnal cough and slept better compared to children in the other groups.

Sprains, Strains and Bruising: The topical (and oral available as a homeopathic preparation and greatly diluted, do ***not*** take the tincture orally) superstar is arnica (Arnica montana) gel or tincture applied topically to the area that is injured or bruised. It is widely available and is clear and odorless with amazing results. Keep a tube around if you (like me) are a week-end athlete.

WARNING: In conclusion if you have any skin lesions that do not heal readily, don't delay consulting with your physician!! These could be pre-cancerous or early skin cancers and may need a biopsy or a specialist referral. Also a spreading infection of the skin may need aggressive oral anti-biotic therapy.

April 7

CATASTROPHIC COSMETICS (PART 1)

"Beauty, to me is about being comfortable in your own skin. That, or a kick ass red lipstick."
—Gwyneth Paltrow

Your skin is the largest organ of your body. Besides its unique ability to heal from wounds, it also cools us when we are hot, prevents bacteria from invading us and even functions as an endocrine gland (Vitamin D production). And caring for that organ is a multi-billion dollar industry with thousands of products developed, all of them holding out the promise of beauty and youth.

One has to just visit the cosmetic counter of the nearby mall to realize how seamlessly they have been integrated into our daily lives. These are products that women and men use on a daily basis without giving it a second thought to the toxic chemicals that are being absorbed by the skin and their long term consequences. I have listed a product related breakdown of the 10 worst offenders.

LIP STICK:BHA (butylated hydroxyanisole) also listed as *Antioxyne B; Antrancine 12* is a preservative and stabilizer; U.S. National Toxicology Program, a part of the National Institutes of Health, has classified BHA as "reasonably anticipated to be a human carcinogen" based on evidence of carcinogenicity in experimental animals. It is also an endocrine disruptor (similar to BPA found in plastic bottles) and has shown neuro-toxicity in animal models.

NAIL POLISH: TOLUENE also known as *benzene* is a volatile solvent and is a potent neuro-toxic agent. Mothers who inhale toluene vapors during pregnancy may cause developmental damage in the fetus. It has been also associated with toxicity to the immune system and a possible link to blood cancer such as malignant lymphoma.

DR. M. P. KHAN, MD/NMD

SHAMPOO: FRAGRANCES: This usually represents a witch's brew of chemicals and the components are usually not listed separately. They can be neuro-toxic and can have an adverse effect on the immune system. It is best to use fragrance free products.

PARABENS: Parabens also known **as** *Propylparaben; Benzoic acid; 4-Hydroxy- Propylester; 4-hydroxy benzoic acid* are preservatives used by the food, pharmaceutical, and personal care product industries. Parabens are estrogen mimics and can act as hormone (endocrine) system disruptors.

SUNSCREENS: OXYBENZONE: Also known as *Benzophenone-3; 2-Benzoyl-5-Methoxyphenol; Durascreen; Solaquin.* This is a common ingredient of some sunscreens and is associated with photo allergic (an allergic reaction when exposed to sunlight) reactions. This chemical absorbs through the skin in significant amounts. And is found in the bodies of 97% of Americans and accumulates in the body. Animal studies have shown possible effects on behavior and cardiac diseases and may also be an endocrine disruptor.

CATASTROPHIC COSMETICS (PART 1)

Please note that not all products in the above categories have these chemicals. www.ewg.org has an excellent list of safe products under the Skin Deep link.

Make a list of all the products that you use in the above categories on a daily basis.

_____

_____

_____

_____

_____

_____

_____

_____

_____

_____

_____

_____

_____

_____

_____

_____

Access the web site www.cosmeticsdatabase.com or the above mentioned link and look up the safety rating of the products you have listed above.

Thank them by making a donation for all the excellent and unbiased information that they provide.

April 9

CATASTROPHIC COSMETICS (PART 2)

*"Cosmetics are a boon to every woman, but a girl's best
beauty aid is still a near sighted man."*
—Yoko Ono

A recent study of teenagers recorded an average use of 17 personal care products each day, while the average adult woman used only 12 products. Teens may unknowingly expose themselves to higher levels of cosmetic ingredients with adverse potential health effects. This, at a time when their bodies are more susceptible to damage from these chemicals which disrupt the signals that hormones send to each other and to organ systems. A whole cascade of sex hormones cause physical and emotional changes in the adolescent years and a very small change can have long term consequences. The same can applied in pregnancy as these chemicals can affect the sexual development of the fetus. So here are the next five culprits.

SOAPS: TRICLOSAN is a common ingredient found in anti-bacterial soaps. Recent studies by the AMA in 2000 have shown that they are no more effective than regular soap in decreasing the bacteria count. It is the actual duration of washing your hands that is more critical. Sing the Happy Birthday song twice (quietly or not). The other concern is the emergence of anti-biotic resistant bacteria. But this chemical also reacts with chlorine and produces chloroform which is carcinogenic and in sunlight breaks down into dioxin which is an environmental toxin.

DEODORANTS/HAIR SPRAYS: PHTHALATES are powerful hormone disruptors and are used widely in the cosmetic industry to improve the consistency of their products. Amazingly, they do not have to be included in the labeling of cosmetic products. Phthalates are also found in children's toys. Phthalates are mostly banned in cosmetics (and toys) in Europe. The male reproductive system of the developing fetus is particularly sensitive to this chemical. There seems to be a strong causal connection with a) **declining sperm count**: Average sperm counts in industrialized countries are declining at a rate of about one percent each year. b) Increased incidence of **hypospadias**: This condition is a physical deformity of the penis in which the opening of the urethra occurs on the bottom of the penis instead of the tip. c) An increase in the rate of **undescended testicles** occurs in two to four percent of full-term boys in Western countries and increases the risk of testicular cancer.

MASCARA: TRIETHANOLAMINE: This is a strongly alkaline substance used as surfactant and pH adjusting chemical. Can cause an allergic reaction and may be contaminated with nitrosamines which are carcinogenic.

HAIR COLORING/DYES: RESORCINOL: This is a common ingredient in almost all popular hair color and bleaching products. It is a skin irritant that is toxic to the immune system and a frequent cause of hair dye allergy. In animal studies, resorcinol can reduce production of thyroid hormone. The federal government regulates exposures to resorcinol in the workplace, but there are no regulations limiting amounts of resorcinol in personal care products. Best to use henna based hair coloring.

April 10

CATASTROPHIC COSMETICS (PART 2)

Please note that not all products in the below categories have these chemicals. Once again, www.ewg.org has an excellent list of safe products.

Make a list of all the products that you use in the above categories on a daily basis.

_____

_____

_____

_____

_____

_____

_____

_____

_____

_____

_____

_____

_____

_____

_____

_____

Once again access the web site www.cosmeticsdatabase.com or the above mentioned link and look up the safety rating of the products you have listed above.

April 11

THE POETRY OF SKIN

"To me, fair friend, you never can be old.
For as you were when first your eye I eyed, such seems
your beauty still."
—William Shakespeare

Lest we forget that our skin is also the largest sensory organ of our body, the poem that follows is the first part of a two-part poem I wrote for Karen; SKIN-1 and SKIN-2. The second part is R-rated and any interested reader can send me a plain brown envelope and I will promptly mail you a copy. SKIN-2 is also in my second volume of collected poems; "Wingless Angels-2" and is available on the Amazon web site.

SKIN-1:

Before I knew your skin, I knew your eyes.
I knew the oceans of tears you cried, Grieving the lifetimes you did not feel me, I would have gladly drowned in that sea, To be washed upon the shores of your beauty.

Before I knew your skin, I knew your laughter. It was the siren song of time immortal, the music of the spheres set to the drumbeat of creation. As Siva's dancing feet spun out worlds, he smiled, knowing one day I would hear the raga of your soul.

Before I knew your skin, I knew your heart.
As child I hid from pain in its wild spaces,
As youth I slaked my anger in its tranquil streams,
As man I slept peaceful under its starry skies,
As lover I stayed warm in its tender fire.

Karen, before I knew your skin, I loved you.

MK/2007

DR. M. P. KHAN, MD/NMD

April 12

THE POETRY OF SKIN

Close your eyes and lightly touch anyone you love (person or pet). Also touch an inanimate object such as carpeting, your sweater, the kitchen counter. Be mindful of the various textures that you feel. Describe them in words.

_____

_____

_____

_____

_____

_____

_____

_____

_____

_____

_____

_____

_____

_____

_____

April 13

SUCROSE = FRUCTOSE + GLUCOSE

*"The taste of sweetness whereof a little. More than a little
is by much, too much."*
—**William Shakespeare**

As every high school boy and girl knows, when the sucrose molecule breaks down by digestion, it gives us a molecule of glucose and fructose. This little fact has created a firestorm in the world of nutrition science. Of course, too much glucose sitting around in the bloodstream results in diabetes and obesity. Its prevalence in our society has resulted in the alarming statistic that the current generation of children will have a *decreased* life span than their parents. But it is fructose found ubiquitously in a very modern laboratory invention called high fructose corn syrup (HFCS), and a creative use of excess corn production, that causes a lot of havoc.

Sugar as we know it was not freely available to the western world till the late 18th century. It originated in India where it was made from sugar canes around 500 BC and known as *shakara* and hence the modern term *sucrose*. Pure glucose is not very sweet and pure fructose can cause indigestion in some individuals. HFCS is a mixture of the two (as is honey). And the body handles the two molecules differently.

Glucose causes the pancreas to release insulin and promotes glycogen production in the liver. Insulin also moves glucose into the cells for energy production. The glucose in sugary foods have a high glycemic index which is an indicator of how rapidly glucose levels rise in the blood stream. Fructose on the other hand has an exceptionally low value which would apparently make it better for diabetics.

Not so! Fructose on the other hand is taken up entirely by the liver and unlike glucose; its metabolism is not tightly regulated by the liver. It subsequently breaks down rapidly causing lipogenesis or conversion to fat. This new fat can accumulate in the liver; a fatty liver. This is one of the more common causes of low level increases in liver enzymes and is seen as anatomical changes on ultrasound of the liver. It can also increase triglycerides and is also stored as fat around the waist. This 'belly' fat produces inflammation products and a waist circumference more than 40" in men and 35" in women is a cardiac risk factor, and time to cut down on the goodies.

If fructose was a problem, people who ate a diet high in fruits would have a disproportionate amount of health issues as discussed in the previous day. A recent South African study put this issue to rest. 17 adults, ages 20-64 were asked to eat a diet high in fruits (20 servings a day) which delivered 200 grams of fructose a day for 12-24 weeks. The results showed that *all* parameters including body weight, lipid levels and blood pressure *improved*! It was the consumption of whole fruit with the soluble fiber and pulp which actually slowed down the *rate* of absorption which made the difference. Juicing the same fruit would probably take away that effect.

April 14

SUCROSE = FRUCTOSE + GLUCOSE

A lot of foods for diabetics replace glucose with fructose as a sweetener. This causes the same kind of metabolic havoc on the body. I recommend all my diabetics to eat an unlimited amount of fresh fruits, and a limited amount of dried fruits as part of their daily food intake and to really limit fruit juices and foods high in any kind of refined sugars. Once again nature triumphs!

Take a look at the foods in your refrigerator and your pantry, especially the sweet goodies!

Make a list of the foods that have high fructose corn syrup or variations of the same.

_____

_____

_____

_____

_____

_____

_____

_____

_____

_____

The next time you are at a grocery store shopping, read the label. HCFS is also called glucose/fructose and high fructose maize syrup. Try to avoid products which list them as a main ingredient. Better still avoid all sodas and make your own lemonade or hot and cold teas using some of the sweeteners outlined below.

Some natural sweeteners are agave nectar and honey. Plant based sweeteners which fool the tongue are stevia and monatin. Alcohol based

DR. M. P. KHAN, MD/NMD

sweeteners are sorbitol and mannitol and are found in various sugar free gums.

Try to limit the use of all of these so as to let the natural taste of the food to come through.

And once in a while go for a thin slice of that triple layer chocolate cake loaded with fat and sugar and cocoa!!

April 15

CHILDWISH

*"Wonder knows that while you cannot look at the light,
you cannot look at anything else without it.
It is not exhausted by childhood, but finds its key there. It
is a journey like a walk through the woods over the usual
obstacles and around the common distractions while the
voice of direction leads,
saying, 'This is the way, walk ye in it."*
—**Ravi Zacharias**

This poem must have emerged from some inexplicable and premonitory childhood memories. When I wrote this poem I was 28 years old. I did not have my own kids until the mid-80. As a child I had a dysfunctional relationship with my mostly absent father. Maybe this poem emerged from a yearning for the guidance that I craved from some idealistic version of a warm and sagacious patriarch.

CHILDWISH:

Lest I forget those halcyon day Of your childhood and mine. When I was the reflection of your innocence And your eyes the sunrise of tomorrows to come.

You were born to the wind, You child of mine you were born not mine. For as a stream that laughs its way through hills, As a breeze through a tree, whispering its song of peace. As water and wind I felt you, yet could not hold you.

When you walked, you ran And when you ran you flew. I could only watched you soar. And if called you back, It was only to say goodbye

MK/1977

DR. M. P. KHAN, MD/NMD

CHILDWISH

My mother eventually moved back with me in tow to live with my grandmother and an extended family of aunts, uncles and a steady stream of nephews and nieces, who as babies, spent the first forty days of their lives along with their grateful mothers in my mamaiji's (grandmother) tender and watchful care. As a result, my childhood memories were full of assisting with diaper changes, the primal aroma of baby powder and burping colicky babies. Fatherhood by proxy!

What are the not so pleasant memories of your childhood? How have you dealt with them?

_____

_____

_____

_____

_____

_____

_____

_____

_____

_____

What are the best memories of your childhood?

_____

_____

_____

_____

_____

_____

_____

_____

_____

_____

April 17

AN ABUNDANCE OF ATTENTION

*"Think of an absentminded professor who can
find a cure for cancer but not his glasses in the mess on his
desk. These are the inventors, creators,
poets -- the people who think creative thoughts because they
don't think like everyone else."*
—Martha Denckla, M.D.,

I have lived for most of my life with the elephant in the room. For a long time, I could not see the pachyderm. Like the blind men of the parable, sometimes it felt like a snake, sometime like the trunk of a tree and sometimes like a rope. It was much later that I saw the entire elephant. Initially I ignored it, hoping that it would go away. Finally I embraced the creature and accepted it for what it was. The next three days of the book are dedicated to my friend, the elephant. He had a name. It was ADHD.

There are three subtypes; AD (Attention Deficit); HD (Hyperactivity Disorder); and a combination of the two or ADHD. These are some of the questions to ask. In adults, this is a diagnosis that is often missed as it is assumed to be a condition unique to children.

1) Predominantly *inattentive* type and a common presentation in adults (AD)

Symptoms may include:

1=MILD; 2= MODERATE, 3=SEVERE.

* Have difficulty maintaining focus on one task. 1 2 3

* Quickly becoming bored with a task, unless doing something enjoyable. 1 2 3

DR. M. P. KHAN, MD/NMD

* Have difficulty focusing attention on organizing and completing a task or learning something new or trouble completing or turning in homework assignments, often losing things (e.g., pencils, toys, assignments) needed to complete tasks or activities. 1 2 3

* Not seem to listen when spoken to, interrupts often.1 2 3

* Daydream, become easily confused, and move slowly. 1 2 3

* Have difficulty processing information as quickly and accurately as others. 1 2 3.

* Struggle to follow instructions. 1 2 3

TOTAL SCORE _____

April 18

AN ABUNDANCE OF ATTENTION

2) Predominantly *hyperactive-impulsive type* (HD) and more often seen in children. *Symptoms may include:*

* Talk nonstop. 1 2 3

* Dash around, touching or playing with anything and everything in sight. 1 2 3

* Have trouble sitting still during dinner, school, and story time; constantly in motion. 1 2 3

* Have difficulty doing quiet tasks or activities. 1 2 3

* Be very impatient. 1 2 3

* Blurt out inappropriate comments, show their emotions without restraint, and act without regard for consequences. 1 2 3

* Have difficulty waiting for things they want or waiting their turns in games. 1 2 3

1=MILD; 2= MODERATE, 3=SEVERE. **TOTAL SCORE____**

Score as below for the AD and HD. Add your score separately for each section. Each section has seven bullets and has a minimum score of 7 and a maximum score of 21.

1-7 = very small chance of AD or HD

8-14= very likely AD or HD but may be other issues such as anxiety, learning disability.

15-21= AD or HD or ADHD depending what you scored in each of the above sections.

DR. M. P. KHAN, MD/NMD

April 19

ADHD.....MMMM; WHAT WAS THAT?

*"I prefer to distinguish ADD as attention abundance
disorder. Everything is just so interesting . . . remarkably at
the same time."*

—**Frank Coppola**

It took me 14 years after being diagnosed to appreciate the humor
of the above quote. My first clue was the behavior of my son. It was like
déjà vu. Initially I refused to accept the diagnosis. After the third round
of testing confirmed the diagnosis, I had to conclude that there was no
doubt as to its validity. It's as if all the pieces fell in place. The class clown,
the expulsion from school, the emotional pain of knowing that something
was wrong, the world always slightly out of focus. To this day, I wonder
how different my life could have been if I had been diagnosed and treated
earlier! But then again, would there have been the poetry and all the crazy
situations I got myself into? Would I be writing this book? Maybe things
happen exactly the way they should, if only we can see that. Most of the
discussion that follows is about the *adult* ADHD

Attention Deficit /Hyperactivity Disorder or ADHD is an actual
problem with the hard-wiring of the brain. There are three sub-types
as mentioned previously**1) AD** Inattentive-difficulty focusing. 2) **HD**
Hyperactive-impulsive and constantly on the go **3) ADHD** Combined-
with features of 1) and 2). It does have a genetic pattern with 33% of
fathers who have ADHD having children with ADHD. A full 67% of
children with ADHD will have it as adults. (The remaining 33% will not
meet all the criteria but never outgrow it completely) What exactly causes
it is not exactly clear but PET scanning using radionuclide tagged with
glucose is shedding new light on what areas of the brain are not active in
ADHD individuals and may soon be used as a diagnostic tool. Currently
no objective diagnostic tool exists except for questionnaires based on past
behavior!

The key word is **help**. *There is probably no role for just treating ADHD with supplements and mind-body modalities.* I speak from personal experience and years of treating individuals with this diagnosis. Some alternative health practitioners believe that by eliminating food coloring, environmental toxins, using the right vitamins and herbs etc. the problem will disappear. Although all of the above are certainly helpful in living a healthy life and is good advice for anybody, and especially in individuals with ADHD, this is one of the few instances when medication* (stimulant or non-stimulant) is very helpful to optimizing learning and to prevent destructive behavior especially in the adult. Our prisons are full of individuals with ADHD who were misdiagnosed or under treated. And a recent study showed that illegal street drug use actually dropped when ADHD individuals were treated with appropriate pharmaceutical products as many individuals with ADHD self-medicate with street drugs or alcohol. As of the date of writing this article, however, I am not on any pharmaceutical medication though I do use all of the suggestions and supplements outlined below. But if at any point, I felt that I needed to restart my medications to control my attention deficit, I would not hesitate at all.

Researchers believe that a large majority of ADHD cases arise from a combination of various genes as well as environmental triggers. Many of these genes affect dopamine production as well as receptors for serotonin and catechol amines. A common variant of a gene called LPHN3 is responsible for about 9% of the incidence of ADHD. In individuals with ADHD cases, when this gene is present are particularly responsive to stimulants such as methylphenidate and amphetamines. Other individuals may respond better to the non-stimulant medications such as Strattera or Wellbutrin.

* *At no point am I advocating that all individuals diagnosed with ADHD be placed on medications. It's like saying that all diabetics should be placed on insulin or oral medications! That is a decision between you and your physician. The question to ask: Is ADHD stopping you in realizing your full potential as a human being in your personal and professional life? For you, this ability (it is not a disorder) may be an actual advantage and we will talk about this one of these days.*

DR. M. P. KHAN, MD/NMD

April 20

ADHD.....MMMM; WHAT WAS THAT?

Here are some of the supplements and other modalities I would recommend for an adult with ADHD. And which can be safely added onto any pharmaceutical regimen. Most of these supplements can be used in the pediatric population but first check with your pediatrician.

Omega-3 Essential Fatty Acids. There is a marked deficiency in the Standard American Diet and I would recommend four x1000 mg salmon oil capsules daily for optimal brain function.

Taurine. This is a powerful neuromodulator of the nervous system. Also good as an add-on to an anticonvulsant. (DL cat #TAU) Dose at one to three daily.

Phosphatidylserine. This is a key ingredient in the production of neurotransmitters. It assists learning and memory. I use this supplement personally before any major exam. This is also useful in dementia patients as it is a precursor of acetylcholine. It is available as a Douglas Labs product called Cogniflex which has Huperizine, a memory enhancer. This product also has gingko in it so be careful if you are on Coumadin.

Nutrition. I cannot stress the importance of a good diet. Eat organic foods as much as possible and avoid all processed food especially those with artificial sweeteners and MSG which is a very common food additive. Also switch to free range chicken and beef with a low pesticide load. Eat fatty fish (wild caught) which is a traditional brain food. Drink lots of good clean water for hydration. And reduce food coloring in diet. The brain is extremely sensitive to inflammation and with a diagnosis of ADHD, it's the last thing you need.

Meditation. This really helps ADHD individuals focus. I suggest 15 minutes a day. Check out some good books by Kabat-Zin on ("Wherever you go, There you are") Zen mindful meditation practices. There is now available a system of neuro-bio-feedback which uses brain wave entrainment and assists in learning about the meditation process. Also try to get adequate sleep (seven hours). Also check out a free smart phone app 'Insight Timer' for loads of guided meditations.

April 21

ADHD........ MMMM! WHAT WAS THAT AGAIN?

"If a man does not keep pace with his companions, perhaps it is because he hears a different drummer. Let him step to the music which he hears, however measured or far away."

—**Henry David Thoreau**

Ansel Adams,

Hans Christian Anderson,

George Burns,

Admiral Richard Byrd,

Andrew Carnegie,

Lewis Carroll,

Cher,

Sir Winston Churchill (Failed the sixth grade)

Bill Cosby,

Harvey Cushing M.D.,

Leonardo da Vinci (my favorite)

Alexander Graham Bell,

Beethoven

Sir Richard Francis Burton

Thomas Carlyle

Jim Carrey

Prince Charles

Agatha Christie

Tom Cruise

Salvador Dali

Although some of the celebrities in the above list above list may have not had a formal diagnosis, their life and their art strongly suggests it. So if you have the diagnosis, you are in good company. But what if ADHD is not a disease after all but an adaptation of the brain to environmental challenge?

Think of our ancestors, the cavemen type, as they ventured out in a wild a hostile world to hunt and gather food for their tribe. What if you were that hunter and could track several game animals simultaneously by shifting your attention quickly to where it was needed. You would naturally be more successful as a hunter. All the good looking cave girls would adore you for all the meat you would bring home. And of course they would want to bear your cave babies as you could provide better for their offspring. And you would pass on your gene for the ADHD trait to your kids and future generations to come..

10,000 years later, and now you are a stockbroker working in Wall Street. All day long you have to track the market. And you have that same gene that made your ancestors so popular with the cave ladies. And you keep getting distracted by the downtown traffic and the chatter by the water cooler. And you miss out on some big trade or something. Well, guess what! You're fired. You definitely want something done about this!

On the other hand, you are the front man for a famous rock band. And every time you do one of your crazy ADHD related antics, you could sell a million more records and wild haired women would throw themselves at you. You definitely *do not* want to do anything about this!

Get the picture?

DR. M. P. KHAN, MD/NMD

April 22

ADHD........ MMMM! WHAT WAS THAT AGAIN?

If you know somebody with ADHD make a list of their positive qualities.

_____
_____
_____
_____
_____
_____
_____
_____

If you have ADHD yourself, or know someone who does, make a list of (yours or theirs) positive qualities.

_____
_____
_____
_____
_____
_____
_____
_____

How have you or that someone adapted your life/work to fit your diagnosis?

_____
_____
_____
_____
_____
_____
_____

April 23

REMEMBERING ALOIS ALZHEIMER

*"You have to begin to lose your memory, if only
in bits and pieces, to realize that memory is what makes
our lives. Life without memory is no life
at all; just intelligence without the possibility of expression
is not really intelligence. Our memory is our coherence, our
reason, our feeling, even our action.
Without it, we are nothing at all."*

—Louis Brunel

If the passage of years endows us with wisdom, the arrow of time also collects a toll on our body. Alois Alzheimer was a German neuropathologist who, in 1906 first noted the changes in the aging brain on pathology specimens and co-related them with the cognitive changes of what we call dementia. Since then, the biochemistry of these changes has been worked out on a cellular level. The end point is a decreased connection between neurons at the synapse because of abnormal protein deposition called amyloid and tau and also accompanied by a decrease in a neuro transmitter called acetylcholine across the synapse. Amyloid protein attaches on the surface of the neuron and changes the structure of the synapse. Tau proteins actually infiltrate the neuron and disrupt the internal transport system of the cell thus causing cell dysfunction.

Early onset dementia may have a genetic component. Most individuals with Down's syndrome will develop it in their 40's due to a triple copy of chromosome #21. The best known genetic risk factor is the inheritance of the of the gene apolipoprotein E (APOE). Between 40% and 80% of people with AD possess at least one APOE4 copy which increases the risk of the disease by three times in heterozygotes (only one gene of the pair carries the mutation) and by 15 times in homozygotes. (Both genes carry the mutation).

DR. M. P. KHAN, MD/NMD

But to this date, there have been no specific test to diagnose this disease or any pharmaceutical compound to cure it. There are currently in the pipeline several tests that can measure the antibodies to the above protein and a vaccine has also been trialed. The only definitive diagnosis is a brain biopsy which has obvious limitations. Recent advances in identifying certain proteins in spinal fluid and functional MRIs hold promise and more evidence is emerging that AD may well be an *inflammatory* disease of the brain. If this is the case, prevention of this disease maybe a better strategy using nutritional modifications and supplements and data already exists to support that.

A recent 10 year prospective European study was done on a population in which the study group was placed on a low fat, high antioxidant diet and the control given a high fat, low antioxidant diet. The study group had a significant decrease in the occurrence of dementia. This would make sense if the *inflammatory* disease hypotheses stands and an anti-inflammatory diet may play a critical role in prevention. The famous "nun" study also showed an inverse relationship between mental stimulation and the age of onset of dementia. 'If you don't use it you lose it' may well be applicable here. Also early retirement based on a recent French study, was also a risk factor for the early onset of dementia.

April 24

REMEMBERING ALOIS ALZHEIMER

The poem that follows is my attempt to understand this condition. And to see if I can find any blessings from what seems to be a curse of old age.

THE GREEN BENCH:

Outside the nursing home,
In dawns light, fresh with the promise of dew and noisy birds
She sits in her paisley dress on the green bench.
In the late afternoon, her aging face adulates the sun,
And the light fracturing through her snowy hair
Is the halo of a timeless angel.
She sits day long following the warmth and the fading light,
Smiling, as if connected to her inner bliss.
　　　　There are questions 1 want to ask her,
But they tell me she lives in another time!
A time of squealing, embracing, children.
Of a husband that once shared her bed,
White sheets, the grass smell in spring
And the fire place crackling in winter.
All the pain and ecstasy of living forgotten,
In a jumble of weary and confused neurons.
　　　　But she does not answer; speech long lost.
Only her eyes, briefly reflect her humanity,
Words and their ambiguity, unnecessary.
Her age lined face holds a simple message:
"At the end of our lives, the only memories that matter
Is the joy we gave to others, and, more importantly,
The joy we gave to ourselves!"　　　　MK/2005

DR. M. P. KHAN, MD/NMD

April 25

EAT THIS, NOT THAT!

"Part of the secret of success in life is to eat what you like
and let the food fight it out inside."
—Mark Twain

Every day I am confronted with the question "What should I be eating?" OR "What should I *not* be eating?" And the average physician has a very brief training in nutrition to give meaningful advice. With all the confusion it is easy to follow Mark Twain's advice and just plain give up in frustration. I have tried to make sense of a moving target of information by applying some common sense principals as in *"The Ten Eating Suggestions."* I hope they will help you, the next time you sit down at a meal. The heading of this day (#5: *Eat This Food, Not That Food*) is one of The Ten Suggestions and is not to be confused with title of a book of a somewhat similar name. (Which is helpful if you are into eating fast/chain restaurant food)

Let us destroy some of the false assumptions about food.

FALSE ASSUMPTION: **Food is the sum of its nutrients.**

Almost every book on nutrition starts with these basic concepts. All foods have two basic constituents: vitamins, minerals, flavonoids, or MICRONUTRIENTS and protein, carbohydrates and fats or MACRONUTRIENTS.

This reductionist approach, though it may help us understand the science of nutrition, it falls apart in real world applications. Nutrition as a science is in its infancy. Food research is limited by the inability to have placebo control groups. How could you have a fake substitute for a steak or a head of broccoli? Food questionnaires are also lengthy and complicated taking almost 45 minutes to complete. Also some of the confounders are that people most of the time *under report* their calorie intake on food questionnaires. For example on an average, 3900 calories were actually consumed vs 2000 calories that were reported.

It is also difficult to define food intake of the control group. For example if they were eating a low fat diet did they cut down on the bad fats (Trans-fats, animal fats) or good (olive oil) fats? Also the higher the social status, and the higher the level of education, the more health conscious you are and subsequently will make healthier food choices.

Isolate a nutrient and there are problems. Beta carotene as a supplement actually increased risk of lung cancer in smokers, but not if you eat carrots. The way your body processes kernels of corn is not the same as high fructose corn syrup (HFCS) which can cause obesity and diabetes in populations that increase its intake. This is seen in Native Mexicans and Native Americans when they move away from their traditional foods based on whole corn based foods and instead ingested foods high in HFCS.

April 26

EAT THIS, NOT THAT!

FALSE ASSUMPTION: **We can manipulate foods to make us healthy.**

There is this belief that if you eat the right foods and you will have good health. So the nutrition scientists tell us. We now have the very scary phenomenon of designer processed foods or DPF. 17,000 DPF are introduced every year with a marketing budget of 30 billion dollars a year. A good example is how a well-known manufacturer of infant formula convinced mothers in third world countries to use their formula instead of breast feeding with disastrous health consequences.

Margarine closely followed by processed cheese was the first fake food. In fact all margarine products by law (passed in the late 1800s and struck down in1898) had to have pink food coloring added to it to make the consumer aware. We switched from saturated fats (butter which is high in omega-3) to margarine (low in saturated fats and omega-3 but high in Trans fats) and now we have margarine which is free from trans fats and has added omega-3! Crazy huh!

Also all fake foods had to have an "Imitation" label (passed in 1938) but struck down by the FDA in 1973 as long as the foods were nutritionally equivalent. Anybody for fake cheese? This opened up the Pandora box of fake food and the whole fad food movement. Think "added omega-3 or "whole grain" cereal. Multigrain corn chips, heart healthy candy, cola with vitamins! The list is endless.

And remember "low fat" or "fat free" foods which we all thought were healthy for us. Well, guess what! Thirty years later we have almost a 10% increase in obesity as a result of this because the manufacturers just added more sugar (and more calories) to their products to make them more palatable.

*The next time you go shopping, see how many food items you can buy **without** shrink wrap and packaging. This is one way to cut down on eating processed foods (and also decrease your exposure to chemicals* *leaching from plastic such as BPA and phthalates) and moving more towards wholesome and natural foods. You can even take your own containers such as glass bottles for bulk olive oil and vinegar and recycling egg cartons. You get the picture! Your body and the planet will bless you!*

HERBAL TEA TIME (PART V)

*"Human beings are more closely related
to plants than to aspirin."*
—Chairman Moo

Continuing with Mrs. Fields and her Garden Club, I have made every excuse to not being able to make the evening meetings. But, by now their curiosity is boundless. And unless I deliver, I have visions of spending the rest of my life in the Senior Citizen Center! This time, one of her friends was diagnosed with colon cancer and the focus of our talk this evening is to discuss herbs that can decrease the risk of various cancers.

1) *Lycopene:* **This is found readily in tomatoes, especially in tomato sauce. It significantly decreases the incidence of prostate cancer. When used in men with prostate cancer, it also slowed down the spread of the cancer. As a supplement, it is used at about 30 mg. a day or just eat tomatoes**

2) *Green Tea:* **Recent NCI study showed that consuming four large cups of green tea (preferably organic) daily showed a lower recurrence rate of breast cancer and a delayed onset of breast cancer. A Chinese study showed the lower the risk of ovarian cancer.**

3) *Soy and Soybeans:* **The phytoestrogens in Soy are protective against breast, colon and prostate cancer. Phytoestrogens are not associated with increased breast cancer risk and are very safe for use even with a history of breast cancer. Levels of consumption must reach 60 mg of soy protein (8oz of soy milk, with 2 tbs. of soy protein powder) on a daily basis over a sustained period to be of benefit, ideally starting in adolescence. Ask your physician if you have a history of a thyroid disorder for long term use of soy.**

4) *Turmeric:* Curcuma longa is a commonly used spice in Indian cooking. 500 mg of turmeric 3xday in recent studies showed biopsy proven improvement in certain cancers (Bladder, colon and stomach) and high doses (8000mg) a day may have a chemo preventive effect.

5) *Chemotherapy agents:* Many new chemotherapy agents come from plants e.g. Taxol for the treatment of breast cancer from the Pacific yew tree and Vinblastine for the treatment of leukemia from the Madagascar periwinkle. Controversial treatments are Laetrile and Mistletoe.

6) *Immune modulators:* These are very useful when added to chemotherapy agents especially in treatment of cancer. These are Astralgus, a plant; Arabinoxylan, made from rice bran and shitake mushrooms; and Inositol Hexaphosphate (IP6) made from legumes, all dosed from 1 to 3 grams a day prevented the toxic effects of chemotherapy including the side effect of leukopenia by improving the Natural Killer cell activity and improving the function of the immune system.

HERBAL TEA TIME (PART V)

I make all the ladies of the Garden Club make a promise to see their physician to get the appropriate age specific cancer screening. An ounce of prevention is worth a pound of cure and Mrs. Fields is in agreement with me. . Below are some of the guidelines for cancer prevention. An important caveat is that different medical societies may have different guidelines and they do change with time so they are not written in stone. www.uspreventiveservicestaskforce.org (UPSTF) is a good evidence based website which I refer to for the latest recommendations.

Screening	Description	Grade	Release Date of Current Recommendation
Abdominal aortic aneurysm screening: men	The USPSTF recommends one-time screening for abdominal aortic aneurysm by ultrasonography in men ages 65 to 75 years who have ever smoked.	B	June 2014*
Alcohol misuse: screening and counseling	The USPSTF recommends that clinicians screen adults age 18 years or older for alcohol misuse and provide persons engaged in risky or hazardous drinking with brief behavioral counseling interventions to reduce alcohol misuse.	B	May 2013*

Aspirin to prevent cardiovascular disease: men	The USPSTF recommends the use of aspirin for men ages 45 to 79 years when the potential benefit due to a reduction in myocardial infarctions outweighs the potential harm due to an increase in gastrointestinal hemorrhage.	A	March 2009
Aspirin to prevent cardiovascular disease: women	The USPSTF recommends the use of aspirin for women ages 55 to 79 years when the potential benefit of a reduction in ischemic strokes outweighs the potential harm of an increase in gastrointestinal hemorrhage.	A	March 2009
Bacteriuria screening: pregnant women	The USPSTF recommends screening for asymptomatic bacteriuria with urine culture in pregnant women at 12 to 16 weeks' gestation or at the first prenatal visit, if later.	A	July 2008
Blood pressure screening in adults	The USPSTF recommends screening for high blood pressure in adults aged 18 years or older. The USPSTF recommends obtaining measurements outside of the clinical setting for diagnostic confirmation before starting treatment.	A	October 2015*

BRCA risk assessment and genetic counseling/ testing	The USPSTF recommends that primary care providers screen women who have family members with breast, ovarian, tubal, or peritoneal cancer with one of several screening tools designed to identify a family history that may be associated with an increased risk for potentially harmful mutations in breast cancer susceptibility genes (*BRCA1* or *BRCA2*). Women with positive screening results should receive genetic counseling and, if indicated after counseling, BRCA testing.	B	December 2013*
Breast cancer preventive medications	The USPSTF recommends that clinicians engage in shared, informed decision making with women who are at increased risk for breast cancer about medications to reduce their risk. For women who are at increased risk for breast cancer and at low risk for adverse medication effects, clinicians should offer to prescribe risk-reducing medications, such as tamoxifen or raloxifene.	B	September 2013*
Breast cancer screening	The USPSTF recommends screening mammography for women, with or without clinical breast examination, every 1 to 2 years for women age 40 years and older.	B	September 2002†

Breastfeeding counseling	The USPSTF recommends interventions during pregnancy and after birth to promote and support breastfeeding.	B	October 2008
Cervical cancer screening	The USPSTF recommends screening for cervical cancer in women ages 21 to 65 years with cytology (Pap smear) every 3 years or, for women ages 30 to 65 years who want to lengthen the screening interval, screening with a combination of cytology and human papillomavirus (HPV) testing every 5 years.	A	March 2012*
Chlamydia screening: women	The USPSTF recommends screening for chlamydia in sexually active women age 24 years or younger and in older women who are at increased risk for infection.	B	September 2014*
Cholesterol abnormalities screening: men 35 and older	The USPSTF strongly recommends screening men age 35 years and older for lipid disorders.	A	June 2008
Cholesterol abnormalities screening: men younger than 35	The USPSTF recommends screening men ages 20 to 35 years for lipid disorders if they are at increased risk for coronary heart disease.	B	June 2008
Cholesterol abnormalities screening: women 45 and older	The USPSTF strongly recommends screening women age 45 years and older for lipid disorders if they are at increased risk for coronary heart disease.	A	June 2008

DR. M. P. KHAN, MD/NMD

Cholesterol abnormalities screening: women younger than 45	The USPSTF recommends screening women ages 20 to 45 years for lipid disorders if they are at increased risk for coronary heart disease.	B	June 2008
Colorectal cancer screening	The USPSTF recommends screening for colorectal cancer using fecal occult blood testing, sigmoidoscopy, or colonoscopy in adults beginning at age 50 years and continuing until age 75 years. The risks and benefits of these screening methods vary.	A	October 2008
Dental caries prevention: infants and children up to age 5 years	The USPSTF recommends the application of fluoride varnish to the primary teeth of all infants and children starting at the age of primary tooth eruption in primary care practices. The USPSTF recommends primary care clinicians prescribe oral fluoride supplementation starting at age 6 months for children whose water supply is fluoride deficient.	B	May 2014*

Depression screening: adolescents	The USPSTF recommends screening for major depressive disorder (MDD) in adolescents aged 12 to 18 years. Screening should be implemented with adequate systems in place to ensure accurate diagnosis, effective treatment, and appropriate follow-up.	B	February 2016*
Depression screening: adults	The USPSTF recommends screening for depression in the general adult population, including pregnant and postpartum women. Screening should be implemented with adequate systems in place to ensure accurate diagnosis, effective treatment, and appropriate follow-up.	B	January 2016*
Diabetes screening	The USPSTF recommends screening for abnormal blood glucose as part of cardiovascular risk assessment in adults aged 40 to 70 years who are overweight or obese. Clinicians should offer or refer patients with abnormal blood glucose to intensive behavioral counseling interventions to promote a healthful diet and physical activity.	B	October 2015*

Falls prevention in older adults: exercise or physical therapy	The USPSTF recommends exercise or physical therapy to prevent falls in community-dwelling adults age 65 years and older who are at increased risk for falls.	B	May 2012
Falls prevention in older adults: vitamin D	The USPSTF recommends vitamin D supplementation to prevent falls in community-dwelling adults age 65 years and older who are at increased risk for falls.	B	May 2012
Folic acid supplementation	The USPSTF recommends that all women planning or capable of pregnancy take a daily supplement containing 0.4 to 0.8 mg (400 to 800 μg) of folic acid.	A	May 2009
Gestational diabetes mellitus screening	The USPSTF recommends screening for gestational diabetes mellitus in asymptomatic pregnant women after 24 weeks of gestation.	B	January 2014
Gonorrhea prophylactic medication: newborns	The USPSTF recommends prophylactic ocular topical medication for all newborns for the prevention of gonococcal ophthalmia neonatorum.	A	July 2011*
Gonorrhea screening: women	The USPSTF recommends screening for gonorrhea in sexually active women age 24 years or younger and in older women who are at increased risk for infection.	B	September 2014*

Healthy diet and physical activity counseling to prevent cardiovascular disease: adults with cardiovascular risk factors	The USPSTF recommends offering or referring adults who are overweight or obese and have additional cardiovascular disease (CVD) risk factors to intensive behavioral counseling interventions to promote a healthful diet and physical activity for CVD prevention.	B	August 2014*
Hearing loss screening: newborns	The USPSTF recommends screening for hearing loss in all newborn infants.	B	July 2008
Hemoglobinopathies screening: newborns	The USPSTF recommends screening for sickle cell disease in newborns.	A	September 2007
Hepatitis B screening: nonpregnant adolescents and adults	The USPSTF recommends screening for hepatitis B virus infection in persons at high risk for infection.	B	May 2014
Hepatitis B screening: pregnant women	The USPSTF strongly recommends screening for hepatitis B virus infection in pregnant women at their first prenatal visit.	A	June 2009
Hepatitis C virus infection screening: adults	The USPSTF recommends screening for hepatitis C virus (HCV) infection in persons at high risk for infection. The USPSTF also recommends offering one-time screening for HCV infection to adults born between 1945 and 1965.	B	June 2013

DR. M. P. KHAN, MD/NMD

High blood pressure in adults: screening	The USPSTF recommends screening for high blood pressure in adults aged 18 years or older. The USPSTF recommends obtaining measurements outside of the clinical setting for diagnostic confirmation before starting treatment.	A	October 2015*
HIV screening: nonpregnant adolescents and adults	The USPSTF recommends that clinicians screen for HIV infection in adolescents and adults ages 15 to 65 years. Younger adolescents and older adults who are at increased risk should also be screened.	A	April 2013*
HIV screening: pregnant women	The USPSTF recommends that clinicians screen all pregnant women for HIV, including those who present in labor who are untested and whose HIV status is unknown.	A	April 2013*
Hypothyrodism screening: newborns	The USPSTF recommends screening for congenital hypothyroidism in newborns.	A	March 2008

Intimate partner violence screening: women of childbearing age	The USPSTF recommends that clinicians screen women of childbearing age for intimate partner violence, such as domestic violence, and provide or refer women who screen positive to intervention services. This recommendation applies to women who do not have signs or symptoms of abuse.	B	January 2013
Lung cancer screening	The USPSTF recommends annual screening for lung cancer with low-dose computed tomography in adults ages 55 to 80 years who have a 30 pack-year smoking history and currently smoke or have quit within the past 15 years. Screening should be discontinued once a person has not smoked for 15 years or develops a health problem that substantially limits life expectancy or the ability or willingness to have curative lung surgery.	B	December 2013
Obesity screening and counseling: adults	The USPSTF recommends screening all adults for obesity. Clinicians should offer or refer patients with a body mass index of 30 kg/m^2 or higher to intensive, multicomponent behavioral interventions.	B	June 2012*

DR. M. P. KHAN, MD/NMD

Obesity screening and counseling: children	The USPSTF recommends that clinicians screen children age 6 years and older for obesity and offer them or refer them to comprehensive, intensive behavioral interventions to promote improvement in weight status.	B	January 2010
Osteoporosis screening: women	The USPSTF recommends screening for osteoporosis in women age 65 years and older and in younger women whose fracture risk is equal to or greater than that of a 65-year-old white woman who has no additional risk factors.	B	January 2012*
Phenylketonuria screening: newborns	The USPSTF recommends screening for phenylketonuria in newborns.	B	March 2008
Preeclampsia prevention: aspirin	The USPSTF recommends the use of low-dose aspirin (81 mg/d) as preventive medication after 12 weeks of gestation in women who are at high risk for preeclampsia.	B	September 2014
Rh incompatibility screening: first pregnancy visit	The USPSTF strongly recommends Rh (D) blood typing and antibody testing for all pregnant women during their first visit for pregnancy-related care.	A	February 2004

Rh incompatibility screening: 24–28 weeks' gestation	The USPSTF recommends repeated Rh (D) antibody testing for all unsensitized Rh (D)-negative women at 24 to 28 weeks' gestation, unless the biological father is known to be Rh (D)-negative.	B	February 2004
Sexually transmitted infections counseling	The USPSTF recommends intensive behavioral counseling for all sexually active adolescents and for adults who are at increased risk for sexually transmitted infections.	B	September 2014*
Skin cancer behavioral counseling	The USPSTF recommends counseling children, adolescents, and young adults ages 10 to 24 years who have fair skin about minimizing their exposure to ultraviolet radiation to reduce risk for skin cancer.	B	May 2012
Tobacco use counseling and interventions: nonpregnant adults	The USPSTF recommends that clinicians ask all adults about tobacco use, advise them to stop using tobacco, and provide behavioral interventions and U.S. Food and Drug Administration (FDA)–approved pharmacotherapy for cessation to adults who use tobacco.	A	September 2015*

Tobacco use counseling: pregnant women	The USPSTF recommends that clinicians ask all pregnant women about tobacco use, advise them to stop using tobacco, and provide behavioral interventions for cessation to pregnant women who use tobacco.	A	September 2015*
Tobacco use interventions: children and adolescents	The USPSTF recommends that clinicians provide interventions, including education or brief counseling, to prevent initiation of tobacco use in school-aged children and adolescents.	B	August 2013
Syphilis screening: nonpregnant persons	The USPSTF strongly recommends that clinicians screen persons at increased risk for syphilis infection.	A	July 2004
Syphilis screening: pregnant women	The USPSTF recommends that clinicians screen all pregnant women for syphilis infection.	A	May 2009
Visual acuity screening in children	The USPSTF recommends vision screening for all children at least once between the ages of 3 and 5 years.	B	January 2011*

April 29

HERBAL TEATIME (PART VI)

"Warning: The Internet may contain traces of nuts"
—Anon

I had just finished the presentation on cancer when another member gets tearful and starts asking me questions about heart disease. She has high cholesterol and is very worried. How can I refuse? Do I have a captive audience or does her Garden Club, a captive speaker! Help

1) *Nuts:* I oz. of nuts 5 times a week including walnuts, almonds, pistachios and even pea nuts reduced bad cholesterol -LDL and triglycerides 7-10% and raise HDL by 4%. (more later on this topic) Cashew nuts have the highest fat content and almonds the least. Would recommend as a snack and this will add an average of 150 calories to the daily intake.

2) *Omega-3/Flax seed or Marine oil:* This was covered previously over several days. Flax seed/oil is a rich source of ALA- alpha linolenic acid and lignans modestly improve lipid profiles. 5-10% Of ALA is converted to EPA-eicosapentaenic acids and DHA-docosohexanoeic acid, fatty acids found in fish oil. Also ground flax seeds are a good source of fiber and may help in lowering blood glucose. ALA was a prime ingredient in the Mediterranean diet and showed a 76% reduction in mortality in post-acute MI patients. In this study, flax seed and not flax seed oil was the source of ALA. The lignan component may have cardio protective effects and lignans are not found in flaxseed oil. Would recommend 3-6 tbsp. of flax seed meal (140 -240 calories) a day or l-2tbsp of flax seed oil (120-240 calories) a day in salads or gel caps OR 2000 mg of mercury free marine oil daily (QUELL Douglas Labs) OR 16 oz. of fatty fish (Salmon-wild caught) once a week. The

new guidelines recommend 16 oz. of fatty fish once a week even for pregnant women because the benefits far outweigh the danger of mercury levels. National Geographic has a calculator on their web site.

3) *Gugul resin:* **Commiphora mukula, a tree resin is an Indian herb used in Ayurveda medicine for thousands of years for the treatment of heart problems. Three hundred tons of resin are used** <u>annually</u> **in India. Blocks the FXR receptor of liver cell and increases the excretion of cholesterol. Average reduction of 14% and no significant side effects. Advise 2 capsules twice a day on empty stomach. Results are seen in 12-16 weeks. Western version may not be as effective as the Ayurvedic preparation.**

4. *Garlic:* **Not as useful in lowering cholesterol with only a modest 4% reduction in total cholesterol levels no significant changes in HDL and LDL. It may be more useful in lowering blood pressure. Use in its raw form after exposure to air so as to activate allicin. Avoid the dried pill forms. Can also be used as an antiseptic and antispasmodic and is a good treatment for the common cold. Also keeps away friends and vampires!**

April 30

HERBAL TEATIME (PART VI)

5) *L-Carnitine*: plays critical role in energy production and can be deficient in patients undergoing dialysis and on valproic acid (an anti-seizure drug) therapy. It improves symptoms of heart failure and chronic angina. May be lacking in vegetarians because it is found in dairy and meat. Many supplements contain D and DL carnitine, which may increase the risk of L-carnitine deficiency. Use 1 gram three times a day. Avoid in patients with history of seizures and liver failure.

6) *CoQ-10:* This was also discussed previously. It is found in whole grains and is also known as ubiquinone, a vitamin like compound. It is used as standard therapy in congestive heart failure in Japan, Russia and Europe. It is also used in chemotherapy to prevent cardio toxicity. Latest use is in high doses in Parkinson's disease and markedly improves symptoms Use from 100mg to 1000 mg. a day preferably in a melt tablet form. Statin drugs may lower Co Q- 10 levels so supplementation is strongly advised. Has synergistic effect with L-carnitine and can be used together with statins.

7) *Hawthorn:* Also known as May or Haw. Used in mild congestive heart failure and has action similar to Digitalis. Also acts as a vasodilator on the coronary circulation and reduces blood pressure. It can be used to prevent benign arrhythmias after an electrolyte imbalance is ruled out. It does have some synergy with Digitalis and it is best to avoid concurrent use. I advise Hawthorn (*Crataegus oxyacantha*) 250 mg two daily between meals Standardized to 2% vitexin-2" rhamnoside in a 100 mg base of non-standardized Hawthorn. (DL Hawthorn Max-V)

Mrs. Fields, there is something I would like to stress to all the members of your garden club. Before you get off your medications and try the above approaches, please consult your physician. Some cardiac drugs cannot be stopped abruptly because of significant and even fatal rebound effects from their withdrawal.

MAY

1-May	NUTS ABOUT NUTS. Another eating suggestion which is actually easy.
2-May	NUTS ABOUT NUTS. And also a very delicious desert recipe using nuts.
3-May	PEEING INTO THE PERFECT STORM (PART-1) The system is broken.
4-May	PEEING INTO THE PERFECT STORM (PART-1). Barriers to an I. M. model of care.
5-May	PEEING INTO THE PERFECT STORM (PART-2) We are the solution; really!
6-May	PEEING INTO THE PERFECT STORM (PART-2) A mandala for the rest of us.
7-May	DOC, I HAVE A COLD. (PART-1)Some natural remedies for a cold.
8-May	DOC, I HAVE A COLD. (PART-1)Some more natural remedies.
9-May	DOC, I HAVE A COLD. (PART-2) Some preventive measures.
10-May	DOC, I HAVE A COLD. (PART-2) Some more preventive measures.
11-May	MENOPAUSAL MISERY. (PART-1) Understanding hormonal changes
12-May	MENOPAUSAL MISERY (PART-1) A natural approach to manage symptoms.
13-May	ONCE THERE WAS AN ANGEL. A poem for Perin.
14-May	ONCE THERE WAS AN ANGEL. Was there an angel in your life?
15-May	EVERYBODY'S PISSED OFF. (PART-1) Mrs. Fields has some concerns.
16-May	EVERYBODY'S PISSED OFF. (PART-1) Mrs. Fields concerns are valid!
17-May	EVERYBODY'S PISSED OFF. (PART-2) A course of action for Mrs. Fields.
18-May	EVERYBODYS PISSED OFF. (PART-2) Changing the negative and finding joy.
19-May	MENOPAUSAL MISERY. (PART-2) Some more natural remedies.
20-May	MENOPAUSAL MISERY. (PART-2) And also a remedy for menarche.
21-May	LUV YA CAMELLIA. A cup of chai, anyone?
22-May	LUV YA CAMELLIA. The health benefits of tea.
23-May	MAGICAL MUSHROOMS. It's not what you think.
24-May	MAGICAL MUSHROOMS. And do not pick your own!
25-May	THE WISDOM OF COMPASSION. (PART-1) The parable of the stray cat.
26-May	THE WISDOM OF COMPASSION. (PART-1) An exercise in compassion.
27-May	THE WISDOM OF COMPASSION. (PART-2) And its conclusion.
28-May	AN IRISH BLESSING. And also Guinness beer and limericks.
29-May	AN IRISH BLESSING. And a long and personal limerick.
30-May	BERMUDA DREAMS. A poem about a perfect memory of summer.
31-May	BERMUDA DREAMS. Remembering a perfect memory of a perfect summer.

DR. M. P. KHAN, MD/NMD

NUTS ABOUT NUTS

"Health nuts are going to feel stupid someday; lying in hospitals dying of nothing."
—Red Foxx

I am not sure at what point in the colloquial that nuts were equated with being crazy or eccentric. Looking out at my back yard and watching the local squirrels gathering nuts and hiding them, usually in a frenzy of manic energy may be the basis of this, as in 'going nuts.' But there is another side of nuts as in 'eating them' and is the next recommendation is #6 for a healthy diet:

"Eat a handful of nuts, any kind, and every day".

This information is hot off the press in a study by Bao et al. Two studies were analyzed, one being the Nurses' Health Study that consisted of 121,700 female nurses and the second was the Health Professionals Follow-up Study of 51,529 male health professionals. Women and men with a history of cancer, heart disease and stroke were excluded resulting in 76,464 women and 42,498 men. Information was collected via FFS (food frequency questionnaires) starting in 1980 for the women and 1986 for men.

Participants were given 1 oz. of nuts ranging from none at all to up to 4-6 times a day with the a category of 'peanuts' 'tree nuts' and 'total nuts.' The end point of the study was death from any cause based on records from the National Death Index. Participants were excluded if they had ever smoked, were underweight BMI, <18.5 or overweight BMI> 40.0 or had a diagnosis of diabetes. It was not clear from the study whether the nuts were raw or roasted and organic vs. non-organic.

At the conclusion of the study, it was found that when compared to individuals who did *not* eat nuts at all there was an inverse relationship between daily consumption and death rate reduction.

May 1

Less than1/week= 7% lower death rate; 1/week= 11% lower death rate;

2-4 times/week= 13% lower death rate; 5-6 times/week= 15% lower death rate.

7+times/week= 20% lower death rate.

The interesting part of the study was that peanuts, which are relatively inexpensive, had a similar beneficial effect to the more expensive tree nuts. There are not a lot of foods out there with the health benefit of nuts; a delicious snack, which is low in fat and calories, and can also lower the bad cholesterol (LDL), the risk of cancer and type 2 diabetes and lower the overall death rate by 20%!! Weight for weight, almonds have the least calories (40-60 for 1 oz.) and cashews the highest. (80-120 for 1oz.) And multiple studies show no association with nut consumption and weight gain.

NUTS ABOUT NUTS

BAKLAVA; A VEGAN VERSION:

1 16 ounce package phyllo dough
1 cup Earth Balance margarine
1 pound chopped mixed nuts including peanuts (avoid if peanut allergies)
1 teaspoon ground cinnamon
1/2 cup agave nectar or 1 cup brown sugar
1 teaspoon vanilla extract
1 cup water

Preheat oven to 350 degrees F (175 degrees C). Grease the bottoms and sides of a 9x13 inch pan with Earth Balance

Chop nuts and toss with cinnamon. Set aside. Unroll phyllo dough. Cut whole stack in half to fit pan. Cover phyllo with a dampened cloth to keep from drying out as you work. Place two sheets of dough in pan, smear margarine thoroughly.

Sprinkle 2 - 3 tablespoons of nut mixture on top. Top with two sheets of dough, margarine, nuts, layering as you go. The top layer should be about 6 - 8 sheets deep.

Using a sharp knife cut into diamond shapes all the way to the bottom of the pan. Bake for about 40-50 minutes until baklava is golden and crisp.

Make sauce while baklava is baking. Boil sugar or Agave nectar and water. (until sugar is melted)Add vanilla and agave nectar. Simmer for about 15 minutes.

Remove baklava from oven and immediately spoon sauce over it.

Let cool and enjoy!

PEEING INTO THE PERFECT STORM (PART-1)

"Happiness is like peeing in your pants. Everyone can see it, but only you can feel it."

—Anon

In case you are wondering what this title is about, it actually is an old sailing expression used for obvious reasons. *"If you have to pee, don't do it against the wind."* This homily, in some ways reflects the state of the American medical system and the frustration felt by physicians and patients alike.

I gave this presentation with the above title to a high level committee of a major hospital system board to try to convince them of the importance of an integrated medicine delivery system. Everyone thought it was a good idea at that time. However, several efforts to follow up on the agenda were met with a polite response which went something like this: "but as soon as we get our new Open Heart unit up and running we might consider it"

In the days that follow, I will make my case and come up with some solutions. I can only speak from thirty five years of practicing medicine and I am sure that wiser and smarter minds may disagree with me.

The system is terminally broken and in the current economic climate, the rising cost of health (or illness) care may hammer the final nail in the coffin!

PEEING INTO THE PERFECT STORM was the title slide of the presentation.

CHALLENGES TO IMPLEMENTING AN INTEGRATED MEDICINE PROGRAM.

1) THE <u>4 P'S</u>: <u>P</u>hysicians; <u>P</u>atients; <u>P</u>roviders *(hospitals)*; <u>P</u>ayors *(Insurance companies) are all PEED off setting up conditions for a <u>PERFECT STORM</u>*

DR. M. P. KHAN, MD/NMD

2) *PHYSICIAN BARRIERS:* PROBLEM: *Integrated Medicine modalities too woo-woo to be taken seriously. Not sure if it is evidence based and advise may hurt their credibility with their peers!!* SOLUTION: *Education via seminars, individual presentations, prominent speakers. Augmenting, not replacing the care they provide.* BELIEF: *Most physicians want what is best for their patients. Also Complimentary Alternative Medicine is now a $10 Billion dollar industry so there is also a financial incentive!!*

3) *PATIENT BARRIERS:* PROBLEM: *The #1 reason for using CAM is to take control of their health. The #2 reason is dissatisfaction with the current "illness" model of health care.* SOLUTION: *Offer an in-patient and outpatient experience which is friendly and congruent with their needs. Hi-tech care delivered in a caring manner.* BELIEF: *If we build it they will come!*

PEEING INTO THE PERFECT
STORM (PART-1)

If you are a physician, what barriers do you see in providing an integrated model of health care? How would you overcome these barriers?

_____
_____
_____
_____
_____
_____
_____
_____
_____
_____

If you are a patient, what barriers do you see in the delivery of an integrated health care system from a physician and a hospital perspective? How would you overcome these barriers?

_____
_____
_____
_____
_____
_____
_____
_____
_____
_____

PEEING INTO THE PERFECT
STORM (PART-2)

"Good health like sunlight. Only miss
it when it not there!"

—**Chairman Moo**

4) *PROVIDER/ HOSPITAL BARRIERS:* PROBLEM: *The current market is a static market. The current model objectifies the patient; treated like small cogs in the big machine. Nursing /staff stressed out, unappreciated with high turnover.* SOLUTION: *Hospitals should be healing places. Employee Wellness is an ideal starting point for CAM programs. There is a slow implementation of this by dollar incentives in reducing health premiums. BELIEF: Perception is everything. Recently I had a chance to visit a hospital (Gilbert Mercy Hospital) in Phoenix AZ. The entire hospital environment was geared towards the comfort of the patient and their families. The nurses carried cell phones set on vibrate so the sound levels were startlingly low. Every patient room was fitted with a day bed so that family members could stay overnight if they wished. But the most amazing thing was that a patient could, at the push of a button, summon a hospital representative if they had a problem with the care they were getting!*

This bears repetition: Hospitals should be places of healing, not just treating illnesses!

5) *BARRIERS FOR PAYORS: (Insurance companies.)*PROBLEM: *Increasing health care costs with rising premiums and employers offering fewer bangs for the buck in the traditional illness based model!* SOLUTION: *promote the value of CAM especially in early intervention of chronic disease states. Pay less now, or more later. This shift is already happening. It is also a great marketing tool for the Employee/Employer dyad. Wouldn't it be great if your health plan included massage therapy?* BELIEF: *The wellness model*

is a profitable one also!! Maintaining health is definitely more cost effective than curing disease.

6) *IN CONCLUSION, WHY RE-INVENT THE WHEEL?*

One way to implement this in a cost effective manner is to use existing practitioners who already practice alternative modalities that are quickly becoming mainstream. Why not utilize the services of a healer trained in acupuncture or Ayurvedic medicine and integrate them into the current system rather than have busy MDs go to expensive and time consuming training programs. And I now hear the chorus that they do not have an MD after their name. In a broad sense we are all "healers". It is easy to set up standards of care based on evidence based outcomes. True, certification is important but difficult at times. (Reiki?). And when was the last time that a patient actually was happy with the care you provided solely based on the number of certificates on your wall? Would you as a patient have the collective wisdom of several world medical systems, or the narrow knowledge base of a singular isolated system?

DR. M. P. KHAN, MD/NMD

PEEING INTO THE PERFECT
STORM (PART-2)

A HEALING MANDALA FOR ALL OF US: This is based on an American Indian mandala that all healers (and patients who can access their inner healer) can strive to establish a balance! The 'warrior' is to remind us to fight for advocacy for our patients and for the wellbeing of our environment.

WARRIOR

VISIONARY   *TEACHER*

HEALER

Each of us, in the role of patients or healers are to make any changes in the health care system, we need to make this mandala a core part of our belief system. On a larger perspective, this change will affect the health of a global community and ultimately the health of this beautiful blue spaceship on which we are fellow travelers: Earth.

May 7

DOC, I HAVE A COLD (PART-1)

"A person often catches a cold when a mother-in-law comes to visit. Patients mentioned mothers-in-law so often that we came to consider them a common cause of disease in the United States."

—Thomas Holmes

Mrs. Fields again: *"Hey Doc, are there any herbal remedies or supplements which will help with the common cold or flu symptoms? I am concerned that I may get really sick this winter."*

Mrs. Fields, if I got a dollar every time I was asked this question, I could retire to the Bahamas. Even in the wild and wonderful world of herbal medicine there does not exist a cure for the common cold. It would be useful to understand why a viral infection occurs in the first place. You and I are exposed to viruses and other miscellaneous nasty bugs all the time! Usually the body recognizes them as foreign and mounts an immune response to destroy them. It is only when the body's immune response is overwhelmed does the virus or the bacteria take over. Which explains why one is more prone to get a cold when one is physically and emotionally (yes, your emotions directly affect the endocrine and immune system) run down. And as one ages, the immune system is not as nimble as it used to be. This is why a young person would quickly recover from an infection while the same infection could prove fatal to an older person. But there are some natural remedies that we can discuss may help cut down on the duration of a cold or a flu infection.

ECHINACEA: There are several herbal products that can cut down the duration of a cold or infection to days instead of weeks. The most popular one is Echinacea of which E. purpurea can be found growing in any decent garden and is also known as the purple coneflower. Widely used by Native Americans for a variety of ailments including snake bites and by naturopaths in the early 1900 in the US it is recently making resurgence.

Echinacea has been shown to increase the level of Natural Killer cells (NK) as well as virus destroying substances called interferon. In animal studies it also has anti-inflammatory properties. Several studies have been done to date, some with conflicting results. One study (Lindenmuth, J Alternative Complement Medicine) which was randomized showed a significant decrease in the duration of cold symptoms as compared to the placebo group. A recent trial on children age 2-11 showed no difference between the placebo and control group. My concern is that many of the studies which show equivocal result were done with inadequate doses of Echinacea. I personally use it, but the key factor is to take the Echinacea (standardized to 4% Echinacosides) 3 capsules 4 times a day at the *first sign of a cold.* I recommend Douglas Labs Echinacea Max V CAT#77321 for 2 to 3 days at the above dose. Of course there is a chance that the immune system is overwhelmed by the bug and there may not be a satisfactory response.

DOC, I HAVE A COLD (PART-1)

To prevent colds try 2 capsules of Echinacea daily for 12 to 16 weeks starting in early November till the end of March. I tell all my patients who come in contact with little kids to try this strategy. It is advisable to avoid Echinacea if you have any immune system disorders such as lupus or rheumatoid arthritis or pregnancy. Also avoid if you are allergic to the daisy family of plants.

Once again 'Prevention' is the buzz word. And even though we will review several natural remedies to prevent and ameliorate viral illnesses let us not forget the importance of vaccination. One of the answers to the above question is that each season, I get my flu vaccine. Although there are no guarantees that you will not get the flu, if you do, it is a much milder illness. Almost every patient who presents in my office with the complaints that they feel like a train ran them over, and other symptoms of a full blown influenza illness, did not get vaccinated.

There is a common myth that the vaccine itself causes the illness. The virus in the vaccine is inactive and the vaccine does not confer 100% immunity against the influenza virus. So there is a small chance that you may get the illness in spite of the vaccination.

If you are allergic to eggs, there are now egg free vaccines available. There are also intranasal vaccines available (live) although they are not recommended in pregnancy. Latest CDC recommendations are that regular egg based vaccines can be given to patients with egg allergies with an observation period of thirty minutes.

DOC, I HAVE A COLD (PART-2)

"I shall not die of a cold. I shall die of having lived".
-Willa Cather

"Hey Doc, all that sounds very helpful. But how come you don't get sick? All these patients constantly sneezing and coughing on you?"

Yes and another question, for which I wish I had a dollar! *LIFESTYLE:* And there is a relatively simple answer. The immune system is just another player in the symphony of the body. And as long as everyone is doing their part, all we hear is beautiful music. But if one of the musicians plays too loud or slow, the orchestration falls apart. Inadequate rest, smoking, high levels of sustained stress, depression, too much alcohol, illegal drug use and lack of exercise are some of the life style culprits. Chronic infections such as Hepatitis C, disease states such as diabetes and poor nutrition also weaken the immune response.

VITAMINS: The first line of defense is the intact lining of the nose and the lungs. *Vitamin A* is important for this lining to function properly. Vitamin A is derived from dietary beta carotene in the presence of thyroid hormone. (Remember the symphony). Also any break in the surface can also lead to entry of the cold virus and this happens often in cold dry weather. I advise a maximum of 15,000 units daily although some studies have used 100.000 units daily for three to five days to dramatically cut down on the duration of a cold. Another powerful immune modulator is *Vitamin C.* A University of Texas study measured the lymphocytes (immune cells) of patients before and after supplementation with 1000 mg of vitamin C daily for 14 days. The number of blood Natural Killer cells (potent against viruses) increased and even though the number of

T-cells remained the same, they were more active following vitamin C supplementation.

GARLIC/GINGER: One of my grandma's remedies for a cold was to chop up some fresh garlic and ginger and mix with a tablespoon of lemon juice and chug it down. I hated it when I was a kid. But there was wisdom in the allicin of garlic which is a powerful antibacterial and anti-viral agent and the anti-inflammatory properties of ginger. Try it the next time you have the sneezies. Also oregano has similar properties and there are several preparations available.

ZINC: There is some evidence that zinc lozenges decrease the duration of a cold by interfering with the cold virus attachment sites on the cell surface. I have not had much success based on clinical experience. I definitely do not advise zinc sprays used intranasal as they can cause significant irritation.

HOMEOPATHY: Preparations such as *Oscillococcinum* (Boiron), can be used to prevent or treat influenza. Try one dose monthly during flu season. Three large randomized controlled trials have shown statistically significant results for the treatment of flu (Vickers AJ, Smith C. *Cochrane Database Syst Rev.* 2000) although some trials have shown equivocal results.

DOC, I HAVE A COLD (PART-2)

And Mrs. Fields, here are some additional approaches you can try:

* Adequate hydration is critical and would advise large amounts of warm herbal teas. Chicken soup is another option. Remember; if there is any coloring your urine, you are dehydrated.

* Another piece of advice even though it's un-American; REST! Let the body's immune system kick in and if you are feeling wiped out, listen to what your inner healer is shouting out to you; REST. Curl up with a good book or your favorite TV show under some blankets. The world will survive without you for a few days!

* And avoid common cold remedies with decongestants. They dry up the mucus which is the primary defense of the body. That pesky mucus delivers the anti-bodies that you need to fight off the virus. By all means use saline to irrigate your nose and OTC guaifenesin at a dose of 600 mg twice a day for comfort measures. A quick way to make saline is to add a pinch of baking soda and a pinch of salt to 8 oz. of water Boil and cool before use. Make a fresh batch daily. Use in a medicine dropper or Neti pot (a small kettle like device with a spout) frequently. Saline is an excellent decongestant.

And REST some more.

May 11

MENOPAUSAL MISERY (PART-1)

"The secret of staying young is to live honestly, eat slowly,
and lie about your age."

—Lucille Ball

Mrs. Fields is now a part of my fan club. She has referred her daughter as a new patient to my practice. Her name is Helena. My nurse has written on the initial encounter form: "Can't take it anymore." When I walk into the room I can see the family resemblance! She leads of the interview with this question.

Hi Dr. Khan, I am experiencing change of life issues, mainly a nasty mood and hot flashes several times a day. I'm only 46 years old. My husband looks kind of weird at me these days and I don't blame him. I want to stay away from the pharmaceutical preparations because of all the publicity. Are there any herbal or natural remedies?

First of all Helena, give my warmest (chuckle) regards to your husband. Tell him help is on its way. You are in the peri-menopausal period which can start at age 45 and has an upper limit of around 55 years of age. The symptoms you are experiencing are a result of falling estrogen levels but also a complete drop in progesterone levels as the menstrual cycles become an-ovulatory ie the ovary is exhausted of its egg supplies with zero production of progesterone. The symptoms you are experiencing may last three to five years and are variable in intensity from woman to woman. Some women may experience no symptoms at all. The medical definition of menopause is the absence of menstruation for a year. What is important to keep in mind is that menopause is not a disease but a natural process of aging. Any treatment for these symptoms should be safe and effective

Black Cohosh or Cimicifuga is a member of the buttercup family and (the root) has been used in Europe for the treatment

DR. M. P. KHAN, MD/NMD

for menopause for the last 40 years in over 1.5 million patients. It truly is an American herb. In fact it was on the USP (United States Pharmacopoeia) in the late 1940's! Used extensively by several American Indian tribes for multiple problems (including rheumatism and to induce the flow of breast milk), it was introduced to early settlers in the 1700's. Its Estrogen-like effect (the exact mechanism is not known) was first seen in 1944 on animal experiments. The first scientific study was done in 1960 using a Black Cohosh tablet taken 3 x day for 8 weeks in 1,256 pre-menopausal and menopausal patients. The study showed significant improvement in hot flashes and depressive moods and sleep disturbances without causing irregular bleeding. A 1985 study using 3 groups; Valium, Black Cohosh and Premarin showed that all three therapies were effective in improving menopausal symptoms and that the Black Cohosh group had very few side effects. From a safety viewpoint, a 1993 study conclusively proved that it is safe to use even in patients with breast cancer and it also helps to reduce the side effect of hot flashes caused by the use of the chemo-prophylaxis drug Tamoxifen.

May 12

MENOPAUSAL MISERY (PART-1)

But aren't there any blood tests that can tell me that my ovaries are failing without having to wait a whole year before I can start treatment for my symptoms?

You can start treatment right away for the symptoms you mentioned. A blood test that measure Follicle Stimulating Hormone or FSH and Luteinizing Hormone or LH can tell. Usually a high range is a sign that ovulation has stopped. There is some data that Black Cohosh may actually be working on the LH and FSH.

The other issue is of estrogen predominance.

I thought that the ovaries stopped producing estrogen and that is why I am having all these crazy problems!

Actually, the adrenal glands and fat stores of the body continue to make small amounts of estrogen so that you have around 30% of your estrogen levels that you had before menopause. It is the progesterone that is non-existent which causes this estrogen predominance. Which is why obesity, and excess estrogen production by the adipose tissues, is a risk factor for uterine cancer.

So why not try progesterone replacement in some kind of a natural way?

We can discuss this at the next visit. Why not try the Black Cohosh first. It is the first line treatment for menopause symptoms in Europe and is available as Remifemin. Then if that is not successful, we can discuss the use of progesterone and other alternative approaches to help the symptoms. I would recommend Douglas Labs as a source of the Black Cohosh as it is standardized. Start with one at bedtime for about 4 weeks and increase it to two at bedtime for the next 4 to 8 weeks if your symptoms do not improve.

DR. M. P. KHAN, MD/NMD

The recommended dose is 40 mg. *of a standardized* dose 2 x day. Menopausal symptoms usually subside after 8 weeks of use and can be used long term. Regular exercise, reducing nicotine and caffeine use, stress reduction techniques, avoiding processed foods and cutting down on non-organic foods (pesticides) and a sense of humor are also useful.

Also keep a daily diary of your symptoms. Use simple symbols and intensity measures. For example hot flashes =H and severity from 1 lowest to 4 highest. Mood changes =M 1-4 and vaginal Dryness=D 1-4.

For example: Monday=H1; M3; D2

And so on so you can see what your progress is. Bring your diary at your next doctor visit.

ONCE THERE WAS AN ANGEL

"Who if I cried out, would hear me among the angel's hierarchies? And even if one of them pressed me suddenly against his heart, I would be consumed in that overwhelming existence".
—**Rainer Maria Rilke**

<u>PERIN:</u>

Some say in antiquity, angels walked the earth. Mine was named Perin: Persian for fairy. I called her "Mamaiji," Gujarati for grandmother. And a Happy Birthday to Mamaiji.

She weaved magical stories of her youth, her eyes misted over.
Reminiscing of genteel Victorian days,
The British Raj, faded pictures of a young Elizabeth;
"God bless the Queen, those were the days."
Never the wise matriarch, innocent childhood was her talisman.
Her father, a physician, made house calls in a horse drawn carriage,
Tales of her two sisters, in the parlor of their home,
She played the viola, the evening air filled with sweet music.
In her presence, in quiet times, I caught these primal strains.
A wistful melody that lingers, a lullaby of childhood dreams,
Escaping memory and yet soothing me to sleep.

In dotage, blinded by the ravages of diabetes,
Lesser souls would have railed
Against the darkness and the eternal night.
How does the light shine through?
How did she transcend sorrow? Is it a gift only angels have?
I saw no wounds, no stigmata!

In her kitchen, I learned to cook, to believe in life again.
The simmer of cardamom, cinnamon,
The warm bubble of ghee, the crisp fry of lamb and fish,
Pungent with chili and coriander.
Around the dinner table, I understood her alchemy of food and love.

On my own pilgrimage in this great continent,
In an Interstate motel, lost somewhere in the Rockies,
A disembodied voice, heavy with tears half a world away,
Conveyed the news of her sudden passage.
I grieved; but after the anguish of loss and empty obituaries,
What burned into my memory was her kindness,
Her special grace, an oasis in my troubled youth.

She was my peace, my Mecca, a haven when the world closed in.
A Mecca now buried with the sands of time,
Thousand times more I could have circled her gentle soul.
I do not know where the sacred returns to?

MK 5/2010

May 14

ONCE THERE WAS AN ANGEL

March was Women's History Month. Every day, on a radio program, I heard about a long list of influential women who made a meaningful and significant impact on society. And it got me thinking about a woman, who, in a very difficult period of my life, accepted me and believed in me. Looking back, she was really an angel disguised as my Grandmother. She is and will always be on the top of my list. The above poem is dedicated to her.

Was there was a person that changed your life in a meaningful and deep way?

_____

_____

What would your life been if that person had not existed?

_____

_____

_____

_____

What lesson did this person teach you that you remember the best?

_____

_____

_____

_____

DR. M. P. KHAN, MD/NMD

May 15

EVERYBODY'S PISSED OFF (PART-1)

> *"When health is absent,*
> *Wisdom cannot reveal itself,*
> *Art cannot manifest,*
> *Strength cannot fight,*
> *Wealth becomes useless,*
> *And intelligence cannot be applied."*
>
> **—Herophilus**

It's Thursday and I am anticipating Mrs. Fields office visit. Her son just gave her a computer for her birthday. My nurse informs me that she has a sheaf of paper that she has printed off the internet. And she is pretty upset about something!

Hello Doctor Khan. I just can't believe this! Excuse the colorful language but I am really pissed off. I thought that we had the best medical system in the world! Look at this stuff I found on the internet!

I hear you Mrs. Fields. As usual you have hit the nail on the head. *Everybody's* pissed off! It seems that the medical system is currently peeing into the perfect storm if you will excuse my French. Nobody is happy! When you talk to physicians, almost one in two doctors are dissatisfied (43%/2007) with the system. We all want to do what is best by our patients. If money was the only issue we could have been CEOs of large corporations with obscene salaries and outrageous pension plans. Instead, we carry pagers that never stop beeping, sometimes spend sleepless nights, deal with the abuse of insurance companies, and go crazier as the years go by. The solution however is staring us in the face!

Maybe Dr. K., but until I read this, I thought we had the best health care system in the world? It's all very disappointing!

Yes and no. As far as medical technology goes, America leads the world. It is in the transfer of this technology to health care that it falls apart. Here are some cold hard facts.

Also check out the information found on May 3-May 6 "Peeing into the Perfect Storm." There are more constructive suggestions that the health system could implement.

May 16

EVERYBODY'S PISSED OFF (PART-1)

- Health care spending in 2004 per person was $6,102 per person per year in the U.S.A. compared to $3,165 in Canada (which has universal insurance). In fact no other industrialized country exceeded Canada with Spain having the lowest at $2,094. This (USA) has probably gone up since then.
- The USA has an infant mortality rate per 1000 of population at 6.5 which is slightly worse than South Korea at 6.3.
- The USA leads the world in the population which is overweight/obesity rates: 66.3% with the UK at 63% and Japan at 24.9%.
- 47 million uninsured (and the only industrialized country *without* universal insurance) with a growing number underinsured and this number is growing as businesses cannot afford rising insurance costs. Hopefully this will change with the implementation of the Affordable Care Act which has been recently implemented.
- Insurance companies uses up 30% of the health care dollar in administrative costs.

This sounds incredible! Maybe I should move to Canada?

There is a saying that Canadians are actually Americans without Guns and with Health Insurance! Before you do that, remember the sun always shines after a storm. American ingenuity invented flight and the light bulb. Surely we can fix the system. But it can only happen when we act collectively. Patients/consumers need to actively demand preventive as well as basic health care services from their insurance companies and their political representatives;

Physicians (at times we are patients too) need to understand that we are healers and that the paradigm is shifting from an illness to a wellness model and that they should also be reimbursed for their time in providing preventive services. Already major payors are incentivizing physicians when they can hit certain quality indicators in patient care

Payors/Insurance companies need to balance profit with access to health care with financial incentives and education for their clients towards a healthier lifestyle. There also needs to be a political vision and will which creatively provides basic health care for all Americans at the same time keeping the free market system in place. So many expenses to treat the major complications of illness could be avoided if money was spent in disease prevention. The Perfect Storm is also the Perfect opportunity for change!

REFERENCES: *One in two doctors is dissatisfied (43%/2007) with the system. Harris Interactive, Strategic Health Perspectives 1995-2007.

* Health care spending in 2004 per person: OECD Health data Volume 26:5, 2007.

* An infant mortality rate per 1000 of population at 6.5; OECD 2002-2007.

May 17

EVERYBODY'S PISSED OFF (PART-2)

"Only two things sure in life; death and change."
—Chairman Moo

The task seems overwhelming, Doctor Khan! How can I as an individual do any of these actions you talk about? Maybe the next generation can fix it.

Mr. Fields, if everybody took that attitude, nothing would change. What kind of a healthcare system will we leave for our grandchildren? If everyone in your Garden Club wrote to their congressmen about their concerns, it would be a beginning. The AARP is a powerful political lobby. Every journey begins with a single step. Every revolution begins with a single idea. Leaving it to the future generation may be too late. The health system is in state of crisis. Medicare is already feeling the pinch, and baby boomers are going to find out that when they are ready for the Golden years (retirement), a couple will have to have at least $200,000 in savings to pay for out of pocket expenses. Here are some tips:

Start with taking a long honest look at your own health. Are there any life style issues that you can change? Start with something small like taking the stairs.

- Initiate a dialogue with your physician so as to provide you options to make these changes. Most doctors would love to help, because it results in a win-win situation for both parties. Contrary to popular belief we do like to see our patients get better (and healthier). Also find out about other resources in your community such as yoga classes, nutrition programs, health clubs etc. Many insurance companies now offer free classes in lifestyle management like Silver Sneakers.
- If you are employed, talk to your HR department that when the time comes to choose an Insurance product, go for one

that also covers complimentary medicine approaches such as acupuncture. (They already do that on the West coast). If you are an employer, provide incentives in premium reduction from payroll if certain target behaviors are met and maintained, for example weight loss. Provide mini-seminars in stress management or nutrition using professionals in the community. Healthy employees are happy employees and result in a healthy bottom line.

- Call your political representatives and ask them where they stand on health reform issues. You elected them so hold their feet to the fire! And if you are dissatisfied there is always election time!! I hope this discussion helps you as a starting point in your journey. As the saying goes," *Don't get pissed off, get healthy!"*

DR. M. P. KHAN, MD/NMD

May 18

EVERYBODY'S PISSED OFF (PART-2)

Believe in your ability to make changes in their lifestyle. If you are a healer, nothing destroys the therapeutic relationship than a cynical attitude. Also be aware that change does not happen until the individual is ready for change. So keep plugging away and one day that patient you have been counseling for years to quit smoking will surprise you with: "Hey doc, guess what, I gave up those cigarettes!"

What are my negative life style issues, and am I ready to change them?

_____

_____

_____

_____

We are all guilty of getting so busy in taking care of others that we forget to take care of our own emotional and physical health. We need to first make a strong commitment to our own wellbeing and that of our families. What activity /hobby bring me joy and how can incorporate this in my life?

_____

_____

_____

_____

If you are a healer, try to find the balance in your professional and personal life. A conference I attended on Mind Body Medicine was a transformative experience for me. It not only put me in touch with my own feelings but also gave me tools to deal with stress in the patient care setting. Is there any CAM modality that I can experience such (as massage, hypnotherapy, biofeedback, journaling, dance, meditation) and how do I use it to reduce my stress levels? Can I help my patients to deal with their stress levels better?

_____

_____

_____

_____

May 19

MENOPAUSAL MISERY (PART-2)

"Real women don't have hot flashes,
they have power surges."

—Anon

Mrs. Fields daughter, Helena returns for her follow up visit. She has tried the Black Cohosh and has had some improvement in her symptoms according to her diary. She was hoping for a better outcome.

Hi Dr. Khan, I kept the diary as you suggested. There is some improvement. My husband and I are friends once again. No more strange looks. I also want to talk to you about my daughter. Sometimes, especially around her period, she is impossible to be around. Now that I am feeling better, I would like some suggestions to help her. Any ideas, Doc?

First let's discuss options so that we can help your symptoms. I feel that there is some room for improvement. We can try topical or trans-dermal cream that you can use daily. A one-year randomized, placebo-controlled trial compared the effects of 20 mg of progesterone cream vs. placebo in postmenopausal women. 55% of women had vasomotor symptoms (hot flushes) at baseline in the placebo vs. 69% in the progesterone group. Of those who had hot flushes, 83% experienced improvement in the progesterone group, compared to 19% in the control group. (Leonetti HB, et al. Transdermal progesterone cream for vasomotor symptoms. *Obstetric Gynecology* **1999; 94:225-228).**

Sounds like a good idea. Where can I get this cream? What about saliva testing to determine the hormone levels?

There is an OTC version that you can buy at any pharmacy but this does not have enough progesterone. I would suggest you try

DR. M. P. KHAN, MD/NMD

the compounded version which has higher levels of progesterone. As far as saliva testing, it is not very accurate and there is no correlation between saliva levels and symptom relief and the amount of progesterone used. *The best indicator to adjust progesterone dosing is the relief of symptoms that you experience.* There is some value in checking red blood cell progesterone levels but this is experimental. And it can be used with the Black Cohosh as an add-on.

I have heard that acupuncture is also useful in preventing hot flashes? Can I try it? How does it work?

We know that Acupuncture increases endorphin levels. It may affect the sympathetic nervous system by its action at the hypothalamic and brainstem levels where the body's heat regulation centers are located. The endorphins seem to stabilize these centers from which hot flushes are initiated. The mechanisms of action of acupuncture also might be related to neurotransmitters by activating the dopamine and serotonin pathways. This explains why drugs like Effexor, which activate the same pathways, work in relieving hot flushes.

MENOPAUSAL MISERY (PART-2)

"Menopause is your return to where you were before, when your hormone levels are the same as a pre-adolescent girls."
—Sandra Tsing Loh

A study called ACUFLASH (Menopause 2009; 16:484-493) found that at the end of 12 weeks, hot flushes decreased by 5.8 in a 24 hour period as well as its intensity in the acupuncture group. The control group, which received self-care advice only, had a decrease of 3.7 per 24 hours with no significant decrease in intensity. The effect did not persist beyond a 6 month period.

Where can I get acupuncture treatment like you suggested? And don't forget my daughter's problem!

I would suggest a practitioner trained in Traditional Chinese Medicine or TCM. It may require between 8-10 sessions before you notice a difference.

Assuming that your daughter's menstrual cycles are regular (when periods first start, because cycles are an-ovulatory or non-egg producing, they can be very sporadic) a good herb is Vitex or Agnes castus. Used as early as 4th century BC it was also later known as "chaste tree" in the mistaken belief that it suppressed woman's libido.

Vitex works by increasing the production of Luteinizing Hormone or LH and causing more ovulatory cycles thus increasing progesterone production and correcting a relative progesterone deficiency. A 1990 German study showed a 90% reduction in PMS symptoms after 25 days on a liquid extract, the average age being 34.7 with a range of 13 to 62.years. I would start on 400 mg of Vitex daily between meals and would also recommend it for at least a 90-120 day period continuously along with a good vitamin-mineral supplement and plenty of exercise. The best approach is to buy products from a reputable manufacturer like Douglas Labs so that it is standardized so as to avoid variation or adulteration.

Try the below web sites as a starting point.
http://www.medicalacupuncture.org/
http://www.nccaom.org/

May 21

LUV YA CAMELLIA

"Come, let us have some tea and continue to talk about happy things."

—**Chaim Potok**

Camellia sinensis or tea or chai is probably consumed by more cultures than any other beverage. To add to the confusion there are now a plethora of teas available. All colors of tea essentially come from the same plant and depends on what point the fermentation process is stopped. (See below) For simplicities sake we will not discuss herbal teas although technically it can be applied to an infusion of a plant or parts of a plant brewed in hot water, like mint tea

White tea; Wilted and unoxidized

Yellow tea; Unwilted and unoxidized allowed to yellow.

Green tea; Unwilted and unoxidized.

Oolong; Wilted, bruised, and partially oxidized

Black tea; Wilted, sometimes crushed, and fully oxidized

Tea contains catechins, a type of antioxidant. In a freshly picked tea leaf, catechins can compose up to 30% of the dry weight and are highest in concentration in white and green teas, while black tea has substantially fewer due to its preparation. Catechins also have anti-cancer properties. Research by the U.S.D.A. has suggested that levels of the other antioxidants in green and black tea are similar. Green tea has an oxygen radical absorbance capacity (ORAC) of 1253 and black tea an ORAC of 1128. Tea also contains caffeine; between 30 mg and 90 mg per 8 oz. cup depending on type, and brewing method. Tea also contains small

DR. M. P. KHAN, MD/NMD

amounts of theobromine and theophylline which are mildly stimulating. Tea is probably one of the heaviest sprayed crops with large amounts of fungicides used to prevent spoilage. Go organic if you are a heavy tea drinker.

Besides the catechins, tea leaves contain more than 700 chemicals, among which are compounds called flavonoids as well as small amounts of vitamins, Tea drinking has recently proven to be associated with improved cell-mediated immune function of the human body. Tea plays an important role in improving beneficial intestinal bacteria, as well as providing immunity against intestinal disorders.

LUV YA CAMELLIA

It has been estimated that up to 30% of the dry leaf weight of green tea consists of polyphenols and levels of EGCG (The major polyphenol found in green tea is epigallocatechin-3-gallate or EGCG) vary according to the method of processing the teas with green tea having the highest levels and black tea, the least.

Previously we talked about tea and catechins being a superstar in any weight loss program. But there are other health benefits to drinking tea. In 2010 researchers found that people who consumed tea had significantly less mental decline than non-tea drinkers. The study used data on more than 4,800 men and women aged 65 and older. (AAICAD 2010; Lenore Arab, PhD; UCLA)

Although there have been no direct clinical trials to date, epidemiologic studies have found the relative risk of breast cancer in women who are consistent tea drinkers, is half that of women drinking less than one cup per month. Tea catechins, especially EGCG, are an active chemo-preventive constituent.

Prostate cancer risk appears to decrease with increasing frequency, duration, and quantity of green tea consumption with higher consumption of green tea over a period of years significantly reducing the risk of developing prostate cancer. A trial conducted at the Mayo Clinic among patients with androgen-independent prostate cancer found that green tea consumption was able to significantly decrease PSA values. The placebo group sustained a PSA increase of 43%.

Tea also prevents dental caries due to the presence of fluorine. Tea is also known to normalize blood pressure, lower cholesterol, and in prevention of coronary heart diseases and diabetes. Tea also possesses bactericidal and bacteriostatic activities against various human pathogenic bacteria.

Green tea is an acquired taste. I would suggest you brew it together with mint tea to make it more palatable. Also stick to the non-caffeinated variety,

The "Republic of Tea" makes a good brand of organic green tea. Start with real hot water and let the tea bag steep for no more than 4 minutes.

For maximum health benefits drink 2-3 cups of green(15mg caffeine/cup) or black tea (30mg to 70mg caffeine/cup) a day.

MAGICAL MUSHROOMS

"All mushrooms are edible. Once!"

—Anon

Strange as it may seem, we are genetically closer to mushrooms than we realize. In a new analysis of genetic relationships among organisms, researchers have concluded that animals and fungi share a common evolution. This new finding, which appeared in the journal Science, suggests that the common ancestor of animals and fungi was a so-called *protest*, a single-celled creature that very likely possessed both animal and fungal characteristics.

A newer approach to studying evolution is by examining genes and analyzing the same genes in many different species and tracking how many mutational changes have occurred in the genes from one organism to the next. Scientists are then able to calculate their connections based on a complex mathematical model. "A lot of the metabolism is so similar that you can't target a fungus sufficiently without gravely affecting the human host as well," said Dr. Mitchell L. Sogin of the Center for Molecular Evolution at the Marine Biological Laboratory in Woods Hole, Mass., and the main author of the report. This could explain why fungal infections (for example ring worm or tinea) in humans are so difficult to treat

We will only consider edible mushrooms as there are a whole bunch of hallucinogenic mushrooms and their use is probably illegal. Mushrooms are also known as macro-fungi and are actually their fruiting bodies. Their active ingredients are the beta-glucans which are widely used in anti-cancer drugs. World production of mushrooms amounted to $18 Billion (same as coffee sales)

Shitake and Reishi mushrooms can be found in your local grocery are one used in the production of Lentinan, a powerful anti-tumor drug. A drug called Krestin is developed from the Turkey tail mushroom and is used in treating a number of cancers in Japan. A study of native population in Brazil, where intake of "almond flavored Portobello" was high showed a very low incidence of adult onset degenerative diseases. This species was the most effective mushroom in its anticancer activity as compared to reishi and maitake. *Reishi mushroom extract* DL cat# 77365 can be taken 1 three times a day to help the immune system.

MAGICAL MUSHROOMS

Also *CNCR support pack* DL cat# 4551 has a blend of mushrooms and other plant based products and I recommend this to patients on chemotherapy or radiation treatments. Mushrooms also contain a large amount of essential amino acids and are a good source of vegetarian protein. They are also a vegan source of Vitamin D.

Going back to the above quote, unless you have a good knowledge of edible mushrooms, do not eat mushrooms growing in your backyard. Some species can cause rapid liver failure and death. The only way to reverse liver failure due to mushroom poisoning is an injectable extract of milk thistle (Sylmarin). This is readily available in most Emergency Departments in Europe where wild mushroom gathering is very popular. Unfortunately, this antidote is not readily available in the US and would have saved the life of one of the inheritors of the Gallo wine dynasty who accidentally ingested a very toxic nightshade variety of mushroom.

Below are some tips on buying and eating mushrooms:

All store bought mushrooms are edible.

It is best not to eat them raw. Eat mushrooms lightly cooked after a thorough washing and drying because of the fertilizers used in their growing. If used in a stir-fry add them last as they cook very quickly. They are best stored unwashed in a brown paper bag in the refrigerator.

Try to get organic mushrooms as they tend to accumulate heavy metals if grown in contaminated soil.

To learn more about this amazing life form, checkout "Mycelium Running" by Stamet. The diverse uses of mushrooms will astound you; from cleaning up diesel fuel to absorbing radioactive wastes!

May 25

THE WISDOM OF
COMPASSION (PART-1)

*"If you want to be happy, practice compassion. If you want
others to be happy, practice compassion."*
—The Dalai Lama

This parable tells the story of the hidden power of compassionate action. Without our knowing, kindness sometimes bears unexpected fruit. This story is loosely based on real events in our life and is a kind of belated birthday gift for Karen.

In the village of Linchow lived a poor farmer, Lo Mein and his wife, Moo Shoo. Although they eked out a difficult existence, they were happy with their lives and each other. Money was always tight and Lo Mein would often worry and spend sleepless nights if his wife spent too much on rice or some other small luxury. But he loved her very much and as the couple was childless, she was all he had in this world.

One night as they were about to go to sleep, Moo Shoo heard a soft meow outside the window of their hut. Lo Mein was fast asleep and snored softly, exhausted from the day's labor. This meowing continued for some time so she went outside to investigate it. In the darkness she could see two amber eyes staring at her. At first she was scared and thought that the she-devil Manu, had come to take her away.

But then, as her eyes adjusted to the darkness, she saw that it was a small black cat. She laughed out loud in her relief and was about to go back to sleep when she heard a plaintive and even louder meow. This time she looked at the poor creature more closely. In the moon light she could see that it looked gaunt and the faint outline of its ribs.

Moved by its plight, she quietly went into the kitchen and scooped out a handful of cooked rice and some left over fish, and returned to where she had last seen the cat. She placed the fish and rice on the grass and soon she could hear the quiet slurp of the cat as it gobbled up the offering. When it was done with the meal, as if to reward Moo Shoo, it came up to her and started to purr and rub against her leg.

Very soon it became a kind of a ritual. Every night, Moo Shoo would wait till she heard Lo Mein snoring. Then she would quietly go to the kitchen and would head out with her scoopful of rice and fish and waited till she saw those amber eyes appear out of the darkness. She even named the cat Manu, and soon she had adopted this wild creature. Or was it the other way around?

DR. M. P. KHAN, MD/NMD

THE WISDOM OF
COMPASSION (PART-1)

When we lived in our Monroeville residence, Karen had fed the two or three outside cats. (And raccoons and possums and deer and backyard birds). We had a large dog house on our front porch which was heated in the winter and was used by several furry nocturnal creatures. We spent a small fortune on pet food every month and unlike Lo Mein, I did sometimes complain about it!

Part two of the story that follows could have actually happened. And then again it could be fiction. Life may be closer to art than we realize.

Has there been a time in your life that you have been compassionate to another being without any thought of a reward or future payback?

_____

_____

_____

_____

_____

_____

_____

_____

_____

How did it make you feel?

_____

_____

_____

_____

_____

May 27

THE WISDOM OF COMPASSION (PART-2)

Soon the weather got cooler. The first snowflakes covered the ground and Moo Shoo worried about Manu. One day when Lo Mein was visiting the nearest town to stock up for the winter, she made a small house of bamboo and thatch at the back of the hut. She lined it with straw. She was gratified when she saw that Manu, on her nightly forays with the fish and the rice, would emerge from the little shelter she had made. To make it easier, she put relatively large bowls of food and water outside the shelter. If Lo Mein knew about it, he did not say anything to Moo Shoo. All he knew was that she seemed happier than ever and that was a good thing.

One evening Lo Mein returned from his day's labor with disturbing news. There were reports of several robberies nearby. The thieves had stolen precious grain and even a couple of pigs. They were probably bacon by now, thought Lo Mein, as he broke the bad news to Moo Shoo. That night they made sure they locked the barn and burnt an extra oil lamp near the entrance to their hut. Of course that didn't stop Moo Shoo from her nightly duty of feeding Manu. She was afraid that she might surprise the robbers if they were nearby. But her love for Manu overcame her fears and after making sure that Lo Mein was fast asleep, she once more ventured out into the darkness.

It was now nearly the end of the growing season. Most evenings he would tell her stories of how another neighbor's farm got robbed or of livestock stolen. It was only a matter of time before his farm would be next on their list. But as the days grew shorter and fall was around the corner and they had not been visited by the robbers, he breathed easier. But then word got around that since his farm was the only one spared by the bandits, he was probably in cahoots with them. Poor Lo Mein. He almost wished that his farm would be robbed so he could stop their wagging tongues.

And then the good news! The local police had a tip and the robbers were apprehended. There was great celebration in the village. Lo Mein was very relieved though he still could not believe his good fortune. Soon there was a trial and the courtroom was filled with villagers. As was the judicial custom, the wronged parties could question the accused to establish their guilt. When they were almost done, Lo Mein, now very curious as to

DR. M. P. KHAN, MD/NMD

why his farm was spared, got on the stand and asked the question that was on every one's mind.

Their answer to Lo Mein's question surprised everybody. The robbers had been by the farm one night and were about to walk away with his prize cow. But when they saw the small house at the back of his hut with the big bowls of food and water, they assumed that a large and fearful dog probably lived there. And when they saw the two glowing eyes peering at them in the darkness they turned and ran. They decided, in the future, to avoid this farm for easier pickings!

May 28

AN IRISH BLESSING

"May you always have walls for the winds,
a roof for the rain, tea beside the fire, laughter
to cheer you, those you love near you and all your heart
might desire."

—Irish Blessing

Sometime ago, I purchased a 12 pack of Guinness stout beer in those dark bottles with a harp in anticipation of St. Patrick's Day. And when I pour that dark brown libation in a chilled beer mug I am reminded of two other quintessential Irish exports; blessings and limericks. Irish blessing remind me of a Zen saying "Bless Everyone." Maybe the act of blessing someone implies that we wish upon them a divine guidance on whatever path they are on. And it also emphasizes that it is the simple things in life (like a warm cup of tea on a cold day besides a roaring fire) that bring us joy.

And the Irish also invented (so they claim) drinking songs and raucous limericks. Which is why, in memory of St. Patrick's Day, I have included this poem (which is really an extended limerick). I wrote this poem as an exercise based on an item of clothing; in this case 'pants.' Only problem is that it turned out more auto biographical than I intended. So raise a glass of Guinness and enjoy today, and this poem!

PANTS:

At first I envisioned a saga about ants.
You know the little critters with a queen.
Instead chronicled the story of my pants!
You know, they cover legs,
And everything in between.

As an infant, my diaper was frequently changed; very frequently.
I was raised by three doting aunts.
No question, I hold the record for being toilet trained,
And at age two, thank God, graduated into pants.

School at St Mary's, all boys and chastity vows, was kind of scary.
Did the Jesuits really invent the position, 'missionary'?
Starched white shorts, blue ties neat as a pin,
And daily admonishments:
"Keep your pants on kids. Masturbation is a sin."

Medical school and anatomy classes;
The customary dissection of cadavers.
Fell in love teasing out the radial nerve,
And the flexor digitorum secundus.*
Aaah! Lara; unlike cadavers, you kept me up forever!
Dropping my pants for you,
Was an experience quite profundus!

And now divorced twice, I will end this doggerel.
Heed me guys, if these silly verses have a lesson or a moral,
Before you mate and shed your trousers indiscriminate,
Pants may be your only protection from a dire fate!

*No such muscle exists. Sorry, poetic license.

MK/7/03

AN IRISH BLESSING

Write a blessing for someone you care for;

_____
_____
_____
_____
_____
_____
_____

Write a blessing for someone you <u>don't</u> care for:

_____
_____
_____
_____
_____
_____
_____

Write a blessing for yourself:

_____
_____
_____
_____
_____
_____
_____

DR. M. P. KHAN, MD/NMD

DREAMING OF SUMMER

"A perfect summer day is when the sun is shining, the breeze is blowing, the birds are singing, and the lawn mower is broken."

—James Dent

BERMUDA DREAMS:

In the soft afternoon
the Rastafarian jogged on the pristine beach
his waist length dreadlocks writhing like
dusty serpents against damp ebony skin.
In this world of pink sands and white bodies
he was an apparition; a disenchanted Island God
waking up from a cocoon of centuries.

In a time before history
an angry volcano poured out its fiery heart to
a cooling sea, a violent orgasm of lava and steam.
When the passion of their meeting subsided, the archipelago of Bermuda was born.
A verdant gem set in the azure sea,
the paradise of Khayyam's dreams.

Where once wild boars rooted,
and cruel men of plunder lured ships to their doom,
equally cruel men now dream of carving up paradise.
But how does one sell:
the evening fragrance of frangipani,
the crimson of tamarind trees, a filigree of green,
the self-proclaiming song of the kiskadee?

I clasp the rock ledge, it's edge soft with seaweed,
the waves embracing me in its primordial bosom.
And the warm noon sun, vies with the perfection of blue green water
and surrounds itself with a rainbow.
The Rastafarian resumes his jog, leaving foot prints on forgiving sand.
I watch him disappear into phantom coves.
In the silence that follows, words fail to describe this enchantment

MK/05

DR. M. P. KHAN, MD/NMD

May 31

DREAMING OF SUMMER

One of the best summer vacations that I have had was a trip to Bermuda. I wrote this poem as a memory of a perfect summer. I had to do some research on the geology and the history of this island of pink sands.

Write down your favorite summer memories, past or future:

_____

_____

_____

_____

_____

_____

_____

_____

_____

_____

_____

_____

JUNE

1-Jun	DON'T BE A WORRY 'WORT.' The merits of St. John
2-Jun	DON'T BE A WORRY 'WORT.' And more botanical approaches.
3-Jun	A GIFT OF LEAVES. Musings and a poem on an early summer's day.
4-Jun	A GIFT OF LEAVES. Becoming one with Nature.
5-Jun	NAVROZ MUBARAK (HAPPY NEW YEAR) BELATEDLY. The Zoroastrian faith.
6-Jun	NAVROZ MUBARAK (HAPPY NEW YEAR) BELATEDLY. Celebrate this day.
7-Jun	LOTSA WATER, NADA TO DRINK (PART-1). Your 'water foot print'.
8-Jun	LOTSA WATER, NADA TO DRINK (PART-1). And how to reduce it.
9-Jun	LOTSA WATER, NADA TO DRINK (PART-2). Plastic bottles and tap water.
10-Jun	LOTSA WATER, NADA TO DRINK (PART-2). Bottled or Tap: www.ewg.org.
11-Jun	LOTSA WATER, NADA TO DRINK (PART-3). Life cannot exist without water!
12-Jun	LOTSA WATER, NADA TO DRINK (PART-2). 'GASLAND' and CDWA
13-Jun	LOTSA WATER, NADA TO DRINK (PART-4). A chemical cocktail recipe for disaster.
14-Jun	LOTSA WATER, NADA TO DRINK (PART-4). A Witch's Brew; definitely.
15-Jun	GOOD BYE, LUDWIG. All about Beethoven.
16-Jun	GOOD BYE, LUDWIG. "A Fifth of Beethoven" poem.
17-Jun	A DARK NIGHT OF THE SOUL (PART-1). A poetic term for Depression.
18-Jun	A DARK NIGHT OF THE SOUL (PART-1). Demographics and Diagnosis.
19-Jun	A DARK NIGHT OF THE SOUL (PART-2). Depression is not a disease!
20-Jun	A DARK NIGHT OF THE SOUL (PART-2). PDB: Paced Diaphragm Breathing.
21-Jun	A DARK NIGHT OF THE SOUL (PART-3). The Stress to Depression cascade.
22-Jun	THIRTEEN YEARS LATER. An Anniversary and a poem
23-Jun	THIRTEEN YEARS LATER. Your thoughts on '300 Years.'
24-Jun	A DARK NIGHT OF THE SOUL (PART-3). To SSRI or Not?
25-Jun	A DARK NIGHT OF THE SOUL (PART-4). Lessons from Winnie the Pooh.
26-Jun	A DARK NIGHT OF THE SOUL (PART-4). Supplements in the Rx of Depression.
27-Jun	A DARK NIGHT OF THE SOUL (PART-5). More Mind-Body approaches.
28-Jun	A DARK NIGHT OF THE SOUL (PART-5). Find your joy!
29-Jun	SOME OF KAREN'S POEMS. "Misanthropic Muse."
30-Jun	SOME OF KAREN'S POEMS. "Seven Veils"

DR. M. P. KHAN, MD/NMD

June 1

DON'T BE A WORRY 'WORT'

"That the birds of worry and care fly over your head, this you cannot change, but that they build nests in your hair, this you can prevent."

—**Chinese Proverb**

Mrs. Fields has referred her daughter Melanie to me for a "supplement consult." She is going through a contentious divorce and is not sleeping well. She is very tearful during the visit. She confides in me that, her physician, because the symptoms were ongoing for the last six weeks had prescribed her an anti-depressant drug but has stopped taking it because of weight gain. It also makes her feel flat, like someone pulled the plug on her emotions.

"Hi, Doctor Khan. Mom feels that you can help me with some of the issues I am going through. I have gained eleven pounds over the last four weeks and I am not sure if I am more depressed about that or the divorce! And no, I am not suicidal. I just need something to help me through a difficult period of my life."

Good news, Melanie! There are several herbal supplements used since ancient times for managing the 'ill humors' as the Greeks would call them. It seems that stress and worry is not a modern phenomenon. The problem is that the pharmaceutical treatments for these conditions, which are an inevitable risk of living life, cause more side effects and dependency issues and so I usually recommend the below listed herbal supplements. Remember that supplements should be obtained from a reliable source and should be used for at least an eight week period as they take a longer period of time before the therapeutic effect is achieved.

1) St John's Wort: Also known as SJW and no it is not a "wart." "Wort" is old English for a plant. Legend has it that if a maiden put this plant under her pillow on the day that St. John was celebrated, she would dream of her beloved! This herbal supplement is one of the main treatments in Europe for treatment of mild to moderate depression. I do not recommend this for depression with suicidal ideation or for depression associated with psychosis. It is just as effective as conventional antidepressants and worked better in lowering anxiety scores. And there is no weight gain or sexual dysfunction to be concerned about!

It should be used as a standardized form of hypericin 0.3% at a dose of 1 or 2 capsules twice a day between meals for 6-8 weeks and up to 1 year if there is a good response. I would avoid direct sunlight exposure when on SJW as it is photo sensitizing and can cause a skin reaction Use in caution with drugs that share the same metabolic pathway and do not mix with other antidepressants, especially the class of anti-depressants known as SSRI's.

June 2

DON'T BE A WORRY 'WORT'

2) Valerian root: An ancient herb and used as early as 150 AD by Galen. Also used by prostitutes in 1700s London and added to wine so that their customers would fall asleep and forget the reason why they were visiting the house of ill repute in the first place! Has a distinct old-sock-dirty feet smell and cats love it (like catnip). It is a good sedative and hypnotic and useful in treatment of insomnia and anxiety disorders. Also useful if you are trying to taper off the benzo diazepam class of drugs such as alprazolam and eases the withdrawal symptoms.

Valerinic acid increases the concentration of GABA in the brain and may cause sedation. Try a dose and see how it affects your motor skills. Be careful about driving until you can see what effects it has on you. There is almost no sedative or hangover effect in the morning-after, but may cause dependency and a withdrawal syndrome with long term use. It can be fatal if used with excess amounts of alcohol. Use 300mg-900mg DL Valerian Max-V standardized to 0.8 % valerinic acid one hour before bedtime and try not to exceed 6-8 weeks of use.

3) Kava kava: This was initially used in a drink by Pacific Islanders. It is a very good herb for anxiety states. Recent reports have shown a potential for liver damage and it is now banned in Switzerland and Germany. This may be a good example of what happens when an herb used traditionally is concentrated into a capsule and used almost like a drug. I would not recommend this supplement until the dust settles.

4) Passion Flower: Passiflora incarnata. A fiery name for an herb that is a sedative, it is useful in anxiety disorders. At a dose of 200 mg three times a day or two at bedtime. It is very safe and has no known drug interactions. It can be mixed with valerian as a sleep aid.

5) *Chamomile:* This is a god herbal tea to sip on before bedtime and can be combined with Valerian to assist with the zzzzzz.

And Melanie, do not forget the importance of exercise, multivitamins, fish oil and vitamin D and meditation and guided imagery and behavioral therapy.

Make a plan of action to help deal with your stress levels and sleep issues:

_____

_____

_____

_____

_____

_____

_____

DR. M. P. KHAN, MD/NMD

June 3

A GIFT OF LEAVES

"It is summer, it is the solstice.
The crowd is cheering, the crowd is laughing.
In detail permanently, seriously without thought."
— **William Carlos Williams**

One of my favorite activities of summer is lying in my hammock and looking up at the lazily swaying canopy of oak trees. A Zen-like experience; you have to be there! The poem that follows celebrates the gift of sight

Since the age of eight, I had been wearing corrective lenses (glasses) and endured taunts of four-eyes etc. So in my forties I leapt at the chance to undergo a new procedure (now old hat) called LASIK. "Leaves" is homage to the marvels of technology and to my own foolish bravado in undergoing it!

LEAVES:

I once saw the world with myopic eyes,
Always slightly smaller than it was.
Smaller stars; smaller trees; smaller minds;
My reality altered by an optical twist of fate.
Can three minutes change the perception of a lifetime?
Can the laser god clicking away with the burn smell of my cornea,
Make me see the world as it really is?
Recipient of this techno-miracle,
Supplicant of to the laser god smiling in her temple,
I perceive the world with newborn eyes!
So I now look up at leaves on a fine June day,
Seeing each perfect shape layered towards an azure sky,
More authentic than its own reality if that is possible.
And by chance if I never see again,
This I know: "I once saw leaves for the first time!"

MK/2000

June 4

A GIFT OF LEAVES

Sit back and try to do nothing for a while. If it is a work day, take a few minutes during lunch time. I know it's almost un-American and quite difficult in our getup and go society! Focus on nature and see it for what it is without any labels or pre-conceptions. If you will excuse the cliché, hug a tree or walk barefoot in the grass. Just be present and in peace with the sky and the sun and the wind.

Write down your impressions of your experience:

_____
_____
_____
_____
_____
_____
_____
_____
_____
_____

DR. M. P. KHAN, MD/NMD

June 5

NAVROZ MUBARAK (HAPPY NEW YEAR) BELATEDLY

"In the Spring a livelier iris changes on the burnish'd dove; In the Spring a young man's fancy lightly turns to thoughts of love"
—Alfred Lord Tennyson

The first day of spring is the 21st of March and is also the spring equinox. Almost six weeks later, the weather in the Berkshires is vacillating between a fall like wet fiftyish and a semi- warm early seventies. The robins and the crocuses are thoroughly confused. Lest you think I too am confused about when New Year actually falls, this day (March 21) is also the first day of the New Year according to the Zoroastrian calendar.

The religion of my birth, it usually elicits a "Huh!" kind of response when I tell them about it. I was raised in that faith and though I no longer practice it, I appreciate its simplicity and its connection to nature. It holds Fire, Earth, Air, and Water sacred. It also was the world's first monotheistic religion, predating Christianity by about 600 years. At one time the entire Persian Empire was of the Zoroastrian faith. After the invasion of Alexander the Great (or The Destroyer) the religion dwindled and was later marginalized by Islam.

Because of religious persecution there was a migration to cities in the great salt deserts, which remain centers of Iranian Zoroastrianism to this day. Crucial to the present-day survival of Zoroastrianism was a migration from Iran (then known as Persia) over 1500 years ago to Gujarat, a state on the western coast of India. The descendants of that group are today known as the Parsees (from Persia). It is also my ethnic identity.

Central to Zoroastrianism is the doctrine of moral choice. We have to choose the responsibility and duty for which one is born, and to never give up on this duty. Similarly, the concept of destiny is rejected in Zoroastrian teaching. Humans bear the final responsibility for all situations they are in, and in the way they behave toward one another. Reward and punishment; happiness, and grief; all depend on how we live our lives.

In Zoroastrianism, good things happen to those who do righteous deeds. Those who do evil have themselves to blame for their ruination. Zoroastrian morality is summed up in the simple dictum which we all do well to live by, "good thoughts, good words, good deeds" There are no monastic or ascetic theologies and there is the belief that life and nature that Ahura Mazda (God) has given to us is to be enjoyed to its fullest.

June 6

NAVROZ MUBARAK (HAPPY NEW YEAR) BELATEDLY

Today there are around a 100,000 practicing Zoroastrians worldwide. It was once the state religion of Iran and Navroz is still celebrated as a weeklong celebration in a pre-dominantly Islamic nation. There are still several pockets of the faithful who did not forget the religion of their ancestors, but the holiday is observed nationally by Muslims too. It is a time of connecting with family, feasting, wearing new clothes and to look forward to a renewal of nature once again!

NAVROZ MUBARAK or Greetings for the New Year! In how many other languages can you say greeting for a Happy New Year?

_____

_____

_____

_____

_____

_____

Celebrate this day as the first day of spring as the first day of the New Year.

Make it a "time of time of connecting with family, feasting, wearing new clothes and to look forward to a renewal of nature once again!"

How could we change our lives with the simple tenets of this faith: "good thoughts, good words, and good deeds?"

_____

_____

_____

_____

_____

_____

June 7

LOTSA WATER, NADA TO DRINK (PART-1)

"In an age when man has forgotten his origins and is blind even to his most essential needs for survival, water along with other resources has become the victim of his indifference."

—Rachel Carson

My almanac assures me that there is a World Waters Day. Not sure why there is a special day to celebrate water. But maybe we need a day like this to not to take clean drinking water for granted. When you realize that 80% of our body weight is water, it brings home the importance of water in our daily lives.

According to the latest figures by National Geographic, the actual amount of potable drinking water worldwide is extremely small (1% of all water)). And as the population of the world rises, this resource may be already be a cause for many wars and genocides. And this is only the beginning. The energy costs to make drinkable water are rising dramatically. The process for desalinating sea water is very energy intensive and is not affordable for third world impoverished countries. And now they are hauling icebergs to Arabia from the Arctic!

Conserving water and at the same time making sure that large corporate conglomerates do not exploit poor countries is a cause that should be embraced by each of us. In the larger picture we are all connected and we need to start thinking not only of a global economy but also of a "global humanity." This is not just a feel good tree hugger philosophy but a moral and economic issue that will affect the health of our children and grandchildren in the years to come. Today in some African countries, water is more expensive than pop. Large corporations buy off local governments to ensure that they do not develop the local water resources. And the water they sell is exported in large quantities

DR. M. P. KHAN, MD/NMD

from aquifers a continent away; a process that also depletes the water from that location.

Yes, we do see images of bottled water being distributed when natural disaster strikes to a grateful population and there is a need in those circumstances. But the images we do not see are that of an undernourished child guzzling a bottle of soda because the family cannot afford a bottle of water, is also a disaster of sorts. A disaster that is man-made and could have been avoided in the "global humanity' scenario. More about bottled water later on.

LOTSA WATER, NADA TO DRINK (PART-1)

There has recently been some talk about our "water" foot print similar to our carbon footprint. Check out: http://environment.nationalgeographic. com/environment/freshwater/water-footprint-calculator/

The average American uses 2000 gallons of water a day and twice as much as the rest of the world. There are several things you can do to cut down on the use of water and also save on your water bill.

My water foot print is _____ gallons/day.

Everything takes water to make. So if we buy less, we shrink our water footprint. Recycle plastics, glass, metals, and paper. Buy re-usable products as it takes water to make mostly everything.

Turn off the tap while brushing your teeth. Millions of us doing even little things can make a difference.

Where does your water come from—the river, lake, or aquifer that supplies your home? Once you know it, you won't want to waste water.

Choose outdoor landscaping appropriate for your climate and if you have to water, use a drip hose.

Install low-flow showerheads and faucet aerators and avoid long baths. Because you're saving hot water, you'll also reduce your gas/electric bill.

Replace your old toilet, with a low-volume, or dual-flush model.

DR. M. P. KHAN, MD/NMD

Call your plumber to fix your leaky faucets. All those wasted drops can add up to 25 gallons a day, besides being very annoying!

Run your dishwasher and washing machine only when full or every other day. When it's time to replace them, buy an energy and water efficient model.

Eat less meat, especially beef and change to more vegetable based diet. A ¼ pound of a beef hamburger needs 600 gallons of water.

June 9

LOTSA WATER, NADA TO
DRINK (PART-2)

"Water is life's mater and matrix, mother and medium.
There is no life without water."
—**Albert Szent-Gyorgyi;** *1937 Nobel Prize for Medicine.*

The next time you drink from a plastic bottle of water; **_STOP_**. The U.S. uses 50 billion water bottles a year, and most of those plastic containers are not recycled and more than 80% end up in landfills. And then there is the problem with BPA which is actually banned in Canada and Europe. Bisphenol-A (BPA) is a chemical linked to reproductive problems and heart disease and an endocrine disruptors. I would advise reusable glass water bottles at home, (not aluminum) and portable stainless steel ones for the road.

A safe plastic if used only once, is #1 (all plastic bottles have a number on them) polyethylene terephthalate (PET or PETE). If reused, as they often are, they can leach chemicals such as DEHA, a carcinogen, and benzyl butyl phthalate (BBP), a hormone disruptor. Because the plastic is porous, reusing the bottles causes you to swallow harmful bacteria with each gulp.

Transporting the bottles and keeping them cold also burns fossil fuels, which give off greenhouse gases besides the oil needed to make the plastic bottles. Water pumped up by bottled-water companies draws heavily on underground aquifers and destroys local watersheds. According to some estimates, it takes up to three liters of water to produce one liter of bottled water. It is then exported to third world countries as previously mentioned. These companies then post huge quarterly profits.

The public drinks 21 gallons of bottled water per capita per year on average, according to the Columbia University's Earth Institute in New York. The bottled-water has outpaced almost all beverages with the exception of beer and is actually more expensive than gasoline. Bottled

DR. M. P. KHAN, MD/NMD

water costs 1000 time more than tap water and is not necessarily safer. More than U.S. $100 billion is spent every year on bottled water globally. In many cities in developing countries where there is not a safe source of tap water, bottled water becomes the only option and is sold to indigent populations that can least afford it.

U.S. cities, San Francisco and Seattle, no longer buy bottled water for city use, and the city of Chicago, has added a five-cent tax on each bottle. Several restaurants in those cities have also given up bottled for filtered tap and New York tap water is a de rigueur dining experience.

June 10

LOTSA WATER, NADA TO DRINK (PART-2)

Check out *www.ewg.org* for a full explanation of bottled water vs tap water. You can also check the safety of your water supply by zip code. If you have well water, it would be a good idea to get your water tested by a local water service like 'Culligans' And while you are at it, send EWG a small donation for this valuable service.

The contaminants in my water supply (well or city) are:

_____

_____

_____

_____

_____

_____

_____

_____

_____

_____

_____

DR. M. P. KHAN, MD/NMD

June 11

LOTSA WATER, NADA TO DRINK (PART-3)

"Water is life. We are the people who live by the water. Pray by these waters.

Travel by the waters. Eat and drink from these waters. We are related to those who live in the water. To poison the waters is to show disrespect for creation.

To honor and protect the waters is our responsibility as people of the land."
　　　　—**Winona La Duke**, *"Like Tributaries to a River,"*

There is an elemental truth to this American Indian prayer that has stood the test of time and will be relevant as long as humans exist on this planet. In fact the primary determinant for life on other planets starts with finding the presence of water. *Life cannot exist without water.*

And yet we are systematically destroying this very resource that we here in North America take for granted. I am not a tree hugger. We have the knowledge to exploit our natural resources. The real question is that do we have the wisdom to do it in an ethical and responsible way. Can we use what is abundant in nature in a sustainable way so that future generations will not look back and define the 21ˢᵗ Century as the period of history that was the beginning of the end?

More down to earth (or water)! We have currently moved to Massachusetts from Western Pennsylvania. The issue that made us environmental refugees is of fracking or hydraulic fracturing of the Marcellus Shale that lies directly beneath the ground of most of the state of Pennsylvania. It is touted as one of the largest natural gas deposits in the world. It will also, if the ads are to be believed, end our dependence on foreign oil and will provide us with large amounts of cheap clean energy. And that is one side of the picture.

And if you are asking what gas has to do with water, it is the process of fracking. Each well, when it is fracked uses two to three *million* gallons of fresh water *each time* which usually comes from a river, lake, or an aquifer. This water, once used, cannot be recycled to usable water with current technology. Failures of the casing have the potential to contaminate the water table with very toxic solvents and which eventually end up in wells which are the primary source of drinking water in rural areas. To compound the problem, the contaminated water with large amounts of heavy metals and solvents is removed from the drill sites and is processed through water treatment plants which are not designed to handle these toxins and make their way into the municipal water supply of large cities, and eventually into our rivers and wetlands. *Is this technology or insanity?*

DR. M. P. KHAN, MD/NMD

June 12

LOTSA WATER, NADA TO DRINK (PART-3)

Watch the movie "GASLAND" now available on most streaming service such as Netflix. You may not agree with its message but keep an open mind as to the environmental impact of this technology. Energy companies are drilling with complete abandon because they are exempt from the CDWA or Clean Drinking Water Act. And they offer large sums of money to lease land for natural gas drilling. Also known as the Halliburton loop hole, they are also exempt from the Clean Air act and the Super Fund cleanup act

If you are thinking of leasing your land to a natural gas company, remember; you can't drink money! Before you sign on the dotted line, have a good attorney with a specialty in Oil/Gas leases read it. And research the health impact of some of the toxic chemicals. Although to date there is no direct causal research, there are some case studies coming out which read like a horror movie on a bad day.

June 13

LOTSA WATER, NADA TO
DRINK (PART-4)

*"Researchers with the U.S. Geological Survey estimate that
42 million Americans use groundwater vulnerable to low-
level contamination by volatile organic compounds (VOCs).
The estimate is based on the first nationwide assessment of
untreated groundwater aquifers, which found VOC levels in
excess of federal drinking water criteria in about 6 percent of
urban wells and 1.5 percent of rural wells... Volatile organic
compounds are found in a variety of products, including
gasoline, paints, plastics, and solvents.*
—U.S. Water News Online, *December, 1999*

By now, you are probably thinking that this is not your problem. And
why devote so many days to this topic. *Because it is that important!* As of the
writing of this topic, there is a firestorm of opposition in my adopted state
of MA as community after community vetoes approval for a right of way
for a thirty-six inch pipeline carrying fracked gas from Pennsylvania at
very high pressures (think explosions) which will be going right through
some pristine wetlands and wildlife areas where we now live to provide
gas to a power plant in the Boston area.

And a more serious problem arises when the water used to fracture
the shale is mixed with chemicals to increase the extraction of gas. 15,000
gallons of these chemicals are used for every million gallons of water
used. Do the math! I have listed some of these chemicals. Around 50%
of the water returns to the surface and now has dissolved minerals and
radioactive materials and along with said chemicals percolate down
into the water table or evaporates into the air causing significant ozone
accumulation and air pollution.

And if that was not enough, if the concrete casing of the well cracks,
gas can leak into the water table, causing dramatic pyrotechnic displays

DR. M. P. KHAN, MD/NMD

at your kitchen tap beside being a fire hazard and rendering your water undrinkable.

But nobody, especially the medical community is looking at the elephant in the room. What are the long term health hazards of these chemicals on our health? Are we going to see diseases that are not related to conscious choices of our life style such as smoking and instead have pathologies which are beyond our control and can only be explained by exposure to environmental toxins? And if we shudder at the cost of Diabetes to the health system in the next 20 years, it may be a bargain when compared to the cost of the latter.

June 14

LOTSA WATER, NADA TO
DRINK (PART-4)

Below is a list verbatim from the Department of Energy web site with a list of the chemicals. Note the focus on how benign they are. Would you drink a glass of water with even very small quantities of these chemicals in them? Here's to your health!

Diluted Acid (15%) *Hydrochloric acid or muriatic acid: Help dissolve minerals and initiate cracks in the rock. Swimming pool chemical and cleaner.*

Biocide: *Glutaraldehyde. Eliminates bacteria in the water that produce corrosive by products. Disinfectant; sterilize medical and dental equipment.*

Breaker: *Ammonium persulfate allows a delayed break down of the gel polymer chains*
Bleaching agent in detergent and hair cosmetics, manufacture of household plastics.

Corrosion Inhibitor: *N,n-dimethyl formamide. Prevents the corrosion of the pipe*

Used in pharmaceuticals, acrylic fibers, plastics.

Cross linker: *Borate salts Maintains fluid viscosity as temperature increases. Laundry detergents, hand soaps, and cosmetics.*

Friction Reducer: *Polyacrylamide: Minimizes friction between the fluid and the pipe. Water treatment soil conditioner. Mineral oil Make-up remover, laxatives and candy.*

DR. M. P. KHAN, MD/NMD

Thickener: *Gel Guar gum or hydroxyethyl cellulose. Thickens the water in order to suspend the sand. Cosmetics, toothpaste, sauces, baked goods, ice cream.*

Iron Control: *Citric acid Prevents precipitation of metal oxides, Food additive, flavoring in food and beverages; Lemon Juice ~7% Citric Acid.*

KCl: *Potassium chloride: Creates a brine carrier fluid Low sodium table salt substitute.*

Oxygen Scavenger: *Ammonium bisulfite Removes oxygen from the water to protect the pipe from corrosion. Cosmetics, food and beverage processing, water treatment.*

pH Adjusting Agent: *Sodium or potassium carbonate. Maintains the effectiveness of other components, such as cross linkers Washing soda, detergents, soap, water softener, glass and ceramics.*

Proppant: *Silica, quartz sand. Allows the fractures to remain open so the gas can escape. Very large amounts of sand is used in the process which has to be shipped from off-site sand deposits by truck. (Read more diesel emissions).*

Scale Inhibitor: *Ethylene glycol Prevents scale deposits in the pipe Automotive antifreeze, household cleansers, and deicing agent)*

Surfactant: *Isopropanol. Used to increase the viscosity of the fracture fluid.*

Here's to your health once again.
Cheers!

June 15

GOOD BYE, LUDWIG

"Music should strike fire from the heart of man, and bring
tears from the eyes of woman."
—Ludwig van Beethoven

The opening notes of the Fifth Symphony are one of the most recognizable introductions to a symphony. What is little known is that it stands for the letter V: **...** - or *dot, dot, dot, dash*. in Morse code and was the opening for BBC broadcasts during W.W. II encouraging the war weary citizens of a besieged Britain to stand firm!

The irony, of course, is that Beethoven was born in Germany.

This bit of trivia aside, the body of his work represents the nadir of Western Classical music composition. It was as if all the music composed before was the foundation for this magnificent edifice. And that all music composed since then has been a copy or variation of his work. (My opinion!)

I just completed reading Stephen Cope's book "The Great Work of Your Life" and by sheer serendipity, he uses the life and times of Beethoven to clarify the expression of *dharma*. Even though he is portrayed in popular culture as a crotchety and misanthropic genius, he had an enduring love for God and the human condition. Listen to the Ninth and even if you do not understand German, the chorale 'Ode to Joy' is as close to divine transcendence that music can take you.

But there is also a personal connection. When I was a child I had frequent ear infections. I had this crazy fear that one day I would go deaf and never hear music again. I tried to memorize all the great symphonies in my head. Beethoven was my favorite. And yet here was also a man, who in modern psychological terms and by a stretch of imagination, very likely had ADD and a profound hearing loss!

There was still hope for me!

DR. M. P. KHAN, MD/NMD

His music, at times, awakens intense emotions, and the protagonist of "A Clockwork Orange" parodies the mayhem that follows. Listen to the Sixth Symphony and its bucolic beauty transports you. And what could be more romantic than the Moonlight Sonata? And to think that he composed all this when he was almost stone deaf implies a divine intervention.

Check out the movie and the soundtrack of *"Immortal Beloved"* with Gary Oldman playing Beethoven. Better still; listen to each of his symphonies for the next nine days. Symphonies 1-9. Rejoice that you have the gift of hearing; something he lacked when he wrote them!

So here's to you, Ludwig. To me you will always be" Immortal" and "Beloved".

June 16

GOOD BYE, LUDWIG

<u>A FIFTH OF BEETHOVEN:</u>

Allegro con brio:
A herald of ominous knocks;
Four notes.
Careful! Hell's fetid breath will greet you.
The gates creak open.
No visions of Elysian Fields,
Or Dionysian fantasies evoked.
If ever love has burned you, enter here.
Gods are not welcome.

Andante con moto:
No spiritual salvation here,
Just the ecstasy of endless sorrow.
If the silence of madness moves you,
Its glory brings you tears.
Behold their cries, the anguished mortals
With no promises of tomorrow.
Yet his muse summon seraphim,
Redemption is near.

Finale:

Embrace the passion!
His gift of wings sets you free.
Our leprous minds, our grievous words forgiven,
A time for rebirth.
Music, a subterfuge, conceals his tears.
The deaf hear, the blind now see.

DR. M. P. KHAN, MD/NMD

Baptized in beauty, drowned in its splendor,
Find heaven's peace on earth!

The fearsome construct of his melody, built to transcend time,
In this brief life, Ludwig, from this primordial slime, you found the song Divine.

MK/09

June 17

A DARK NIGHT OF THE SOUL (PART-1)

"Why do you stay in prison when the
door is so wide open?
Move outside the tangle of fear-thinking.
Live in silence."

—Rumi

The next few days will be dedicated to the "disease" of depression. And yet the current state of Psychiatry as it is practiced in the era of managed care is problematic. So ubiquitous is the problem of getting adequate mental health care that it reminds me of a macabre yet an appropriate cartoon that I saw in a local newspaper after a recent shooting in Tucson, AZ by a very disturbed young man. In the cartoon a man was standing at the bottom of a tall mountain looking up. On the top of that mountain was perched an office with the sign "Mental Health Services-Appointment Necessary" and at the base of the mountain was a store which read "Joe's Gun Store-No Waiting Period."

And sometimes a joke has more hidden truths if we look beyond the absurdities.

Ring! Ring!

You have reached Dr. Fraud's economical mental health services. Please listen carefully as our options have changed.

If you have OCD please press "1" repeatedly.

If you are Co-dependent please ask someone else to press "2".

If you have multiple personalities please press "3, 4, 5, and 6".

If you are paranoid/ delusional, we know who you are and what you want. Simply stay on the line so we can trace the call.

If you are schizophrenic, listen carefully and a little voice will tell you what number to press.

If you are manic depressive, it doesn't matter what number you press, no one will answer.

DR. M. P. KHAN, MD/NMD

The purpose of this little vignette is not to belittle the anguish of mental illness. There are situations when we need the intervention of trained professionals and powerful drugs. But if you have an ounce of humor, you must have cracked a smile. And laughter is one way to overcome depression. But is depression really a disease or are we caught up in messy semantics describing the down slope of the minds expression of life's difficulties? Are we 'medicalizing' depression so that we can treat it with drugs? Are there other ways to treat the *dark night of the soul?*

June 18

A DARK NIGHT OF THE SOUL (PART-1)

Let's start with some very "depressing" statistics:

- *Depression is the most disabling of fatal conditions in the US and around the world as per the W.H.O. (20% worldwide).*
- *Worldwide, Depression results in 12% of total productive years lost.*
- *$50 Billion loss of productivity in the USA alone.*
- *14 Million Americans will suffer with depression.*
- *10% of population at any time will meet the criteria for Major Depression (DSM) and one in five will have a lifetime risk of depression. The US has the highest incidence of depression in the world and climbing.*
- *One-fifth of all adolescents will experience a major depression episode by the time they are twenty.*

DSM DEFINTION OF DEPRESSION: Five (or more) of the following symptoms have been present during the same 2-week period and represent a change from previous functioning; at least one of the symptoms is either (1) depressed mood or (2) loss of interest or pleasure.

(1) Depressed mood most of the day, nearly every day, as indicated by either subjective report (e.g., feels sad or empty) or observation made by others (e.g., appears tearful). Note: In children and adolescents, can be an irritable mood.

(2) Markedly diminished interest or pleasure in all, or almost all, activities most of the day, nearly every day (as indicated by either subjective account or observation made by others).

(3) Significant weight loss when not dieting or weight gain (e.g., a change of more than 5% of body weight in a month), or decrease

DR. M. P. KHAN, MD/NMD

or increase in appetite nearly every day. Note: In children, consider failure to make expected weight gains.

(4) Insomnia or hypersomnia nearly every day.

(5) Psychomotor agitation or retardation nearly every day (observable by others, not merely subjective feelings of restlessness or being slowed down)

(6) Fatigue or loss of energy nearly every day

(7) Feelings of worthlessness or excessive or inappropriate guilt (which may be delusional) nearly every day (not merely self-reproach or guilt about being sick)

(8) Diminished ability to think or concentrate, or indecisiveness, nearly every day (either by subjective account or as observed by others)

(9) Recurrent thoughts of death (not just fear of dying), recurrent suicidal ideation without a specific plan, or a suicide attempt or a specific plan for committing suicide

B. The symptoms do not meet criteria for a Mixed Episode. (Bipolar)

C. The symptoms cause clinically significant distress or impairment in social, occupational, or other important areas of functioning.

D. The symptoms are not due to the direct physiological effects of a substance (e.g., a drug of abuse, a medication) or a general medical condition (e.g., hypothyroidism).

E. The symptoms are not better accounted for by Bereavement, i.e., after the loss of a loved one.

A DARK NIGHT OF THE SOUL (PART-2)

"It seemed like this was one big Prozac nation, one big mess of malaise. Perhaps the next time half a million people gather for a protest march on the White House green it will not be for abortion rights or gay liberation, but because we're all so bummed out."
—**Elizabeth Wurtzel**

I am going to get lawyered up and make the case that depression is not a disease.

Let's start with the medical definition of a disease. There are three criteria that must be met as outlined below.

1) *A disordered or incorrectly functioning organ, part, structure, or system of the body*
2) *Resulting from the effect of genetic or developmental errors, infection, poisons, nutritional deficiency or imbalance, toxicity, or unfavorable environmental factors; illness; sickness; ailment.*
3) *AND is the end-point of pathology and is usually irreversible.*

Consider #1. Type 1 Diabetes is a disorder of the endocrine system because it is due to the failure of the pancreas to produce insulin and it meets the first criterion.

Consider #2. It is usually due to an auto immune disease which destroys the pancreas and meets the second criterion.

Consider #3. Type 1 Diabetes is irreversible and also meets the third criterion too. Type 1 Diabetes meets all criteria of a disease.

Now apply the same criteria to Depression and it falls apart.

Consider #1. Depression is an emotional and physical expression oı imbalances of brain neurotransmitters and barely meets the first criterion.

Consider #2. It is usually triggered by stress and there is sometimes a genetic predisposition but not always and responds to placebo drugs almost as effectively as pharmaceutical drugs.

Consider #3. It is almost always reversible and is almost never the end point of pathology.

In conclusion, depression barely meets the criteria of a disease!!

A DARK NIGHT OF THE SOUL (PART-2)

Try this out the next time you are stressed out. It is called paced diaphragm breathing or PDB. I can almost guarantee you that at the end of this exercise that you will be relaxed.

Part one:
Place one hand on chest and one hand on abdomen.
While breathing IN try to push the hand on the abdomen OUT.
While breathing OUT try to push the hand on the abdomen IN.

Part two
Inhale over a slow count of four.
Hold for a slow count of four.
Exhale over a slow count of four.

Part three
Do the inhale; hold; exhale; cycle using the four count.
Wait for six seconds using a clock or a very slow count of six.
Repeat every six seconds for about two minutes. Increase gradually to 8-10 second intervals.

Rationale for PDB:

* Direct connection from the Hypothalamus/Amygdala (anxiety center) via the vagal nerve to the diaphragm.

* Moves x 3 amount of oxygen to the brain.

* Cessation of stressful thoughts. Changes focus to the activity. (Meditation!)

The discussion that follows is the state of the art understanding about what causes depression. A very common and poorly understood cause is chronic stress. It would be a natural response to be depressed as per the DSM criteria if you were going through a divorce or if your house burnt down or you lost a loved one. But chronic stress! Here is how it works.

June 21

A DARK NIGHT OF THE SOUL (PART-3)

"Hiding in my room, safe within my womb,
I touch no one and no one touches me.
I am a rock, I am an island.
And a rock feels no pain,
And an island never cries."

—**Paul Simon**

From the song **'I Am a Rock'**

There is a six step cascade with the end point being depression:

1) Chronic stress causes an epigenetic change in the DNA with a change in the expressions of proteins by the RNA or a change in the gene expression influenced by external or environmental factors. This puts the whole notion of a fixed genetic destiny theory upside down.

2) This results in a *decrease* in BDNF or Brain Derived Neurotropic Factor: a kind of growth hormone responsible for repair of brain cells.

3) Which in turn causes a *subsequent imbalance* in the HPA or Hypothalamic Pituitary Adrenal axis and this results in

4) Stimulation of the adrenal glands, which in turn *increases* the cortisol levels continuously instead of intermittently.

5) This causes a *decrease* in levels of brain neuro-transmitters such as serotonin, dopamine and epinephrine

6) *Low levels* of these feel good chemicals results in the emotional and physical expression of depression.

Chronic depression also suppresses the immune system due to high levels of cortisol and actually increases the incidence of cancer and viral related illnesses. This cortisol increase also causes changes in the endocrine system and increases the risk of diabetes and thyroid problems. The increased cortisol levels also causes a decrease in the BDNF which causes down regulation of the cells in the hippocampus, an area of the brain responsible for short term memory. Pseudo-dementia, or symptoms that appear to look like dementia, is subsequently very common in the elderly who are depressed.

So having made the diagnosis of a disease that is really not a disease in the true sense, how do we treat it? Of course Prozac immediately comes to mind but before you buy into that, remember that depression is not a Prozac deficiency. In fact there is no real understanding as to how it works. A recent UK study showed that the SSRI class of drugs was no more effective than placebo in treating mild to moderate depression. And some SSRI drugs like paroxetine actually increased the risk of suicide in adolescent populations!

DR. M. P. KHAN, MD/NMD

June 22

FOURTEEN YEARS LATER

"Infatuation is when you think he's as sexy as
Robert Redford, as smart as Henry Kissinger,
as noble as Ralph Nader, as funny as Woody Allen, and as
athletic as Jimmy Connors.
Love is when you realize that he's as sexy as Woody Allen,
as smart as Jimmy Connors, as funny as Ralph Nader,
as athletic as Henry Kissinger and nothing like Robert
Redford - but you'll take him anyway."
—Judith Viorst, *Redbook, 1975*

Fourteen years ago, we tied the knot on this day. And in spite of our best efforts to untie this knot, and the trials and tribulations that are the essence of every relationship, this day is a celebration and a milestone. Today, I cannot imagine life without Karen. Although I will never admit it, over the years, she has changed my life in subtle ways. I value her gentle guiding comments (and sometimes downright nagging) which has shaped my life for the better. And some of the chapters in this book were directly inspired by her.

And at times when the creative dragon inside me has gotten unruly, she has stood by me and accepted my shortcomings. I could not ask for a better friend and teacher. But just in case you want to bestow on her a seemingly well-deserved sainthood, I must advise you that she has her lion's share of eccentricities; quirks which are mostly amusing and sometimes downright frustrating.

The poem that follows was inspired by the teaching of the Buddha. That in 300 years all the pettiness and problems that we see are so insurmountable will not matter. I would like to think that the manifestation of true love will survive forever.

300 YEARS:

In the molding and primal passage of ancient centuries,
We will exist once again, but only as faint apparitions.
Snippets of memories, flashes of flat singular images
Haunting the rusted ticking of temporal illusions.

But search not for sacred texts,
Or hieroglyphs of a gospel truth.
All your efforts will find but a faded papyrus
Writ largely with gentle musings
Of flawed prophets and blessed sinners.
Between the dawn and the dusk of their lives,
They dared to be flesh and spirit, love and tears,
Valiantly struggling to find the garden and the manger.

I was the thirteenth angel, heaven's pariah.
My only crime was passion for your touch.
Forgive me; it was I who blindly plucked
The fruit of your naked innocence.
God, my judge and jury, was the mythical serpent.
His venomous wrath, or unrequited love,
Cast me out of Eden into the Paradise of your embrace.

Herald angels, pristine in their absolution,
Will not understand the mystical convolution of our love.
How does eternity in its constant monotony
Capitulate to the random fire that is a lover's curse?
Even perfect Zeus in a perfect Olympus,
Asleep in the obsidian night of Morpheus' embrace,
Will moan with longing for human imperfection,
And dream of the ecstasy of our tangled lives.

MK/2010

DR. M. P. KHAN, MD/NMD

FOURTEEN YEARS LATER

This poem has yet to be completed and like our marriage, is a work in progress. Lately the muse has deserted me. I must be patient.

If you have a significant other in your life, how do you plan to celebrate your anniversary?

_____

_____

_____

_____

_____

_____

List the joys and sorrows you may have shared over the years with your significant other.

_____

_____

_____

_____

_____

_____

What are your hopes and dreams for the years to come?

_____

_____

_____

_____

_____

_____

June 24

A DARK NIGHT OF THE SOUL (PART-3)

Of course there are always exceptions. There are individuals who have 5-HTP polymorphisms or gene defects and this prevents the hydroxytryptophan (raw material) to be converted to serotonin. As a result they may be more prone to depression, though not necessarily so. This may explain why they need long term use of SSRI agents just like diabetics needing insulin.

<u>*To SSRI or not; that is the question?*</u>

- *No clear theory on action. Serotonin levels increase immediately but therapeutic effect takes 4-6 weeks.*
- *Possibly increases BDNF levels and reverses hard wiring changes caused by chronic stress!*
- *Therapeutic effects of SSRI drugs slightly better than placebo, cognitive behavioral therapy, biblio- therapy (SELF-HELP BOOKS), exercise, journaling and talk therapy.*
- *Significant side effects in short term use such as nausea, headaches and sexual dysfunction and even suicide (black box adverse drug warning).*
- *Long term use may cause dependence, and weight gain. It may also deplete dopamine in the brain, and cause Parkinsonian type side effects such as tremors at rest, psychomotor retardation and a shuffling gait.*
- *Potential for overdose with about 100 deaths reported a year from "serotonin syndrome" due to high levels of serotonin. Do not combine with Saint John's Wart.*
  The sign and symptoms of "serotonin syndrome" are as below: The symptoms are often described as a clinical triad of cognition, autonomic, and somatic (related to the body) dysfunction.

Cognitive effects: headache, agitation, hypomania, mental confusion, hallucinations, coma.

Autonomic effects: shivering, sweating, hyperthermia, hypertension, tachycardia, nausea, diarrhea.

Somatic effects: myoclonus (muscle twitching), hyperreflexia manifested by clonus (or a rapid contraction and relaxation of muscle), and tremor.

June 25

A DARK NIGHT OF THE SOUL (PART-4)

"It's snowing still," said Eeyore gloomily.
"So it is."
"And freezing."
"Is it?"
"Yes," said Eeyore. "However," he said, brightening up a
little, "but we haven't had an earthquake lately."
                                                    —A. A. Milne

From the book 'Winnie the Pooh'

SUPPLEMENTS: *If only we could be like Eeyore and see the brighter side of things. The U.S. has some of the highest incidences of depression on the planet. The irony is that we have the "pursuit of happiness" guaranteed by our constitution. Maybe it is because the expectation of happiness is not often met that we have become a Prozac nation. And maybe it is because we have so many choices in our day-to-day lives. If I choose Toothpaste X instead of Y, could I be missing out on something? And Madison Avenue is constantly reminding us of the next big thing that we need to make us "happy!" And out comes the pills, those SSRI's with the promise of a chemical Nirvana.*

Although there are several ways to treat I have outlined below some supplement/herbal approaches as alternatives to the SSRI (and other classes) class of pharmacotherapy.

1) 5-HTP (HYDROXY TRYPTOPHAN): FORMULA 5HTP; 1-4 AT BED TIME.

USE: *This is my go-to supplement to support depression, anxiety and sleep issues because of its safety profile.* Serotonin, an important brain neurotransmitter, is a key chemical in the regulation of appetite, mood and in the production of melatonin. The presence of serotonin in the brain is associated with a balanced emotional state. This is achieved in part by decreasing the activity of certain excitatory hormones, including dopamine and noradrenaline. Serotonin also acts as a satiety signal in the brain, thereby naturally regulating food intake. Additionally, as a precursor of melatonin, serotonin is involved in regulating sleep patterns.

Serotonin is unable to cross the blood-brain barrier and is therefore synthesized in the brain .Tryptophan, an essential amino acid, is converted to L-5-Hydroxytryptophan (5-HTP), which in turn is converted into serotonin. Unfortunately, tryptophan faces many obstacles during its journey into brain tissue. First, dietary intake directly affects body levels of tryptophan, as the body cannot produce it endogenously. High protein diets often provide greater amounts of tryptophan, yet higher carbohydrate diets appear to enhance tryptophan uptake into the brain. Secondly, tryptophan must compete with other amino acids for entry into the brain. Finally, tryptophan may be taken up by other tissues for protein or niacin synthesis, and thus is not exclusively for use by the brain.

June 26

A DARK NIGHT OF THE SOUL (PART-4)

5-HTP offers a number of advantages over tryptophan. 5-HTP is derived naturally from the seeds of the Griffonia plant, unlike tryptophan which is produced synthetically or through bacterial fermentation. 5-HTP crosses into the brain more readily than tryptophan as it is able to cross the blood-brain barrier without competition for uptake. 5-HTP is significantly more effective than tryptophan; one 50 mg capsule of 5-HTPis roughly equivalent to 500 mg of tryptophan. Finally, research studies have shown 5-HTP to be safe at levels as high as 900 mg. As a result, 5-HTP is a safe and effective means of increasing brain serotonin levels.

2) ST. JOHN'S WORT MAX-V; FORMULA 77373; 1 TWICE A DAY BETWEEN MEALS. IMP: TAKE FOR 8-12 WEEKS BEFORE EFFECT IS NOTED!!

USE: St. John's Wort extract is widely recognized for its positive, supportive effects on mental and emotional function. *(This herbal product was discussed previously in the entry of June1, but it bears repeating.)* Numerous scientific studies have addressed the effectiveness and safety of standardized St. John's Wort extract. The activity of St. John's Wort extract is often attributed to its hypericin content .Interestingly, new evidence indicates that hypericin may not be solely responsible for the beneficial properties of St. John's Wort extract. Which of these many other components may be active in extract preparations and how they may exert their activity are unknown. Because St. John's Wort may act through the synergistic action of many components, it is important to ensure not just standardized hypericin content of an extract, but also the availability of these other ingredients

Warning: If you are pregnant, trying to become pregnant, nursing, or taking any prescription medication (especially anticoagulants, oral contraceptives, antidepressants, anti-seizure medications, drugs to treat HIV or prevent transplant rejection), consult your physician before using

DR. M. P. KHAN, MD/NMD

this product. This product may cause skin rashes or photosensitivity in some people. Avoid excessive exposure to sunlight, tanning lights or UV sources while taking this product. This product may cause serotonin syndrome if taken with SSRI agents. It may also cause hair loss.

3) SAM-e (S-adenosyl-methionine):100 to 200mg.daily.

USE: As a major source of methyl groups in the brain, SAM-e, in conjunction with other methyl donor metabolites such as betaine, choline, or folate, may optimize the synthesis of neurotransmitters, i.e. serotonin and dopamine. With few side effects SAM-e has been shown in multiple studies to offer support for improving symptoms of depression.

A DARK NIGHT OF THE SOUL (PART-5)

"This life is yours. Take the power to choose what you want
to do and do it well. Take the power to love what you want
in life and love it honestly. Take the power to walk in the
forest and be a part of nature. Take the power to control your
own life. No one else can do it for you. Take the power to
make your life happy."
—**Susan Polis Schultz**

Here are some mind-body approaches in dealing with depression. There is no one size shoe fits all approach and what may work for you may not work for another. I would also encourage you to see a physician or counselor qualified in treating depression. Having suffered with depression myself in the past, I know that it is more painful than any physical condition I have ever experienced. And especially if you feel that life is not worth it anymore! Life is *always* worth it, and a gift that will not be given to you ever again.

CBT: A very useful modality of treatment uses psychotherapy called CBT or Cognitive Behavioral Therapy. Study after study shows that combining this approach with a pharmaceutical or herbal approach causes significant improvement in recovery and remission from depression. It is also used in the treatment of a host of anxiety disorders and for PTSD, insomnia and AD/HD. Below is the Wikipedia definition of CBT:

"Cognitive behavioral therapy (CBT) is a psychotherapeutic approach that addresses dysfunctional emotions, maladaptive behaviors and cognitive processes and contents through a number of goal-oriented, explicit systematic procedures. The name refers to behavior therapy, cognitive therapy, and to therapy based upon a combination of basic behavioral and cognitive principles and research. CBT is "problem focused" (undertaken for specific problems) and "action oriented" (therapist tries to assist the client in selecting specific strategies to help address those problems)."

DR. M. P. KHAN, MD/NMD

CBT has six phases and is usually delivered in six 2-hour sessions.

1. Assessment or psychological assessment;
2. Reconceptualization;
3. Skills acquisition;
4. Skills consolidation and application training;
5. Generalization and maintenance;
6. Post-treatment assessment follow-up. (*Continued*)

DBT: My favorite type of mind-body therapy is DBT or Dialectical Behavioral Therapy. It is a hybrid of CBT and Buddhist meditative techniques using Mindfulness training to provide insight into behaviors. It is increasingly use as an essential tool in modern day psychotherapeutics. Here are some of the key components of Mindfulness Training as used in the DBT approach:

"What" skills: OBSERVE: This is used to nonjudgmentally observe one's internal and external environment. DBT recommends developing a "Teflon mind," the ability to let feelings and experiences pass without sticking in the mind.

DESCRIBE: This is used to express what one has observed with the observe skill. It is to be used without judgmental statements in regards to yourself or others.

PARTICPATE: This is used to become fully focused on, and involved in, the activity that one is doing.

"How" skills: NONJUDGEMENTAL: This is the action of describing the facts, and not thinking about what's "good" or "bad," "fair," or "unfair." These are judgments because this is how you feel about the situation but isn't a factual description. This avoids the subjectivity of a judgmental statement which someone will disagree with.

ONE-MINDFFUL: This is used to focus on one thing at a time. This strategy is helpful in keeping your cognitive mind from straying into the emotional mind.

EFFECTIVELY: This is simply doing what works for you in using the "What" and "How" skills effectively.

AUTOGENIC BIOFEEDBACK: Remember the last time that you were stressed out (and remember the link between stress and depression) and you had the physical sensation of your hands and feet getting cold. This is because the body's flight-or flight response directed all your blood to the large muscles. Biofeedback, in this case using a thermal sensor attached to your hand teaches you to increase the blood flow to your hands and thus reverse the stress response. With some training, it is an excellent tool to get in touch with your body and its response to stress. It is also a great tool to abort migraine headaches and works really well in childhood migraines.

EXERCISE: Yoga is an exceptional exercise program to help with depression as it involves breathing, stretching and isometric exercises and is a wonderful way to reconnect to your body. However any physical activity is helpful in reducing the symptoms of depression. So get off the couch, put on your walking shoes and say hello to the neighborhood. (more later)

DR. M. P. KHAN, MD/NMD

June 28

A DARK NIGHT OF THE SOUL (PART-5)

<u>*Alternatives to SSRI:*</u> *Mind-Body approaches.*

*Find your joy: *There is a saying "Find your own bliss" and in these four words lies the secret of happiness and it's really not a secret. All of us at some time of our lives have been truly happy or in joy with what we have been doing. The question to ask is "What activity brings you joy?" and then no matter what the answer is, pursue that activity. The sun has to rise on the dark night of the soul eventually. Finding what you enjoy is the answer. And it may be the answer to finding our spiritual connection; our inner power to heal. As in a Rumi poem "The soul is here for its own joy."*

What do you really enjoy doing? When did you last do it? How did you feel thinking about that time? After you have written the answer try to do what you enjoy at least once a week.

_____

_____

_____

_____

_____

_____

_____

_____

_____

June 29

SOME OF KAREN'S POEMS

<u>MISANTHROPIC MUSE:</u>

Hapless wanderings in January blue,
Lead me to you so spatially poised and hungry.
Your thoughts so immaculate, a sweeping sum,
The surreal equation of you;
A tender instrument of well-wrought quality.
Capable of golden moments,
That melt self- possession...all else.

You can touch me past winding fields of other selves,
Gently admiring and affecting my instrument.
Admonishing, I am in danger of losing myself.
I find I must touch my center to love you.
Truly, are you there for real?

Our nights of anxiety matrices,
Issue a heroic attempt to do all.
God would forget, to control.
I am the featured catalyst
For sacrificial rites of passage,
To die at puberty, or now.

But loose threads of night time do also intend,
To weave dreams of vivid desire.
Rock hard ecstasies issue silent screams.
Angel lips so palpable relieve,
All the fatalities that straight- jackets can bear.
Alert in trauma all these years.

DR. M. P. KHAN, MD/NMD

You are a difficult gift to me,
Morbidly sensitive are we.
Emotions that can't stand to be felt,
Fear vulnerability.
Can we accept what we see,
And be free in the blessings of time?

KBK 3/2010

SOME OF KAREN'S POEMS

<u>SEVEN VEILS:</u>

Count the arrows that fall like rain,
As his countenance passes my domain.
Scintillating moments catch like wild fire,
As I satiate my sumptuous sire.
Midnight magic sheets, naked thighs,
And lips so desired tales these Arabian nights.
Yes whatever you say, tame my
Passions fey. Wildly will I consent
To enter Heaven.

Lay, weigh upon me your laughter,
Scripted in melodious touches.
A vagabond princess wearing tattered stars,
Torn from the sky, framed by and by,
Acting out creation from on high.
Thorn pricks of red dot sleeping beauty's bed.
Searching sighs cry, never ever lies,
This hour devour inspired muses bower.
Should dawn awaken my fate lies
In yet another story.

KBK 6/2011

DR. M. P. KHAN, MD/NMD

JULY

1-Jul	THE? IS BLOWIN' IN THE WIND. (Part-1) All about air pollution.
2-Jul	THE? IS BLOWIN' IN THE WIND. (Part-1) What we can do about it.
3-Jul	THE? IS BLOWIN' IN THE WIND. (Part-2) They call it 'prana'.
4-Jul	INDEPENDENCE DAY. And "Immigrant Dreams."
5-Jul	A DRAGON UNLEASHED. An environmental poem by Karen.
6-Jul	A DRAGON UNLEASHED. How will you be the change?
7-Jul	ADAPTING TO ADAPTOGENS (PART-1) There ain't nothing like this!
8-Jul	ADAPTING TO ADAPTOGENS (PART-1) Really, Really.
9-Jul	ADAPTING TO ADAPTOGENS (PART-2) All about HPA and SAS.
10-Jul	ADAPTING TO ADAPTOGENS (PART-2) And their effect on them.
11-Jul	ADAPTING TO ADAPTOGENS (PART-3) Some commonly used ones.
12-Jul	ADAPTING TO ADAPTOGENS (PART-3) And their dosing. And a jam.
13-Jul	ADAPTING TO ADAPTOGENS (PART-4) All about Panax and Rhodiola.
14-Jul	A CIVIL WAR (PART-1)" I Said, She Said" and another poem.
15-Jul	A CIVIL WAR (PART-1) This relationship did not work out.
16-Jul	A CIVIL WAR (PART-2) A lesson in building 'Walls."
17-Jul	A CIVIL WAR (PART-2) And tearing them down.
18-Jul	A CIVIL WAR (PART-3) The "Fire Fight" begins.
19-Jul	A CIVIL WAR (PART-3) And some lessons are learned.
20-Jul	HERBAL TEA TIME. And how to get some ZZZZZ......
21-Jul	HERBAL TEA TIME. Some indications for Acupuncture.
22-Jul	WHAT ME WORRY! Words of wisdom from Chairman Moo.
23-Jul	WHAT ME WORRY! Complimentary approaches to stress.
24-Jul	INTEGRATE THYSELF (PART-1) Hippocrates had it right.
25-Jul	INTEGRATE THYSELF (PART-1) Physician as a holistic healer.
26-Jul	INTEGRATE THYSELF (PART-2) A pop quiz on the BODY.
27-Jul	INTEGRATE THYSELF (PART-2) A pop quiz on the MIND.
28-Jul	INTEGRATE THYSELF (PART-2) A pop quiz on the SPIRIT.
29-Jul	INTEGRATE THYSELF (PART-3) Strategies for the BODY.
30-Jul	INTEGRATE THYSELF (PART-3) Strategies for the MIND.
31-Jul	INTEGRATE THYSELF (PART-3) Strategies for the SPIRIT.

July 1

THE? IS BLOWIN' IN THE
WIND (PART-1)

"Oh Beautiful for smoggy skies, insecticided grain,
for strip-mined mountain's majesty above
the asphalt plain.
America, America, man sheds his waste on thee,
and hides the pines with billboard signs,
from sea to oily sea."

—George Carlin

I remember a time when we attended a meeting by the Sierra Club at a nearby college campus in Pittsburgh. It was a forum to discuss the quality of air in our fair city of which I was a longtime resident. In the past, on my travels, the very mention of my former hometown would immediately elicit a reaction which goes something like this; "Isn't that the Smoky City?" complete with images of people walking about with coal blackened clothes in streets where the lights were on in the afternoon because of heavy smog.

Although Pittsburgh has come a long way from that national stereotype, it still has a ways to go. The city was recently rated as the fifth worst city for FPM or Fine Particulate Matter, particles smaller than 2.5 microns which can reach all the way into our alveoli or the small air sacs of our lungs. (Much later, this along with the hydro-fracking was a deciding factor in our move to the Berkshires).The particles are the same size as the medication used in an inhaler used for the treatment of asthma. Only problem is that these FPM particles are made up of a complex of heavy metals and organic compounds with profound effects on our health. In fact there are 188 HAP or Harmful Air Pollutants of which benzene, ozone, lead, mercury, tetra-chloro-ethylene and coke ash are the chief culprits, most of which are a byproduct of coal fired electric plants.

And the U.S. is one of the leaders in emissions (6,500 million metric tons of CO_2/yr.) with levels close or exceeded only by China. We are also the number one consumer of energy. It is estimated that we would need 4 planets like Earth to support us if the almost 7 Billion people on our planet consumed energy at the same rate as the U.S.! In fact the average American is burning a *10 Kw light bulb per person every **second** of every hour* compared to the rest of the world at a puny average of *5Kw light bulb/ person/every hour.*

The primary source of emissions (20%) nationwide are coal fired plants producing electricity with 1950's technology where water is boiled by firing coal and producing steam which drives a turbine, a very inefficient way to produce electricity. And the byproducts of this technology are the emissions we discussed above.

Even though some of these plants have installed scrubbers, to clean the emissions, the stuff finally left behind is fly ash. This is a toxic blend of heavy metals including arsenic. The fly ash is stored in open storage pits and with time these toxic chemicals leach into the ground and contaminate the water table.

So what is the health impact of this outrage and what can we do about it?

July 2

THE? IS BLOWIN' IN THE
WIND (PART-1)

Check these web sites out with excellent links to air pollution related topics:

www.sierraclub.org
www.epa.gov
www.ewg.org
www.GASP-pgh.org

So what can we do to cut down on air pollution?
Sign up and volunteer with groups like GASP or Sierra Club and get active in your area. They can't do it without your time and money. Yes, some sacrifices need to be made but our fair planet and our lungs will thank you, along with your grandchildren.

Petition your elected representatives. Think 'elected' and 'representative' and that this is America. It was a people's revolution that drove the British out. I am not advocating violence but a Gandhian approach. The pollution of our environment using nonrenewable resources with antiquated technology is unacceptable and immoral when we can be using zero CO2 emission sources of energy.

Take a long hard look in the mirror at ourselves and our energy habits. Each of us has a moral imperative to cut down our use of energy and at the same time educate others about what can be done to cut down our carbon footprint. If you are a technophile, think of yourself as astronauts on a spaceship with limited resources. If you are a New Ager, that we are all children of the Earth Mother! It does not matter.

Invest in companies that are eco responsible and buy products that are renewable. We need to move away from disposable products and focus on using our resources wisely. When you buy products, or go grocery shopping tell them you don't need those nasty plastic bags or better still take your own cloth bags. Use washrags instead of paper towels. Washable plates instead of paper or plastic plates.

We are all part of one inter-connected web after all.

Namaste!

July 3

THE? IS BLOWIN' IN THE WIND (PART-2)

"Humankind has not woven the web of life. We are but one thread within it. Whatever we do to the web, we do to ourselves. All things are bound together. All things connect."
—**Chief Seattle, 1855**

The Hindus call it Prana and it is the very essence of life. We start our life with the first gasp and end with the last. And in between, in an average lifetime we will breathe 63 million times and move a million gallons of air per year or around *75 million gallons over an average life span!* And if you were not concerned about air pollution till now, this little bit of trivia should make you sit up and take notice.

At the same conference sponsored by the Sierra Club in Pittsburgh, we viewed an excellent documentary by two well respected news reporters who followed several families over a nine year period and also the impact of air pollution in several surrounding communities. The project was called "Mapping Mortality." In the areas they studied, there were 14,636 *excess* deaths over the nine year period in populations living downstream from the Ohio valley (home to several coal burning power plants) from heart disease, asthma and cancer above the national average when compared to the rest of the U.S. population and conclusively showing a causal relationship between the two.

A recent JAMA article (March 23/30.2011-Vol 305, No. 12) concluded that air pollution was the *eighth* leading cause of death in industrialized countries accounting for 2.5% of all deaths. EPA safety levels in the US for FPM are 15ug/m3 although that is an arbitrary number and the safest level should be "0". (In the Pittsburgh area, they average 16-17).

The authors noted a co-relation between strokes and air quality. When the level of FPM reached over 20 ug/m3, the risk for stroke *doubled* and hospital admissions for strokes increased by 13%. Another finding was that the risk for a stroke was greater with *short term high* FPM exposure vs. populations who were exposed to *low levels of long term* FPM.

And the impact is even greater in developing countries like India where burning coal and wood accounts for the *sixth* leading cause of death and stroke and accounting for 10% of total deaths; more than HIV and TB combined.

So if you live in an industrialized area of the U.S. and before you put on your spandex jogging shorts and expensive running shoes for your morning spin, take a whiff of the air. Because of the cooler night air settling the pollutants at ground level, it may not be the best time of the day to jog. Also check the FPM levels by checking the Air Quality Index or AQI*. This is an Index ranging from 0-500 with 50 being good and 300 being hazardous to your health. Check out *www.AIRNOW.gov* or sign up at: *www.enviroflash.info* to get updates of the air quality of your location directly to your e-mail.

AQI: (There is a color scale overlaying a map on the web version).*
*Good
0-50

Air quality is considered satisfactory, and air pollution poses little or no risk.
*Moderate
51-100

Air quality is acceptable. However, for some pollutants there may be a moderate health concern for a very small number of people who are unusually sensitive to air pollution.
*Unhealthy for Sensitive Groups
101-150

Members of sensitive groups (smokers, asthmatics) may experience health effects.

The general public is not likely to be affected.

Unhealthy: For almost everybody. Especially high risk groups.
150-200

Unhealthy for Everybody. Minimize all outdoor activities.
201-300

Hazardous: Time for gas masks!
301-500

DR. M. P. KHAN, MD/NMD

July 4

INDEPENDENCE DAY

In a very indirect kind of way, each of us reading this are immigrants or descendants of immigrants. We each have a story as to why we or our forefathers and mothers left their roots. If we are to live in harmony with each other, after the fireworks and the picnics are over, it is important to remember and respect that story.

I left because I believed in the American Dream and it did not disappoint me. Today, I cannot imagine what my life would have been if I had stayed in India. I wrote this poem in the summer of 1977. I had just immigrated to the U.S. and had landed in a small town in Oregon, population 700 and 12,000 miles from my home town of Bombay (Mumbai) with a population of fifteen million. As you can tell, I was a little homesick.

IMMIGRANT DREAMS:

I bear the onus and glory of my countrymen.
I have left my motherland for this land!
Will it nurture me and hold me in its bosom?
Or will it be a cruel stepmother?
I do not know.
For I have left behind more than a land.
Sunsets and warm summer rains;
Friends and coffee-shop talks;
The fragrant aromas of the market place.
Some of the essential roots of my existence.
Left behind parts of myself,
To seek the missing parts of myself.
Reality to find a dream,
Or is it the other way around?
Sometimes I forget!

MK/77

A DRAGON UNLEASHED

"There is a sufficiency in the world for man's need but not for man's greed."
—Mohandas K. Gandhi

DRAGON:

A steam shovel digs in the dirt, it crumbles.
I feel the pain of the earth,
laid low by the fire of rape;
a red hot incision.
The sky is a buffer of soothing grace,
its blue testament witnessing all.

Thought boxes suspended on the horizon,
tall buildings scrape at the darkening sky.
A plague of locusts mimics in continuum,
"So say we", stripping bare the earth of
our dying planet- our Mother.

Where is the golden moment of light inside me?
A low hush suppressing her tongue;
A babbling stream thwarted;
The dear hypodermics at hand,
extruding the feared times we live in.

A picture torn open locked in perpetuity,
stands apart bending another staircase,
to climb so free form unending.
Cars pass by in rainy protest.
swarming in the night,
then falling away in a wash of cement.

DR. M. P. KHAN, MD/NMD

A railway track in one pointed perspective,
the rapid train careens out of control,
in hallowed fields of corn.
A voice whispers absurdities.
a cell phone punctuates at will,
three undisciplined dots repeating:
"No Gentleness, no Sanctuary, no Love."

KBK / 6/10

July 6

A DRAGON UNLEASHED

There are sacred trusts that we all have to uphold. To love our children, respect our elders, protect what we hold dear are obvious and acceptable trusts. But these are also sacred trusts that are so ubiquitous that we take them for granted. When I see what can happen to our air and water, elements that our critical to our survival, it strikes an emotional cord.

In America we have been blessed with good air and clean water; the lack of which, in developing countries, has resulted in outbreaks of war and genocide. And yet we are systematically destroying the very essence of life for immediate profits and greed. The above poem, written by Karen, is very visual and has a powerful message.

What emotions are evoked by this poem?

_____

_____

_____

_____

_____

_____

Think of Gandhi's words. If you feel despair on reading this, remember what Gandhi also said, "Be the change you want to see in the world."

What change do you want to see in the world?

_____

_____

_____

_____

_____

_____

DR. M. P. KHAN, MD/NMD

How will you be the change?

_____

_____

_____

_____

_____

_____

_____

ADAPTING TO ADAPTOGENS (PART-1)

"All plants contain adaptogenic compounds,
because plants have to contend with a good deal of stress
themselves."
—James Duke, PhD

"Adaptogens" was a term coined by Russian scientists, Lazarev and Brekhman in 1947 to a class of substances which by definition are:

1) Nontoxic to the person taking them,
2) and produces a non-specific response in the body to resist physical, chemical, and biological stressors,
3) And has a normalizing influence on the physiology irrespective of the stressors direction of change (positive or negative) on the physiology. That is, they are *bi-directional.*

At first glance this sounds too good to be true, especially since there are no modern pharmaceutical products that can mimic the activity of these compounds. But these agents have been successfully used in traditional Indian Ayurvedic (IA) and Traditional Chinese Medicine (TCM) for several thousand years and constitute *tonic* herbs.

The best known being Panax ginseng or Asian ginseng and 'Panax' (which means Panacea) suggests the importance of this herb, especially in TCM. And only Panax is the true ginseng. An interesting bit of history trivia is that many of the missions built in the 1600s along the California coast (the swallows of San Capistrano, San Bernardino) were paid for by the sale of Panax ginseng by enterprising Jesuit monks; it was valued by their Oriental buyers more than gold for its medicinal properties.

To this date the exact mechanism of action has been poorly understood but there are some theories that may explain their almost miraculous effect on our physiology. Most of the early scientific studies on adaptogens, in this case Elutherococcus or Siberian ginseng, were done in Russia in the early 60s with unbelievable results.

Study: One thousand mine workers in Siberia.

Results: 66% decrease in incidence of cases during an Influenza epidemic.

Study: Fourteen thousand factory workers.

Results: 30% decrease in symptoms of fatigue, high blood pressure and anxiety.

Study: One hundred and seven patients receiving drugs for gastric cancer.

Results: 50% decrease in damage done to the immune system and similar reduction in dosing of chemo agents needed to be effective.

July 8

ADAPTING TO ADAPTOGENS (PART-1)

This is a very complex field and to simplify this discussion, we will limit it to the below listed adaptogens which are more easily available:

American ginseng*=Panax quinquefolius.

Ashwagandha=Witharia somnifera or Winter cherry or Indian ginseng. My favorite.

Asian ginseng =Panax ginseng.

Eleuthero=Eleutherococcus senticosus or Siberian ginseng.

Rhodiola=Rhodiola rosea.

Licorice= Glycrrhiza glabra.

*CAUTION: Asian ginseng is one of the most over harvested herb on the planet and because of the high demand is literally worth its weight in gold. As a result any product on the market is suspect to adulteration and need to be researched thoroughly. In fact in a recent study of over 200 Panax ginseng products, only a handful (32) had adequate amounts of P. ginseng. About 30 had none!

An interesting research project would be to visit the nearest nutrition store and check out the various supplements containing the above mentioned adaptogens. If you have any questions regarding the purity or content, see if the manufacturer of the product can send you information on the GMP or Good Manufacturing Practice with any other data confirming the purity of the herb.

DR. M. P. KHAN, MD/NMD

July 9

ADAPTING TO ADAPTOGENS (PART-2)

*"Heyam duhkham anagatam." (Sanskrit: Avert the danger
that has not yet come).*
—Yoga sutras of Patanjali

So how do adaptogens 'avert the danger?" Our current knowledge of their action is that they essentially work on the HPA or Hypothalamic Pituitary Adrenal Axis and the SAS or the Sympatho Adrenal System. These two systems are part of the NEI or Neuro Endocrine Immune system (or for you New Agers; the Mind Body Connection.)

All stress manifests through the HPA and the SAS systems and in most cases our response to acute stress actually is a survival mechanism in critical situations. But it is the *chronic* stress of day to day living which actually causes a lot of damage at the physical level and results in exhaustion of the delicate feedback needed to maintain the body in homeostasis or a state of normalcy.

This is why Zebras don't get ulcers. They run like crazy when they are chased by a lion. And when the lion is gone they go back to their grazing and completely forget about the lion. Not so in humans. Chased by a lion, most of us will probably obsess about the beast for quite some time with all kinds of dire consequences to our body, long after the lion has gone! So the stress response goes something like this;

HPA: A Stressor may or may not be filtered by higher levels of brain areas such as the neo cortex and the perceived threat to survival is first registered by the Hypothalamus. In a chronic stress state, this cascade is continuous and not intermittent (acute stress).

> Production of Corticotrophin Release Hormone (CRH) by the Hypothalamus....

> CRH causes Stimulation of the Pituitary gland......

> Which produces Adreno Cortico Trophic Hormone (ACTH)....

> ACTH causes Stimulation of the Adrenal cortex.....

> Which releases Cortisol which releases energy (glucose) from cells for the 'fight or flight' response.....

> Increased Cortisol also causes Suppression of the immune system...

> And as a result there is Decreased resistance to pathogens....

> Increased Cortisol also causes Loss of feedback to the hypothalamus....

> Which results in Decreased production of neuro-transmitters. Remember the talk on depression?

DISEASE STATES that can be a result of the HPA cascade described above: Decreased resistance to illnesses (Colds, Influenza,) Suppression of the Immune system (Cancer), and decreased production of neurotransmitters (Depression) and excessive production of cortisol (Diabetes).

SAS: Stressor is registered by the Hypothalamus. Once again in chronic stress, this cascade is continuous.

- ➤ There is activation of the Sympathetic Nervous system....
- ➤ The Adrenal Medulla is stimulated with the production of adrenaline which prepares the body for the fight or flight response.....
- ➤ Stimulation of the cardio vascular system results in increased heart rate and blood pressure.....
- ➤ Increased blood flow and stimulation of the muscles for the flight or fight response results in increased muscle tone.....
- ➤ Decreased blood flow and decreased activity of the Gastro Intestinal system.

By one estimate, around 80% of illnesses that present to a family physicians office are rooted in some form of chronic stress. I often kid my patients that if the current model of medical practice could eliminate chronic stress, I would have to close the doors of my office and sell shoes or cars for a living.

July 10

ADAPTING TO ADAPTOGENS (PART-2)

It is the long term release of the stress hormones, cortisol and adrenaline which causes most disease states. In fact the long term effects of stress may be the number one cause of chronic disease states such as hypertension, insulin resistance and anxiety states (too much Cortisol and adrenaline) and Chronic Fatigue and Fibromyalgia (too little Cortisol and adrenaline) when the adrenal glands get literally fatigued out!(this is controversial)

And this is where the magic of adaptogens happens. They work at ALL levels of the stress response and I will let the science guys figure out their exact mechanism of action on the Stress Response. Sufficed to say they work and have worked for the last 3000 years and that is enough proof for me!

There is a test to see if there is Adrenal Fatigue. It measures the variation of Cortisol in the saliva over several collections in a 24 hour period. With Adrenal fatigue* the normal diurnal (am and pm) variations in secretions of Cortisol is lost and results in a generally flat measurement. Although this test is not a fool proof test for adrenal fatigue, it can help establish a base line and the response to treatment.

This test is not available from a conventional lab and is done by some specialty labs such as Genova Diagnostics.

Check out www.GDX.com for more details.

*There is considerable controversy about whether Adrenal Fatigue actually exists as a disease state and may elicit a visceral response from your local endocrinologist although this syndrome is well established in the functional medicine model!

DR. M. P. KHAN, MD/NMD

ADAPTING TO ADAPTOGENS (PART-3)

"There are very few certainties that touch us all in this
mortal experience, but one of the absolutes is that we will
experience hardship and stress at some point."
—Dr. James C. Dobson

Now that we understand the neuro physiology of stress, we can see the importance of controlling stress better. Of course the best approach is to not react to the stressor using mind body techniques. Adaptogens are just another tool to deal with the gorilla in the room. Almost 80% of the visits to my office are related to the direct or indirect effects of stress. I may actually be putting myself out of business but living in a stress free world may be well worth it. So here are some of the adaptogens I use and their dosing.

1) American ginseng OR Panax quinquefolius:

This plant is a native to the Eastern US and it takes seven years to grow from seed to root which is what is used in the preparation. It is best to avoid products which say "wild American ginseng" and to use the cultivated form from a reputable manufacturer.

Daniel Boone made his fortune trading ginseng (not the same as Panax ginseng which is much more difficult to cultivate and find in its natural form) to the Chinese and the sale of this rare commodity actually helped George Washington during the revolutionary war. Used widely by the Cherokee and Seminole Indians for multiple ailments (Panax) and also as a love potion, it did not enter the American Materia medica except as a bitter tonic.

Today it is used as an adaptogen in fatigued individuals with an elevated Cortisol levels and is used sometimes for individuals prone to catching colds as well as in individuals with allergies and asthma. It has a reputation as a "male sexual tonic" but its exact effect on libido and erections is not well known.

DOSE: 1 CAPSULE THREE TIMES A DAY FOR 8-12 WEEKS; DOUGLAS LABS FORMULA (#77332) 1 Vegetarian Capsule Contains:

American Ginseng .... 200 mg

(Standardized to 5% ginsenosides, mainly Rb1)

2) *Ashwagandha OR Withania somnifera (Winter cherry):*

A native of South East Asia, its roots are used widely in the Ayurvedic tradition. Because of its short growth time, it is relatively inexpensive with very little adulteration and is one of my go to herbs. It smells a bit like horse sweat and it gives the user the 'virility of a stallion'; hence its name! It is also used externally as a poultice for boils and sores.

July 12

ADAPTING TO ADAPTOGENS (PART-3)

Whereas most adaptogens are stimulating, Ashwagandha has a calming effect and also has a direct stimulating effect on the thyroid gland and can be helpful in hypothyroidism or an underactive thyroid. It is also used in fatigue situations associated with excess anxiety and in stress induced insomnia.

It has high iron content and is used in herbal medicine for the treatment of iron deficiency anemia. In India it is used as add on to cancer protocols to prevent drops in the blood count secondary to chemotherapy.

DOSE 1 CAPSULE TWICE A DAY; 8-12 WEEKS/MAX LENGTH OF USE 24 WEEKS:

DOUGLAS LABS FORMULA (#7670)

1 Capsule Contains:

Ashwaganda .... 300 mg

(Withania somnifera, standardized to 1.5% withanolides and 1% alkaloids)

A widely used Ayurvedic preparation with multiple adaptogens including Ashwagandha is called "Chyavanprash." It is actually a jam with a distinct sour-spicy taste (definitely acquired) and is available in any self-respecting Indian grocery store. It is named after an elderly sage named Chyavan who invented it so that he could keep up with his young wife. In fact most adaptogens have fabled aphrodisiac properties but the proof of the pudding (or jam in this case) is in the eating.

I normally recommend Ashwagandha as my go-to adaptogen as it is affordable, effective and non-stimulating. It is important to buy it from a reliable source so as to get a standardized preparation.

I advise its use for no longer than six months continuously as the body can "adapt" to the adaptogens. Also have your physician check your thyroid functions every twelve weeks or so when using it as it can elevate thyroid levels.

July 13

ADAPTING TO ADAPTOGENS (PART-4)

"The mark of a successful man is one that has
spent an entire day on the bank of a river without feeling
guilty about it."

—**Anon**

3) Panax ginseng OR Asian ginseng:

This is one adaptogen that I do not use. It is extremely expensive, difficult to obtain in its pure form and is a mainstay of TCM; a system I am not familiar with.

The most stimulating of the adaptogens, it is best not used in conjunction with caffeine and interacts with Coumadin. It is helpful when there is complete exhaustion of the HPA or Adrenal fatigue (low Cortisol levels) based on saliva testing. It is best obtained from a reputable TCM practitioner and it is best to avoid ordering it on the web because of wide spread adulteration.

4) Rhodiola rosea OR Golden root:

Found mostly in the circumpolar region of Asia and Europe, its cut root has a rose like smell, hence the name. It is now being cultivated in Sweden. Its active ingredients are rosavin (adaptogens) and salidrosides (anti-oxidants) and animal studies show that it has a stimulating effect on ALL the neurotransmitters. Its action on the cholinergic receptors actually increases the cognitive improving memory and may have a role in Alzheimer's disease.

These rosavins also modulates the release of opioid peptides which is released by the HPA and also modulates the adrenal and corticoid levels and has an anti-stress effect.

A study of (42) competitive skiers (20-25 years of age) took 100 mg of Rhodiola extract or placebo 30 minutes before 30 km training races and a biathlon. The athletes taking the R. *rosea* extract had statistically significantly increased shooting accuracy with less arm tremor and better coordination than that on placebo. Thirty minutes after the races, the heart rate in the R. *rosea* group was around 20 beats lower in the treatment group than placebo.

DOSE OF RHODIOLA IS 1 TAB THREE TIMES A DAY FOR 8-12 WEEKS

ROSAVIN (TRADE NAME) Ameriden: 100MG TABS 1 TAB THREE TIMES A DAY

A CIVIL WAR (PART-1)

*"It's the heart afraid of breaking that never
learns to dance. It's the dream afraid of waking that never
takes a chance. And it's the soul afraid of dying that never
learns to live."*
—**Nancy Griffith** from the song *"The Rose"*

<u>I SAID, SHE SAID:</u>

*Once in the dark corner of a relationship,
I ambushed her with the tired rhetoric;
"Are we lovers or friends?"
And SHE said "Same difference!"
And I Said: "As lover you have been the pied piper of lust,
Luring me to rivers of promised passion,
And then the music stops.
As friends we have laughed and lived well,
Broken warm bread and spilled crimson wine,
Shared summer's dreams and winter's tears,
So what gives?"
And SHE said: "Before you swim with me,
Let our lips drink vermillion sunsets.
With measured steps, walk with me in sylvan woods.
Awake with me to the music of morning song birds.
And when our souls blossom, there will be,
No love, no friendship.
Just an eternal bond,
a stillness in the present;
Before and beyond time itself!"*   MK/2000

July 15

A CIVIL WAR (PART-1)

After the glow of a new love wears off, there is the delicate dance of discovery. And sometimes, one steps on toes. This poem is a dialogue between the spiritual and physical that are intrinsic parts of our nature. It explores the eternal question of what men and women want in a relationship. And the answer is staring us in the face.

The male voice is interested in the obvious. The female voice wants a spiritual union before she surrenders. Read between the lines and you realize that both voices have the same longing expressed differently.

The woman who inspired this poem never did ask me for an explanation. When I presented this poem to her, she promptly framed it and placed it on a wall in her living room; lost among the sepia portraits of her ancestors and the Kodachrome images of her kids!

What is the role of lust and love in a relationship that you are currently in or were? And how did you find a balance between the two?

_____

_____

_____

_____

_____

_____

_____

_____

_____

A CIVIL WAR (PART-2)

"He taught me housekeeping;
when I divorce I keep the house."
—Zsa Zsa Gabor

<u>WALLS</u>:

Some walls in relationships are six inches high,
Made up of clean squares of misunderstanding
Hidden amongst the weeds of aggravation.
Accidentally stumbling, you swallow your pride, bruise your ego,
Strain your feelings; shed your tears, pick yourself up, hobble for a while,
Kiss and have great sex, and heal with the bond of friendship.

Some are rice paper thin partitions of Japanese screens.
Shadowy manikins flitting against a translucent light
Cast by the glow of pretensions.
Thai cutout puppets acting out a familiar tragedy,
Set to the score of a discordant symphony.
Always reaching for the form;
Never touching the substance.

Then there are bunker thick edifices of tempered steel and reinforced concrete
Crowned with insurmountable thorns of grief.
Accretions of hope and sweat, lust and semen, tears and trepidations,
Scraps of bleached wedding dresses and crumpled divorce decrees.
Crushed skeletal remains of expectations unmet,
Mangled corpses of broken dreams held together with the glue of angst and sorrow.

But having built them,
Was it rapture that collapsed the ramparts of Jericho?
Was it unrequited longing that finally crushed the Berlin Wall?
*In the end, will it be that oft used word: '**love**',*
That will clear the path of misunderstanding;
Soar over the heights of despair;
And pierce the parchment of our isolation?

MK/2000

DR. M. P. KHAN, MD/NMD

July 17

A CIVIL WAR (PART-2)

With the divorce rate close to sixty percent, there is one in two chance that if you are reading this and of a certain demographic, that you have been through one! It's almost an American tradition, a badge of valor for having survived a relationship that went sour. On the other hand if you are in a happy relationship, sing Hallelujah and celebrate your blessings. The above poem was written in the midst of a very contentious divorce

The requiem of a relationship, usually heralded by the silent trumpets of rejection, is the dreaded statement:

"I am building a wall against you"!

I'm not sure at what point in our lives that we start erecting barriers; emotional breakwaters that protect us against future disappointments. It's probably when we realize the impermanence of love and the realization of how vulnerable it can make us. *Still, is there any other choice but to love once more? The alternative is isolation and bitterness and the very denial of our angel natures.*

If you have ever been through a divorce or a separation from a significant other at any time in your life, what lesson did you learn from the experience?

_____

_____

_____

_____

_____

_____

_____

_____

July 18

A CIVIL WAR (PART-3)

*"In every marriage more than a week old, there are grounds
for divorce. The trick is to find, and continue to find,
grounds for marriage."*

—Robert Anderson

<u>FIRE FIGHT:</u>

I stand in still waters;
Reflections of my life.
In the distance I hear the thunder jets,
Harbingers of my Antietam.
In this war, they soon fly overhead
Dripping with the napalm of my memories.
Once I remember,
Waters babbled under foot
And in drunken laughter,
I called ancient birds,
My friends.
Once I remember,
The wind from peaceful valleys
Fragrant with scent of jasmine,
The heady balm of youthful days.
I stand in still waters;
Reflections of my life.
Love scars us all; heals us all.
Leaving no victors,
Only the vanquished.

MK/1998

DR. M. P. KHAN, MD/NMD

July 19

A CIVIL WAR (PART-3)

Fire Fight was written in the throes of an acrimonious divorce. To this day I can vividly recall the marble parquet pattern of the floor of the Family Court that is housed in the old County Jail in downtown Pittsburgh that was recently renovated. The name, Family Court is of course, an oxymoron if ever there was one. And the interminable parade of suited attorneys and their bewildered clients, waiting. Always waiting!

And when it is your turn, you were hauled before a judge whose weary eyes told you that they had heard it all before. And that your case is just another sorry docket before lunch. And to stop loving is a crime. And that you deserve to be raked along the hot coals of the legal system anyway. And try not to take it personally, it is just the system.

Dante missed this version of hell!

If you are in a committed relationship, what are the common grounds or the glue of your marriage or your relationship?

_____

_____

_____

_____

_____

If you are separated or divorced from your significant other, what role did you play in the break up? As the Sufi saying goes, you cannot clap with one hand alone!

_____

_____

_____

_____

_____

_____

July 20

HERBAL TEA TIME (CAN'T GET ENOUGH ZZZ...)

> *"Sleep that knits up the ravelled sleeve of care, The death of each day's life, sore labour's bath, Balm of hurt minds, great nature's second course, Chief nourisher in life's feast."*
> —William Shakespeare, *"Macbeth"*

Mrs. Fields shows up for her regular visit, although she does not seem her usual perky self. This time she does not have her usual list of supplements.

Hi Doctor Khan, I have not slept for three nights and my husband thinks I should try acupuncture. Is there any basis to this approach? If anything, all those needles in my body would keep me up!

Mrs. Fields, how nice to see you again! Amazingly, 10 % of adults in the US have chronic insomnia (insomnia lasting greater than 6 months) and almost everybody has an occasional night when sleep is difficult. It is a symptom and not a disease and a result of multiple causes ranging from medical, psychiatric and side effect of medications and results in significant problems such as poor memory, lack of concentration, an increased risk of car accidents and poor job performance.

The most important step, is to establish a sleep pattern. This means going to bed at the same time and awakening at the same time. Even on weekends. Also make your environment as dark and quiet as possible. Also keep any clocks out of sight so you can't see how late it is, which can create a lot of anxiety. Set up an alarm (or two) if waking up at a certain time is critical. Try not to do any activity that is too stimulating before bedtime.

DR. M. P. KHAN, MD/NMD

Before you try acupuncture, try Valerian root (standardized capsules, 100 mg-200 mg) on a regular basis one hour before bedtime. There are good studies that ongoing use of Valerian improves sleep architecture over a period of 8-12 weeks.

You can also try a combination of a long acting melatonin (3 mg and can gradually increase to 12 mg.) supplement along with a short acting (3 mg) melatonin supplement an hour before bedtime. This only helps if you are deficient in melatonin but it's worth a try as it is very safe. Melatonin can also be combined with Valerian root to help with sleep.

In Traditional Chinese Medicine (TCM), insomnia reflects an imbalance of the mind and is treated with acupuncture and herbs. In one clinical trial, 18 volunteers age 30-50 yrs. with moderate to severe insomnia were treated with Acupuncture 2/week for five weeks with significant improvement in sleep quality and anxiety levels. Interestingly enough there was an increase in urine melatonin levels thus providing a rational explanation as to how acupuncture worked. In conclusion, Acupuncture has been used in Chinese Medicine for hundreds of years and recent studies have confirmed its effectiveness in treating Insomnia.

HERBAL TEA TIME (CAN'T GET ENOUGH ZZZ...)

www.medicalacupuncture.org is a good resource to find licensed acupuncture practitioners. I have listed some indications for acupuncture in the below table. If needles scare you, consider acupressure which is basically applying pulsed pressure or tapping to the same acupuncture points and can be self-administered. Almost any <u>chronic</u> illness will probably respond to acupuncture

ACUTE PAIN

□ Migraine □ Muscle tension headaches □ Temporomandibular joint pain(TMJ) □ Frozen shoulder □ Joint pain(Arthritis-arthrosis) □ Bursitis, tendonitis, epicondylitis (tennis elbow) □ Neuralgias: Trigeminal, Post herpetic, □ Nerve entrapments (Carpal tunnel, Piriformis syndrome, etc.) □ Plantar fasciitis

ADDICTIONS

□ Substance abuse problems □ Alcohol problems □ Smoking cessation □ Obesity

MENTAL AND EMOTIONAL DISTURBANCES

□ Anxiety □ Excitability □ Irritability □ Early stages of depression □ Anorexia-bulimia □ Sleep disturbances □ Insomnia □ Attention Deficit Hyperactivity Disorder

IMMUNE DYSREGULATION DISORDERS

□ Inflammatory disorders □ Asthma □ Bronchospasm □ Sinusitis □ Bronchitis

WOMEN HEALTH

☐ Menstrual cramps ☐ Menopause ☐ Hot flushes ☐ Infertility ☐ Pelvic pain ☐ Dysmenorrhea ☐ Endometriosis

FUNCTIONAL GASTRO-INTESTINAL DISORDERS

☐ Gastroenteritis (stomach-flu) ☐ Nausea and vomiting ☐ Esophageal spasm ☐ Hyperacidity (GERD) ☐ Slow gastric emptying ☐ Irritable Bowel Syndrome Hepatitis ☐ Hemorrhoids ☐ Constipation ☐ Diarrhea

GENITO-URINARY DISORDERS

☐ Frequent urination ☐ Nocturia ☐ Irritable bladder ☐ Urinary incontinence ☐ Retention (neurogenic, spastic, adverse drug effect)

July 22

WHAT ME WORRY!

"Worrying brings you back full circle;
planning moves you ahead."

—Chairman Moo

Mrs. Fields returns to my office sans the usual can of cookies. She apologizes to my staff for her oversight.

Hi! Doctor Khan. Where to begin? Your advice on sleep is helping me somewhat. But due to some recent losses in my personal and business dealings, I am worrying a lot about my finances. My daughter feels that I am stressed out. My adrenal glands are not working, she says. Like she is an MD or something! That I should be on drugs and that I will not get better without them. I disagree with her. Are there any tests that can tell me if stress is causing me problems?

Mrs. Fields, on the previous topics on Adaptogens, we covered some approaches to treating stress using specific herbs to manage stress and I can print out the handouts for you. But there are two lab tests, which may be useful when dealing with diseases of the adrenal gland.

The first one is the Dexamethasone Suppression Test. This test is useful when there is a suspicion that the adrenal glands are not under the control of the Hypothalamus as in a disease called Cushing's disease. It classically presents as a moon face, fat around the abdomen, skinny legs and a high blood sugar and emotional changes, all related to excessive cortisol production by the adrenal glands (a condition also seen in excessive oral or intravenous use of steroids i.e. prednisone).

Dexamethasone in normal individuals should shut off the ACTH production in normal patients and decrease the body's own cortisol. In Cushing's disease this does not happen. The reverse condition is Addison's disease and Shy-Drager where the adrenals shut down

DR. M. P. KHAN, MD/NMD

completely thus producing a poor response to stressful situations causing a very low blood pressure, low energy levels and possible shock. In fact in *chronic fatigue syndrome* levels of cortisol are very low (current thinking is that *fibromyalgia* and *CFS* are variations of the same problem).

The second test is the Adrenocortex Stress Profile, which is a saliva test which checks the ratio of DHEA to Cortisol and the kit is available from my office (Genova Diagnostic Labs).We discussed this previously. Its advantage over the blood test is that it measures the *free* levels of cortisol/DHEA versus blood tests, where there can be protein binding, and this makes accurate measurement of free levels difficult.

July 23

WHAT ME WORRY!

Below are some herbal and complimentary approaches in managing stress based on a high or low cortisol situation.

Low Cortisol: I would recommend Adaptogenic Herbs. These are unique to Chinese and Ayurvedic medicine. The stars are American Ginseng (Chinese) and Ashwaganda (Ayurvedic). These are also useful after a chronic illness or surgery and are tonic herbs. Do not use them for more than 8-12 weeks. (Incidentally Ginseng is the most commonly adulterated herb). Other herbs are Licorice, which prolongs the action of cortisol, and Sarsaparilla, which is a cortisol building block.

High Cortisol: Phosphatidyl Serine may resensitize the hypothalamus thus establishing control of the adrenal glands. Calmative herbs are Valerian, Hops, Passion Flower (Douglas Labs: Neurosed 1 or 2 at bedtime) and chronic use can lead to dependency so limit to 8-12 weeks or use intermittently. Low dose adaptogenic herbs may also help.

General Measures: Lifestyle change are critical and the most important intervention. These include stress reduction, prayer, meditation, sufficient sleep eliminating food allergies (IgG mediated delayed type) and restoration of normal bowel function is helpful. A good multivitamin/mineral supplement, omega-3 fatty acids and probiotics (yogurt) and clean water with a reduction of animal based proteins are the foundation of these changes. And of course the more we interact with our fellow beings we can find joy and rediscover the miracle that life truly is.

Write down three things that you are "worried" about the most.

_____

_____

_____

DR. M. P. KHAN, MD/NMD

Write down your "plans" to deal with these three "worries."

_____

_____

_____

_____

_____

_____

_____

_____

July 24

INTEGRATE THYSELF (PART-1)

"It is more important to know what sort
of person has a disease than to know what sort
of disease a person has."
—Hippocrates (460-377 B.C.)

I have listed below the ten guiding principles of the Board of Integrated and Holistic Medicine or ABIHM, directly from their exam application. I could not have said it better.

1. *Optimal health* is the primary goal of integrative holistic medical practice, deriving from the conscious pursuit of the highest level of functioning and balance of the physical, environmental, mental, emotional, social and spiritual aspects of human experience. The result is a state of being fully alive, a condition of well-being transcending the mere absence or presence of disease.

2. *The healing power of love:* Integrative holistic physicians strive to relate to patients with grace, kindness and acceptance, emanating from an attitude of unconditional love as life's most powerful healer.

3. *Wholeness:* Illness is a dysfunction of the whole person – body, mind and spirit – or the environment, in which they live, rather than simply a physical disorder or a random isolated event.

4. *Prevention and treatment:* Integrative holistic practitioners promote health, prevent illness and manage disease processes. Integrative holistic medical treatment balances relief of symptoms with mitigation of causes.

5. *Innate healing power:* All persons have innate powers of healing of body, mind and spirit. Integrative holistic physicians evoke these powers and help patients utilize them to affect the healing process.

6. *Integration of healing systems:* Integrative holistic physicians embrace a variety of safe and effective options in diagnosis and treatment,

including education for lifestyle changes and self-care, complementary approaches, and conventional drugs and surgery.

7. *Relationship-centered care:* The quality of the relationship between physician and patient is a major determinant of healing outcomes which encourages patient autonomy and values the needs and insights of patient and practitioner alike.

8. *Individuality:* Integrative holistic physicians expend as much effort in discerning a patient's uniqueness as they do in establishing what disease may be present.

9. *Teaching by example:* Integrative holistic physicians continually work toward the personal incorporation of the principles of holistic health, in turn profoundly influencing patients by their own example and lifestyle choices.

10. *Learning opportunities:* All life experiences including birth, illness, suffering, joy, and the dying process are profound learning opportunities for both patients and integrative holistic physicians.

July 25

INTEGRATE THYSELF (PART-1)

I am often asked if I am a holistic doctor. I sincerely hope that this is a question that will not be relevant as we move towards the future. The answer is of course a resounding' yes'. It's not like I have access to special knowledge or that I am an anomaly. All physicians should be holistic in their approach.

That was how medicine was practiced in almost every culture in the past. Much as we need the specialization of conventional medicine in acute illnesses, we also need the integrated overview in chronic disease states.

Do you feel that your physician or healer is practicing with these principles in mind?

If not how would you initiate a dialogue with your partner in healing?

_____

_____

_____

_____

_____

_____

_____

If the answer is yes, the next time you have a visit; give him or her, an appreciative hug and a warm thank you!

July 26

INTEGRATE THYSELF (PART-2)

"Health is the proper relationship between microcosm,
which is man, and the macrocosm, which is the universe.
Disease is a disruption of this relationship."
—**Dr. Yeshe Donden, physician to the Dalai Lama**

Its POP-quiz time and remember there are no right or wrong answers. This is not a competition to get the highest score. Just answer with yes or no or both if it is a two part question. It is a questionnaire I use when I do a consult and it may give you valuable insight into where you are on the Body-Mind-Spirit spectrum and what areas you need to focus on. There are no right or wrong answers. Just a friendly tool to see which areas you need to work on

BODY: Physical and Environmental Health

_____ 1. Do you maintain a healthy diet? (Low fat, low sugar, fruits, grains & vegetables fish proteins and probiotics and whole foods; organic and non-GMO)?

_____ 2. Is your water/fluids intake adequate (60-80 oz. /24 hrs.)?

_____ 3. Are you within a 20-25 range of your BMI?

_____ 4. Do you fall asleep easily and sleep soundly and awaken well rested

_____ 5 Do you have more than enough energy to meet your daily tasks?

_____ 6. Do you take time to experience sexual pleasure and do you find it gratifying?

_____ 7. Do you engage in regular workouts lasting at least 30 minutes and do you have good endurance?

_____ 8. Do you do paced diaphragm breathing daily for at least a few minutes?

_____ 9 Do you do some stretching exercises or yoga on a regular basis?

_____ 10. Are you free of any chronic disease states such as hypertension; diabetes etc?

_____ 11. Do you have regular effortless bowel movements without the use of laxatives?

_____ 12. Are you free of any drug or alcohol dependency (including nicotine and caffeine) or addiction to food or sex?

_____ 13. Do you live in a healthy indoor and outdoor environment?

_____ 14. Do you feel a strong connection with and appreciation for your body, your home, other beings and nature?

_____15 Do you have any frequency or urgency of urine

July 27

INTEGRATE THYSELF (PART-2)

"The competent physician, before he attempts to give medicine to the patient, makes himself acquainted not only with the disease, but also with the habits and constitution of the sick man."

—Cicero

MIND: Mental and Emotional Heath

_____ 1. Do you have specific goals in your personal and professional life?

_____ 2. Can you meet your financial needs and desires in an ethical manner?

_____ 3. Can you see he brighter side of a situation even when it is a difficult one?

_____ 4. Are you very self-critical or critical of others?

_____ 5. Do you forgive yourself and others easily?

_____ 6. Does your job utilize all of your greatest talents in an enjoyable and fulfilling setting?

_____ 7. Do you deal with others in a kind and open manner?

_____ 8. Are you able to learn from painful experiences and adjust beliefs and attitudes?

_____ 9. Do you have a sense of humor and take yourself lightly?

_____ 10. Are you free from the need to be right always?

_____ 11. Are you able to fully experience and accept (feel) your painful feelings such as fear, anger, sadness, and hopelessness and deal with them in a constructive manner?

_____ 12. Do you engage in meditation, self-witnessing or counselling to better understand your thoughts and feelings?

_____ 13. Do you take the time to let down and relax, or make time for activities that constitute the abandon or absorption of play?

_____ 14. Do you experience feelings of joy and peace of mind?

_____ 15 Do you enjoy high self-esteem?

July 28

INTEGRATE THYSELF (PART-2)

"We live in illusion and the appearance of things. There is a reality. We are that reality. When you understand this, you see that you are nothing, and being nothing, you are everything. That is all."

—Kalu Rinpoche

SPIRIT: Spiritual and Social Health

_____1. Do you believe and actively commit time to the spiritual side of your being?

_____ 2. Do you take time for prayer, meditation, or some quiet time free from distractions?

_____3. Do you have any creative activities which are not related to work?

_____4. Do you have believe in a God, a higher power, spirit guides, or angels?

_____5. Do you count the blessings that are present in your life?

_____6 Do you commune with nature on a regular basis?

_____7. Are you very attached to material thing in your life and does their loss affect you adversely

_____ 8. Does your life have a sense of purpose or destiny?

_____ 9. Do you have a sense of commitment to a marriage, a long-term relationship or a cause you believe in?

_____ 10. Do you experience intimacy, besides sex, in your committed relationships?

_____ 11. Do you confide with one or more close friends?

_____ 12. If you have experienced the death of a loved one, have you fully grieved that?

_____ 13. Has your experience of suffering enabled you to grow spiritually?

_____ 14. Do you practice random acts of kindness?

_____ 15. Do you feel a sense of belonging to a group or community or a church/temple/mosque?

Go over the three part questionnaire and no matter if you have a disproportionate number of negative answers, the awareness of our shortcomings is the first step in transformation. We all have an enormous potential and need to believe that. It is the journey that is important and no matter what the outcome, it is your own unique voyage! All you need is a strategy that can help you make those positive changes. Over the next three days, write down a plan for the negative areas in the BODY, MIND, and SPIRIT quiz. Come up with realistic and practical approaches you can implement over the next three to six months.

July 29

INTEGRATE THYSELF (PART-3)

Write down some strategies to improve your negatives in the BODY quiz.

_____

_____

_____

_____

_____

_____

_____

_____

_____

_____

_____

_____

_____

_____

_____

_____

_____

_____

_____

July 30

INTEGRATE THYSELF (PART-3)

Write down some strategies to improve your low scoring areas in the MIND quiz.

_____

_____

_____

_____

_____

_____

_____

_____

_____

_____

_____

_____

_____

_____

_____

_____

_____

_____

_____

_____

DR. M. P. KHAN, MD/NMD

July 31

INTEGRATE THYSELF (PART-3)

Write down some strategies to improve your low scoring areas in the SPIRIT quiz.

_____

_____

_____

_____

_____

_____

_____

_____

_____

_____

_____

_____

_____

_____

_____

_____

_____

_____

_____

_____

_____

_____

AUGUST

1-Aug	SPORTS 'N' SUPPLEMENTS. It's quite legal.
2-Aug	SPORTS 'N' SUPPLEMENTS. Creatine and egg whites.
3-Aug	SPORTS 'N' SUPPLEMENTS. All about ATP and energy.
4-Aug	SPORTS 'N' SUPPLEMENTS. And minerals and Co-Q-10.
5-Aug	SPORTS 'N' SUPPLEMENTS. And also glutamine.
6-Aug	SPORTS 'N' SUPPLEMENTS. And remember the adaptogens.
7-Aug	A PARABLE OF INNER BLISS. Akbar asks Birbal a question.
8-Aug	A PARABLE OF INNER BLISS. A question of happiness.
9-Aug	A PARABLE OF INNER BLISS. And Birbal finds the answer.
10-Aug	A PARABLE OF INNER BLISS. Perform random acts of happiness.
11-Aug	THANK YOU, JOHN MUIR. A poem. Nature and mankind thank you.
12-Aug	THANK YOU, JOHN MUIR. How will you help the environment?
13-Aug	CELEBRATING GAIA. A poem about SILENCE.
14-Aug	CELEBRATING GAIA. If the English language disappeared!
15-Aug	OF BIRDS AND BEES. Another poem. ONCE THERE WERE BEES.
16-Aug	OF BIRDS AND BEES. And buy some native bee friendly plants.
17-Aug	POT POURRI. All about that steak and breast cancer.
18-Aug	POT POURRI. That yellow spice, turmeric and cucuminoids.
19-Aug	POT POURRI. Those precocious probiotics.
20-Aug	POT POURRI. And how to use them (pro and pre biotics).
21-Aug	POT POURRI. Meditation and Inflammation.
22-Aug	POT POURRI. All about cocoa and cognition.
23-Aug	POT POURRI. No need to be SNP y about it.
24-Aug	POT POURRI. What is all the fuss about "kefir?"
25-Aug	CONCERNINGKRISHNAMURTI. What are we seeking?
26-Aug	CONCERNINGKRISHNAMURTI. Gratification or Happiness?
27-Aug	CONCERNINGKRISHNAMURTI. Who creates our problems?
28-Aug	CONCERNINGKRISHNAMURTI. In oneself lies the whole world!
29-Aug	CONCERNINGKRISHNAMURTI. To live without any belief!
30Aug	CONCERNINGKRISHNAMURTI. Carry a cup.
31-Aug	AND NOW FOR SSOMETHING DIFFERENT. 'A SSerpent's Ssorrow.'

DR. M. P. KHAN, MD/NMD

August 1

SPORTS 'N' SUPPLEMENTS (PART-1)

"Serious sport has nothing to do with fair play. It is bound
up with hatred, jealousy, boastfulness, disregard of all
rules and sadistic pleasure in witnessing violence. In other
words, it is war minus the shooting."
—George Orwell

If you ever participated in organized sports, the above quote has a lot of truth in it. Just recently a famous baseball player, and a former Pittsburgh Pirate, was indicted for perjury in a case involving performance steroids. And a 1997 survey of Olympic athletes asked the question; "Would you take a drug which would in five years assure you a gold medal, even though the drug would kill you?" Half of the athletes amazingly, said *yes*! As a result of this fierce drive to win, most major athletic events have extensive testing for illegal drugs before the event and it is crucial that athletes are aware of the safety and legality of the supplements that they are taking.

Even though anabolic or performance steroids are illegal in sports, there are a whole bunch of non-prescription vitamins, nutritional supplements and herbs available, some with doubtful value, to the athlete trying to get that crucial edge over the competition. For the purpose of this discussion, we can divide them into LEGAL and ILLEGAL for use in competition sports.

LEGAL:

Protein Powders: These are usually available in your local nutrition store and sometimes have pictures of muscle bound men on the label. There are three major sources of proteins. These are milk or whey protein, soy protein and pea or legume based protein. The only time I recommend them are in the elderly with documented protein deficiency. They are no better than eating fish or eggs or other vegetable food based proteins.

Because of the high concentration of protein in the supplements, there is a real concern for kidney failure.

Creatine: This is one of the most popular supplements, especially among high school football and baseball players. Creatine forms a complex with phosphate called creatine phosphate (CP) that is required to replenish ATP stores in muscles. ATP or adenosine tri phosphate, by the action of CP, releases a phosphate molecule to convert to AD (di) P and results in an energy packet that is used by the cell. The system is called the ATP-CP system and it kicks in when there is an immediate and intense need for energy such as sprinting. But it is quickly exhausted. Almost all supplements have the rationale that they will increase the production of this ATP molecule. Creatine was first used by athletes in the 1990s when Olympic sprinters admitted they were using it. Creatine is not banned by the International Olympic Committee (IOC) or the National Collegiate Athletic Association (NCAA).

Phosphates: Representing the second half of the CP molecule, it stands to reason that increasing phosphate stores in the muscles theoretically might allow the ATP system to function longer and help hasten recovery of depleted ATP stores. Phosphate loading is done by the athlete taking 1 g of phosphate salts three or four times daily for up to seven days.

DR. M. P. KHAN, MD/NMD

August 2

SPORTS 'N' SUPPLEMENTS (PART-1)

But does it really help? Creatine supplementation does not appear to improve sustained exercise. Improvements here would not be expected since the ATP-CP system is not a significant player with these types of exercise.

Creatine supplementation, on the other hand, appears to provide benefit for specific types of intense, short-duration exercise such as sprinting, short football plays and weight lifting followed by a recovery cycle. This system provides a burst of energy for ten seconds and is obviously more consistent with the ATP-CP cycle.

Creatine supplementation usually consists of a loading period of 20 g/d for four to six days and is then followed by 2 g/d as a maintenance dose. Some of the protein supplements mentioned above have creatine mixed with it. There is some concern that creatine may cause kidney problems in those already predisposed to kidney disease. One study followed a group of athletes using creatine for up to five years. The authors concluded that creatine supplementation has no harmful effects on the kidneys. The ACSM or American College of Sports Medicine recommends against creatine supplementation for those under 18 years.

Currently, the research basis for phosphate loading is hazy at best and can be of concern for long term use. Elevated plasma levels of phosphate lead to secretion of parathyroid hormone, which increases kidney excretion of phosphate. Calcium is reabsorbed from bone to help this excretion, leading to concerns about osteoporosis.

A label from a typical protein supplement shows it has the same amount of protein per serving (22 grams) as three egg whites! Almost all protein supplements are egg based, whey (milk) based, soy protein or pea protein based and the last one is what I usually recommend because of safety concerns

August 3

SPORTS 'N' SUPPLEMENTS (PART-2)

> *"I think my favorite sport in the Olympics is the one in which you make your way through the snow, you stop, you shoot a gun, and then you continue on. In most of the world, it is known as the biathlon, except in New York City, where it is known as winter."*
> —**Michael Ventre, L.A. Daily News**

Although the ATP-CP system is the jump starter, it is *glycolysis* or the conversion of glucose to the ATP molecule via the Krebs cycle that is the real workhorse of the endurance athlete. It is done in the presence of oxygen or *aerobic* when enough glycogen (a form of storage of the glucose molecule) is available and *anaerobic* when not enough oxygen is available and which results in lactic acid build up or *burn* as endurance athletes describe it. Which is why eating large amounts of pasta the day before an endurance event makes sense, as it increases the amount of glycogen stored in the muscle?

Glucose is released from the glycogen stores and by glycolysis results in the release of small amounts of ATP and *pyruvate*. Pyruvate can produce large amounts of ATP as long as there is enough oxygen (aerobic) and can sustain endurance for hours depending on the activity and training level of the athlete. But if oxygen demand gets too high, the pyruvate breaks down to lactic acid and small amounts of ATP and can provide energy for the next 30 minutes or so before complete fatigue sets in or the athlete hits the proverbial *wall*.

Pyruvate: A study done by Stanko used a combination of 25 g pyruvate with 75 g dihydroxyacetone (DHA), a precursor of pyruvate. The mechanism by which pyruvate might be helpful in athletics is unknown. 66% of the research participants had diarrhea and stomach cramps, which could potentially interfere with their sport. This study has not yet been

DR. M. P. KHAN, MD/NMD

replicated. This may benefit those seeking to lose weight and is sometimes used by competitive wrestlers. Commercial preparations advice the use of 2 grams of pyruvate daily and a different proportion of DHA, or none at all. Long-term effects of supplementation have not been examined and use of pyruvate is *not* recommended

Carnitine: When glycogen stores get exhausted, production of ATP switches to anaerobic where fat stores are broken down to fatty acids and used by the cell to produce that all important ATP molecule. Carnitine assists the movement of the fatty acids into the cell and can theoretically improve performance. Carnitine dose is usually is recommended at 2 g/d. The most common short term side effect is diarrhea but the long-term effects of taking carnitine have not been tested. Carnitine is available in two isomeric forms: D-carnitine and L-carnitine. L-carnitine is the only form that should be used, since D-carnitine may block the production of L-carnitine, leading to its deficiency. This could result in muscle weakness.

August 4

SPORTS 'N' SUPPLEMENTS (PART-2)

Chromium: Chromium is more popularly used in weight-loss products, but also to increase muscle mass and burn fat. Chromium is an essential trace element involved in the function of insulin. . Insulin helps with the transport of glucose, fatty acids, and amino acids into muscle cells. Several studies of athletes given 200 mcg/d of chromium over several weeks showed no change in muscle mass.

The Adequate Intake Level for chromium set by the Institute of Medicine (IOM) in 2001 was 25 mcg/day- 35 mcg/day. (Of chromium picolinate) although a dose up to 100mcg/day is considered safe.

Calcium/Magnesium/Sodium: Every football season sees players sidelined by muscle cramps. The above triad is critical in the prevention of muscle cramps along with adequate hydration. Although sport drinks provide adequate sodium, the other two elements such as calcium and magnesium are just as important. I would recommend that athletes take a Calcium/Magnesium supplement at a 2:1 ratio on a daily basis (750 mg Calcium: 375 mg Magnesium) to prevent cramps and an additional benefit in preventing osteoporosis in the female athlete.

Coenzyme Q-10: Coenzyme Q-10 (also called ubiquinone) plays an important role in the electron transport chain (ETC) which allows oxygen to release energy from nutrients. For this reason, CoQ-10 supplementation may be helpful for endurance athletes. Early reports from several studies appeared to support this finding though recent studies showed no benefits. No adverse effects were reported after taking 70-150 mg/d CoQ-10 for several weeks.

Cal-Mag 2001

DOUGLAS LABS FORMULA (#2001)

Three Tablets Daily Contain:

Calcium .... 750 mg

Magnesium .... 375 mg

Vitamin D-3 .... 75 I.U.

Citrus Q-10 100

DOUGLAS LABS FORMULA (#200053)

Each Tablet Daily Contains:

Natural Coenzyme Q10 .... 100 mg

August 5

SPORTS 'N' SUPPLEMENTS (PART-3)

"Left hand, right hand, it doesn't matter.
I'm amphibious."
—**Charles Shackleford of the NCSU basketball team**

When you consider the gazillion dollar deals that are made by not-so-smart professional athletes, it makes sense why performance enhancing agents are so widely used. Meanwhile most of us poor uncoordinated slobs have to slog along and write books like these to make a living. (Yes, I am envious) Improving performance stats in their particular sport by any means possible can result in salary differentials of several million dollars in future contract negotiations.

Glutamine: Glutamine is a nonessential amino acid and the body, under normal circumstances does not need it. But in some situations, the body is unable to make sufficient glutamine and supplementation may be required. Glutamine plasma levels are lower during conditions causing muscle breakdown, such as those following surgery, trauma, and extended, high-intensity exercise. The body's largest stores of glutamine are in skeletal muscle, which can be broken down to restore plasma glutamine levels. Protein breakdown can also occur because of elevated cortisol levels, as a result of prolonged physical stress and exercise.

Glutamine is an important energy source for many cells in the immune system. Several studies have demonstrated that athletes have higher incidences of upper respiratory tract infections following prolonged, high endurance exercise. For example, 13% of athletes who completed the Los Angeles marathon had Upper Respiratory Infections the week after the race compared to 2.2% of athletes with similar training regimens who did not compete on that day. There is little clinical evidence to support the use of glutamine supplements. It may have a role after an intense endurance event to reduce the chances of developing a URI. Glutamine

DR. M. P. KHAN, MD/NMD

is a very safe supplement with no known side effects. It other uses are in any detoxification program as it carries ammonia to the liver for excretion. It is also a crucial nitrogen donor in times of stress when the body's own glutamine is depleted and helps the immune cell in the gut function better. This explains the frequent URI's with the LA marathoners.

L-Glutamine:
DOUGLAS LABS FORMULA (#7940)
Each Capsule Contains: 500 mg of L-glutamine
Advice 1 capsule daily

August 6

SPORTS 'N' SUPPLEMENTS (PART-3)

Adaptogens: Ginseng is one of the most popular herbal remedies sold in the United States. An adaptogens by definition is: "A substance that helps the body adapt to stressful situations." Ginseng is one of the few herbal remedies that have been investigated extensively in its role in sports medicine. Siberian ginseng or Eleuthero has been used by Soviet Olympic Sports teams since the late 60's and has a different group of steroidal glycosides called eleutherocides which have an adaptogenic effect. (See previous month of July for more detailed information of Adaptogens)

Clinical trials on ginseng for sports performance date to the early 1970s but the quality of the early studies often was poor; several of them were not controlled in any way, Animal studies have found that ginseng consistently helped animals adapt to stress. Those studies have tended to use much higher doses (up to 100 times higher) than in human research and many studies of herbs in humans may be inconclusive because sub-therapeutic doses may be used.

Although ginseng is not banned by the IOC or NCAA it is often contaminated with ephedra, a banned substance. One athlete at the 1988 Seoul Olympics tested positive for ephedrine, which was traced to a ginseng product. This is a common problem with severe consequences for the athlete. If used, it is best to get it from a reliable source. Overall, there is little research support for the use of ginseng to improve performance. Its real role may be in aiding a quick recovery from severe physical exhaustion that follows competitive sports by restoring Cortisol levels!

Eleuthero MAX-V
DOUGLAS LABS FORMULA (#77336)
Each Vegetarian Capsule Contains:
Eleutherococcus senticosus ....200 mg
Standardized to 15% Eleutheroside B and 0.5%
Eleutheroside E Total 0.8% Eleutherosides
(China, Russia [Eastern Siberia], Manchuria, Korea)

Take one capsule three times a day between meals.

DR. M. P. KHAN, MD/NMD

August 7

A PARABLE OF INNER BLISS

*"Thousands of candles can be lighted from a single candle,
and the life of the candle will not be shortened. Happiness
never decreases by being shared."*

—Buddha

In ancient India, during the time of the Mughal dynasty almost four hundred years ago, there lived a wise and curious king named Akbar. Such was his renown that emissaries from the four corners of the world would seek him out for he ruled his subjects with wisdom and compassion.

But rumor had it that there was an even more learned individual in his court, the Grand Vizier, Birbal. It was said that Akbar made no important decision in the day to day ruling of his Kingdom without consulting Birbal first. And although Birbal never sugar coated the truth, unlike some of his courtiers, Akbar respected Birbal and valued him as a friend and confidant.

One summer night, Akbar woke up from a dream feeling very joyful. He could not remember the dream but he remembered the feeling. So in the morning he summoned Birbal and asked him the question that mankind has asked for millennia. "What is the nature of happiness?"

Wise as he was, this was a question that he could not answer with some clever remark or with some obscure philosophy. So he told Akbar to give him seven days. At the end of this time he may have an answer. Akbar agreed and Birbal set out on a long and arduous journey to seek the answer to this eternal conundrum.

For days he travelled over mount and vale and on the third day of his travels came upon a holy man or sadhu sitting in meditation on the river bank. Respectfully he approached the holy man and upon reaching him, Birbal posed him the question for surely he would know. Much to his amazement the man roused from his practice got quite red in the face with anger. At first Birbal could not understand his reaction. "Please great sadhu, it was a simple question. I certainly did not mean to upset you." Sensing Birbal's humility and recognizing him as the renowned Birbal, he calmed down.

"O' Great Vizier, for years I have contemplated on what is true happiness. I have starved myself, made long pilgrimages to holy places and even consecrated temples to the Gods. And yet the answer eludes me. So when you ask me about the true meaning of happiness, my frustration comes through. I hope that before I die I have the revelation of what it actually means. I am sorry to have offended you. And if you do find the answer promise me that you will share it with me and the rest of the world."

Although Birbal was disappointed by the sadhu's answer, he knew that someone out there would be able to answer this question. So he took leave of the sadhu and continued on his travels and asked the same question to all he met and never quite received a satisfactory answer.

DR. M. P. KHAN, MD/NMD

August 8

A PARABLE OF INNER BLISS

What is the nature of your happiness? OR What makes you happy?

_____
_____
_____
_____
_____
_____
_____
_____
_____
_____
_____
_____
_____

When was the last time you were happy? What did it feel like?

_____
_____
_____
_____
_____
_____
_____
_____
_____
_____
_____
_____
_____

A PARABLE OF INNER BLISS

"When all your desires are distilled;
you will cast just two votes:
To love more, and be happy"

—Rumi

And so Birbal continued on his travels. Passing through a small village, he heard the sound of a woman laughing with great gusto and joy. On investigating the sound of this merriment, he came upon an old lady playing with her grandchildren. They were running around her and pulling on her garments and giggling with abandon. "Surely" Birbal thought "here is a happy person."

So he asked her the same question and the old lady answered promptly; "Can't you see my happiness. Of course I am happy. What a foolish question." Birbal persisted "but are you truly happy?" At this the old lady got very upset and scolded Birbal for wasting her time and if he could not see how happy she was, no explanation was necessary. But Birbal was not to be put off so easily. So he asked her another question. "Would you still be happy if something happened to your grandchildren like a disease or they just grew up and did not want to play their childish games?" This greatly saddened her and after she recovered, she started cursing Birbal and his ancestors as being snakes and pigs for ruining her happy moments with her grandchildren and to never visit this village again.

The week was almost up. Birbal despaired that he would have to tell the great King Akbar that he did not have an answer to his question and so he turned around with a heavy heart and began to make the long journey back to the palace.

The Monsoons had just begun and the rains were torrents. As he was making his journey, he came upon a woman crying by the roadside. From the state of her clothes and her look, Birbal could tell she was very poor. Her bullock cart was stuck in the wet mud and much as she tried to coax the bullock, Birbal could see that it did not move. Although the road was busy, no one stopped to help her. The cart was loaded with bananas on their way to the local market and without the money from their sale, her family would probably starve.

DR. M. P. KHAN, MD/NMD

Seeing her plight, Birbal wordlessly went to her assistance. He gently coaxed the bullock, at the same time pushing on the spokes of the wheel that was stuck. Although he was wet and muddy, he eventually got the wheel free. The woman thanked him profusely and this time her tears were of relief and happiness. Soon, she, and her cart full of bananas were on their way. And then Birbal smiled as his heart filled with joy for helping another human being. He finally had an answer to his question.

He now knew about the true nature of happiness. If you want to be happy, make others happy!

August 10

A PARABLE OF INNER BLISS

What is your interpretation of this parable?

_____
_____
_____
_____
_____
_____
_____
_____

How will you use this wisdom in your daily life?

_____
_____
_____
_____
_____
_____
_____
_____

What random acts of happiness can you do on a regular basis?

_____
_____
_____
_____
_____
_____
_____
_____

DR. M. P. KHAN, MD/NMD

THANK YOU, JOHN MUIR

"God has cared for these trees, saved them from drought,
disease, avalanches, and a thousand tempests and floods.
But he cannot save them from fools."

—**John Muir**

THANK YOU, JOHN MUIR:

When the vultures of avarice circled,
he heard the wails of the Earth Mother.
Her cry of lament was the spark,
igniting this simple wanderer into her fiery Apostle.
For this prophet, no epiphany, no Burning Bush,
just a lover's surrender, falling, drowning, into Her beauty.

A sacred man, he walked softly into Her secret places.
Over the peaks of the high Sierras;
through the lush valleys of Yosemite;
amidst groves of the Great Sequoias.
And in quiet nights, serenaded by wolf howls,
She whispered to him her ancient songs.

The mountains of the Sierra Nevada murmured
stories of the Great Beginning of time itself.
When Earth and Sky embraced in mighty spasms,
and Man was just a dream in the sleep of The Great Spirit.

The granite gorges of Yosemite bespoke
of violent glaciers, fingers of ice sculpting solid rock.
Of gentle streams, that burbled through the millennia,
their constant caresses, burnished smooth their roughness.

And the majestic baritone of the Sequoias summoned him.
Before they were giants, they were tender saplings.
When another gentle Carpenter walked the Earth,
and a Prince, under another tree, was enlightened.

Finally, The Great Spirit itself,
Awakened from slumber.
And moved by the tears of the Mother who birthed Him,
was grieved into words:

"This Beauty I have given you, is who I am,
This Beauty I have given you is who YOU are.
Celebrate Mass in this cathedral, ring the Bells of this temple,
and spread your Prayer rugs in this mosque, read the Torah in this synagogue.
Let the waters of these rivers be your baptism into joy,
and in this Paradise, this other Eden, you will surely find grace!"

MK/2009

DR. M. P. KHAN, MD/NMD

August 12

THANK YOU, JOHN MUIR

Born in 1938, he is one of my heroes. I first heard about him in a PBS documentary of our National Parks. If not for him, Yosemite, the Grand Canyon and Yellowstone would by now be commercialized and covered with tacky hotels and arcades.

The first time I saw Niagara Falls was one of the great disappointments of my life. The falls were magnificent. It was the surroundings that were completely bereft of nature. If not for his vision, Niagara would have repeated itself and we would have lost the beauty of those wild places forever.

His life inspired this poem. It is also posted on the Sierra Club's web site as a tribute.

http://www.sierraclub.org/john muir exhibit/life/ thank you john muir poem mp khan.aspx

I am not a tree hugger. But with the climate changes that we are experiencing, there is a real possibility that the great Sequoias which are also the oldest and largest living organisms on the planet may become a memory for our grandchildren.

Join an organization (Sierra Club: www.sierraclub.org is a good one) which is dedicated to protecting our natural resources. Remember that we are interwoven with them and if nature falls, so do we!

What single act, however small or large can you do to preserve the environment?

_____

_____

_____

_____

_____

_____

August 13

CELEBRATING GAIA

SILENCE: *(for a few moments after the end. Glossary to follow poem)*
       Over the banks of the Orinoco, my people the Yanomani,
Have slept for a thousand moons and have woken
To the calls of the living forest Urihi.
What the white Napepe call the Amazon.
       But in two weeks, my son Remori,
We will not roam the wildness and teach you the art
Of the blowgun and the deadly flight of the curare dart
So that, someday, you too may hunt the bounty of Urihi.
       In two weeks, my daughter Smita,
You will not hear the songs of the mountain spirits
That calmed you to sleep at night,
Safe from the panther's growl and the jackal's cry.
       In two weeks from now, my wife, Alara
There will be no more brave tales of my waipe days.
No more will I praise the painted beauty of your body,
Or whisper of our love's passion around the evening fire.
       In two weeks, my people, offspring of Omama
The yakoana visions of the shamans will not protect us.
The smoke-clouds of Yaosi with his army of evil ne-waipe
Will silence the voices of the Yanomani forever.
(For audience recitation)
Every two weeks a language disappears, (repeat)
       A language disappears, (repeat)
         Disappears. (Repeat)

                MK/2006

DR. M. P. KHAN, MD/NMD

August 14

CELEBRATING GAIA

John Muir is celebrated around the world as a reminder that we cannot keep raping Mother Earth or GAIA without having grave consequences for our future survival as a species. Destroy the environment and you run the risk of destroying an entire culture, and eventually the human race. For we intimately connected with and are part of the natural world.

This poem was inspired by a National Geographic special on the Orinoco Indian tribes that live along the Amazon River. Every two weeks, the exploitation of their land for oil, wood and other natural resources destroys an entire culture and its language; a sacrifice to man's avarice.

The native words are authentic and a meager effort to illustrate the beauty of the language. I have included the translations of some of the words. It is essentially a read aloud poem and the last three lines of the poem require audience participation followed by silence for a minute or so!

Napepe=foreigners
Waipe=warrior;
Yakoana=a hallucinogenic plant
Ne-waipe=zombie warriors;
Omama=the creator of the forest and its inhabitants
Yaosi=the destroyer of life

What would your life be like if the English language disappeared?

_____
_____
_____
_____
_____
_____
_____

OF BIRDS AND BEES

*"The world was really one bee yard, and the same rules
work fine in both places. Don't be afraid, as no life-loving
bee wants to sting you. Still, don't be an idiot; wear long
sleeves and pants. Don't swat.
Don't even think about swatting. If you feel angry, whistle.
Anger agitates while whistling melts a bee's temper. Act
like you know what you're doing, even if you don't. Above
all, send the bees love. Every little thing wants to be loved."*
—Sue Monk Kidd

ONCE THERE WERE BEES:

The Earth is sad, her life enraged in heaving pain.
Continual tears overripe, grieving days gone by,
The beaten breast of self, awash in a toxic soup.
Her head is bent, she beckons the seasons,
And a final spring shrugs the strength to grow no more.

Birds urgently call to deaf ears of men;
Sleep walkers, these ugly lords of greed and power.
Failed stewards of nature, they spin on relentless treadmills,
Vertically raping the virgin soil, deaf to her spirit.

The souls of lost bees look on; this year's flower will not seed.
Forsaken beauties, now infertile, empty eyed, wave goodbye.
In memory of forsaken pollen, they shed their grace,
Yielding only sterile fields and trees bereft of fruit.

DR. M. P. KHAN, MD/NMD

The sun broken heartedly, hangs in the sky,
The grand experiment of earth has failed.
All creatures great and small mourn
Of destroyed habitats, impure water, air choking.
Connected to a brighter world, they whisper of paradise lost.

Soon, the last harvest moon this fall will come.
Men will scramble to survive, lost bounties gambled.
Climate will find no friend, and seeds will sell for gold.
Hope will kneel belatedly to hard lessons learnt,
And the grim reaper will claim his karmic due.

KK/2004

OF BIRDS AND BEES

It is mid-summer. By now the garden would be buzzing with the sounds of bees and hummingbirds. In this poem, Karen mourns the avarice of humans and the lack of these creatures that are so critical to our food supply.

Bees are supreme pollinators and if they collapse, there is no technology existing today that can mimic their function. Food prices especially that of fruits and nuts will go through the roof. But there is still hope we will see those winged creatures soon! Karen wrote the above poem and I tweaked it a little.

Find a list of native flowering plants that are bee friendly.

(Google "native plants" for your geographical area).

Go to your local nursery and plant a few in your garden. If you don't have a garden, find a vacant field or place them in containers on your porch.

If you buy potted plants from a local nursery, be sure they are not grown from seeds or in soil treated with a pesticide called neo-nicotinoids. These chemicals actually affect the immune system of bees and may have contributed to the wide spread collapse of bee colonies in North America.

Make a list of the naïve plants in your geographical area and the time of the year to plant them.

_____

_____

_____

_____

_____

_____

_____

_____

August 17

POT POURRI

For the next few days, I want to share with you some pearls about how the mind body approach is used in the healing process. All the recommendations are evidence based and are the results of rigorous peer reviewed studies and I have also included the references so that the next time you meet a skeptical healer, you can share the study with them in a credible way.

Breast cancer and red meat:

Breast cancer is the second leading cause of cancer in the U.S. population and the number one cause of cancer in women. In 2014, around 40,000 deaths occurred due to breast cancer. This study found that women who had an intake of 1.5 servings (6-8 oz.) of red meat per day in early adulthood (though not in midlife) had a 22% increased risk of breast cancer compared to women with the lower intake of 0.14 serving/day. Each extra serving of red meat increased the risk of breast cancer by another 13% in women. Because of the high incidence of breast cancer, dietary intake of red and processed meats may be a significant risk factor.

What is confounding in the study is that: Was the red meat raised in feed lots with cows pumped with antibiotics, hormones and feed containing recycled cow parts and GMO corn heavily sprayed with pesticides? Would there be the same results if the beef was free range and pasture fed?

Processed meat is treated with nitrates as a preservative to keep them fresh and pink looking. They undergo a process called nitrosation which converts them into compounds which are considered "probable human carcinogens" by the International Agency for Cancer Research. Were these compounds responsible for the increased risk?

So here is what I would recommend:

If you have to eat red meat at all, limit it to one or two servings a week. Also eat grass fed free range beef which is also low in fat and cholesterol (10% vs 30% for feed lot beef). I would avoid all processed meat. Switch to a Mediterranean style of eating. This would include EVOO (Extra Virgin Olive Oil), tomatoes, garlic, large amount of greens, whole grain pastas and brown rice and small amount of free range chicken and large amounts of sustainable fish and sardines along with nuts, fruits (dried and fresh) and natural sweeteners such as honey and agave. And if you want to reduce your carbon foot-print further switch to a pesco-vegetarian or a completely vegetarian or vegan diet

REFERENCES

Cho E, et al. Red meat intake and risk of breast cancer among premenopausal women. Arch Intern Med 2006; 166:2253-2259.

DR. M. P. KHAN, MD/NMD

POT POURRI

That yellow spice that everybody is talking about (Turmeric):

In a previous day I discussed the anti-inflammatory properties of turmeric. The researchers in this study wanted to study the analgesic or pain relieving properties of turmeric in osteoarthritis of the knee. This is a synopsis of the study using a polysaccharide component of turmeric rhizome, in the form of the extract HR-INF-02. This was studied in 120 people with moderate osteoarthritis in a placebo-controlled, four-arm, and a 42-day study. The four arms of the study were

1) Placebo; 400mg of cellulose twice/day
2) Turmeric extract HR-INF-02; 500mg twice a day.
3) Glucosamine sulfate; 750 mg twice a day
4) Glucosamine + Turmeric extract as per above doses twice a day.

The group taking only turmeric not only had better improvements, when compared to placebo, in pain severity using three separate scoring systems, but also experienced fewer side effects over the course of the research study.

My recommendation is that turmeric be added to *any* chronic inflammatory condition such as arthritis, Crohn's disease or rheumatoid arthritis without a concern for side effects. I have used it empirically with very satisfying results and patient satisfaction and minimal side effects. There is now some exciting news that turmeric may slow down the progression of dementia of the Alzheimer's type (it is an inflammation of the brain!) if used earlier at disease onset. Make sure to use a high quality formulation as described below.

TURMERIC MAX-V.

FORMULA (#77377) DOUGLAS LABS

1 Vegetarian Capsule Contains:
Turmeric (standardized to 95% curcuminoids) ....100 mg
In a 100 mg base of non-standardized turmeric
TAKE THREE CAPSULE THREE TIMES A DAY WITH FOOD

REFERENCES:

1. Gregory PJ, et al. Dietary supplements for osteoarthritis. Am Fam Physician 2008; 77:177-184.
2. Henrotin Y, et al. Biological actions of curcumin on articular chondrocytes. Osteoarthritis Cartilage 2010; 18:141-149.
3. Dahmer S, Schiller RM. Glucosamine. Am Fam Physician 2008; 78:471-476?

DR. M. P. KHAN, MD/NMD

August 19

POT POURRI

Those precocious probiotics:

URTI: This was a study to determine if a daily intake of a single strain probiotic supplement (Bl-04) was associated with a decreased risk of upper respiratory tract infections (URTI) in healthy adults. This was a 150-day study (randomized, double-blind, placebo controlled trial) RCT of 465 healthy adult volunteers (mean age 37 years old). The study was done in three groups.

1. *Bifidobacterium animalis* subsp. *lactis* Bl-04 (2 x 10^9 cfu/day);
2. *Lactobacillus acidophilus* NCFM and *Bifidobacterium animalis* subsp. *lactis*
3. Placebo.

   At the end of the study, participants taking the Bl-04 had about a 27% reduction in risk of URTI compared to the placebo group. There was no significant difference in the number of URTIs between the NCFM/Bi-07 group and the placebo group although interestingly, both probiotic supplement regimens were associated with a delay in time to a URTI of approximately 3 weeks compared to placebo. My recommendation is to find yogurt or take probiotic capsules with Bifidobacterium on a regular basis. *REFERENCES: Hao Q, et al. Probiotics for preventing acute upper respiratory tract infections. Cochrane Database Syst Rev 2011; CD006895. doi: 10.1002/14651858.CD006895.pub2.*

BLOOD PRESSURE: This was a meta-analysis (where several existing studies are placed in mathematical model and the finding compared and the results reviewed) of nine clinical trials was completed to determine the effect of probiotics on blood pressure. The total number of participants was 543 and the included studies were all RCT.

Of the nine studies, three included healthy participants. Two included patients with hypercholesterolemia. One included patients with hypertension. One included overweight and obese subjects. One included patients with metabolic syndrome.10 billion cfu to 100 billion cfu of single and multiple strains of probiotics were used with various delivery systems such as yoghurt, sour milk and kefir with a duration ranging from three to nine weeks.

Eight of the studies reported a lowering of systolic blood pressure (SBP) with a mean reduction ranging from 1.07 to 14.10 mmHg. Results in lowering systolic blood pressure were better with multiple strains and longer duration of the study. There was no significant impact on diastolic BP. Participants with a blood pressure greater than 130/85 were more likely to show significant improvement compared to those with BP less than 130/85. REFERENCES: *Khalesi S, et al. Effect of probiotics on blood pressure: A systematic review and meta-analysis of randomized, controlled trials. Hypertension 2014; 10.1161/HYPERTENSIONAHA.114.03469.*

DR. M. P. KHAN, MD/NMD

August 20

POT POURRI

I would recommend a good quality yogurt or kefir (both organic) to mix this supplement with as the yogurt/kefir improves the delivery of the below probiotic that I feel delivers a good mix:

MULTI PROBIOTIC-40 BILLION

FORMULA (#57649P [powder], 202115 [v. capsule]) DOUGLAS LABS

Proprietary Blend...............40 Billion CFU

Short Chain Fructooligosaccharide (NutraFlora®; FOS®), *Bifidobacterium bifidum, Bifidobacterium breve, Bifidobacterium lactis (infantis), Bifidobacterium lactis HN019,*

Bifidobacterium longum, Lactobacillus acidophilus, Lactobacillus brevis, Lactobacillus bulgaricus, Lactobacillus casei, Lactobacillus gasseri, Lactobacillus paracasei, Lactobacillus plantarum, Lactobacillus rhamnosus, Lactobacillus salivarius, Lactococcus lactis, Streptococcus thermophilus

Multi-Probiotic contains 16 potent strains of Lactobacillus, Bifidobacterium, and Streptococcus cultures, including the clinically researched Bifidobacterium lactis HN019 that supports enhanced gastrointestinal and immune function. Also included in the symbiotic blend, is FOS® prebiotic fiber that is well tolerated and works synergistically (a prebiotic) with probiotics to flourish the intestinal tract. These Probiotics are acid and bile resistant and undergo a patented cyroprotectant stabilization process for shelf stability.

Capsules: Adults take 2 capsules daily or as directed by a healthcare professional. May gradually increase to 4 daily.

Powder: Adults take 1/2 teaspoon daily or as directed by a healthcare professional. May be increased to 1 teaspoon daily. Mix in unheated liquids (yogurt/kefir) or sprinkle on room-temperature food.

CAUTION: Consult a healthcare professional before use if you are immune-compromised.

SIDE EFFECTS: START SLOWLY to avoid symptoms such as gas, bloating and diarrhea may occur in sensitive individuals. To minimize these effects, start at 1 capsule or 1/4 tsp powder daily and gradually increase over time.

STORAGE

Store in a cool, dry place, away from direct light. After opening, keep refrigerated with lid tightly sealed for optimal results. Keep out of reach of children.

August 21

POT POURRI

Meditation OR Medication:

A research group conducted a small study of blood biochemical and gene markers associated with stress in convenience samples of experienced 19 meditators and 21 non-meditator controls. Certain blood cells called monocytes were separated out and used for assessment of (for all the technophile readers of this book) cytosolic proteins, histones (precursors of chromatin), and for genetic analysis (specifically, the following genes: HDAC1/2/3/5/9, SIRT1, SET7, G9a, LSD1, DNMT3A, RIPK2, CCR7, CXCR1, and genes controlling expression of COX2, IL-6, and TNF-α) *All you need to know is that they are blood markers for inflammation.* Saliva samples were also collected before and during the study and used to assess how quickly the cortisol (which is also a stress hormone) returned to base line.

Selection was based on meditation experience of at least 3 years and 30 minutes or more of daily meditation, and completion of at least three retreats of at least 5 days each in the last three years. For the study, the meditators completed a 1-day intensive program that drew extensively on the mindfulness-based stress reduction program developed by Jon Kabat-Zinn (which included both sitting and walking meditation). Also there were inspirational talks and a healthy lunch along with a video on "mindful eating". The control group participated in a program of the same time frame that included reading, watching documentaries, playing computer games, and walking. Neither group had access to electronic devices or the Internet, or other external distractions.

The result of the study at the end of 24 weeks showed that the meditators had more favorable changes than the controls (an average reduction of 17% vs an average increase of 3%) in the decreased expression of some epigenetic markers of chromatin modification of the genes that produce the inflammatory markers mentioned above. They also showed a quicker recovery of the saliva cortisol to base line.

The only flaw in the study was that the study groups were seasoned meditators and it is hard to evaluate if they already had the skills to lower their markers. It would have been more meaningful if they had measured the markers of Type A personalities before and after training them in meditation techniques to demonstrate the true impact of meditation.

But having said that, the above study still proves the value of a meditative practice. And besides the reduction in stress markers, meditation has been shown to reduce the risk of heart disease, improve cognition in dementia, reduce your risk of getting the common cold and improve the symptoms of menopause. So sit down in a quiet place, turn off your PC and cell phone and anything else that could distract you, close your eyes and let your thoughts come and go. Set a timer for 5 minutes and gradually over a few weeks increase to 20 minutes. Do the practice twice a day and I promise you that you will see some really positive benefits.

August 22

POT POURRI

All about cocoa and cognition:

A group of 41 healthy but sedentary 50- to 69-year-old subjects were randomly assigned to four groups.

1) High dietary flavanols (900 mg cocoa flavanols and 138 mg of epicatechin per day) and active exercise.
2) High dietary flavanols and no exercise,
3) Low dietary flavanols (10 mg cocoa flavanols and < 2 mg epicatechin per day) and active exercise,
4) Low dietary flavanols and no exercise for duration of 12 weeks.

Active exercise consisted of 1-hour exercise sessions, including 40 minutes of aerobic activity four times a week. Exercise was performed at a target heart rate of 65-80% of maximal heart rate. The study was blinded to observers and the participants. What the observers were looking for were changes in a part of the hippocampus (the sea horse shaped structure in the brain which is responsible for processing memory) called the dentate gyrus. Aging causes decline in the functional activity of the dentate gyrus, a change that can be measured by functional MRI imaging (like a regular MRI but tagged markers are injected intravenously and are taken up by various parts of the brain and these are imaged by the MRI scanner)

In order to measure cognition, The BVRT or Benton Visual Retention Test was used to see how fast the dentate gyrus would respond. Normally BVRT reaction time worsens with aging so this could be an indirect way to measure changes in cognition (memory, recall etc.) At the end of 12 weeks it was found that the high cocoa flavanol group independent of exercise (above groups 1 & 2) was 1997 milliseconds (faster) compared to 2627(slower) milliseconds of the low flavanol groups 3) & 4). Since the BVRT times normally worsen by 220 milliseconds every decade of life lived, the improvement was *an incredible reversal comparable to 2-3 decades or thirty years of aging.*

Since flavonoids are bitter they are usually processed out of chocolate. A good rule of thumb is that old adage; you can have any color of chocolate as long as it is DARK! (70% and higher cacao content.) In fact the more bitter the chocolate, the better it is for you.

For example, chocolate syrup has 26mg of flavanols per serving while baking chocolate has 227 mg per serving. Four servings of the latter would replicate the above study. Beside the cardiovascular benefit of eating chocolate, this finding is one more delicious reason to add it to your daily snacking and to add it as a supplement in the management of dementia.

August 23

POT POURRI

No need to be abusive, MTHFR:

Every time you turn on the news, there is some talking head scientist rapturing on the new era of genetic testing. How in the future, your physician will know if you will have a response to a drug just by reading your genome. Although this scenario is soon to be a reality, a more common use of gene testing is for SNP or Single Nucleotide Polymorphisms. These are very small defects on the gene which can have significant consequences on human health.

One of the most common testing for SNP is for a polymorphism or gene defect called MTHFR or a mouthful: Methyl Tetra Hydro Folate Reductase. This is an enzyme that converts homocysteine to folate. It is usually suspected when a routine blood test shows a high platelet count, the patient has repeated episodes of venous blood clots (DVT) or a woman has frequent miscarriages and there may be an elevated plasma homocysteine level and a low folate level.

At first there was also the theory that a high homocysteine level increased the risk for heart disease but there is currently some controversy about this finding. The two most common polymorphic variants that affect enzyme activity are the C677T and the A1298C variants and these are the most common ones tested for by labs in the U.S. There are also 34 rare and somewhat harmful mutations and genetic SNP testing for these is not widely available. Similar copies of the gene or homozygous have a 70% reduction in MTHFR activity and will have a high homocysteine level. Dissimilar or heterozygous will have 35% reduction in MTHFR activity and will have a normal homocysteine level. There is an increased risk for a woman with homozygous expression having a child with a neural tube defect because of a lack of folic acid and also an increased risk of venous blood clots in men and women

But before you run to your physician and insist on this test, it is usually an out of pocket (and expensive) expense. Instead ask your physician to check your Folate and Homocysteine level. (Low and High in MTHFR SNP respectively). This can be easily correctable by adding supplemental folate 200ug of 5-MTHF (see below) and 200ug of folic acid) daily irrespective of the MTHFR genotype (homo or heterozygous) and then rechecking levels of folic acid and homocysteine in 6-8 weeks. Also supplementation with Betaine which is a methyl donor will also help.

5MTHF

FORMULA (#201181) DOUGLAS LABS

Folate.......................... .... 1,000 mcg

(L-methylfolate, Metafolin®)

One capsule daily, do not exceed more than 5000 mg a day.

August 24

POT POURRI

"There's a lot of blood, sweat, and guts
between dreams and success."
—**Paul Bryant**

The praises of Kefir:

So what is Kefir?
A wonder food for your gut, it was discovered in ancient times when nomadic shepherds in the Caucasus Mountains of Eastern Europe found that the milk they carried in leather sacks occasionally fermented into a bubbly drink. It's kind of like yogurt, the obvious difference between the two is that Kefir is drinkable and contains much more variety (sometimes up to 8-10 *vs* yogurt which has 2-4) of the friendly bacteria known as "probiotics." Its name originates from the Turkish word "Keif" meaning "good feeling" which is experienced after drinking it.

And how is it made?
Kefir can only be produced from dairy and cannot be made out of non-dairy bases such as water, fruit juices, teas, and coconut water, soy milk and almond milk. There is no such product as "nondairy Kefir." The fermentation of milk is triggered by Kefir "grains," consisting of various species of symbiotic healthy and nonpathogenic (safe) bacteria and yeast. Bacteria ferment lactose, the sugar found in milk; yeasts perform alcohol fermentation, producing negligible amounts of alcohol. The resulting drink has a pleasantly tangy taste which bubbles on the tongue.

Where can I buy kefir "grains"?
If you are my patient, I will be happy to share my stock of kefir "grains" with you. They are actually clumps of the healthy bacteria called probiotics which I have discussed in several topics in the past few days. You can also buy the "grains" from Amazon (or if you live in the Berkshires; at

Guido's grocery) and is actually a one-time purchase. Basically as long as you keep making Kefir by adding it to milk, (see below) the culture line is 'immortal.'

And how do I make Kefir?
Take a tablespoon (always use plastic spoons as metal spoons can affect the taste) of the kefir grains and mix them with whole or low fat organic milk (do not use skim) in an 8 oz. canning jar and cover it loosely with a square of muslin cloth. Do not place a tight lid on the jar as there is production of carbon dioxide in the fermentation process and the culture needs to 'breathe.' Let the jar sit overnight at least 8-10 hours in a relatively warm space (75F-85 F). The fermented milk will tend to separate out over a relatively clear liquid at the bottom. Mix thoroughly the contents of the jar with a plastic spoon. Pour out ¾ of the contents of the jar into a large glass. I usually add salt and pepper to the contents of the glass, use a hand blender to whip up the somewhat clumpy kefir contents of the glass and drink it immediately.

Add more milk to the jar until full, mix well with the kefir at the bottom of the jar with a plastic spoon and cover the jar for the next day and *repeat the process forever.* (Also available as a You Tube video if you need more visual instructions.

DR. M. P. KHAN, MD/NMD

August 25

CONCERNING KRISHNAMURTI

"Freedom and love go together. Love is not a reaction. If I love you because you love me, that is mere trade, a thing to be bought in the market; it is not love. To love is not to ask anything in return, not even to feel that you are giving something- and it is only such love that can know freedom."
—Jiddu Krishnamurti

Jiddu Krishnamurti was born in British India on 12 May 1895 and died on 17 February 1986 In early adolescence, he had a chance meeting with the theosophist and mystic, Charles Webster Leadbeater in the grounds of the Theosophical Society headquarters at Adyar in Chennai (Madras) who saw a very pure aura around him. He was an Indian speaker and writer on philosophical and spiritual matters. In his early life he was groomed to be the new World Teacher. Later after the death of his beloved brother, he rejected this destiny and disbanded the organization behind it. His subject matter included psychological revolution, the nature of mind, meditation, inquiry, human relationships, and bringing about radical change in society. He constantly stressed the need for freedom in the psychology of every human being.

He came to the U.S. as a young man and settled in Ojai, California. He claimed allegiance to no nationality, caste, religion, or philosophy, and spent the rest of his life travelling the world, speaking to groups of all sizes and individuals and was emphatic that a guru was not necessary for seeking the truth. He wrote many books, among them "The First and Last Freedom" which I will be quoting and explaining extensively in the form of questions over the next few days.

Many of his talks and discussions have been published and he was widely read by luminaries such as Aldous Huxley, Nehru and the Dali Lama. When I was living in Bombay, I had the good fortune of listening to one of his talks in the early seventies on leading the spiritual life. His last public talk was in Chennai, India, in January 1986. He died a month later at his home in Ojai.

WHAT ARE WE SEEKING? Krishnamurti asks this question of us. He feels that most of us want in a world full of strife and war, is a small measure of peace and happiness! And like Birbal in the above parable, he asks whether we are seeking gratification or happiness. Truth be told, most of us are actually seeking an ends to a mean; that is gratification. Are we actually seeking permanent pleasure or the ultimate truth? And where do we seek this? From self-help books, an organization we can belong to, a guru who can give us the answers we seek?

CONCERNING KRISHNAMURTI

His answer is an emphatic NO. This happiness we seek cannot be given by someone else. It is only through our own self-knowledge and experience of who we really are can we come to this point of ultimate truth. This sounds very simple but is extremely difficult. For it requires a complete awareness of our relationship to ourselves, others and to our environment. And to do this we need to live in the moment so that we can be aware of the moment. And this means getting out of automatic thoughts and rituals that the ego loves and seeking tranquility by daily meditation on the nature of our self. Only by taking the time for self-reflection can we come to that place of inner bliss.

What are you actually seeking? Gratification or Happiness? How do you tell the difference?

_____

_____

_____

How will you bring awareness to yourself?

_____

_____

_____

How will you bring awareness to your relationships?

_____

_____

_____

How will you bring awareness to your environment?

_____

_____

_____

How do you plan to live in the moment?

_____

_____

_____

August 27

CONCERNING KRISHNAMURTI

"You must understand the whole of life, not just one little part of it. That is why you must read, that is why you must look at the skies; that is why you must sing and dance, and write poems and suffer and understand, for all that is life."
—Jiddu Krishnamurti

WHO IS THE CREATOR OF OUR PROBLEMS?

We live in a society full of complex problems related to race and religion and resources. One only has to turn on the 6 pm news to see the depth that human beings and society has devolved to. Would it not be nice to know the cause of our problems? Who is responsible for these issues that we face on a daily basis? Of course the answer is obvious. It is not a government or a religious body or some far-fetched international conspiracy. According to Krishnamurti, "the creator of these problems is the individual, *you and I*, not the world as we think of it."

The only way to transform the world is to begin the change on a personal level. Only by transforming ourselves can we transform the world. In other words a personal revolution. Not a revolution of right leaning or left leaning political values but a personal revolution. And in order to do that, we must first understand what makes us tick. We need to have an intimate knowledge of self. We need to first understand our prejudices and weaknesses. Then we can have a starting point from which change can begin.

Once again he exhorts us that self-knowledge cannot be given by others and is not found in a book or from a guru. If you are full of greed and envy and do not know it, what use is it to talk about peace and non-violence and generosity of spirit? They just remain empty words. But to be aware that one is full of greed and envy requires considerable courage and honesty. It is the true beginning of transformation to non-greed and

DR. M. P. KHAN, MD/NMD

altruism. Knowing yourself is the beginning of virtue. Only in virtue is there true freedom.

But he cautions us. There is a difference in being virtuous and becoming virtuous. The former is through the understanding of what *is*. The latter is postponement, the covering up of what *is* with what you would like to be. But to understand what *is* according to him is very difficult for it is always in a state of movement, never standing still. It cannot conform to a certain ideal as it would then be fixed or married to that ideal. To understand what *is* one must observe how one feels and thinks from moment to moment. To have a state of mind where there is no judgment or condemnation, a mind that is fully alert and yet fully passive.

And to understand what *is*, we cannot follow a system or a guru for the end result will be a product of the system or the teachings of the guru. Therefore there is no one method of self-knowledge. In conclusion, the understanding of oneself is not an end point; it is the result of seeing ourselves from moment to moment in the mirror of our relationships to things and people.

August 28

CONCERNING KRISHNAMURTI

"In oneself lies the whole world and if you know how to look and learn, the door is there and the key is in your hand. Nobody on earth can give you either the key or the door to open, except yourself."
—Jiddu Krishnamurti

Name a few things that are the negative aspects of your nature.

_____

_____

_____

_____

_____

Take each one separately and write down how you will begin the transformation towards a more virtuous self.

_____

_____

_____

_____

_____

DR. M. P. KHAN, MD/NMD

CONCERNING KRISHNAMURTI

"When you call yourself an Indian or a Muslim or a Christian or a European, or anything else, you are being violent. Do you see why it is violent? Because you are separating yourself from the rest of mankind. When you separate yourself by belief, by nationality, by tradition, it breeds violence. So a man who is seeking to understand violence does not belong to any country, to any religion, to any political party or partial system; he is concerned with the total understanding of mankind."

—**Jiddu Krishnamurti**

Krishnamurti believes that it is belief that separates us from each other and which causes intolerance for others and breeds violence to those who do not share the same belief system as ours. So he makes a very radical suggestion;

"To live without any belief system at all!"

You might ask how this is possible. But if we have no belief, what will happen to us? If we had no basis to our actions based on dogma or what we are conditioned to, will we not be utterly lost? He makes the case that if you are free from all beliefs, then you will meet each situation anew from moment to moment and without any expectations based on past belief systems so that there is nothing that comes between you and what *is*.

And now he makes a brilliant insight:

"Belief is based on fear."

A mind empty of belief is like an empty cup. Try putting more liquid in a full cup. It will overflow and make a mess. It is the fear of the empty cup that we fill our minds with assertions and quotations and past experiences that color our actions. And these belief systems act as a screen in the process of understanding ourselves and also others. How much richer and full of wonder our lives would be (and of our relationships) if we always kept our cup empty.

> *"Another side of belief is knowledge. Is knowledge necessary to understand truth? Or is it an obstruction to knowing truth?"*

When you say "I know" it is the same as saying "I believe." What is it that we actually know? In fact our knowledge is based once again on our readings and indoctrinations and what our experiences (or our interpretation of our experiences) have made us know or believe in. And in the end it is knowledge and belief that stand in the way of love and compassion for our fellow beings.

> *"So you should always carry an empty cup!"*

DR. M. P. KHAN, MD/NMD

August 30

CONCERNING KRISHNAMURTI

*"The moment you have in your heart this extraordinary
thing called love and feel the depth, the delight, the
ecstasy of it, you will discover that for you the world is
transformed."*
—Jiddu Krishnamurti

*Write down your feelings (agree or disagree) of the above statements in
italics from the topic of August 29.*

_____

_____

_____

_____

_____

_____

_____

_____

_____

_____

_____

_____

_____

_____

_____

_____

_____

_____

_____

_____

_____

August 31

AND NOW FOR SSOMETHING DIFFERENT

<u>A SSERPENT'S SSORROW:</u>

(A poem best read aloud and ssee if you can find any of the 'ss' words I missed)

Whereass most animalss thank their maker
I for one would like to meet that joker!
He made critterss warm and cuddly, and even a whale.
As for me, I was cursed with a forked tongue and sslithering sscales.
They were blesssed with flipperss to sswim and armss to hold.
All I got was a venomouss bite and a blood that runss cold.
You have to admit, Creator, that'ss quite a bummer,
Oopss! Ssorry. Forgot! I don't' have a bum either!!

Whereas most animals thank their maker
I for one would like to meet that joker!
Consider them forbidden appless in the Garden of Eden,
I sore got a bum rap by you know who, for them being eaten.
Really! It wass Eve that tempted Adam, that husssy.
Though a beauty, it wass how sshe flashed her p.......!
Oopss! Ssorry again! Forgot I am in mixed company,
(You know the female anatomy that rhymess with 'husssy')

Whereass most animalss thank their maker
I for one would like to meet that joker!
Just to be funny, he created uss, 3000 or sso, in quite a variety,
The Cobra's dance will hypnotize you, ass you forget your mortality.
And when you get to know my buddiess, we are not all thugss,
My coussin, the Boa constrictor; can give you quite an affectionate hug.
And a Rattler will sshake her tail for you, sshe has quite a beat,
Look ma, no armss! Swallowing our meal whole iss quite a feat.

‹430›   DR. M. P. KHAN, MD/NMD

Whereass most animalss thank their maker
I for one would like to meet that joker!
But it's not all bad newss and terrorss and, rumorss ssalacious,
Ass a symbol of healing, wrapped around an sstaff, it'ss called a Caduceuss.
And once I was an ssymbol of America, home of the brave, land of the free,
Coiled on a flag of the early Coloniess that read "Don't tread on Me!"
So next time you come acrosss a ssnake in the grasss, don't' be coy,
Come on over, (I don't bite, really) I promisse to be nisce, and ssay- "Hi!"

MK 04/2013

SEPTEMBER

1-Sep	A NEW RESOLUTION (PART-1) Mr. Smith goes to York.
2-Sep	A NEW RESOLUTION (PART-1) The PAFP and Resolution # 3.
3-Sep	A NEW RESOLUTION (PART-2) Taking an environmental history.
4-Sep	A NEW RESOLUTION (PART-2) Biomonitoring and the CDC.
5-Sep	SUPER FOOD, SUPER SMART. Mrs. Fields has a request.
6-Sep	SUPER FOOD, SUPER SMART. All about how food makes us smart.
7-Sep	SUPER FOOD, SUPER SMART. All about Newton, Einstein and Hawkings.
8-Sep	SUPER FOOD, SUPER SMART. And some reading material.
9-Sep	SUPER FOOD, SUPER SMART. Meditation, Yoga and Tia Chi.
10-Sep	SUPER FOOD, SUPER SMART. Some definitions and core concepts.
11-Sep	3000 LIVES. Remembering that day of infamy.
12-Sep	SUPER FOOD, SUPER SMART. Not just nutrition, Food is information.
13-Sep	SUPER FOOD, SUPER SMART. All about BDNF and a recipe.
14-Sep	SUPER FOOD, SUPER SMART. How to increase BDNF and another recipe.
15-Sep	SUPER FOOD, SUPER SMART. The Aliens have already invaded.
16-Sep	SUPER FOOD, SUPER SMART. The Gut Brain connection and RA.
17-Sep	SUPER FOOD, SUPER SMART. To treat diseases using probiotics.
18-Sep	SUPER FOOD, SUPER SMART. Inflammation and the MGBA.
19-Sep	SUPER FOOD, SUPER SMART. Antibiotics and the MGBA and dessert.
20-Sep	SUPER FOOD, SUPER SMART. Must Eat Foods: Fermented
21-Sep	SUPER FOOD, SUPER SMART. Health benefits of Fermented Foods
22-Sep	SUPER FOOD, SUPER SMART. Turmeric and its Benefits.
23-Sep	CELEBRATING AN EQUINOX. My gold and crimson hues!
24-Sep	CELEBRATING AN EQUINOX. Some personal reflections.
25-Sep	SUPER FOOD, SUPER SMART. Sea Food, Beef (Grass Fed)Eggs(Free Range)
26-Sep	SUPER FOOD, SUPER SMART. Must Eat: The bliss of Dark Chocolate.
27-Sep	SUPER FOOD, SUPER SMART. Broccoli, Blueberries & Vi.t D & a Smoothie!
28-Sep	ANOTHER LOVE POEM. Flying the Garuda.
29-Sep	IT AIN'T (NEW YORK). The resolution of the Resolution.
30-Sep	AND A HEINOUS CRIME OF LOVE. Not so loud, please.

DR. M. P. KHAN, MD/NMD

September 1

A NEW RESOLUTION (PART-1)

"It is useless for the sheep to pass resolutions
in favor of vegetarianism, while the wolf remains
of a different opinion."
—William Ralph Inge

Five years ago to this day I submitted a resolution. The eventual failure of this resolution was one of the reasons we moved to the Berkshires. More on that later. Returning to that day, I was planning a trip to York in the eastern part of Pennsylvania. It reminded me of the movie "Mr. Smith goes to Washington" where this unassuming man (me) takes on big government. (Harrisburg). I had always prided myself in being apolitical, like the Swiss. But this time, the issues were too hard to ignore. I had lived close to thirty four years in this state and they had been good years. Two wonderful kids, a good second marriage, and professional satisfaction, combined with relatively close access to nature and the big city culture of small city Pittsburgh.

But this way of life was under imminent threat. Human greed had subverted common sense. Everyday there was news of environmental disasters which had caused irreversible damage to our health and our way of life. In just the previous week, there was a large spill of toxic waste water from fracking (hydraulic fracturing, a drilling process used in the extraction of natural gas from shale) into the river system of Bradford County. And the list kept growing. From personal tragedies to accidents which affect entire communities. And the reality was that with the application of modern drilling techniques and with state of the art waste water disposal, these catastrophes could largely be avoided. But that would impact their bottom line of profits

So with the assistance of the PAFP (Pennsylvania Academy of Family Practice) I had drafted a resolution (see next page) that I would present when the representatives of the PAFP next met. The irony that York was only a short drive away from Harrisburg (the state capital) with a Governor (Corbett) willing to bend over backward for the natural gas industry, and whose party received close to a million dollars in campaign contributions from the same industry, was not lost on me.

During my presentation, I had already seen a ground swell of interest from physicians from the Bradford County which had been directly impacted from the violations of fracking. The NY Academy of Family Practice has already called for a moratorium on drilling until the health and environmental hazards have been studied more thoroughly. And New York had listened. Eight million people get there drinking water from the Delaware water shed and they understood the consequences if this precious resource was contaminated. Maybe all States should adopt that approach that NY had. (As of this publication, it has been banned in NY). Prove to the people who lived and worked in PA and other states that the process was safe and that there were safeguards built in before granting drilling permits! Instead it was and still is the other way around as was seen in Bradford County where Chesapeake Gas had stopped drilling operations because of the spill it was responsible for. *Somebody left the gate open and the horse had already left the stable!*

September 2

A NEW RESOLUTION (PART-1)

RESOLUTION NUMBER 3: THE PUBLIC HEALTH IMPACT OF GAS FRACKING FROM MARCELLUS SHALE.

AUTHOR: Mehernosh Khan MD

WHEREAS, the PAFP has a mission to assume a leadership role in issues that may impact public health, and also to increase the awareness of members and patients on these issues, a

WHEREAS, the PAFP supports cost effective, public health initiatives that can be implemented with low cost educational programs, and

WHEREAS, the health impact of chemicals released by the by products of the gas fracking process on air and water will adversely impact the health of our patients, families and communities as per the CHEC presentation on the health impact of gas fracking/ Dr Volz /UPMC, and

WHEREAS, family physicians by virtue of education and in their role as patient advocates, will be in a unique position to recognize and treat these health effects, and

WHEREAS, the PAFP and its members recognizing these effects on public health, will advise and interface with appropriate government and environmental agencies and make necessary recommendations. Therefore, be it

RESOLVED, the PAFP actively promote educational programs to educate the membership in recognizing and treating the health effects of chemicals released in the environment by the gas fracking process through continuing medical education programs and its communication tool such as its magazine and newsletter. Be it further,

RESOLVED, the PAFP, with information and feedback received from its members, will advise and interface with appropriate government and environmental agencies with timely data related to these effects.

Later I will share with you the final outcome of this resolution. It was disappointing but predictable. It was not adopted because members of the board felt it was too premature to be endorsing it and it really was not a problem * at this time.

*The real irony is that the residents of Western Massachusetts, me included, as of the writing of this second day of September, are fighting the presence of a high pressure pipeline that will transport fracked gas from Pennsylvania! And the residents of PA are finally realizing the health and environmental impact of uncontrolled hydro fracking.

September 3

A NEW RESOLUTION (PART-2)

*"Be stirring as the time, be fire with fire, threaten the
threatener, and outface the brow of bragging horror; so
shall inferior eyes, that borrow their behaviours from the
great, grow great by your example and put on the dauntless
spirit of resolution."*
—**Shakespeare from "King Lear"**

After the presentation of 'The Resolution', frankly, I was concerned
that I would be trivialized and dismissed as another Chicken Little or
even worse, a trouble-maker that would be making the already busy
and stressed out family physician deal with questions about the patient's
environmental exposure. On the other hand, I can't help feeling that it
may make us better physicians and advocates for the health and the well-
being of our patients.

So I have put together a list of questions that physicians can ask (or
you can ask them yourself). Knowing the time constraints that we operate
in, it is a very short list. These questions may give you or your physician
important clues in diagnosing conditions that usually do not fit the usual
medical template and especially in chronic disease states.

ENVIRONMENTAL HISTORY QUESTIONS:

1) *What occupations/ jobs that you have held continuously for more than 1yr
   since you graduated from high school?*
2) *What hobbies do you have besides your job?*
3) *Are you concerned currently about exposure to toxins or chemicals in your
   food, air, or water in your home or work place?*
4) *Did you notice a recent change in your health that defies diagnosis and cannot
   be explained by conventional medical testing?*

5) *Did you notice a change in your internal environment (new carpeting, a faulty furnace) or your external environment (oil or gas drilling nearby, a chemical or coke/coal plant) which coincided with your illness?*

6) *Have you seen a pattern of illnesses in your friends, family members and neighbors (a higher incidence of cancers, birth defects, heart attacks) or other unexplainable illnesses?*

DR. M. P. KHAN, MD/NMD

A NEW RESOLUTION (PART-2)

If you suspect that you may have exposure, there is testing available through the CDC called bio monitoring where almost 450 chemicals can be tested from small samples of blood and urine. It is fairly expensive and it may be a good idea to check with your health insurance company about coverage. Below is the web address to read an excellent article on this subject and to get more information related to this.

http://www.cdc.gov/biomonitoring/pdf/AS_article_biomonitoring.pdf

Also some references to landmark studies that the above article was based on:

Bibliography:

DeCaprio, A. P. 1997. Biomarkers: coming of age for environmental health and risk assessment. *Environmental Science* & *Technology* 31:1837-1848. Mendelsohn, M. L., j. P.

Peeters and M. J. Normandy, eds. 1995. *Biomarkers and Occupational Health: Progress and Perspectives.* Washington, IX: joseph Henry Press. Mendelsohn, M. L., L. C. Mohr and j. P.

Peeters, eds. 1998. *Biomarkers: Medical and Workplace Applications.* Washington, DC: joseph Henry Press. Needham, L. L., and K. Sexton. 20C10.

Assessing children's exposure to hazardous environmental chemicals: An overview of selected research challenges and complexities. *Journal of Exposure Analysis and Environmental Epidemiology* 10 (Part 2):611-629.

Needham, L. L., D. C. Patterson, Jr., V. W. Burse, D. C. Paschal, W. E. Turner and R. H. Hill, Jr. 1996. Reference range data for assessing exposure to selected environmental toxicants. *Toxicology and Industrial Health* 12:507-513. Pirkle, J. L., E. J.

Sampson, L. L. Need ham, D. G. Patterson, Jr., and O. L. Ashley. 1995. Using biological monitoring to assess human exposure to priority toxicants. *Environmental Health Perspectives* 103 (supplement 3):45-48.

DR. M. P. KHAN, MD/NMD

September 5

SUPER-FOODS; SUPER-SMART

"When life gives you weeds (dandelions) in your garden,
make a salad!"

—Chairman Moo

I was looking forward to my appointment with Mrs. Fields and I knew that she really enjoyed the office visits as she always came up with questions to try to stump me; and occasionally she did. So I was perplexed when she accused me of not sharing some very important information with me. It went something like this:

"Doc, you are keeping something from me!"

"I'm sorry Mrs. Fields, but I am not sure what you are talking about?"

"I heard you have a list of foods that can make you sharp and smart. I want it. Also could you give the talk to the gals at the Garden Club?"

I remembered then that Mrs. Fields niece worked at the psych department of the hospital and recently I had given Grand Rounds at the Department of Psychiatry titled "Super-Foods for Super-Cognition." There was no refusing Mrs. Fields as she would threaten to shut off the office supply of her cookies which in turn would have created a minor rebellion in the staff. So one Saturday afternoon I showed up at her Garden Club with my projector and the power point presentation of the above topic.

Over the next few weeks of the daybook we will explore the slides with some work book assignments; so enjoy the show. This is a large and sometimes complicated topic and necessitated it being spread out over several days. Below is the title slide. The rest of the slides follow on subsequent days.

SUPER FOODS FOR SUPER COGNITION

M.P.KHAN MD/NMD

SUPER-FOODS; SUPER-SMART

WHAT KIND OF A VORE ARE YOU?

CARNI-VORE=All animal based products.

HIGH CARBON-VORE= Produce from big chain grocery stores.

HERBI-VORE=Nothing with legs or eyes except potatoes and sometimes dairy.

GUIDO-VORE= Fruits, vegetables and dairy from

local smaller family owned groceries.

LOC-AVORE= Fruits, vegetables from farmer's markets and roadside stands.

HOME AVORE= The best option

HIGH-CARBON-avore means you shop at large chain grocery stores where a tomato may have travelled a thousand miles (and a high carbon foot-print) to get to the store.

GUIDO-avore is an inside joke as there is a popular family grocery store by that name where they sell locally grown and organic food, and is a popular shopping destination.

LOC-avore is a term for shopping at local farmer's market and road side stands.

HOME-avore should be our ultimate goal growing and eating food FRESH from our own backyard!

A PSYCHIATRIST'S SHOPPING LIST

Asparagus Syndrome.

Corn Addiction Disorder

Manioc-Depressive

Peasonality Disorder

Swiss-Cheesicidal

Brie-Polar Disorder\

Re-Freud Beans

This is a shopping list and a play on words for various psychiatric conditions. See if you can figure them out?

ASPERGER'S=Asparagus

PORN=Corn

MANIC=Manioc

PERS=Peas

CHEESICIDAL= Suicidal

BRIE= Bi

RE-FREUD=Re-Fried

SOME DEFINITONS

FOODS: What we buy in a grocery store.

NUTRACEUTICALS: What the FDA considers most herbals and supplements.

AYURVEDA: What we eat and everything we Perceive as nourishment for the "body and soul."

As you can see Ayurveda has a more expanded definition of "food" and perceives all input as nourishment. The physical food that we eat is like what our eyes see, our ears hear and our nose smell; in other words 'information."

Nutraceuticals is a broad term covering all supplements such as herbs (gingko), proprietary preparations (Co Q 10), and vitamins (Vitamin D.) It does not apply to complex herbal preparations found in Traditional Chinese Medicine TCM and in Ayurvedic Medicine.

MORE DEFINITIONS.

COGNITION as per Webster.
per Webs Conscious mental activity, the activity of Thinking, understanding, learning and Remembering AND imagination and Creativity.

I have added imagination and creativity to the definition. If cognition is what makes us human, then lab rats can possibly fulfil the first part of the definition but no lab rat is going to wake up some day and manifest as Michelangelo or Mozart!

TOOLS TO MEASURE COGNITION.

OFFICE: MMSE. Mini-Cog, Clock Drawing

NEURO-PSYCH TESTING: Mattis, Boston

Naming Test, Constructional Praxis.

MRI: Focal Anatomical Deficits, Cortical thickness

And Hippocampal morphology.

FUNCTIONAL MRI, SPECT, PET: Metabolic activity and synaptic delays.

There are several office based and imaging tools we can use of which the functional MRI is the most objective way of measuring cognition when compared to young normal groups of individuals or cohorts. Just like measuring Bone Mass Density which your physician may have ordered, we can compare the anatomical changes in the brain of younger cohorts.

In the past we could only measure cognition indirectly such as the MMSE or Mini-Cog as discussed on a previous day of the daybook.

SUPER-FOODS; SUPER-SMART

COGNITION AS A NEWTONIAN MODEL.

Sir Isaac Newton invented calculus. Mechanistic view of the Universe and along with Descartes established the schism between mind and body; essentially the mind belonged to the church and the body to science (or the mind to the psychiatrist and the body to the rest of the specialties).

"I can calculate the motion if heavenly bodies but Not the madness of people."

AS AN EINSTEIN/ QUANTUM MODEL

Albert Einstein's theory that energy and matter are inter-convertible gave rise to the Atomic age (and the nuclear bomb) and also opened the door to "Quantum" physics.

He first imagined a non-mathematical model of the theory of relativity but also that science is more closely relates to the divine than we can imagine!

"The true sign of intelligence is not knowledge but imagination."

AS A HAWKING- HIGGS-BOSON MODEL

Stephen Hawking came up with the "theory of everything" marrying the mechanistic world of Newton with the relative world of Einstein, initially denied the God particle and now acknowledges the mystery of the Universe.

"Not only does God play dice, but He sometimes throws them where they cannot be seen."

September 7

SUPER-FOODS; SUPER-SMART

DARK MATTER OR??

According to theoretical physicists, what holds the universe together is something called 'dark matter' otherwise the universe would fly apart and self-destruct! In a computer simulation of what this 'dark matter' would look like if visible, there are billions of 'nodes" or stars all connected by this substance. Stretch your imagination and this looks a lot like a neuronal network in the brain. The macrocosm and the microcosm!!

SO WHAT DO THESE THEORIES

HAVE TO DO WITH COGNITION?

Our thoughts create our actions. My nose itches, I scratch it! But what of an Olympic level ice dancer who is performing a complexities of moves, analyzing some very complicated physics equations of rotation; all in the sequence of milliseconds. The fastest neural pathways conduct impulses at 200 miles per sec. We cannot explain physiologically.

The next time you do an activity which you really enjoy and you have spent years of your life training for, like the above ice dancer and time stands still and you feel really connected with what you are doing or maybe connected with life itself and have a mystical experience, is it possible that the brain now instead of an initiator of action has become a processor of the action, using the template imprinted on the quantum field?

There are still mysteries to be solved *"he sometimes throws them where they cannot be seen"*

DR. M. P. KHAN, MD/NMD

September 8

SUPER-FOODS; SUPER-SMART

I would encourage you to concurrently read the books I have outlined below to get a better understanding of some of the concepts that we will be discussing.

1) *The Omnivore's Dilemma: Michael Pollan*

2) *Cooked: Michael Pollan*

3) *Food Rules: Michael Pollan*

4) *Probiotics and Prebiotics: Where are we going? Gerald W Tannock (a little technical at times)*

5) *Probiotics: A Clinical Guide: Floch and Kim (also quite technical)*

SUPER-FOODS; SUPER-SMART

MEDITATION AND IMPROVEMENT IN GRAY MATTER.

A study looked at meditation naïve patients

Before and after an 8 week mindful meditation

Course (Kabat –Zinn). Post study MRI showed an

Increase in gray matter in the Left Hippocampus,

Posterior Cingulate, Temporo-Parietal Junction

And Cerebellum.

I would like to do a study in cognitive decline in long term meditators such as Buddhist monks with a follow up MRI scans before and after years of meditation.

The Hippocampus and other anatomical terms are areas of the brain associated with memory and cognition.

Mindfulness meditation is a system of meditation which can be easily taught.

MEDITATION AND THE POTENTIAL FOR AGING REVERSAL.

The length of telomeres which are at the end of A chromosome shortens with each division. Telomerase promotes the growth of telomeres. In people who just completed a course there was a significant increase in telomeraseactivity.

Aging is usually associated with cognitive (memory) decline and anything we can do to slow this process means we can slow down this decline. Meditation of almost any kind is an important tool to improve cognition.

MIND-BODY APPROACHES IN THE TREATMENT OF MENTAL DISORDERS.

Significant improvement in PTSD in the yoga group comparable to psycho-pharmaceuticals. Improved in MDD in the exercise group comparable to anti-depressant meds as did Tai Chi and Qigong.

PTSD= POST TRAUMATIC STRESS DISORDER
MDD=MAJOR DEPRESSIVE DISORDER
Tai Chi and Qi gong are Chinese forms of exercise and related to the movements in martial arts such as Kung Fu. Yoga is well known especially in the Berkshires. Both are widely taught by trained practitioners in the U.S.

September 9

SUPER-FOODS; SUPER-SMART

If you live in Western Mass, a great resource for yoga is the "Kripalu Center for Yoga" which is located in Stockbridge. www.kripalu.org. We are fortunate as our residence is almost in walking distance of the center.

Look up a yoga class or teacher in your area and sign up today for a class. If you are a guy concerned about the girly aspect of it, it is much harder than it looks and it will challenge any preconceived notion you might have about yoga.

September 10

SUPER-FOODS; SUPER-SMART

SOME ABBREVIATIONS.

MGBA=Microbiota Gut Brain Axis.
BDNF=Brain Derived
Neurotrophic Factor
CNS= Central Nervous System
ENS= Enteric Nervous System
IBD=Inflammatory Bowel Disease
IBS=Irritable Bowel Syndrome
IFN-y= Interferon Gamma
SP= Substance P
GABA= y Amino Butyric Acid
CRP=C Reactive Protein

These are some of the abbreviations we will be using in rest of the presentation. Don't bother remembering them as you can always refer to this slide for reference

AND BACTERIAL
CONDIMENTS.

Probiotics

Antibiotics

Prebiotics

Psychobiotics

Probiotics are the helpful bacteria found in most fermented foods such as yogurt, kefir and sauerkraut.
Prebiotics are foods such as bananas apples and kiwi which provide a good food source for the probiotic bacteria.
Psychobiotics are bacteria in the gut that produce neuro transmitters such as serotonin and can affect our mood (depression, anxiety)

FOOD AND COGNITION: CORE CONCEPTS

1) The gut is the interface between the inner And outer world.
2) Food is not just nutrition, it is information. We are what we absorb!
3) Plasticity of the CNS is modulated by the BDNF.
4) The gut biome bacteria play an integral part in modulating absorption of food, pathogens non pathogens and the PNI system.
5) There is connection between the gut & brain MGBA.

> Spend some time reviewing this slide.
> It has five key concepts in understanding the connection between the digestive system or gut, the bacteria that reside in it and the brain and our mental health and well-being.
> We will consider each of them in detail in subsequent slides.

1) THE GUT IS THE INTERFACE BETWEEN THE INNER AND OUTER WORLD

Absorption of digested foods occurs in the small intestine which is lined by small finger like projections called villi which in turn are lined by columnar or villous cell. The total surface area of the villi in a single individual if they were stretched out flat would be the same as that of two tennis courts.

The spaces between the villous cells (see large arrow) are where food absorption occurs at a molecular level. You may have heard of the "leaky gut syndrome" This space is controlled by an enzyme called 'zonulin.' like a gatekeeper. When you eat non organic wheat which is sprayed with Round Up, a weed killer which ensures that only wheat is harvested, it can trigger "leaky gut syndrome." Round Up has a compound called glycophate which increases zonulin which allows gluten molecules (a wheat protein) to enter the blood-stream.

You can then develop gluten intolerance or worst case scenario; if you are HLA positive (a genetic marker) you will get celiac disease. This may be why we are seeing an increase in celiac and gluten sensitivity. Also celiac disease can also cause central nervous system manifestations such as anxiety, foggy thinking and depression. Which makes a strong case for eating organic wheat based products.

3000 LIVES

"Today, we gather to be reassured that God hears
the lamenting and bitter weeping of Mother America
because so many of her children are no more. Let us now
seek that assurance in prayer for the healing of our grief
stricken hearts, for the souls and sacred memory of those
who have been lost. Let us also pray for divine wisdom
as our leaders consider the necessary actions for national
security, wisdom of the grace of God that as we act,
we not become the evil we deplore."
—Rev. Nathan Baxter, Dean of Washington
National Cathedral

This is a day of solitude and remembrance. A day that will go down in history when a few fanatics distorted their religion and claimed thousands of innocent lives. A day of infamy and cowardice; a day when we came together not only as Americans, but also as a common people. All of us were affected by this tragedy and even years later, some of us grieve this day when we lost our loved ones. But we also grieve as a nation for the loss of our innocence and our sense of security in our daily lives.

There will always be anger and the need to lash out against the perpetrators and anyone closely resembling them as was seen post 9-11. But all of life is a lesson and what can we learn from this atrocity? Victor Frankl found beauty in a fish head in a concentration camp in Auschwitz and it was this belief in the goodness of humanity that kept him alive. *"That as we act, we not become the evil we deplore."*

Where were you on September 11 2001?

_____

_____

What were your first thoughts on that day in 2001?

_____

_____

_____

_____

What are your thoughts of that event 14 years later?

_____

_____

_____

_____

_____

_____

_____

DR. M. P. KHAN, MD/NMD

September 12

SUPER-FOODS; SUPER-SMART

2) FOOD IS NOT JUST NUTRITION,
IT IS INFORMATION.
WE ARE WHAT WE ABSORB.

FOOD IS NOT JUST NUTRITION, IT IS ALSO INFORMATION. If you can remember this line every time you eat something, it will remind you to make healthy choices. Digestion begins in the brain first, also called the cephalic phase, which is why delicious food makes one salivate.

Let us compare a typical fast food hamburger to a healthy garden salad. But what if I told you that the 'burger' is actually a whole grain organic bun with a salmon patty, wild greens, vine tomatoes and hummus as dressing?

3) PLASTICITY OF THE BAIN IS MODULATED BY BDNF.

BDNF acts on certain Neurons of the CNS and the peripheral Nervous System, helping to support the survival of existing neurons, and encourage the growth and differentiation of new neurons and synapses. In the brain, it is active in the hippocampus, cortex and basal forebrain-areas vital to learning, memory and higher thinking.

BDNF or Brain Derived Neurotrophic Factor is one of four neurotrophic factors and expressed by the BDNF gene and is responsible for brain plasticity.

More is not necessarily a good thing. For example in chronic stress and anxiety states, it is higher in the amygdala, the anxiety center of the brain where it is theorized that it can strengthen anxiety circuits and less in the hippocampus (memory center) where it may cause memory problems.

September 13

SUPER-FOODS; SUPER-SMART

DISEASE STATES ASSOCIATED WITH ALTERED /DECREASED BDNF LEVELS IN THE BRAIN.

DEPRESSION
ALZHEIMER'S DISEASE
EPILEPSY
OCD
SCHIZOPHRENIA
HUNTINGDON'S DISEASE
ANOREXIA/BULEMIA
AGING
OBESITY
DRUG ADDICTION (PLEASURE PATHWAYS)

In depression, chronic stress releases cortisol from the adrenal which by a feedback loop decreases BDNF and causes atrophy of the hippocampus (pseudo dementia).

Decrease in BDNF in Alzheimer's dementia patients on post mortem brain study but relationship is not clear. In epilepsy, polymorphisms in gene expression of BDNF cause reinforcement of excitatory pathways and suppression of inhibitory pathways. Ditto for OCD and Huntington's disease

It has been shown that in schizophrenic patients BDNF mRNA levels are decreased in cortical layers IV and V of the dorsolateral prefrontal cortex. This area is known to be involved with working memory. Since schizophrenic patients often suffer from impairments in working memory, BDNF deficiency may have something to do with this neuro developmental disorder.

There is an inverse relationship between BMI (Body Mass Index) and BDNF. Obesity (a BMI > than 30) may be a risk factor for dementia. That is the more obese one is, the lower the level of BDNF and a higher risk for dementia.

BDNF may reinforce pleasure circuits in the brain and contribute to opiate/alcohol addiction

September 13

SUPER-FOODS; SUPER-SMART

Recipe for Honey-Soy-Spice Salmon Bake:

This recipe is for a single serving and can be made in a small square Pyrex glass dish in a toaster oven. Or more servings just multiply all the ingredients based on the number of servings and use a regular oven.

Combine two tablespoons of soy sauce, one tablespoon of honey, a pinch of cumin, red pepper, salt to taste, black pepper and one tablespoon of olive oil. Blend all ingredients together in a small bowl.

Place two tablespoons of the above mixture in a small Pyrex dish. Place a 6 oz. filet of wild caught salmon, fresh or defrosted if frozen(or if you want a vegetarian option, try a 6 oz. piece of tofu) on the mixture and pour rest of the mixture over the salmon (or tofu). Marinate for 30 minutes (optional).

Cut up a small head of broccoli or cooked brown rice or whole wheat or rice noodles and place around the filet. Place in a preheated toaster oven at 400 degree F for 15-20 minutes or till fish flakes easily.

SUPER-FOODS; SUPER-SMART

WHAT INCREASES BDNF LEVELS IN THE BRAIN.

EXERCISE
CURCUMIN (TURMERIC)
EGCG (GREEN TEA) (Epi Gallo Catechin Gallate)
MEDITATION
DHA (FISH OIL)
CALORIC RESTRICTION
INTELLECTUAL STIMULATION
NIACIN

One more benefit of consistent exercise is the increase in gray matter.

Turmeric binds to amyloid which is the protein found in the brain of Alzheimer patients and may also upregulate BDNF and also a cox-2 inhibitor. (Anti-inflammatory)

Green tea a polyphenol same as above and also a chelating agent

We already discussed the effect of meditation on cognitive anatomy of the brain.

DHA or fish oil or fatty fish in most cultures is considered brain food, critical in pregnancy, significant decrease in IQ points when maternal diet is low in DHA

Caloric restriction also increases telomerase and hence increased telomere length.

You have all heard of the nun study where long term intellectual stimulation delayed the onset of Alzheimer's in a population of nuns in a monastery.

Niacin, which is a B vitamin, upregulates BDNF production.

September 14

SUPER-FOODS; SUPER-SMART

This is a recipe for fish curry which uses nuts, fatty fish, and lots of turmeric and you might need access to an Indian store or you can buy it on line.

- *2 lbs. fish fillets of salmon or halibut or tilapia, cut into 3" lengths.*
- *2 tablespoons garlic or garlic- ginger paste.*
- *2 inches ginger root*
- *5 teaspoons mustard seeds*
- *4 bay leaves*
- *½ tablespoon coriander powder*
- *2 medium onions, quartered.*
- *7 red chilies*
- *½ cup of cashews.*
- *1 tablespoon cumin seed*
- *3 teaspoons turmeric powder*
- *3 tablespoons salt*
- *2 big tomatoes, cubed.*
- *2 bay leaves*
- *2 tablespoons of coconut oil to pan fry fish*
- *3 cups water*

DIRECTIONS 1) In a food processor, grind the onions, ginger, 2 bay leaves, red chilies, mustard seeds, cumin seed and cashews altogether. 2) Take a big plate, put the fish in it and sprinkle 2 teaspoon of salt, two teaspoon of turmeric powder and the garlic paste.3)Mix all of them properly. Allow to marinate for 1/2 hour.

4) Take a pan, heat it on medium and put oil to pan fry the fish turning after about 2 minutes on each side. When all the pieces are fried, remove the fish and place aside. Clean all the black residues from the oil in the pan with the spatula and put 2 tablespoon of fresh oil in the pan.

5) Then put a pinch of cumin seed, a pinch of mustard seed, 2 red chili, 2 bay leaves, and allow them to splutter. Put the cut onion pieces and fry until slightly brown. Add all the ground paste, tomatoes, left over turmeric powder and salt to taste. Keep stirring it until the paste becomes a little brown (it takes around 10 minutes). The paste will start leaving the oil and paste will now no more stick on the pan. The paste is now perfectly fried.

6) Now pour 2-3 cups of water to it, adjusting for desired thickness. Once the gravy comes to boil, start dropping the fried fish pieces and allow to simmer for 15 minutes.

Use coarsely chopped coriander leaf for garnishing and serve with rice or flatbread (naan).

DR. M. P. KHAN, MD/NMD

September 15

SUPER-FOODS; SUPER-SMART

4) THE GUT BIOME PLAYS AN INTEGRAL PART IN MODULATING ABSORPTION OF FOOD, THE RECOGNITION OF PATHOGENS AND NON PATHOGENS AND ALSO PROVIDES FEEDBACK TO THE PNI SYSTEM.

The Aliens have already invaded us. Your Immune system thanks you for that.

Some less known facts about probiotics:
   The sub title of this slide sounds like a blurb from a bad Sci-Fi movie script. The 'aliens' in this case are the trillions of bacteria that live in and on areas of our body called "biomes." and of course the bacteria do not look anything like the scary creature from the movie of the same name!
   There are four microbiomes; Skin, Mouth, Vagina and Gut. The Gut has 10 to the power of 14 number of bacteria or 100 trillion as compared to human cells which number about 10 trillion in a single individual. 30% of the weight of fecal matter in a bowel movement is made up of bacteria!
   The human genome has 20,000 genes (human) while the bacteria in the above biomes have 2-20 million genes. So actually we have not really studied the human genome until we also study the bacterial genomes which we co-exist with.
   The entire biome weighs 2-3 lbs. which is coincidentally the same weight as the brain!
   We are born from the womb as sterile individuals and pick up lactobacillus from the vagina and Bifidobacterium (two types of pro biotic bacteria species) from breast feeding.
   Babies delivered by C-section colonize the gut with bacteria from the skin biome and as a result have decreased immunity and are more prone to infections. One way to prevent this is to place a swab in the vagina during child birth and as soon as the baby is delivered by C-section, to smear the baby with the swab and thus colonize the baby with the vaginal bacteria.
   80% of the body's immune system is around the gut and the gut biome plays a critical role in in keeping the body healthy by interacting with the cells of the immune system. As we shall see later also has feed back to the nervous system and has a direct influence on the NPI (Neuro Psycho Immune) system.
   Understanding the function of the gut as an organ for immune modulation may be a key to understanding the dysfunction of the immune system in Inflammatory Bowel Disease and also in auto immune diseases such as Rheumatoid Arthritis and Multiple Sclerosis. The biome plays an integral role in up or down regulation of the immune system.

September 16

SUPER-FOODS; SUPER-SMART

It is critical to understand the connection of the gut to the brain via the MGBA. In fact 70 % of serotonin production of the body is in the gut. Your gut biome plays a significant role in the functioning of the PNI and disturbances in this system may play a significant role in the development of auto immune diseases such as Hashimoto's and Rheumatoid arthritis

---

MGBA= Microbiome Gut Brain Axis

Brain to Gut= directly by the Vagal Nerve and indirectly by the endocrine system (Adrenaline, Cortisol)

Gut to Brain= directly by the Vagal Nerve and indirectly immune responses (Inflammatory reflex) and neuro transmitters and production of metabolites.

PNI= Psycho-Neuro-Immunological

At this point one of the ladies from Mrs. Field's Garden Club raised her hand and asked a question as to how she had these joint pains and she feels she may have rheumatoid arthritis. Below are the criteria for the diagnosis of RA. Of course this has nothing to do with the present topic. So here goes.

The diagnosis of rheumatoid arthritis (RA) can be made when the following clinical features are ALL present:

- *Inflammatory arthritis involving three or more joints. It does not have to be the hand only as it can be warmth, swelling and stiffness of any three joints.*

- *Positive rheumatoid factor (RF) and/or anti-citrullinated peptide/protein antibody testing. Your doctor can order these above tests from a blood sample.*

- *Elevated levels of C-reactive protein (CRP) or the erythrocyte sedimentation rate, also a blood test.*

- *Diseases with similar clinical features have been excluded, particularly psoriatic arthritis, acute viral polyarthritis, polyarticular gout or calcium pyrophosphate deposition disease, and systemic lupus erythematosus. These can be separated out by history physical exam and blood testing.*

- *The duration is more than six weeks.*

September 17

SUPER-FOODS; SUPER-SMART

ABSTRACT

Animal studies have demonstrated that the early phase of enteric infection is accompanied by anxiety-like behavior, which is mediated through vagal ascending pathways.

Chronic infection alters gut function, including motility and visceral sensitivity, as well as feeding patterns, anxiety and depression-like behavior.

These effects are likely immune-mediated, and involve changes in pro-inflammatory cytokines and altered metabolism of kynurenine/tryptophan pathways.

Most of the next slides that follow are from a chapter in a textbook titled:

"The Effects of Inflammation, Infection and Antibiotics on the Microbiota-Gut-Brain Axis" and I have quoted an abstract from that article by Premysl Bercik & Stephen M. Collins

In human terms, this means that infection/inflammation of the gut can affect our mental health.

This concept of microbiota-gut-brain interactions opens a new field of research aimed at developing microbial-directed therapies to treat a broad spectrum of human conditions, including chronic gastrointestinal and psychiatric disorders.

To which I might add "and auto immune diseases such as RA and MS and even some cancers.

We will probably live to see the day when we will be able to tweak the immune system using specific types of probiotics to treat a host of disorders including obesity

DR. M. P. KHAN, MD/NMD

Clinical studies have shown that chronic gastrointestinal infections lead to malnutrition and stunting, resulting in impaired cognitive function. Accumulating evidence suggests that in addition to pathogens, the commensal gastrointestinal microbiota also influences gut function and host's behavior.

Both animal and clinical studies have demonstrated changes in behavior and brain chemistry after induction of intestinal dysbiosis by administration of antibiotics.

Dysbiosis is a term used when the pathogenic bacteria outnumber the beneficial bacteria in the gut.

Clinical signs of dysbiosis include indigestion, bloating and gas and also an altered stool pattern.

Commensal are the healthy bacteria that coexist in our gut.

September 18

SUPER-FOODS; SUPER-SMART

INFLAMMATION AND THE MGBA
DEPRESSION:
Increase in cytokines and CRP in MDD. Also increase in incidence of depression and cognitive dysfunction in chronic illnesses associated with immune activation. (RA, COPD, DM -1, CAD) Interferon Rx in cancer increases depressive like behavior.

> Cytokines and CRP (or C Reactive Protein) are markers of inflammation found in the blood.
> They are increased in chronic diseases such as diabetes and coronary artery disease and also in RA and chronic lung diseases all of which also have a high incidence of MDD or Major Depressive Disorder. Interferon is a drug used in cancer which has an inflammatory effect on the immune system.

INFECTIONS AND THE MGBA

Robust connection between IQ and parasite stress. Infectious disease remains the most powerful predictor of average *national* IQ.

DBPC study on Jamaican school children with treating and eradicating a non-invasive parasite; *Trichuris trichura* resulted in significant increase in short and long term memory.

> MGBA if you recall is the Microbiome Gut Brain Axis.
> DBPC means a double blind placebo controlled study.

INFECTIONS AND THE MGBA

Early child hood diarrhea resulted in impaired physical growth as well as cognitive function 6-9 yrs. later.

A five country study over 20 years concluded that early infancy diarrhea showed physical and cognitive stunting at 24 months and for every five episodes of diarrhea the adjusted odds of stunting increased by a ratio of 1.3.

Mice infected with Campylobacter jejuni showed increased anxiety behavior *without* increase in inflammatory markers due to vagal ascending pathways.

Diarrhea in infancy can result in physical and intellectual stunting and the incidence increases if the child has frequent episodes of diarrhea.

Campylobacter jejuni is also a bug that causes diarrhea in humans and in a rat study caused anxiety by a direct connection to the brain by the vagus nerve.

September 19

SUPER-FOODS; SUPER-SMART

ANTIBIOTICS AND THE MGBA

PENICILLINS, QUINOLONES (C I P R O F L O X A C I N), MACROLIDES (AZITHROMYCIN) and SULFONAMIDES are the most common antibiotics that can induce psychosis.

The psychotic events generally develop within five days and stop after withdrawal of treatment.

Cause may be intestinal dysbiosis (bacterial overgrowth) leading to alterations in neurotransmitters produced by the biome thus affecting CNS function.

> The next time you take an antibiotic, see how it affects your mood and cognition.
>
> Which is why it is critical to take probiotics when taking antibiotics *and to continue with probiotics for at least another 2 weeks after you stop the antibiotics.*

ANTIBIOTICS AND THE MGBA

Intestinal dysbiosis may be the precursor of Irritable Bowel Syndrome or IBS.

IBS could be explained by bacterial overgrowth, increasing conversion of tryptophan to serotonin causing increased gut motility AND modulation of the MGBA by vagal afferent nerve pathways as a top down response to stressors

In 19 RCT studies, probiotics, specifically Bifidobacterium bifidum was more effective than placebo. (47% vs. 11%)

> Frequent treatments with antibiotics may actually predispose to Irritable Bowel Syndrome and probiotics are now increasingly used in the treatment of IBS.

DR. M. P. KHAN, MD/NMD

September 20

SUPER-FOODS; SUPER-SMART

MUST EAT FOODS: FERMENTED FOODS: The ones that come to mind are yogurt and kefir.

Most yogurts available in your local super market have 1-4 strains of pro biotics. A very heavily advertised form of yogurt has only one strain: Bifidus regularis. Or Bifidobacterium infantis.

A readily available form of kefir (which is a liquid or drinkable form of yogurt) has:

Lactobacillus lactis

Lactobacillus rhamnosus.

Streptococcus diacetylactis

Lactobacillus plantarum

Lactobacillus casei

Saccharomyces florentinus

Leuconostoc cremoris

Bifidobacterium longum

Bifidobacterium breve

Lactobacillus acidophilus

Bifidobacterium lactis

Lactobacillus reuteri

As you can see, kefir is the winner. Kefir is 99% lactose free so f you have lactose intolerance, no worry. Also try to buy or make organic kefir for obvious reasons. If dairy is not your thing, sauerkaraut, fermented soy products such as miso and kim chee are other examples of fermented foods which as far as I am concerned should be a distinct food group.

September 21

SUPER-FOODS; SUPER-SMART

MUST EAT FOODS: *Below are some of the uses of probiotics in various disease states:*

1) *Acute infectious diarrhea: Prevention data is not available but can assist in the recovery phase. Would recommend 4 oz. of kefir daily for at least two weeks.*

2) *Traveler's diarrhea. Strains such as Saccharomyces boulardii, Lactobacillus acidophilus and Bifidobacterium bifidum are helpful in the prevention of Traveler's diarrhea.*

3) *Radiation induced diarrhea: Probiotics found in kefir and yogurt are helpful in the prevention and treatment of this problem in patients getting radiation therapy (? prostate cancer).*

4) *Clostridium difficile associated diarrhea: This very troublesome diarrhea is associated with long term or multiple use of antibiotics and causes a significant illness burden. The milder form of this problem is Antibiotic Associated Diarrhea or AAD as discussed previously and I would strongly recommend that ALL antibiotic therapy be accompanied with probiotic therapy! Fecal tranpalntation is now an accepted treatment for chronic treatment resistant C diff infection where the healthy biome from a fecal extract of a healthy individual is processed and adminstered to the host with very good treament outcomes.*

5) *Helicobacter pylori infection: Helicobacter pylori is a bacteria associated with gastric ulcers and is detected by a blood test and more commonly by biopsy when an endoscopy is done for upper gastrointestinal problems or by a breath test. It is usually treated with a triple therapy of antibiotics(clarithromycin) and inhibitors of acid production such as omeprazole. Probiotics such as Saccharomyces boulardii and Lactobacillus are helpful in treatment of this problem.*

6) *Crohn's disease/Ulcerative colitis: Kefir would be a good add on for ulcerative colitis and inflammatory bowel disease along with omega-3 EFA and turmeric (both anti-inflammatories) although no specific studies are available to support this.*

7) *Irritable Bowel Syndrome or IBS: Bifidobacterium bifidum found in a commercial preparation (Philips Colon Health) is helpful in the treatment of this very common and sometime debilitating condition which is actually an imbalance in the feedback loop of the gut brain axis.*

DR. M. P. KHAN, MD/NMD

September 22

SUPER-FOODS; SUPER-SMART

MUST EAT FOODS: TURMERIC (CURCUMIN)

* CAN CONSUME UP TO 10G A DAY WITH NO SIDE EFFECTS.

* BINDS TO IRON SO CAN CAUSE FE DEFICIENCY.

* BINDS TO AMYLOID SO MAY SLOW PROGRESSION IN ALZHEIMER'S. INDIA HAS SOME OF THE LOWEST INCIDENCE OF AD.

* ANTI INFLMMATORY COX-2 INHIBITOR BUT NO STUDIES ON BRAIN METABOLISM.

* INCREASES BDNF.

Turmeric is easily available in bulk at your local Indian grocery store and is very cheap in this form. It is also available as a capsule, usually 100 to 200 mg. and is used at a dose of 2-4 capsules 3 x day with meals although this can get pricy very quickly,

The Ayurvedic approach also known as Golden Milk involves heating 6 oz. of milk (Soy or Rice milk is also OK) almost to boiling. Add a heaping teaspoonful of turmeric and a teaspoon of agave or honey and stir well.

Let sit for 3-5 minutes, stir well and gulp it down.
Repeat up to three times a day or as tolerated.

Turmeric is a member of the Ginger family. Lot of RCT studies pending especially in cancer prevention and treatment AND in prevention of AD. Also activates the Nrf2 pathways and increase glutathione production, a powerful anti-oxidant.

September 23

CELEBRATING AN EQUINOX

Today is the first day of fall. From now on the days will get shorter until we hit the winter solstice. Below is a poem I wrote about the inevitable arrival of the chill and snow.

FALL EQUINOX:

I am the sullen handmaiden of winter,
And my presence, a reminder of life's fragility.
I am the destroyer of summer's promise,
As I morph the sun filled hours into darkness.

My gold and crimson hues are deceitful in their beauty,
For I herald the great southward migrations that cloud the skies
Of Sand Cranes and Canada Geese,
And signal the grizzly to fatten for slumber.

Very soon I will embrace my icy mistress
With open arms of bare gnarled trees.
Enslaved, I will satisfy her frigid lust to slumber,
And she will awaken; pregnant with the child of spring!

MK 11/2012

September 24

CELEBRATING AN EQUINOX

*"An equinox is an astronomical event in which the plane of
Earth's equator passes the center of the Sun. The Astronomical
Almanac defines it, on the other hand, as the instants when
the Sun's apparent longitude is 0° or 180°. The two definitions
are almost, but not exactly equivalent. Equinoxes occur twice
a year, around 21 March and 23 September."*
—Wikipedia Definition

What is it that you like most about autumn?

_____

_____

_____

_____

_____

_____

_____

_____

What is it that you like least about autumn?

_____

_____

_____

_____

_____

_____

_____

_____

September 25

SUPER-FOODS; SUPER-SMART

MUST EAT FOODS: SEA FOOD, GRASS FED DAIRY, FREE RANGE EGGS.

* ALL OF THE ABOVE ARE GOOD SOURCE OF OMEGA-3 EFA.

* 16oz OF FATTY FISH/WK. (not farm raised) WILL GIVE ENOUGH OMEGA-3 EFA &

VITAMIN D SO YOU DO NOT NEED TO SUPPLEMENT.

* WATCH FOR MERCURY (montereybayaquarium.com has a good download of a chart that tells for safe vs unsafe vs overharvested fish; see below.) AND THIS CAN BE MONITORED BY PERIODIC URINE OR BLOOD TESTING.

> *Omega-3 are like grease for the neurons.*
>
> *Omega-3 fatty acid levels are lower in major depression vs. normal controls and lower levels are significant predictors of future suicide risk.*
>
> *Higher DHA levels associated with better performance on tests of nonverbal reasoning, mental flexibility, working memory, and vocabulary*
>
> *MIXED DATA, EPA>DHA appears best for improved cognition.*

SEAFOOD-WATCH FOR MASSACHEUSETTS: You can download a guide for your state form the web site for the Monterey bay aquarium or look for a link at ewg.org.

BEST CHOICES:
Buy first; they're caught or farmed in ways that cause little harm to habitats or other wildlife.

Cod: Atlantic (Canada & US)
Crab: Atlantic Rock & Jonah (US)
Crab: Canned (imported)
Crab: Red King (Russia)
Haddock (Gulf of Maine)
Halibut: Atlantic (US)
Mahi Mahi (imported)
Orange Roughy
Salmon: Atlantic (farmed)
Sardines: Atlantic (Mediterranean)
Sharks
Shrimp (imported)
Squid (imported)
Swordfish (imported longline)
Tuna: Albacore (except US troll, pole and line, and longline)
Tuna: Bluefin
Tuna: Skipjack (imported purse seine)
Tuna: Yellowfin (except troll, pole and line, and HI longline)

GOOD ALTERNATIVES:
Buy, but be aware there are concerns with how they're caught or farmed.

Bluefish (US gillnet and trawl)
Branzino (Mediterranean farmed)
Cod: Atlantic (Georges Bank trawl, hand line and imported)
Crab: Blue & King (US)
Croaker: Atlantic
Haddock (Georges Bank)
Hake: White (US)
Halibut (US Pacific gillnet and trawl)
Lobster (Bahamas & US)
Monkfish (US)
Pollock (Canada & US)

Scallops (wild)
Shrimp (Canada & US wild,
Ecuador farmed)
Snapper (US)
Squid (Mexico & US)
Swordfish (US)
Tilapia (China & Taiwan)
Tuna: Albacore (US longline)
Tuna: Skipjack (free school, imported troll, pole and line, and US longline)
Tuna: Yellowfin (free school, imported troll, pole and line, and HI longline)
Arctic Char (farmed)
Barramundi (US & Vietnam farmed)
Bass: Striped (US hook and line, farmed)
Bluefish (US hook and line)
Catfish (US)
Clams, Mussels & Oysters

AVOID:

Take a pass on these for now, they're overfished or caught or farmed in ways that harm other Marine life or the environment.

Cod: Atlantic (imported hook and line)
Croaker: Atlantic (beach seine)
Mahi Mahi (US Atlantic troll, pole and line)
Prawn: Spot (AK) (Continued)
Rockfish (CA, OR & WA)
Salmon (AK & New Zealand)
Scallops (farmed)
Seaweed (farmed)
Shrimp (AK wild, US farmed)
Swordfish (Canada & US buoy, hand line, harpoon)
Tilapia (Ecuador & US)
Trout: Rainbow (US farmed)
Tuna: Albacore (Pacific troll, pole and line) Tuna:
Skipjack (Pacific troll, pole and line)

September 26

SUPER-FOODS; SUPER-SMART

MUST EAT FOODS: DARK CHOCOLATE.

BVRT TESTING IN THE DENTATE GYRUS USING f MRI SHOW (220 millisecs per decade) REDUCTION OF RESPONSE TIMES EQUIVALENT TO THREE DECADES (OF AN INDIVIDUAL 30 YEARS YOUNGER) IN THE HIGH FLAVONE GROUP VS CONTROLS (4 pieces bakers choc or 700mg of coca flavones for 12 weeks). BEST TO BUY ORGANIC AND FAIR TRADE CHOCOLATE.

In order to measure cognition, The BVRT or Benton Visual Retention Test was used to see how fast the dentate gyrus (an area of the brain associated with memory) would respond. Normally BVRT reaction time worsens with aging so this could be an indirect way to measure changes in cognition (memory, recall etc.)

At the end of 12 weeks it was found that the high cocoa flavone group independent of exercise (above groups 1 & 2) was 1997 milliseconds (faster) compared to 2627(slower) milliseconds of the low flavone groups 3) & 4). Since the BVRT times normally worsen by 220 milliseconds every decade of life lived, the improvement was an incredible reversal comparable to 2-3 decades or thirty years of aging.

Since flavonoids are bitter they are usually processed out of chocolate. A good rule of thumb is that old adage; you can have any color of chocolate as long as it is DARK! (75% and higher cacao content.) In fact the more bitter the chocolate, the better it is for you. For example, chocolate syrup has 26mg of flavones per serving while baking chocolate has 227 mg per serving. Four servings of the latter would replicate the above study. Beside the cardiovascular benefit of eating chocolate, this finding is one more reason to add to your diet.

September 27

SUPER-FOODS; SUPER-SMART

MUST EAT FOODS: VITAMIN D IS REALLY MORE LIKE A HORMONE (SUCH AS INSULIN) AS THE BODY CAN MAKE IT WITH SUNLIGHT EXPOSURE. IT IS CRITICAL TO HAVE ADEQUATE LEVELS; SO RECOMMEND SUPPLEMENTATION IN HIGHER LATTIUDES AND IN WINTER MONTHS.

VITAMIN D HAS ANTI INFLAMMATORY AND ANTI DEPRESSANT EFFECTS.

VITAMIN D REDUCES CALCIUM ION INFLUX AND EXCITATION OF NEURONS

INCREASES BDNF AND SUPRESSES GLUCOCORTICOID PRODUCTION.

ADVISE 5000 IU DAILY YEAR ROUND WITH LEVELS IN 6-12 WEEKS. 40-50 IS A GOOD TARGET RANGE.

FOODS HIGH IN VITD: FATTY FISH AND MUSHROOMS.

FOODS LOW IN VIT D: DAIRY, EGGS.

KEY POINTS ABOUT VITAMIN D:

A low Vitamin D level that is less than 30 can predispose to rickets, a condition that is relatively rare and results in defects in bone formation.

Since normal levels are 30-100 in blood test levels, toxicity is also very rare. In fact it is not known what the upper level of Vitamin D really is.

Some individuals with specific SNP variations for Vitamin D may need up to 10,000 iu. Daily. Frequent testing of levels is important.

If you have a diagnosis of sarcoidosis or certain kidney calcium metabolism disorders, it is advisable to supplement with Vitamin D very carefully.

DR. M. P. KHAN, MD/NMD

September 27

SUPER-FOODS; SUPER-SMART

MUST EAT FOODS: BROCCOLI AND OTHER CRUCIFEROUS VEGETABLES:

Cruciferous vegetables are vegetables of the family Brassicaceae (also called Cruciferae) such as cauliflower, cabbage, garden cress, Bok Choy, broccoli, Brussels sprouts and similar green leafy vegetables. The family takes its name Cruciferae, from the shape of their flowers, whose four petals resemble a cross.

This is my favorite way to eat cruciferous vegetable such as Brussel sprouts, Cauliflower an of course Broccoli:

Cut up the head into bite size pieces. Leave the Brussel sprouts whole. Steam for 3-8 minutes and check frequently so that they remain slightly crunchy. Remove from the stove and transfer to a bowl. Sprinkle the florets with a teaspoon of roasted sesame oil and a teaspoon of tamari. Add black pepper to taste, toss the veggies and enjoy hot or cold.

THE BROCCOLI EFFECT: CRUCIFEROUS VEGGGIES ARE HIGH IN SULPHORAPHANE WHICH ACTIVATES THE Nrf2 PATHWAY AND INCREASES GLUTATHIONE,

GLUTATHIONE IS A POWERFUL ANTIOXIDANT AND CRITICAL FOR DETOXIFICATION OF THE BRAIN.

ALSO PROTECTS AGAINST CARCINOGEN EXPOSURE.

Also be careful about eating large amounts of cruciferous veggies as they interfere with the uptake of iodine and can decrease thyroid production of thyroxine. (Hypothyroidism)

SUPER-FOODS; SUPER-SMART

MUST EAT FOODS: ALL BERRIES BUT MOSTLY BLUEBERRIES:

BLUEBERRIES ARE RICH IN A PHYTONUTRIENT CALLED PTEROSTILBENE, A MOLECULE SIMILAR TO RESVERATROL (RED WINE) BUT MUCH MORE POTENT AND ALSO AN ACTIVATOR OF THE Nrf2 PATHWAY WHICH ALSO UPREGULATES GLUTATHIONE PRODUCTION

My favoirite way of eating blueberries is to heap them on buckwheat flour pancakes with a generous helping of Maple syrup. I will also eat them alongside realy dark 80% chocolate to cut the bitter taste and talk about an anti-oxidant boost! A smoothie recipe follows.

<u>*Dr. K's r Super Duper Smoothie:*</u> *This heavenly concoction is loaded with anti-oxidants, omega-3 and probiotics.*

> *1 cup organic Blueberries.*
> *2 Tbsp. Of Unsweetened Dark Cocoa powder.*
> *1 cup Organic Soy (or Almond or Rice) Milk*
> *1 Tbsp. of Flax seeds.*
> *½ to 1 cup Kefir*
> *1 banana (optional)*
> *Agave syrup adjusted for sweetness.*
> *Blend all ingredients until smooth*

And remember:

"If life gives you dandelions, make a salad"

—Chairman Moo

SUPER-FOODS; SUPER-SMART

Here is another recipe for all that zucchini that you will be given by well-meaning neighbors.

Peel two or three large zucchinis.

Cut lengthwise slabs of zucchini about ½ inch thick.

In a zip lock bag, place one Tbsp. of olive oil and 1 Tbsp. of tamari (soy) sauce.

Add salt and pepper to taste.

Add zucchini to the bag, zip shut and mix thoroughly.

Marinate overnight.

Grill zucchini the next day about two minutes on each side with the burner on medium heat.

Garnish with fresh cilantro and serve hot!

September 28

ANOTHER LOVE POEM

<u>GARUDA</u>:

*All I know is the freedom of flight
And the bright blush of wings
Lifting me towards the rare skies
And the comforting darkness of solitude.*

*Look for me in the breaking dawn.
I am the consort of soaring eagles,
Circling, seeking in endless spirals,
Hungry for the crimson flash of love.*

*If you would love me, loosen your hair.
Come ride with me in naked splendor.
I will lift you to the face of the sun
And burn you in the ecstasy of my longing.*

*Nest with me in the high mountains,
Together we will greet the virginal day.
Drink from crystal springs of another time
Feed from the nectar of a thousand flowers.*

MPK/06

DR. M. P. KHAN, MD/NMD

September 29

IT AIN'T (NEW) YORK

If Columbus had an advisory committee he would probably still be at the dock.
— Arthur J. Goldberg

This is a follow up to the Resolution that I proposed to the PAFP (May-1) and the outcome of that Resolution like I had promised earlier.

It was a rainy Thursday evening. As the cloud covered sun dimmed, the wet road reflected an increasing number of truckers whizzing by. I grabbed a sandwich at one of the Quinzo's located in a plaza that cater to the turnpike crowd and merged back into the swiftly moving traffic, glad that I didn't do this for a living. Almost four hours later, after starting out, my GPS informed me that I had arrived at my destination in York, PA; a town about 20 miles south of Harrisburg. I checked into a local Holiday Inn and turned in early.

The meeting was the next day at a local golf club and the session was part of a three day conference that included a golf outing. If this reinforces the stereotype of the golf playing physician who takes his emergency calls on the 13th hole, rest assured that I have never held a golf club and don't plan to in the future.

I arrived bright and early at the Heritage Hills Resort on a still rainy Friday morning. I was fortunate to hook up with Kevin Wong, a physician from my neck of the woods, relieved to have someone guide me through the daunting agenda projected on a large screen. As I sat down to munch on a muffin and fruit, I realized with a sickening feeling that I had left the copy of the resolution on my laptop. Same said laptop was sitting on my bedside table at home. Kevin assured me that the resolution was going to be projected and that it was already reviewed by the board. You can guess by now that I was just a wee bit nervous, but relaxed as the meeting progressed.

I was surprised to learn that the key note speaker was Dr. T, a Texan, and the current President of the AAFP (American Academy of Family Practice). If anyone could understand the ecological disaster that PA could face someday, it would be him. Texas was beginning to be the poster boy of what can go wrong with oil and gas exploration. But, sadly most of his presentation was about the upcoming discussion in Congress to make payments more equitable to family physicians so as to narrow the gap between primary care and specialists. And that is another story.

Then it was time for resolution Number Three. Not familiar with the complex parliamentary protocol, I jumped in with an opening statement, arguing that it was vital that the Academy get involved with the health impact of gas fracking. After my little speech it was time to vote on the "Resolved" issues. There was some discussion with one member disapproving both of the Resolved. There was a move to separate the two. The first "Resolved" outlined below was motioned, seconded and approved by a 68% YES vote.

RESOLVED, the PAFP actively promote educational programs to educate the membership in recognizing and treating the health effects of chemicals released in the environment by the gas fracking process through continuing medical education programs and its communication tool such as its magazine and newsletter.

The second "Resolved" was deferred to the board for future discussion and was not approved, as they wanted to know more about what that involved. I personally thought that it was very straight forward in its intent as you can see from the language!

RESOLVED, the PAFP, with information and feedback received from its members, will advise and interface with appropriate government and environmental agencies with timely data related to these effects.

When one of the delegates stepped up to the mike and remarked that this second issue could be brought back to the table at next year's meeting, something snapped inside me. I was slightly taken aback at the emotional quaver in my voice as, almost involuntarily, I went up to the mike. These were my very words.

DR. M. P. KHAN, MD/NMD

"It's me again! This is not a political issue, but a human issue. By next year there may be 50,000 plus wells nationally and 10,000 in Pennsylvania alone. And some of them will fail. I sincerely hope that we are not sitting here still discussing this resolution a year from now. It is imperative that we deal with this issue as soon as possible."

I must have been pretty vehement as this was followed by an awkward silence. One of the board members as if to placate me, came up to the mike and assured me that this issue would be discussed as soon as the board meets. This opened up the flood gates, as several physician delegates from Bradford County which already has 90% of the land leased for drilling, expressed their concern about the health impact of gas fracking. Later over lunch, several of the delegates thanked me for bringing up this issue.

On the ride home, I pondered on my actions. Guess I had my "Mr. Smith" moment and one out of two is OK for now. We shall see!

Have you ever felt strongly about a social issue that impacts society, your community or your immediate family? What is it and what do you plan to do about it?

_____

_____

_____

_____

_____

_____

_____

_____

_____

_____

_____

_____

A POEM BY KAREN ABOUT A CRIME

A CRIME OF LOVE:

Was it a dream?
She was imprisoned in wood,
Cut up in pieces and compartmentalized.
Non-threatening, unreal,
Her visage no longer shown in his eyes,
Just furniture framed by blinders.
Her fractured mind could still synthesize,
Aspects of reality.
These forces were so much greater than she,
That played upon her body.
The howling continued obliterating speech.

How to continue immobilized and dead,
Red hues seeped into her head.
Burning her soul in painful agony,
She now fit into his world lifeless,
Shut up with nails, carved and sealed,
Finely engraved, oiled and replete.
The heaviness sunk deeply depressing time,
How to utter he was no longer mine?
The spoken word was strangled, a voice was lost,
The howling continued obliterating speech.

His indifference cemented her helplessness,
A pressure clamp stamped her body, snapped her bones,
Forgetful of who committed a crime,
He wore blinders. She knew,
The wasting of time, the pin prick truth,
The tremulous notes that would not leave.
Their sacred trusts lie broken and bereaved,
The howling continued obliterating speech.

KK 2/2010

OCTOBER

1-Oct	MRS. SMITH AND METHUSELAH. Detoxification Nation.
2-Oct	MRS. SMITH AND METHUSELAH. Super Detox Hummus recipe.
3-Oct	MRS. SMITH AND METHUSELAH. So tell me more, Doc.
4-Oct	MRS. SMITH AND METHUSELAH. Toxic exposure, it's very scary.
5-Oct	MRS. SMITH AND METHUSELAH. A 4 week program of Rejuvenation.
6-Oct	MRS. SMITH AND METHUSELAH. Put the good in, keep the bad out.
7-Oct	MRS. SMITH AND METHUSELAH. Are you or are you not: toxic.
8-Oct	MRS. SMITH AND METHUSELAH. Testing for toxins.
9-Oct	MRS. SMITH AND METHUSELAH. A urine test from Genova.
10-Oct	MRS. SMITH AND METHUSELAH. Where I introduce you to A NERD.
11-Oct	MRS. SMITH AND METHUSELAH. All about chelation and saunas.
12-Oct	MRS. SMITH AND METHUSELAH. A recipe for a Super Detox Spicy Salsa.
13-Oct	A POEM IN YOUR POCKET. The praises of Rumi.
14-Oct	A POEM IN YOUR POCKET. And you meet 'Wingless Angels.'
15-Oct	SPORTS 'N' SUPPLEMENTS. (PART-4) Illegal performance enhancement.
16-Oct	SPORTS 'N' SUPPLEMENTS. (PART-4) More not so legal ways.
17-Oct	TWO PARABLES: IMPERMANENCE & ENVY. A Master and a Rock cutter
18-Oct	TWO PARABLES: IMPERMANENCE & ENVY. And reflections on the same.
19-Oct	EATING AND MEDITATING. (PART-1) Manja with your friends.
20-Oct	EATING AND MEDITATING. (PART-1) And some friendly advice.
21-Oct	EATING AND MEDITATING. (PART-1) Manja slowly.
22-Oct	EATING AND MEDITATING. (PART-2) And some really slow advice.
23-Oct	HOLLOW VICTORIES. (Pt-1) A poem: Battle Cry!
24-Oct	HOLLOW VICTORIES. (Pt-1) A mother named Martha.
25-Oct	HOLLOW VICTORIES. (Pt-2) Anna, a woman he loves.
26-Oct	HOLLOW VICTORIES. (Pt-2) And a soldier named Troy.
27-Oct	HOLLOW VICTORIES. (Pt-3) His death and a mother's grief.
28-Oct	HOLLOW VICTORIES. (Pt-3) And a lover's lament.
29-Oct	TYPE-2 DIABETES- A NEUTRACEUTICAL APPROACH. Micronutrients.
30-Oct	TYPE-2 DIABETES- A NEUTRACEUTICAL APPROACH. Botanicals.
31-Oct	TYPE-2 DIABETES- A NEUTRACEUTICAL APPROACH. A recipe for rice.

DR. M. P. KHAN, MD/NMD

October 1

MRS. SMITH AND METHUSELAH*

Mrs. Smith has not been to my office for several months. So imagine my surprise when I see her on my schedule with the time and the blurb next to it "wants to discuss detoxification." This is how it went.

Hi Doc! Long time no see. Sorry about being familiar but that's how my granddaughter talks. You know, teenagers! Anyway she keeps talking 'Grandma you need to detoxify." She is driving me crazy. So here I am. At my age, really! But I want to live to a hundred and then some; like Methuselah.

Mrs. Smith, you have a very savvy granddaughter. So let me give you some information on it and you then can decide, OK.

Every day our body is exposed to toxins. We absorb it by digestion in what we eat. Pesticides on our food are one of the biggest exposures and one reason to use the 'dirty dozen' list so as to increase organically grown foods in our diet and to decrease the pesticide burden Also through our skin in the form of some cosmetics and skin products such as insect repellants. What we breathe in also adds to our toxic load. This could range from car fumes to industrial pollutants such as paint and cleaning solvents to household cleaning products and chemicals off gassing from carpets and clothing.

Detoxification occurs through various natural systems in our body. We can detoxify using the liver (bile and then through evacuation by bowel movements), our skin (through sweating), our lungs (alcohol is a good example), and by the kidneys through urination.

So why do I need your help, doctor? Just kidding you. You know me by now, huh!

You are absolutely right if we lived in a perfect world. A long as the body is in good health it can handle a certain volume or load of

toxins. The problem becomes when the toxic load overwhelms the body and then we start seeing chronic diseases and organ failures. So we need some help with the process in the form of supplements that we will discuss later on.

Sounds complicated. I am not sure I can do this at my age. My Sally will be disappointed.

Not so fast. I use a 28-day "Metabolic Rejuvenation" program from Douglas Labs, which makes it really easy. I have used it myself with really good results. Of course there are other reputable detoxification programs which are also effective. I like DL "MR" program because it is convenient and easy. The supplements are prepackaged so all you have to do is remember to take them twice a day before meals. The real hard part is the lifestyle changes you need to make to ensure the program is successful.

October 2

MRS. SMITH AND METHUSELAH*

Here is a healthy versatile food you can prepare before you start your detox program. Hummus is made from chick peas and is very affordable if you make it from scratch

2   *8oz. Cans of Chick Peas. (preferably organic and a BPA free can) Drain fluid in can and wash and drain the Chick Peas in a colander.*

> *2 cloves of garlic. (Omit if you do not like garlic)*
> *2Tbsp of tahini.*
> *1Pinch of cumin. (I like to use more)*
> *1 Pinch of turmeric.*
> *1 Pinch of cayenne pepper.*
> *1 Pinch of salt. (Add to taste later on if needed*
> *1 Pinch of black pepper.*
> *2 Tbsp. of olive oil.*
> *2 Tbsp. of chopped parsley or cilantro.*
> *1 Tbsp. of lemon juice.*

Place all ingredients in a food processor and process until smooth and creamy. If too thick, add a small amount of water,

Can stay frozen for six months. Use as a dip with raw broccoli and cauliflower; as dressing on a salad or in a sandwich instead of mayo.

MRS. SMITH AND METHUSELAH*

> *"Methuselah lived to be 969 years old. You boys and girls*
> *will see more in the next fifty years than Methuselah saw*
> *in his whole lifetime."*
> —Thomas Tusser.

So can you tell me more about detoxification, Doc.? How does it work?

Detoxification is a complex process and requires optimal functioning of the kidneys, lungs, skin, the lymphatic systems and most importantly, the liver.

Phase I detoxification: Almost every toxin that your gut absorbs is processed by the liver in two distinct steps. Some toxins are fat soluble (in that if they are not processed, they get stored in the fat stores). These are the end products of body metabolism, contaminants, pollutants such as insecticides and pesticides, food additives in processed foods, pharmaceutical agents and also alcohol. They undergo *phase I detoxification* by a family of over 50 enzymes called *cytochrome P450* which converts the fat soluble toxins to intermediate molecules. This process produces free radicals and other harmful compounds and an increased load of toxins can overwhelm the system leading to multiple chronic health problems

The *phase II detoxification* is carried out by enzymes called *conjugase*s which attach to the above molecules by pathways such as glucoronidation to molecules of glucoronic acid and glutamine and sulphurated phytochemicals (found in broccoli and garlic and wasabi) which make them water soluble and these are in turn, are eliminated by the kidneys (urine) and the bowels (bile). For efficient detoxification, *phase I* and *phase II* must work seamlessly. If the specific nutrients, for example glutamine, are not available, the

DR. M. P. KHAN, MD/NMD

phase II system becomes backlogged and is overwhelmed as *phase I* keeps producing as usual, This once again scores the importance of good nutrition as most of the *phase II* chemicals are food sourced.

So if there are inadequate nutrients such as vitamins and minerals, increased exposure to certain pharmaceutical agents, poor liver health such as obesity or chronic viral diseases such as Hepatitis C, excessive alcohol and acetaminophen use, chronic constipation, decreased kidney function as measured by GFR (a number which should be greater than 60 based on a blood test as part of a routine chemistry profile); they can all increase the toxic burden.

Hence the equation:

Total Toxic Exposure minus Body's Natural Detoxification= Toxic Burden

October 4

MRS. SMITH AND METHUSELAH*

Here are some frightening stats on toxic exposure.

- 2100 chemicals including pesticides, herbicides, PCB's medications such as antidepressants and other recreational drugs are in our water supply. Water Treatment plants do not have the capacity to remove all of them.
- Over 80% of foods we commonly eat are genetically modified. Foods that are GMO do not have to be labeled in the US so by default foods have to say 'non-GMO' on the labeling.
- The EPA estimates the average US citizen has over 400 toxic compounds in their body. Check out www.EWG.org video clip "Ten Americans." Its content is scarier than the horror flick "Friday the 13th".
- There are 82,000 chemicals in use today but only a fourth have been tested for toxicity. Toxicity data is not easily available and often the FDA allows small parts of an individual chemical as safe. What has not been not researched has been the impact on human health when you combine several chemicals at 'safe' levels!

Because a toxic build up increases free radical activity, it can cause premature aging, affect joint health and gastrointestinal health. It can also affect the immune system and increase fatigue and brain fog. And because pesticides and herbicides are similar to the molecules of estrogen, they can cause significant hormonal imbalance (endocrine disruptors) in men and women. A good detoxification program is often the starting point of the treatment of most chronic conditions.

OK Doc! Stop trying to scare me. Is there an easy way to detoxify? I am sold on the idea but once again it sounds complicated.

DR. M. P. KHAN, MD/NMD

October 5

MRS. SMITH AND METHUSELAH*

Yes there is. Below is a direct copy of the 4 week program which outlines the supplements used and their functions. It is all prepackaged and convenient to use and takes all the guess work out of the process.

DESCRIPTION "Metabolic Rejuvenation" by Douglas Laboratories is a comprehensive 28-day, 3 phase detoxification support program with nutrients specifically chosen to prepare the body through elimination, detox through support of phase 1 and 2 liver detoxification, and repair the body and intestinal tract. One Metabolic Rejuvenation box includes 4 bottles (one for each week) with convenience packs and a patient guidebook.

FUNCTIONS <u>*Week 1- Prepare.*</u> *The goal of the first week is to open pathways for elimination and prepare the body to properly detoxify in the next phase. The proprietary blend supplies a significant amount of detoxifying herbs, fibers, minerals, probiotics and vitamin C for proper bowel elimination and intestinal support. Fiber from citrus pectin and psyllium seed husks can naturally stimulate the bowel. Bentonite powder has properties that tightly bind and immobilize toxic compounds in the gastrointestinal tract. Vitamin C acts as a free radical scavenger to cells. Magnesium may support infrequent bowel movements.*

<u>*Week 2 and 3- Detox.*</u> *The goal of week 2 and 3 is to support phase 1 and phase 2 detoxification of the liver. As the body's main detoxification organ, the liver is responsible for removing all potentially detrimental molecules. This detoxification process occurs in 2 phases. The supplements in week 2 and 3 convenience packs help to maintain liver structure and function in response to environmental toxins. Choline, betaine, and methionine are involved in methyl group metabolism, which is essential for normal liver function. Isothiocyanates (ITCs) found in Wasabia*

japonica (Wasabi or Japanese horse radish) are naturally occurring compounds that have the ability to stimulate detoxification pathways, and are 10-25 times more potent than ITCs found in cruciferous vegetables.

Sulforaphanes in broccoli (cruciferous) have been found to significantly increase the activity of Phase II enzymes. For efficient Phase two detoxification, the liver cells require sulphur-containing amino acids such as taurine, methionine and cysteine.

N-Acetyl-L-cysteine is a biologically active precursor for glutathione synthesis, therefore raising intracellular glutathione levels. L-Glutathione scavenges toxic free radicals and inhibits peroxidation by slowing down free-radical catalyzed chain reactions. Glutathione is involved in DNA synthesis and repair, protein and prostaglandin synthesis, amino acid transport, metabolism of toxins and carcinogens, immune system function, prevention of oxidative cell damage, and enzyme activation.

Dietary sulfur assumes a major role in detoxification as part of the hepatic sulfur conjugation pathways. Glutathione, sulfur and NAC support mercury detoxification. High mercury in the body can inhibit antioxidant enzymes and deplete intracellular glutathione. B vitamins, vitamin C and lipoic acid perform as antioxidants to scavenge free radicals. Garlic appears to prevent endothelial cell depletion of glutathione, which may be responsible for its antioxidant effects.

<u>Week 4- Repair</u> The goal of week 4 is to replenish lost nutrients through the detoxification phase and provide specific nutrients to repair the gut. A multivitamin/mineral with an organic fruit and vegetable blend provides adequate amounts of vitamins, minerals, and antioxidants to nutritionally replenish the body. Omega-3 fatty acids from fish oil support normal inflammatory processes.

Glutamine helps maintain normal intestinal permeability, mucosal cell regeneration and structure, especially during periods of physiological stress. Glutamine also carries potentially toxic ammonia to the kidneys for excretion, which helps maintain normal acid-base balance.

DR. M. P. KHAN, MD/NMD

Healthy bacteria in the intestinal tract can be removed during extensive or frequent bowel elimination, thereby making supplementation with probiotic bacteria cultures necessary after a detoxification regimen. A normal intestinal microflora rich in lactobacilli creates acidic conditions that are unfavorable for the settlement of pathogenic microorganisms.

October 6

MRS. SMITH AND METHUSELAH*

This program sounds very technical and complicated, Doc! Can you explain this to me in plain English?

OK Mrs. Smith, to understand this well, you need to understand the concept of 'Functional Medicine.' Here is a short version of the definition of this branch of medicine. It is essentially "Taking out the bad and putting in the good."

"Functional Medicine is dedicated to prevention, early assessment, and improved management of complex chronic disease by intervening at multiple levels to correct core clinical imbalances and thereby restore each patient's functionality and health to the greatest extent possible."

So Dr. Khan, if it is that simple, why do I need to go through this complicated program of twenty eight days?

First let's consider the multiple plant based supplements used in the twenty eight day program. These supplements are also called phytochemicals. They are chemical compounds found in plants (and caffeine is a good example, a chemical found in coffee beans) can modulate this detoxification system. Some modulate Phase I or Phase II (mono-functional modulators) and some modulate both phases (multi-functional modulators).

Most phytochemicals (with the exception of St. John's wort which increases drug metabolism and grapefruit which decreases drug metabolism and can result in toxic levels of a drug and therefore no medication should be taken with grapefruit juice), derived from plant foods have important effects on the detoxification pathways. And actually if you eat a diet rich in the below foods and supplements as part of your daily diet, you may never need to go through a detoxification program.

DR. M. P. KHAN, MD/NMD

Onions, garlic, cruciferous vegetable such as broccoli, garden cress and Brussel sprouts, chlorophyll (wheat grass juice, kale), terpenoids such as Gingko biloba, bioflavonoids such as grape seed and green tea, the aplaceae family (eat your carrots please) are all foods that are multi-functional modulators of the detoxification pathways.

Also vitamins play a critical role in the detox pathways. Deficiency of Vitamin A results in a slowing down of the Phase II pathway.

Hormones, such as the thyroid hormone (triiodothyronine or T3) require Vitamin A to also affect Phase II pathways.

Gut bacteria play a critical role in both pathways and are influenced by dietary fiber such as wheat bran, carrot fiber and oat bran which are pre-biotics and nourish the healthy gut flora, also modulate Phase I and II pathways. Also fiber moves stool along the gut more rapidly (transit time) thus removing the chemicals in the bile that the liver has detoxified and also reduce bacterial enzymes that reverse the conjugation of the toxins (Phase II). Also by decreasing intestinal permeability, they reduce the absorption of toxic compounds.

Adequate amounts of protein, specifically L-glutamine, methionine, L-cysteine and N-acetyl cysteine NAC are examples of Phase II modulators. Lipoic acid supplements and whey protein greatly increase levels of glutathione, a powerful anti-oxidant which helps soak up free radicals.

Special attention to Sylmarin or milk thistle which is a powerful inducer of the Phase II pathway in the liver. In fact it is also protective to the liver cells and the injectable form is one of the few agents that can reverse nightshade mushroom poisoning; a poisoning which quickly destroys the liver and is usually fatal. It is also useful in patients with active Hepatitis C, reducing the inflammatory effect on the liver.

An adequate amount of minerals is important. An iron deficiency can lead to increased lead absorption and aluminum absorption. A selenium deficiency increases mercury retention. Mercury needs to bind to glutathione for excretion and a zinc deficiency can result in decreased production of this compound.

Boy, this sounds complicated. I see the need for supplement support. My daughter also thinks I should fast when I am on this program of detoxification. Not sure I can do that. I love to eat, Doc!

Mrs. Smith, you are in luck. I do not recommend long term fasting. Phase II pathways are dependent on various compounds present in food. Complete fasting may result in slowing down of Phase II (and accelerate Phase I) which may result in an increase in toxic intermediate compounds and could potentially make you very sick.

Another suggestion. Reduce carbohydrates in your diet. These affect the Phase I pathways, reducing their activity. Adequate protein intake is also important to provide the amino acids needed as noted above. Also increase soluble fiber intake (Metamucil anyone?) and insoluble fiber. (Bran)

And increase your water intake (at least 64 oz. /daily) to assist elimination by the kidneys. Also regular exercise for 30 minutes a day, which increases antioxidant enzymes and increases sweating which is an important method of removing heavy metal toxins.

Sounds good, Doc. But are you sure that it is necessary? Am I toxic?

October 7

MRS. SMITH AND METHUSELAH*

"If, having endured much, we have at last asserted our "right to know," and if by knowing, we have concluded that we are being asked to take senseless and frightening risks, then we should no longer accept the counsel of those who tell us that we must fill our world with poisonous chemicals; we should look about and see what other course is open to us."
—Rachel Carson, Silent Spring

The question is not that you *are or are not* toxic. Living in the times we do, *everybody* is carrying a toxic load. The question to ask is that whether the toxic burden is a cause of illness or an obstacle to cure and what can be done to help the patient. I recommend a detoxification protocol to *any* patient with a chronic illness. The first step is to get a good history. The mnemonic **C (H2) OP (D4)** is helpful. Below is the questionnaire I would ask you to complete before your next visit. Circle any positives and expand on them if you need to in the space provided.

Community..... City and neighborhood air quality.

_____

_____

_____

Hobbies......... Toxic chemicals, paints, solvents.

_____

_____

_____

Occupation......Workplace air, toxic chemicals.

_____

_____

_____

Personal Habits. Smoking, alcohol, illicit drugs, sleep patterns, exercise.

_____

_____

_____

Diet............. A food diary is helpful and also organic vs. non and processed vs whole. Are there food allergies or intolerance? Is there disruption of healthy gut bacteria? (Dysbiosis or Small Intestinal Bacterial Overgrowth or SIBO which can be detected by a breath test)

In the space below, write down a list of foods you eat for Breakfast, Lunch and Dinner as well as the snacks and beverages you consume in a typical day.

Breakfast _____

_____

Lunch _____

_____

Dinner _____

_____

Snacks _____

_____

Beverages _____

_____

Drugs............ What prescription pharmaceuticals as well as herbal supplements and OTC drugs are you taking?

_____

_____

_____

_____

_____

_____

_____

DR. M. P. KHAN, MD/NMD

Dental............ Any amalgams or root canal procedures?

_____

_____

Development..... Maternal history of toxic exposure during pregnancy or childhood exposure to leaded paints, pesticides?

_____

_____

_____

_____

_____

_____

October 8

MRS. SMITH AND METHUSELAH*

"We need to accept the seemingly obvious fact that a toxic environment can make people sick and that no amount of medical intervention can protect us. The health care community must become a powerful political lobby for environmental policy and legislation."

—Andrew Weil MD

So Mrs. Smith, I see you have completed your toxin exposure history. You have, from your answers, had extensive dental work done in the past with multiple fillings. As you know, the amalgams used then were based on mercury compounds. We will have to focus on that issue. You are also on a statin drug for cholesterol which can affect liver function. And you use a brand of cosmetics which has high levels of certain toxic chemicals.

Wow Doc! Now you have me worried. Before I do anything about this is there any testing that can be done? Like a blood test or something?

Yes, Mrs. Smith, there are tests developed by specialty labs which measure metallothionein profiles. These include serum zinc, serum copper, serum ceruloplasmin, whole blood glutathione and copper/zinc ratios. These test are a bit complicated to interpret but they may help in understanding how efficiently the body is detoxifying.

There are also challenge tests where patients are given aspirin as a standard dose and the urine is collected and the levels of chemicals produced by Phase I and Phase II pathways is measured. These tests are useful mostly in evaluating the efficiency of liver detoxification processes.

There are also tests for measuring organic toxicants such as PCBs, BPA, organochloride pesticides, fire retardants, furans and dioxins. As these are all fat soluble and are stored in the fat cells of the body. A small sample of adipose tissue is taken from just under the belly button and sent for analysis. This sampling is important as blood or urine samples may show low or no levels of organic toxins.

Blood tests are also available, which run into thousands of dollars. These can test for over two hundred different environmental toxins and are mostly used for research purposes. (See EWG.org video "Ten Americans").

In your case, Mrs. Smith, My primary concern is mercury toxicity. A hair analysis is one way you may have heard of. This may not be accurate as high levels of mercury may be due to normal excretory patterns of mercury. A urine specimen for heavy metals may be useful but may not reflect tissue levels. Since sampling of tissue is impractical, *provocative urine* testing is probably the most reliable way to test for heavy metals. In provocative testing, urine can be collected following the administration of a challenge agents such as EDTA, DMSA, DMPS, and D-penicillamine which are chelating agents for specific toxic elements, which can help identify tissue levels from prior exposures to the specific heavy metals. Depending on the agent administered, urine collection may be spot or short-term ie 2-6 hours, intermediate ie 8-12 hours or a complete 24-hour collection. This approach is best utilized when the clinician suspects specific heavy metal toxicities.

October 9

MRS. SMITH AND METHUSELAH*

Below is a one page description of the test as performed by Genova Diagnostics. (www.GDX.net) and can be ordered by your health care provider.

The Toxic Element Clearance Profile: This profile offers an advanced, comprehensive assessment of toxic and potentially toxic elements excreted in the urine. In addition to measuring classic elemental toxics, this profile includes elements used in medical, aerospace, nuclear and high-tech electronics industries. Use of these potential toxins is increasing.

Sources of Exposure: *Accumulations of these toxics can occur in the human body in response to occupational exposures or to environmental exposures from toxic release in air, soil, or industrial waste streams. These include:* • *Metal refining* • *Fabrication of nuclear reactor fuel assemblies* • *Alloying* • *Electronics and computer manufacturing* • *Plating and parts manufacture in aerospace and machine tool industries*

According to the EPA, the U.S. has the largest electronics (including computers) workforce in the world. Exposures to the measured elements can occur in other occupations as well, including: • *Welding and metal shaping* • *Military or police service (with weapons use)* • *Plumbing* • *Handling and disposal of wastes* • *Oil refining* • *Petrochemical production* •

Health Consequences of Exposure: *Evidence suggests that chronic toxic element exposure can adversely affect:* • *Energy levels* • *Neurological development and function* • *Reproductive function* • *Respiratory, cardiac, hepatic and immune functions* • *Cancer risk* • *Cognitive and emotional health* • *Degenerative conditions*

DR. M. P. KHAN, MD/NMD

Researchers are discovering detrimental health effects of toxic heavy metals at lower and lower exposure levels. This raises the issue of whether any toxic element level in the body is safe. The Toxic Element Clearance Profile assesses urinary excretion of elements acquired through either chronic or acute exposure. The test enables practitioners to effectively monitor the progress of detoxification regimens and nutrient element status during treatment. All toxic metals are reported as micrograms/g creatinine or as micrograms per 24 hours (if a 24-hour urine specimen is provided).

Analytes: - Toxic Elements (ratioed to creatinine): aluminum antimony arsenic barium bismuth cadmium cesium gadolinium gallium lead - Nutritional Element: sulfur

Specimen requirements: 2 tubes of urine •Before Patient Takes this Test: - Avoid taking creatine supplements (2 days before test) - Check with your healthcare provider about what medications and supplements to avoid (2 days before test) - Do not collect urine during a menstrual period - See instructions inside test kit for details

This Toxic Element Clearance Profile measures urinary excretion of a diverse range of potentially harmful elements, both well-known toxics such as lead and mercury, as well as new technology toxics such as niobium, mercury nickel niobium platinum rubidium thallium thorium tin tungsten uranium.

October 10

MRS. SMITH AND METHUSELAH*

> *"All this has come about because of the sudden rise and prodigious growth of an industry for the production of man-made or synthetic chemicals with insecticidal properties. This industry is a child of the Second World War. In the course of developing agents of chemical warfare, some of the chemicals created in the laboratory were found to be lethal to insects. The discovery did not come by chance: insects were widely used to test chemicals as agents of death for man."*
> — Rachel Carson, *Silent Spring*

Mrs. Smith returns for a follow up office visit. Her testing showed (as expected) high levels of mercury. She went to a special dentist trained in safe removal of mercury amalgams and had them replaced with non-toxic dental fillings. A follow up urine test shows a greatly reduced burden of mercury. She reports that she feels mentally sharper and also has less muscle and joint pains.

Hey Doc! I had no idea about all that nasty mercury in my body. Thanks for all your help in this matter. I feel so much better. My granddaughter keeps saying "I told you so, Grandma;" the little brat. Are there any lifestyle changes I can make to prevent this problem in the future?

Yes, a good way is to remember the mnemonic "A NERD".

Avoid: This is obvious. Avoid exposure to polluted water. Alcohol in moderation. Avoid tobacco products and illicit substances. Avoid processed, deep fried and junk foods and sugary beverages as well as foods with artificial sweeteners. Also check your home for leaded paints.

Nutrition: Try to eat mostly organic foods (remember the Dirty Dozen list) and emphasize an alkaline diet (fish, vegetables, fruits, nuts and soluble fiber) and avoid acidic foods such as red meat and pork. Eat generous amounts of garlic, onions, olive oil, and cruciferous vegetables such as broccoli.

Supplementation with trace minerals, multivitamins, omega-3 EFA and NAC along with lipoic acid and grape seed/green tea extracts also support detoxification.

Exercise: This increases lymphatic flow and also induces sweating; a key pathway for eliminating heavy metal toxins

Rest: Relaxation and stress management and a good sleep pattern are important features of the detox life style.

Detoxification: I recommend the process on a six month interval to keep up with elimination of the toxic load. As discussed previously, prolonged fasting is not a good idea but a juice fast for one or two days before the twenty eight day Douglas Labs Metabolic Rejuvenation Program is very helpful in kick starting the bodies detox systems.

October 11

MRS. SMITH AND METHUSELAH*

*"Why should we tolerate a diet of weak poisons, a home
in insipid surroundings, a circle of acquaintances who are
not quite our enemies, the noise of motors with just enough
relief to prevent insanity? Who would want to live in a
world which is just not quite fatal?"*
—Rachel Carson, "Silent Spring"

*A NERD! That's very helpful, Doc. Can't wait to tease Elsie. Bet she does not know
this one, Ms. Smarty Pants! Is there anything else that I can do about this mercury
issue? How about chelation? And sauna therapy?*

Mrs. Smith, you have certainly done your research on this issue.
God bless Google. Since you have responded so well to some of the
measures you have undergone, these are not interventions that would
help you. But I will explain them to you anyway. First chelation.

Chelation is a process by which a chemical compound taken
orally or by intravenous route binds to heavy metals such as lead
and mercury and this the excreted out in the urine.

The most common form of an oral chelating compound is DMSA
or *dimercaptosuccinic acid*. It is approved by the FDA for safety and is
efficient in removing heavy metals such as lead, mercury and other
heavy metals when used in as specific protocols. .It is available
by prescription under the brand names of Chemet and Succimer
and is administered at the dose of 30 mg/Kg and is even safe in
children and infants although the final dosing is up to your health
care provider.

Two protocols are used. The first: Three days of DMSA followed
by eleven days without and then the cycle is repeated if needed. The
second protocol is five days of DMSA followed by nine days without
and the cycle repeated. A urine test for heavy metals can be done on

every fifth cycle and it is not uncommon to go up to twenty cycles before stopping which is a testament to its safety.

On DMSA free days, supplement with low levels of zinc, copper, molybdenum and manganese. Also there is significant loss of magnesium so it is important to supplement with high dose oral or injectable magnesium.

Sauna therapy involves excessive sweating (like exercise) and is helpful in removing fat loving compounds such as pesticides and PCBs and certain pharmaceuticals also known as xenobiotics as well as heavy metals such as mercury and lead. Sauna therapy is also known as 'thermal depuration' and patients state that they can actually smell the chemicals released during the process and some have reported staining and destruction of their clothing!

October 12

MRS. SMITH AND METHUSELAH*

<u>Dr. K's Detox Salsa.</u>

This salsa uses ingredients which can ramp up your detoxification pathways.

Ingredients: (Try to go organic as much as possible.)

Five x 1 pound cans of stewed tomatoes. Chop the tomatoes into small pieces and do not discard the juice. If you would rather use fresh tomatoes, score the top of five pounds of raw tomatoes, blanch them for a minute in boiling water, cool and remove the peels. Core them, chop into small pieces. Retain any juice that separates.

Two x 7oz cans of chopped green chilies. If you want to use fresh chilies, use a cup of chopped Jalapenos after deveining and removing the seeds. Eliminate this step if you do not like a spicy kick to the salsa.

> *1 ½ cups of chopped onions*
> *4 large cloves of garlic minced*
> *½ inch of ginger grated.*
> *1 ½ cup of loosely packed chopped cilantro*
> *2 tsp of dried oregano or 1/2 cup of chopped fresh oregano*
> *1 cup of broccoli (florets only) finely chopped*
> *½ tsp. of ground cumin*
> *2 tsp. of salt*
> *1 tbsp. of sugar.*
> *1/2 cup of apple cider vinegar*

Combine all ingredients in a stainless steel pot (never use aluminum utensils for cooking as any acidic foods will leach aluminum compounds into the food) and bring to a boil and let simmer for 10 minutes. Cool and store in jars. Refrigerate or can using a water bath canner or pressure cooker as per instructions.

DR. M. P. KHAN, MD/NMD

October 13

A POEM IN YOUR POCKET

*"For poems are not, as people think, simply emotions (one
has emotions early enough)—they are experiences."*
—Rainer Maria Rilke

Jelaluddin Rumi was born in 1207 in Balkh, Afghanistan. Fleeing the
invading Mongol armies, his family settled in Konya, Turkey. He spent
many years as a religious scholar, steeped in convention until he met
Shams of Tabriz in 1244. Although Rumi was well versed in the horizontal
of a learned and secular life, Shams connected him to the vertical of
spiritual union. And the poetry started flowing. The translations of his
poems are widely available in English and in almost all major world
languages. Amazingly, he is the most widely read poet in America today!

The poems were originally written in the Persian language called
Farsi. (It is also the language of the Khordeh Avesta, a collection of holy
books of the Zoroastrian religion.) Rumor has it that there was a large pole
planted in the backyard of Rumi's house. He would hold the pole and walk
around it in a trance like state. And as he walked the verses flowed through
him and were promptly transcribed. All 44,000 of them; making him the
most prolific poet of all time. But his real genius lies in the timelessness
of his poems and how relevant they are to the times that we live in.

Rumi felt that human beings were like reeds pulled out of the river
mud. God fashioned these reeds into a flute with seven holes (yes, the
human body does have seven apertures) and our speech and our songs are
actually a longing to return to the divine mud. And as per Rilke, maybe
the experience of poetry is finally to return us to our divine nature!

*"In your light I learn how to love; in your beauty, how to make poems.
You dance inside my chest where no one sees you."*

2007 was the 800th Anniversary of his birth and was widely celebrated.
UNESCO declared that year as "International Rumi Year" and issued a

special medal in commemoration. Rumi died in 1273 AD. He was buried in Konya. His shrine became a place of pilgrimage. His followers, and his son Sultan Walad, after his death, founded the Mawlawīyah Order of Sufis. Also known as the Order of the Whirling Dervishes, they are famous for its dancing where the participants twirl in a divine trance.

One of my favorite poems and in my top ten list is the translation by Coleman Barks titled "Someone Digging in the Ground" which I cannot reproduce here for copyright reasons. It is in a collection of poems "The Essential Rumi" by the above author. These poems are truly essential food for the spirit; like our daily bread!

October 14

A POEM IN YOUR POCKET

This was a poem I wrote in 1994 and was dedicated to a woman who I thought would have been my soul mate and the great love of my life (she wasn't). Much later I realized that it could have been a metaphor of the meeting between Rumi and Shams or maybe the yearning of all human beings to fuse with the divine! It is also the title of my two poetry books published by Trafford Press that are now available on Amazon.

WINGLESS ANGELS

We are wingless angels,
Born in separate times.
Outcasts of Eden and Nirvana,
Children of lesser Gods.

We have wandered through time,
Tasting the dust of eternity.
Our foot prints crossed Acropolis and Atlantis,
But we never met until now!

Like water and fire,
Like Ying and Yang,
Like lightning and summer rain,
Our souls united between heaven and earth,
Embracing with a quiet thunder.

MK/1994

Make a copy of your favorite poet and carry it in your pocket. If you don't have one check out some of these web sites.http://poems.com/ http://www.poets.org/

October 15

SPORTS 'N' SUPPLEMENTS (PART-4)

"Once and for all, I did not use steroids or any other illegal substance."
—**Mark McGwire**

"Performance-enhancing drugs are an illusion. I wish I had never gotten involved with steroids. It was wrong. It was stupid."
—**Mark McGwire**

In a previous month we had discussed the use of LEGAL supplements to enhance athletic abilities. Below are some that are <u>not</u> LEGAL!

In a previous discussion, we talked about legal supplements that can be used in competitive sports. But in the month of October in my other life in PA, there was the inevitable preparation for the next season of school sports. As school physician for a large school district, I got to do the honors. There was always a concern of the use of illegal supplements when I examined members of the varsity football team. Especially when I saw a participant who had packed on twenty pounds of muscle since the last physical and had acne; a sure sign of anabolic steroid use.

1) DHEA: DHEA is a testosterone precursor or a pro hormone that has been used to enhance performance in sports. DHEA also is present in the blood as its sulfate. (DHEAS) and together are the most abundant steroid in humans. Much remains unknown about DHEA's effects. Levels peak when people are in their 20s, and then gradually decrease as a person ages; hence its wide spread use in Anti-aging medicine. Only humans and a few primates have the ability to synthesize DHEA and DHEAS.

DR. M. P. KHAN, MD/NMD

In human research, a few small studies have found some benefits when older men and women take DHEA supplements. (Usually 100 mg/day) This returned blood DHEA levels to their levels a chronological age of their 20's with women (but not men) also having some increase in androstenedione and testosterone levels. Another study done on untrained men, showed no significant differences in serum testosterone levels in both the study and control groups.

Prolonged use of DHEA use is associated with acne, increased facial hair, and loss of scalp hair, deepening of the voice, weight gain, decreased HDL cholesterol, abnormal liver tests, and sleep disturbances. The quality of commercial products available is also a problem. There is little reason to support the use of DHEA by athletes. The IOC and NCAA has banned its use.

SPORTS AND SUPPLEMENTS (PART-4)

> *"In his new book, baseball slugger Jose Conseco said he took steroids when he played for the Texas Rangers, and that owner George W. Bush knew all about it. In response President Bush said that's ridiculous. I've never known all about anything."*
> —Conan O'Brien

If you participate in sports or know someone who does and are contemplating the use of performance enhancing drugs, review or share the information presented in this article. It may save their life!

2) EPHEDRA: Recently banned by the FDA, it was widely used in sport drinks and weight loss supplements until recently. Several deaths directly related to its use caused the directive to make it unavailable in the US. Also known as Ma Huang, it is widely used in TCM (Traditional Chinese Medicine) in appropriate disease conditions. This is a good example how the improper use of an indigenous herbal system can cause problems. Its synthetic form is ephedrine and pseudo-ephedrine.

Its use is associated with stroke, cardiac arrhythmias, tachycardia, acute myocardial infarction, and sudden death. Another review reported to the FDA of adverse events found that hypertension was the most common adverse event.

Ephedra is also associated with psychiatric effects, including euphoria, neurotic behavior, agitation, depressed mood, and anxiety. It stimulates the adrenergic receptors and causes release of dopamine, the feel good neuro-transmitter. Ephedra users had almost four times the risk of mild psychiatric symptoms compared to placebo.

3) ANABOLIC ANDROGENIC STEROIDS (AAS): These are a group of steroids related to testosterone. Although there is a question of

DR. M. P. KHAN, MD/NMD

how effective they are, the current belief is that they do increase muscle mass and strength. There is a heated debate about their adverse effects and almost all AAS users minimize them.

Nearly 30% of users report mild adverse effects. Common ones are loss of libido, mood changes, reduced testicular volume, and acne. The incidence of all-cause mortality of 62 Finnish powerlifting champions suspected of using AAS was compared with 1094 population controls. Over a 12-year period, 12.9% of the study group died compared to 3.1% of the controls. The causes of death among the users were suicide, acute myocardial infarction, hepatic coma and non-Hodgkin's lymphoma.

AAS can cause cardiac disease via several mechanisms. Studies have found that AAS cause major changes in lipid metabolism by reducing HDL levels and raising LDL levels and promote platelet aggregation and promote coagulation along with direct damage to coronary arteries and myocardial cells, a sure fire recipe for a heart attack. Other serious adverse events reported include liver toxicity and cancer, hirsutism (excess hair) in women, and gynecomastia (or breast formation) and reduction in testicular size in men

The psychiatric effects of AAS are harder to study. In controlled studies, most subjects given smaller physiological doses did not display mood changes but higher doses elicited mania and hypomania. Increased aggression and violence with AAS have been coined "roid rage." and may have contributed to the double murder-suicide of professional wrestler, Chris Benoit, and his wife and son in June 2007.

Having said that, there is a role for AAS in the treatment of male hypogonadism (or the drop in testosterone levels as men age) also known as 'andropause'. This can easily be tested by a test which should measure total and free testosterone with a blood draw first thing in the morning. This test is also called a Free Androgen Index.

A total level of 300 units or less along with the complaints of fatigue, low libido and depression is usually an indication for treatment with AAS usually in the form of a daily topical gel. This level is arbitrary and has no real clinical value except that your insurance plan will not cover the testosterone gel unless the level is less than 300 units.

October 17

TWO PARABLES:
IMPERMANENCE & ENVY

Below are two Zen parables.

The first is about the transient nature of life and how we are just guests in this world.

Gudo, a famous Zen spiritual master came to the front door of the King Baisal's palace. None of the guards tried to stop him as he entered and made his way to where the King himself was sitting on his throne.

"What do you want, Zen Master Gudo?" asked the King, immediately recognizing the visitor, whose fame was well known throughout the kingdom.

"I would like a place to sleep in this inn," replied the Master.

"But this is not an inn," said the King, outraged at this request. "It is my palace."

"May I ask who owned this palace before you?" said Gudo.

"My father. He is dead," said King Baisal.' May he rest in peace," still agitated by the questions asked by the Zen Master.

"And who owned it before him?" continued Gudo.

"My grandfather. He too is dead." replied King Baisal, amazed and intrigued now, by the man's impudence.

"And this place where people live for a short time and then move on – did I hear you say that it is NOT an inn?"

The second one is acceptance of the life and circumstances given to us and the folly of envying others.

There was once a stone cutter named Rustam who was dissatisfied with himself and with his profession. Each day as he toiled in the hot sun, cutting the hard rock with his chisel, he wished his life was different. One afternoon, tired from his toils, he fell asleep and had a dream:

In this dream, Rustam passed a wealthy merchant's house. Through the open door way, he saw many beautiful possessions and important visitors sitting around and

DR. M. P. KHAN, MD/NMD

drinking tea. "How powerful that merchant must be!" thought Rustam. He became very envious and wished that he could be like the merchant.

To his great surprise, he was suddenly transformed into a powerful merchant, enjoying beautiful objects and friends and more power than he had ever imagined, but envied and hated by those poorer than himself. Soon a tax collector passed by. He was carried in a fancy carved and embroidered sedan chair, with a retinue of attendants and escorted by soldiers accompanied by the sound of heraldic trumpets. Everyone, no matter how rich, had to bow and curtsy before the procession. "How powerful that person is!" he thought. "I wish that I could be that tax collector!"

Then, just as suddenly he became a tax collector, carried everywhere in his embroidered sedan chair, despised and feared by the people everywhere he travelled. It was a hot summer day, so Rustam felt very uncomfortable in the richly upholstered sticky sedan chair. He looked up at the afternoon sun. It shone proud and bright in the sky, unaffected by his presence. "How powerful the sun is!" he thought. "I wish that I could be the sun!"

Then he became the bright sun, shining fiercely down on everyone, scorching the fields, cursed by the farmers and laborers for the drought they faced. But a huge black thundercloud moved between him and the earth, so that the sun could no longer shine on everything below. "How powerful that storm cloud is!" he thought. "I wish that I could be a thunder cloud!"

Then he became the cloud. Soon he let loose a huge rain storm flooding the fields and villages and destroying their crops. He heard the villagers now cursing him more vehemently.. He did not like this. Soon he found that he was being pushed away by some great force, and realized that it was the wind. "How powerful it is!" he thought. "I wish that I could be the wind!"

Then he became the wind, blowing tiles off the roofs of houses, uprooting trees, feared and hated by all below him. But after a while, he ran up against something that would not move, no matter how forcefully he blew against it – a huge, towering pillar of granite. "How powerful that rock is!" he thought. "I wish that I could be a rock!"

Then he became that pillar of granite, more powerful than anything else on earth. But as he stood there, he heard the sound of a hammer pounding a chisel into the hard surface, and felt himself being changed. "What could be more powerful than I, the rock?" he thought.

He looked down and saw far below him the figure of a stone cutter. As this figure once again held up the hammer and chisel, Rustam awoke with a start from his sleep. He was filled with gratitude about the position of his life. Never would he envy others.

Perfection is within us, we just have to look for it.

October 18

TWO PARABLES:
IMPERMANENCE & ENVY

Impermanence:

What is your perception of death? Do you fear it, accept it as inevitable or see it as a transition to a higher and more beautiful level of existence?

_____

_____

_____

_____

_____

How would you live your life differently if you knew you had only six months remaining?

_____

_____

_____

_____

Envy:

Have you ever envied another person for their beauty, money, power or intelligence? (Of course we all have at some time or another) Write down what is positive about your life and also the downside of what you envy in another. For example a beautiful woman would have to try really hard to establish her intelligence and that she is just not another pretty face!

_____

_____

_____

_____

DR. M. P. KHAN, MD/NMD

October 19

EATING AND MEDITATING (PART-1)

"One of the delights of life is eating with friends, second to that is talking about eating. And, for an unsurpassed double whammy, there is talking about eating while you are eating with friends."
—Laurie Colwin

On my way to work, (when I lived in Pittsburgh, my present commute is very short and bucolic) I often saw the driver of a car eating a breakfast sandwich and at the same time balancing a cup of coffee resigned to the inevitable Parkway traffic. And sometimes when I could slip away at lunch time to my home, Karen and a sandwich, I swear I saw the same drivers, this time with a hamburger or something equally portable, going this time in the opposite direction.

One of the things I dread is the solo trip to a restaurant. One is usually given a table next to the entrance to the restrooms by a smirking maître de and then the waiters generally ignore you." How sad that you had to come alone to a restaurant" they whisper under their breath. And if one of them takes pity on you, they may actually start up a conversation with you. In the meanwhile it helps to fiddle with your Blackberry or makes voluminous notes on a legal pad as if to give the message that you are too busy for company anyway!

And yet look around at your fellow drivers or in a fast food restaurant and you will see the singletons as they wolf down their meals and head back to the office. And some of us (yours truly included) occasionally skip lunch completely as we use that precious time to *catch up on work!*

Which brings me to Eating Suggestion #9: *Eat with family and friends, not alone.*

Food is more than a sum of its calories! Each of us have an emotional attachment to food. What we eat is our history and our geography and our culture and our bogeymen and our dreams. Most of us, in the US have never gone hungry unless we are engaged in some fad diet or other. And yet so much food ends up in dumpsters. Mealtimes are generally scattered according to the various schedules of the individuals involved. Hence the expression "I will grab something on the way!" or "Just zap the leftovers for dinner, dear!"

We have made eating food irrelevant and one more chore to be done in the course of a busy day. In most other countries and cultures, there is time and space reserved for this very important part of our lives. We are social creatures and when we get together around a table for a meal or on the carpet around a large dish of food as in some Middle Eastern countries, we reestablish the communal bonds that are so critical to our mental health. And there is something primal about going to a restaurant and ordering different items and then sharing the colors and aromas of the dishes that follow!

EATING AND MEDITATING (PART-1)

This is an exercise you can do and it is a lot of fun as it is done with almost everybody's favorite food: chocolate. You will need a piece of chocolate (dark, organic and fair trade) so splurge a little. I actually did this exercise at a local management retreat of over 250 participants and was wildly popular.

INTRODUCTION: You are probably full of mindfulness by now. And you are looking at the dish of chocolates and thinking: "The heck with all this touchy feely stuff and just let me eat it." My talk will consist of three parts.

Let's start with a show of hands.
The first: How many of you work through lunch?
The second: How many of you eat while driving?

1) The historical origin of chocolate.
2) The health benefits of chocolate.
3) Some tips on mindful eating

> *1) Let's start with some botanical facts. The word cacao is not a typo. Theo broma is Greek for "food of the gods." Kakaw is an Aztec word. First introduced to the Western world to the Spanish by the Aztecs in 1519. Grows mostly in South America and the Ivory Coast of Africa and in 15 other countries. Each tree yields 20 pods a year and the beans or seeds (20-60) from the pods are processed to make cocoa paste which yields a pound of chocolate. Worldwide annual production is around 5 million tons. Agricultural practices vary so try to eat organic chocolate and also fair trade which means that the farmer gets a fair price for the beans.*

2) We already covered the health benefits of chocolate in previous days so I will not repeat it but it is probable one of the healthiest foods you can enjoy as long as it is dark chocolate. The active ingredients of chocolate can affect brain chemistry in several ways. The main ingredient is theobromine which has a similar effect as caffeine. Chocolate is high in tryptophan which is the raw material of serotonin, a mood elevator. Another effect is the release of endorphins which also causes the release of dopamine, the brains 'feel good" chemical. But the more interesting action of chocolate is due to a neuro peptide called anandamide (anand = joy; Sanskrit) which binds with the same receptors as the active chemical in marijuana; THC. But before somebody makes chocolate an illegal drug, one would have to consume several pounds of chocolate daily to have any significant impact (get high) on brain chemistry.

DR. M. P. KHAN, MD/NMD

October 21

EATING AND MEDITATING (PART-2)

"One of the very nicest things about life is the way we must regularly stop whatever it is we are doing and devote our attention to eating."

—Luciano Pavarotti

And the last one;

Eating Suggestion # 10. *Eat Slowly: It's (food) not going anywhere!*

As the title suggests, eating can be a form of meditation. It involves being more mindful of the moment when we begin to eat. Pavarotti, well known for his girth and his zest for a good meal, followed his own advice often! But he can be forgiven because of that heavenly voice. It was like manna for the ears even though he was not exactly a good role model for sensible gustatory behavior.

An easy exercise to start with is the process of eating a single piece of chocolate) Here is how it works.

Take the piece of chocolate and hold it in your hand. Feel the surface and the shape. Closing your eyes sometimes helps to appreciate its uniqueness. Smell the aroma of the chocolate.

Now bite off a small piece. Do not start chewing on it right away. Fell the texture of the chocolate with your tongue.

Next bite into the chocolate and gently chew it mixing it with your saliva. Notice how it melts as it breaks up. Remember digestion begins in the mouth. Appreciate the flavors that are released as you chew on it.

Swallow the well chewed piece. What is the aftertaste?

Most of us, after completing this exercise, often comment on how different the chocolate tasted when we were more mindful of the experience. I think you get the picture! And you thought meditation was all about sitting cross legged and chanting!

Of course there are times when it is not possible to meet and eat with friends and family members. But if you are going to eat alone, (or not) here are some ideas that may make you enjoy your meal and at the same time help in cutting down on calories. The behavior of eating is getting a lot of attention these days and like any change in long established patterns, needs to be made slowly and consistently over a period of time. Try to incorporate most of the ten guidelines which follow on the next page, the next time you sit down for a meal.

October 22

EATING AND MEDITATING (PART-2)

Here are some recommendations to help with changing eating behaviors.

1) *Eat slowly. It takes about 20 minutes before the satiety center in the brain kicks in after we begin eating. Most of us eat as if the food will disappear if left alone. This is not true. Really! Take your time, It may help to set a kitchen timer, first for 15 minutes and increase it till you can spend a leisurely 30 minutes eating your meal. This is harder to achieve than you think, but soon you will actually feel more relaxed after a meal.*

2) *Put your fork and knife down between bites and chew your food as this will also help you with #1) and with digestion. Remember, it begins with your mouth!*

3) *Do not do any other activity while eating and especially not while driving or watching TV. Food commercials are powerful triggers to impulsive eating. This will prevent 'unconscious' eating and also make you more aware when you are 'full' so that you can stop eating.*

4) *Don't worry if there is food on your plate. Save it for another meal. This is one time you do not listen to your mother's advice to finish everything on your plate.*

5) *Conversely, do not keep the main serving dish on the table. It is too tempting to have a second helping which you probably don't need. Keep it on the kitchen counter or better still put it away in the refrigerator.*

6) *If you get a snack attack, do not grab food from the refrigerator or a handful of potato chips and start eating. Instead put it in*

a small bowl and stop after you are done with the contents of the bowl

7) *If you are a stress eater, keep a diary of WHY you consumed a certain food! This will give you insight into what emotion triggers the consumption of food and also what other behaviors you can substitute instead of food.*

8) *The next time you feel hungry, you actually may be thirsty. Drink a large glass of water instead. This is also a way to lose weight, especially by consuming that same glass of water before a meal.*

9) *And once again if you get the munchies, wait for fifteen minutes and then see if you are still hungry! Chances are you will not be hungry anymore!*

10) *And above all, be in joy with your food. It is a gift and a part of nature's bounty!*

HOLLOW VICTORIES (PART-1)

"How could man rejoice in victory and delight in the slaughter of men?"

—**Lao Tzu**

Turn on the news and all you hear is the drumbeat of wars. There is a refugee crisis not seen since World War II as thousands flee their war torn homes risking their lives to seek a better and peaceful life. I cannot imagine their heartbreak. And yet there will be ceremonies honoring the brave young men and women who have fallen or been injured in battle. And the Generals will hand out the medals and there will be solemn funerals. The history of humanity has been a succession of wars. But to all of us who have lost loved ones in the madness, right or wrong, I wonder if war for any reason, is justified. Maybe if more world leaders were women who were fearful of losing their sons and husbands, we would have fewer conflicts?

The poem that follows is an anti-war poem reflecting the emotional costs on its protagonists. The love that women have for their men is universal. It is set to the music of the quintessential American composer, Aaron Copeland. *"Appalachian Spring"* was originally written as a ballet for another American great; choreographer Martha Stewart. The original music symbolizes the beginning of life. I have used it to celebrate the redemption of death!

To feel the full impact of the poem, it needs three distinct voices and timed to the numbers at the beginning of the verse.

<u>BATTLE CRIES</u>: *A Poem for Three Voices*

(A variation on "Appalachian Spring" by Aaron Copeland)

The voices: **Martha**; *the mother and her memories.*
Anna; *the love he leaves behind.*
Troy; *a soldier, his youth soon to be lost.*

Martha:

Do you remember that night 0.46
When the cicadas,
With their songs monotone and comfortable
Lulled you into a dreamless sleep?
Summer ending and the first leaf-fall.

In the years before, 1.35
You were my child of springtime.
Together we rested under a shady elm,
Watching a tender brook tumbling through sylvan meadows,
Shimmering westwards towards an impossible sunset.

Into your hair I had weaved the first crocus flowers,
And called you Adonis, a mother's fantasy.
While you chased elusive butterflies,
I had foreboding visions of a Greek tragedy.

Anna:

She had called you Adonis, my friend of childhood, 2.30
But in my arms, you were no God, just a man.
Love blossomed between us, twice spring again.
And I knew why birds have wings and the grace of flight.
And why this can be our salvation,
And hatred our demise.

DR. M. P. KHAN, MD/NMD

Troy:

The Valkyries are restless on sullen steeds, 3.14
Shrouded ominously in crimson war clouds.
Bewildered, for once they culled heroes,
Warriors who believed,
Warriors who died with valor and passion.

For the legions of Mammon battle
The armies of the Mujahedeen.
Howitzers and RPGs rip the desert night,
The merciless sun never sets for them,
And they, all too soon,
Will knock on Valhalla's gate.

The fanfare of marching sons. 4.30
The fanfare of marching daughters.
The fanfare of God, paradise, and shallow promises.
The fanfare of glorious fallacy and bitter tears.
The fanfare of death, finally mocking hope.

At dusk taps sounds clear in this barren land, 6.50
It's lament merging with the Muezzins call to prayer.
Fanfare for the body bags and clean pine boxes
And souls promised a paradise lost.
We lay one more comrade to an eternal sleep.

HOLLOW VICTORIES (PART-1)

Did you know that since 1900 there have been over a hundred wars? In World War II alone, fifty million people died in the conflict. That would be like the US losing one sixth of its total population.

Do you, or do you know someone who has lost a friend or a loved one to a conflict? What are your feelings about that?

_____

_____

_____

_____

_____

_____

_____

_____

What are your views about wars? Are they sometimes necessary?

_____

_____

_____

_____

_____

_____

_____

HOLLOW VICTORIES (PART-2)

*"No one ever goes into battle thinking
God is on the other side."*
—Terry Goodkind

This movement is my favorite. As you can tell Copeland uses a traditional square dance tune and the words represent a going away party for Troy as he deploys for the desert.

Martha:

That enchanted night before you left, 10.12
We had danced bare feet on the grassy forest floor.
As Orion whirled in the heavens above us,
I swear fairies joined the revelry.
Half-drunk I had asked myself
"Do the Gods make light on their feet,
Those they wish to embrace"?

Whirl to the left, 10.46
Whirl to the right.
Swing you partner, Do si Do.
Hold her by the waist,
Hold her by the hand.
Whirl to the left,
Whirl to the right.

Whirl to the left, 11.04
Whirl to the right.
Swing you partner, Do si Do.
Hold her by the waist,
Hold her by the hand.

Whirl to the left,
Whirl to the right.

Troy

That Labor-day dance I first met Anna, 11.38
My Prima love, My Prima Ballerina.
Effortless, she waltzed into my arms,
A dervish of my sultry dreams.
Spinning my heart with each pirouette
She tightly weaved my soul to hers.

Whirl to the left, 11.48
Whirl to the right.
Swing you partner, Do si Do.
Hold her by the waist,
Hold her by the hand.
Whirl to the left,
Whirl to the right.

Martha & Anna:

I thanked God for the morning mist. 12.01
"No tearful goodbyes "you had said.
The C135, landed, engines screaming.
You walked into its maw.
In my endless nightmares, it was always
A bloated war vulture with bloodied beak,
Solitary, lurking on the mirrored tarmac.

Troy:

In the Humvee, 5 hours into lead patrol, 13.26
130 degrees Fahrenheit,
I hallucinate soft visions of Anna.
In this desert hell there are no seasons,
Only the acrid smell of corpses and cordite.
I hear the cicadas screeching summer's end,
They sing a lullaby of sweet endings
And burnt offerings under the shady elm.

October 26

HOLLOW VICTORIES (PART-3)

"Battle not with monsters, lest ye become a monster"
—Nietzsche

The final movement reflects the grief of the two women as they mourn the loss of son and lover. It is more poignant when accompanied by Copeland's score and if you followed the timing.

Martha & Anna:

You had said "No tears please" 16.36
Dry eyed, each spring, I await the first crocus.
By the shimmering brook,
Under the shady elm tree of our memories,
The cicadas sing to me.

I pray the first snowfall will make me forget my Adonis,
For in the winter stillness I hear the Valkyrie's grieve.
Weeping for mothers hidden behind veils and bourkas,
Reaching out into the void of Valhalla for redemption.

Martha:

Do you remember that night 17.38
When the cicadas,
With their songs monotone and comfortable
Lulled you into a dreamless sleep?
Summer ending and the first leaf-fall.

In the years before,
You were my child of springtime.
Together we rested under a shady elm,
Watching a tender brook tumbling through sylvan meadows,
Shimmering westwards towards an impossible sunset.

Into your hair I had weaved the first crocus flowers,
Called you Adonis, a mother's fantasy.
While you chased elusive butterflies,
I had foreboding visions of a Greek tragedy.

Anna:

She had called you Adonis, my friend of childhood, 18.54
But in my arms, you were no God, just a man.
Love blossomed between us, twice spring again.
I knew why birds have wings and the grace of flight,
And why this can be our salvation,
And hatred our demise.

MK 09/2004

October 27

HOLLOW VICTORIES (PART-2)

To get a feel for this poem, download or purchase a CD of Copeland's "Appalachian Spring." It is a relatively short piece and even has a Shaker folk tune embedded in it Even if you are not a classical music fan, I can guarantee you that you will enjoy the music. It is quintessentially American.

See if you can time it to the poem. I had three actors playing the various roles read the lines timed to the music. If you are interested, email me your address and I will send you the MP3 file.

October 28

HOLLOW VICTORIES (PART-3)

What can each of us do to make this world more peaceful?

_____
_____
_____
_____
_____
_____
_____
_____

What can each of us do to make our inner lives more peaceful?

_____
_____
_____
_____
_____
_____
_____
_____

October 29

TYPE-2 DIABETES- A NEUTRACEUTICAL APPROACH

"Millions of Americans today are taking dietary supplements, practicing yoga and integrating other natural therapies into their lives. These are all preventive measures that will keep them out of the doctor's office and drive down the costs of treating serious problems like heart disease and diabetes."
—Andrew Weil

Type-2 Diabetes is probably the most common chronic illness that I see in a busy family practice. By the year 2030, it is estimated that 400 million people will be affected worldwide. In the US it is of epidemic proportion and with the increase in child hood obesity, the numbers are expected to climb with a potential to bankrupt the current medical system unless measures are taken in the early stages to prevent it (Pre-diabetes). Unlike Type-1 Diabetes, which can only be treated with insulin, Type-2 is very responsive to dietary changes, weight loss and exercise. Unfortunately I cannot distill life style changes in a bottle and tell you to take one daily. But there are some micronutrients and herbs which can prevent diabetes and also help augment conventional pharmaceutical approaches in the treatment of diabetes.

So first let us consider micronutrients or *vitamins and minerals.*

ZINC: A deficiency of zinc increases the risk of getting diabetes and diabetes actually induces a zinc deficiency. So supplementation with zinc is de facto for every diabetic patient. 30 mg. of zinc sulphate daily is enough to meet the needs and it can actually lower the HbA1c (a long term bio marker and which every individual with diabetes is familiar) by half a point. There is not enough evidence for zinc in preventing T2DM.

DR. M. P. KHAN, MD/NMD

CHROMIUM: At this time the evidence is mixed although earlier studies supplementing with 200mcg (micrograms of chromium picolinate daily and do not exceed that dose) reduced HbA1c by a whole point. Supplementation may actually be helpful if one is deficient in chromium. Brewer's yeast is a good food source of chromium.

MAGNESIUM: There is almost a universal deficiency in the American diet of this element and a deficiency can aggravate glucose control as well as increase the risks of diabetic complications such as retinopathy and neuropathy. Magnesium is also thought to prevent the onset of diabetes as determined by a fifteen year study involving over 2000 patients. I recommend 400mg. of magnesium oxide daily for everybody or eat lots of nuts and dark chocolate.

VITAMIN D: It seems that this is one more example of having adequate Vitamin D levels (blood levels around 50) as it seems to regulate the release of insulin by the pancreas and also sensitizes the insulin receptors. I recommend 5000 international units of Vitamin D3 daily, rain or shine.

ALPHA LIPOIC ACID (LA): Not to be confused with alpha-linolenic acid, (ALA,) this supplement increase blood flow to the nerves and is also a powerful anti-oxidant. It is my go to supplement in treating diabetic neuropathy and the optimal dose is 600-800 mg daily.

October 30

TYPE-2 DIABETES- A
NEUTRACEUTICAL APPROACH

"As obesity creeps into preschools, and hypertension and type
II diabetes become pediatric problems for the very first time,
the case for starting preventive health care in the cradle has
become too compelling to keep ignoring."
                                            —Heidi Murkoff

When you consider that almost one in ten Americans have Type 2 DM (T2DM)with combined direct medical cost and loss in productivity at a staggering annual cost of $250 billion, it really brings home the impact of this largely preventable disease. In our office we have started an initiative to identify pre diabetes and intervene with diet and exercise and weight loss to prevent new onset diabetes.

Here are some *herbal or botanical supplements* that may help in the management of T2DM.

CINNAMON: This is one of the more popular food supplements used in the treatment of diabetes. The two common varieties are Ceylon and Chinese cinnamon. Most studies have shown that cinnamon reduces fasting blood sugars but has little or no effect on the HbA1c levels. But some studies have shown that a gram of Chinese cinnamon a day can lower the HbA1c levels by ½ a point. In light of the mixed data I recommend the liberal use of cinnamon in the diet. French toast, anyone?

GOLDEN SEAL: Also known as berberine and used in the treatment of intestinal diarrhea was also noted to act like the commonly used drug, *metformin*. In fact a recent study showed that berberine 500 mg three times a day was as effective as the same dose of metformin in lowering HbA1c. Caution: Berberine is contraindicated in pregnancy as it can cause uterine contractions.

DR. M. P. KHAN, MD/NMD

FENUGREEK: Long used as a spice in Indian cooking, it has a long tradition in Ayurveda medicine in the treatment of diabetes. It works like the drug *glyburide* in that it stimulates the pancreas to produce insulin. It is also high in fiber and slows down the absorption of carbohydrates and sugars from the gut, thus modulating the insulin response. Common dosing is 2.5 grams as powdered seeds in capsule form twice daily.

IVY GOURD: Also known as baby watermelon, it has an important role in Ayurveda medicine and the fruit and leaves seem to mimic *insulin*. Trials are still ongoing but it holds a lot of promise in the managing diabetes. Although there are no specific dosing recommendations, it can be purchased in an Indian grocery and served as a vegetable side dish. This is not to be confused with bitter melon which is also used in Ayurveda and as food. Unfortunately, like another herb (Gymnema, also Ayurveda) there are no good studies available for bitter melon in its use in T2DM but the research is ongoing.

October 31

TYPE-2 DIABETES- A
NEUTRACEUTICAL APPROACH

Here is a recipe for using cinnamon and is a traditional Indian way to prepare rice for a festive occasion.

1 Cup of Basmati Brown or White rice
2 large cinnamon sticks broken I half
1 Tsp. of cardamom
4 whole cloves.
1 Tsp of cinnamon powder
½ tsp of salt
3 Cups of water
1 Tbsp. of coconut or canola oil

In a large heavy pan, heat oil on moderate heat and when hot, sauté cinnamon sticks, cloves and cardamom for a minute or so, then add basmati rice and sauté for another minute. (At this point you can transfer the contents of the pan to a rice cooker but this is optional). Add water, salt and cinnamon powder, stir, bring to boil and then simmer till all water is absorbed. Inhale the aroma of this heavenly dish before eating!

DR. M. P. KHAN, MD/NMD

NOVEMBER

1-Nov	YUGO YOGA. Mrs. Fields has another question.
2-Nov	YUGO YOGA. Experiencing a pranayama.
3-Nov	YUGO YOGA. The eight paths of yoga.
4-Nov	YUGO YOGA. Some resources for yoga & meditation.
5-Nov	A GREAT IDEA. A parable about impermanence.
6-Nov	A GREAT IDEA. And how this shapes your life.
7-Nov	TOBACCO A NO-NO. Some positivity about cessation.
8-Nov	TOBACCO A NO-NO. Some negatives about continuing.
9-Nov	TOBACCO A NO-NO. Smoking is a cause of statistics!
10-Nov	TOBACCO A NO-NO. Some ways to help you quit.
11-Nov	A MEDICALLY SPEAKING POEM. All about a ' Life Vest.'
12-Nov	A MEDICALLY SPEAKING POEM. The pitfalls of technology.
13-Nov	DRINK LOTS OF WATER (PT-1). The magic of water.
14-Nov	DRINK LOTS OF WATER (PT-1). You are half water.
15-Nov	DRINK LOTS OF WATER (PT-2). Evian spelt backwards is?
16-Nov	LETTER TO NERUDA (PT-1). A homage to Neruda & a postman.
17-Nov	LETTER TO NERUDA (PT-1). And the letter to Neruda.
18-Nov	LETTER TO NERUDA (PT-2). And the postman writes a poem.
19-Nov	LETTER TO NERUDA (PT-2). And you write a love poem.
20-Nov	THE PARABLE OF THECROOKED TREE. Accepting imperfection.
21-Nov	THE PARABLE OF THECROOKED TREE. In yourself and others.
22-Nov	AN ENGAGING FRIDAY. Finding another's weirdness.
23-Nov	AN ENGAGING FRIDAY. A 'mirror' of first love.
24-Nov	THE MIRACLE OF SPICE. Something warm for a cold day.
25-Nov	THE MIRACLE OF SPICE. Of Liquorice and Garlic.
26-Nov	THE MIRACLE OF SPICE. Of Cloves and Black Pepper.
27-Nov	I WILL TELL YOU A SECRET. The mystery of life and SECRETS.
28-Nov	I WILL TELL YOU A SECRET. And you tell me yours.
29-Nov	TWO CASE STUDIES: THE ENVIRONMENT. Lead.
30-Nov	TWO CASE STUDIES: THE ENVIRONMENT. Pesticides.

DR. M. P. KHAN, MD/NMD

YUGO YOGA

"Yoga is bringing suppleness in body, calmness in mind,
kindness in heart and awareness in life."
—Amit Ray

Friday morning and the tail end of a busy week. My Medical Assistant gave me a heads up. "It's Mrs. Fields. She has pulled up some articles on yoga and wants to know more about it!"

Hi Doc, remember me? I want to pick your brain about this yoga thing. It seems like all the media is talking about it. My good friend Dottie is taking classes at a place nearby called Kripalu. Is it something that can help my health?

Hello Mrs. Fields. I can give you some theory of yoga. But it's like describing the taste of honey. You have to actually taste it! My best advice to you is to take a Yoga class. So here is a brief explanation of a very complex science.

"Yoga" literally means to yoke together and in this case mind and body and spirit. Although the Western concept of Yoga is a series of postures and breathing techniques, it is far more complex than that. Yoga originated in India over 3,500 years ago and the sage Patanjali was the first to document the various paths of yoga. It was primarily designed as a system to alleviate suffering and promote physical and emotional wellbeing. The system he outlined, *Raja Yoga*, was a path of meditation and it had Eight divisions.

1) Moral Observance:

Ahimsa = Non-violence *Satya* = Truthfulness *Asteya* = Non-Stealing *Brahmacharya* = Moderation of senses *Aparigraha* = Non-greedy

2) Self-disciplines:

Saucha = Cleanliness *Santosha* = Contentment *Tapas* = Austerity
Svadhyaya = Self-reflection *Isvara Pranidhana* = Surrender

3) Postures:

Asanas = Different poses taught in a typical yoga class
Vinyasa = Breath linked movement of poses

4) Breath regulation:

Pranayama = Nostril or mouth breathing with and without sound;

Breath retention using various periods of breath holding at various ratios of in and out breath.

November 2

YUGO YOGA

"Exercises are like prose, whereas yoga is the poetry of movements. Once you understand the grammar of yoga; you can write your poetry of movement."
—Amit Ray, 'Yoga and Vipassana: An Integrated Life Style'

Here is a breathing exercise almost guaranteed to relax you. It is very similar to paced diaphragm breathing and is also known as three part pranayama.

Sit in a comfortable posture.

1) *Place both your palms on your belly. Take a deep breath though the nostrils filling the lower part of your lungs by pushing the palms and belly out (and pushing the diaphragm down). Exhale slowly.*

2) *Next place your palms now on each side of the ribcage. Now fill the mid- lung by raising your palms and the chest wall. Exhale slowly*

3) *Next place your palms under your collar bones. Last fill the top of the lung and when you cannot take in anymore air, breath in just one more sip of air. Exhale slowly.*

4) *Now do stages one to three in succession without exhaling with a slow count of five. Hold it for a slow count of five.*

5) *Closing the throat partially, exhale the air through your nostrils over a slow count of five. If you are doing this right, it should sound like a continuous sound of ocean waves. If you have difficulty with the "ocean wave" breath, just exhale naturally.*

6) *Repeat the above steps five times.*

7) *You can add arm movements by starting with your arms on your side, sweeping them up so your palms touch above your*

head with the *in breath*, and then slowly sweeping them down to your side with the *out breath*. Try to make the movement smooth and effortless.

8) Congrats! You have just completed a basic yoga three-part breath 'pranayama' or breath technique.

DR. M. P. KHAN, MD/NMD

November 3

YUGO YOGA

"The rhythm of the body, the melody of the mind and the harmony of the soul, create the symphony of life."
—B K S Iyengar

Continuing with the eight paths of Raja Yoga:

5) Pratyahara:

Sensory withdrawal using relaxation and inward minding techniques. Mindfulness meditation is one technique.

6) Dharana:

Single pointed focused attention using effort and object-based (like focusing on a burning candle or the in and out breath)

7) Dhyana:

Unbroken flow of attention. This requires years of practice to sustain the attention and train the "monkey mind."
Open monitoring and effortless

8) Samadhi:

This is the final stage. There is no more duality and the object and subject merge.

The stage of self-realization and transcendental consciousness.

Doc, boy this sounds complicated. Maybe I will just stick to walking as an exercise. I cannot even pronounce all those Indian names. And at my age I am not going to attain, umm what's the last one? Samadee?

It's 'Sama-thee". Before you give up on yoga, I would suggest you go to a yoga class. There is even chair yoga where you do not have to get on the mat on a floor and is designed for individuals who have difficulty in that area. And once you see the benefit of yoga you can even purchase a DVD and do it at home.

If you want to go high tech, you can subscribe to GAIA TV, a subscription channel which streams on the internet and has several shows ranging from easy to difficult by well-known yoga teachers.

YUGO YOGA

"Yoga is the dance between control and surrender-between pushing and letting go, and when to push and when to let go becomes part of the creative process, part of the open ended exploration of your being."
—Joel Kramer

Here are some suggestions on books on yoga. Also check out GAIATV.com

* *Hatha Yoga Illustrated: Martin Kirk and Brooke Boon (also delivered on Kindle and easy to follow.)*

* *Yoga for Beginners/An easy Guide to Relieve Stress, Lose Weight and Heal Your Body: Sophia Cannon*

* *The Yoga Bible: Christina Brown*

* *Yoga Fan; Practice Guide for Everyday: Jill Camera & Adrienne Burke*

And some books on the practice of mindful meditation.

* *Peace Is Every Step; The Path of Mindfulness in Everyday Life: Thich Nhat Hanh*

* *Wherever You Go, There You Are: Jon Kabat-Zinn (my favorite)*

* *Mindful Meditation for Beginners; From Zero to Zen in Ten: Grace Stevens*

And some DVD's on yoga and meditation.

* *Simply Yoga-30 Minute DVD: Yolanda Pettinato*

* *Rodney Yee's Yoga for Beginners:* <u>*Rodney Yee*</u>

* *Meditation and Stress reduction for Beginners; The Garden of NOW.* <u>*Dr. Derek Turesky*</u>

Also good meditation techniques on GAIAMTV.

Check out this free smart phone app "Insight Timer" for excellent guided imagery exercises.

November 5

A GREAT IDEA

**"Often the difference between a successful man and a
failure is not one's better abilities or ideas, but the courage
that one has to bet on his ideas, to take a calculated risk,
and to act."**

—Maxwell Maltz

The parable that follows is not directly attributed to the Buddha although it may well be something that the Buddha may have taught his disciples.

One day the Buddha asked all his disciples to gather around him. They had learned at his feet for many years and even though he was Enlightened, he also knew that he was mortal. He wanted to be sure that his teachings would live on after him. He wanted to pick a successor. So he asked two of his brightest monks what they would do to propagate his wisdom to the world. The monk who would come up with the best solution would lead the monastery after his death.

The first monk he asked was named Sunder(beautiful). He thought for a while. Then he replied:

"I will dedicate to you a giant statue in rock carved out of a granite cliff. And for centuries mankind will see your likeness in granite and remember your teachings. I will also devise elaborate rituals to honor you."

The Buddha was somewhat pleased but as he could foresee the future, he had a vision of the statue bearing his likeness. In the vision he saw that several millennia had passed and the wind had worn down his features. The rituals were long forgotten. Now it was an archeological oddity and no one could remember why this artifact was made or who it represented. When the Buddha conveyed his vision to Sunder, he also likened the statue to the Impermanence of all material things.

The second monk was named Santosh (peaceful) and he was asked the same question by the Buddha. After much contemplation he replied.

"I will write down all your teachings in books. Although they will be written on flimsy paper, I will use these books to teach other monks. They in turn will teach others and so on and your wisdom will spread throughout the world."

The Buddha was even more pleased. This time when he looked into the future, he saw that even several millennia later, his teachings flourished. No one remembered what the Buddha actually looked like and yet he was remembered through his teachings. He conveyed to Santosh that indeed that was the way and that a great idea or philosophy did not need statues and rituals to flourish.

And it came to pass that after the Buddha transitioned, Santosh assumed the head position in the monastery and true to his word, spread the teachings of the Buddha.

DR. M. P. KHAN, MD/NMD

November 6

A GREAT IDEA

Write down three great ideas or philosophies or words of wisdom that you live by. How do they make you a better person or improve your life and your relationship with others?

1)_____

_____

_____

_____

_____

_____

2)_____

_____

_____

_____

_____

_____

3)_____

_____

_____

_____

_____

_____

November 7

TOBACCO A NO-NO (PART-1)

"They're talking about banning cigarette smoking now in
any place that's used by ten or more
people in a week, which, I guess, means that Madonna
can't even smoke in bed."

—**Bill Maher**

PS: If you are a non-smoker, share this information with a smoker. There is a world wide effort by WHO to cut down on the use of tobacco. As someone once said, *smoking is the leading cause of statistics* and tomorrow we will discuss the statistical impact of smoking. And if you are a smoker, you are thinking that you can't possibly be in that number. It boggles the mind so it is easier to ignore it all together. But eventually ALL smokers quit! The real question is; even if you live as long as a non-smoker, what is the quality of life that you wish to experience?

You have heard of all the negative aspects of smoking cessation. But what are the plus points of giving up on those cigs?

20 MINUTES: The effects of quitting start to set in immediately. Less than After 20 minutes, your heart rate will already start to drop back towards normal levels .Nicotine is a stimulant

2 HOURS: Without a cigarette, your heart rate and blood pressure will have decreased to near normal levels. Your peripheral circulation may also improve, but around that time Nicotine withdrawal symptoms usually start.

12 HOURS: Carbon monoxide (CO) is released from burning tobacco and inhaled as part of cigarette smoke. In fact if you inhaled the entire CO amount from a 20 cig pack, it would kill you. Because carbon monoxide bonds so well to blood cells and oxygen, high levels of the substance can

DR. M. P. KHAN, MD/NMD

causes serious heart problems. In just 12 hours after quitting smoking, your blood oxygen levels increase to normal.

48 HOURS: Smoking specifically ruins your sense of smell and taste. After 48 hours without a cigarette, your ability to smell and taste is enhanced. In just a little while longer, you'll be back to appreciating what food really tastes like and you will also smell aromas better.

72 HOURS: Nicotine will be completely out of your body by then. That means that the symptoms of nicotine withdrawal will generally peak around this time. You may experience some physical symptoms such as headaches, nausea, or cramps in addition to the emotional symptoms.

2 WEEKS LATER: you'll be able to exercise and perform physical activities without feeling fatigued. Your circulation will improve, and your lung function will also improve significantly. After two or three weeks without smoking, your lungs will start to feel clear, and you'll start breathing easier.

4 WEEKS LATER: Your lungs begin to regenerate. Inside them, the cilia that push mucus out; will start to repair themselves and function properly again. With the cilia now able to do their job, they will help to reduce your risk of infection. With properly functioning lungs, your coughing and shortness of breath will continue to decrease dramatically but you also may have increased coughing in the morning with gray sputum as your lungs clean themselves of all the crud. Men will also see an improvement in their erections and libido.

1 YEAR: After a year without smoking, your risk for heart disease is lowered by 50 percent compared to when you were still smoking. Another way to look at it is that a smoker is more than twice as likely as you are to have any type of heart disease

5 YEARS: Almost 4000 substances are released in the burning of tobacco – carbon monoxide chief among them, which increases your risk of having a stroke. After 5 to 15 years of being smoke-free, your risk of having a stroke is the same as a non-smoker.

10 YEARS: Smokers are at higher risk than non-smokers for a long list of cancers, with lung cancer being the most common and followed by oral cancers in people chewing tobacco. Smoking accounts for 90 percent of lung cancer deaths worldwide. It'll take 10 years, but if you quit, eventually your risk of dying from lung cancer will drop to half that of a smoker's and your risk of cancer of the mouth, throat, esophagus, bladder, kidney, and pancreas also decreases.

And if you are a pack a day smoker you would have saved around $15,000.00 at the end of ten years.

So how about giving it a go? You are worth it!

DR. M. P. KHAN, MD/NMD

November 8

TOBACCO A NO-NO (PART-1)

A month after you quit smoking, your lungs regain 30% of their function. If you continue to smoke, you are a day closer to emphysema. There is no basis to the myth that some individuals have no health effects from chronic tobacco use. There are no exceptions!

If you are a smoker, you have almost certain lung damage after 10 pack years. (Multiply the number of packs you smoke in a day by the number of years you have smoked. For example; 1pk/day x 1year = 1 pack year). You would have also spent around $15,000 over that ten year period or the price of a new compact automobile.

If you chew tobacco, you may escape the impact of smoking on your lungs, but you will have an increased risk of oral cancers, esophageal cancers, gastric ulcers and dental problems.

Chronic tobacco use, especially smoking, increases the risk of erectile dysfunction and if you are a guy, this fact may be a very significant reason (as far as I am concerned) to quit smoking! It can also cause a nasty condition called Thrombangitis obliterans and as the name suggests, smoking damages the small arteries of the legs causing progressive pain initially when walking and then all the time. There is no good treatment for this condition, as the endothelium of the small arteries are irreversibly destroyed.

Your physician may order a low-dose CT scan of your lungs on an annual basis if you are identified as high risk as defined by: age 55-74 with a greater than 30 pk yr. smoking history. If no longer smoking, smoking cessation within the last 15 years. Also if there is one additional risk factors such as a high blood pressure or diabetes, screening can start at age 50 with a 20 pk yr. smoking history and to repeat this annually although the number of CT scans needed is not clearly defined.

In the next topic we will cover statistics and some strategies to help you quit.

TOBACCO A NO-NO (PART-2)

"Thank you for not smoking. Cigarette smoke is the residue
of your pleasure. It contaminates the air, pollutes my hair
and clothes, not to mention my lungs. This takes place
without my consent. I have a pleasure, also. I like a beer
now and then. The residue of my pleasure is urine. Would
you be annoyed if I stood on a chair and pissed on your
head and your clothes without your consent?"
—**Sign from 'Ken's Magic Shop'**

In the same vein as the above quote, someone once said that having a smoking section in a restaurant or other establishment is like having a pissing only section in a swimming pool! And the awareness of the harmful effect of smoking has come a long way from the Camel cigarette ads featuring a doctor in a white coat puffing away with the blurb below:

"Your Doctor Recommends Camels" or something to that effect.

Today, the above blurb is laughable. But spend a few days in my practice and I will show you the horrific end results of years of tobacco use. It is not only a dirty habit but a dangerous one. I often tell my patients that they should find a new bad habit such as picking their nose or something similar. At least it won't kill you!

Here are some global statistics related to tobacco use:

- *Tobacco kills 6 million people worldwide annually.*
- *More than 5 million of the above are users or ex users.*
- *600,000 of the above number are due to secondary exposure to smoke.*
- *After high blood pressure, tobacco use is the second most significant factor in diseases such as heart attacks, stroke and cancer.*

- *100 million people died in the 20th century due to tobacco use and may kill a billion people by the end of the 21st century.*
- *Tobacco use is growing fastest in developing countries and by 2030, 80% of tobacco related deaths will be in those countries and will impact the poor and middle class who have limited access to health care.*

Of course if statistics could scare a smoker to quit, no one in their right mind living on this planet would continue to use tobacco products. And I know of no two patients who quit using tobacco the same way. I am also convinced that the majority of smokers would really like to quit. So why is it so difficult? To answer that question, we need to understand what nicotine is an extremely addictive compound. And incidentally, you can buy nicotine over the counter without a prescription.

Below are some strategies to help you quit.

TOBACCO A NO-NO (PART-2)

*"Avoid using cigarettes, alcohol, and drugs as alternatives
to being an interesting person."*
—Marilyn Vos Savant

<u>*Nicotine Substitutes:*</u> *Most of them are available over the counter
without a prescription. The most common one is the nicotine patch
available in strengths of 21; 14; 7 mg/24 hrs. If you are a heavy smoker,
start with the 21mg/24hrs. patch. The patch is applied daily on the skin.
I suggest removal of the patch before bedtime as it can cause nightmares
if kept on during the night.*

*I have had more success with the lozenge which is available in two
strengths of 2mg and 4mg. It mimics the release of nicotine if sucked on
and parked periodically which is how a cigarette releases nicotine. My
concern for the nicotine gum is that mostly everybody chews the gum
continuously thus releasing large amounts of nicotine without the peak
and valleys like smoking does. The nicotine inhaler is a prescription
and is closest to a smokeless cigarette. Each cartridge is the nicotine
equivalent of two cigs. It also satisfies the whole hand- to-mouth habit.
There is no good data that e-cigarettes help with smoking cessation.*

*Of course you should not be smoking cigs when using a nicotine
substitute or you could end up with a bad case of nicotine overdose.*

<u>*Medications:*</u> *Wellbutrin (Bupropion) is widely used as it fools the
nicotine receptors in the brain. Start the drug as directed by your
physician two weeks before your quit date. Every day cut down two
cigs (20 to 18 to 16 and so on) until you are down to zero by your quit
date. Stay on the medication for at least 12-24 weeks.*

DR. M. P. KHAN, MD/NMD

Chantix is another drug which can also help with cessation but I have had several patients complain of mood changes and depression (which is a known side effect of this drug) and I usually do not recommend it.

Behavioral Approaches: Most smokers have learned to use nicotine to calm down or to get more energy and mental clarity. So coming up with behavioral strategies is critical. I suggest getting rid of all smoking paraphernalia such as lighters and ash trays and also avoiding places for a while where people smoke such as bars, so as to avoid triggers. Also an exercise program is very helpful. You will also crave sweet foods so keep some dried fruits around. You will also notice an increase in appetite so make healthy choices. Also check out local smoking cessation programs that are offered by your local hospital.

If you were a pack a day smoker, place 5-10 dollars into a piggy bank daily (what you would spend on a pack of cigs) and at the end of the month reward yourself to a fine restaurant meal or a shopping spree.

Other approaches that might help are acupuncture and hypnosis. Once again use the method that works for you. An average smoker takes 5-6 attempts at smoking cessation before quitting for good. So hang in there. You will succeed eventually

A MEDICALLY SPEAKING POEM

LIFE VEST:

1

A man in white,
With a crooked smile and a Texan twang
And a small red heart embroidered on his lapel proclaimed
With a condescending chuckle:
"We are sending you home today.
This vest will be your talisman.
Wear it at all times, except when you shower of course!"
And with a leer he added:
"Yes, you need to have it on when you have sex;
Could die in the saddle, you know. Ha Ha Ha!*"*

2

A woman in white,
Somewhere in a dark room in Australia, half a world away,
Waits and watches the fluorescent squiggles of an oscilloscope,
As geo positioned satellites transmit a Wi-Fi translation of his beating heart.
Waiting and watching; watching and waiting.
For a skip or a pause or for the dreaded saw tooth pattern of fibrillating myocardium.
Then, she will summon warriors, also in white, on chariots of pulsating lights
Who will swoop down to battle death, with siren whoops of victory!
Or maybe,
She will summon seraphim or dark angels or karmic promises of an afterlife.
Then, at the end of her shift, she will sign off to the next woman in white,
Shut the door and go shopping for groceries.

MK 10/2012

DR. M. P. KHAN, MD/NMD

November 12

A MEDICALLY SPEAKING POEM

A 'Life Vest' is medical device that looks like a deflated life preserver. There are electrodes embedded in the vest that are strategically placed to pick up the electrical activity of the heart that is electrically transmitted to a monitoring station which actually maybe half a world away. It is a great example of technology helping the health and well-being of patients.

Counter to that is the reliance on technology and how it interferes with the direct human connection between the physician and the patient. How easy it is to forget about that component of healing as we continue to be more and more enamored by the technical advances made in medicine in the 21ˢᵗ century.

What do you think are the three greatest technical advances in medicine that you know of?

_____

_____

_____

_____

_____

How have these advances benefited you?

_____

_____

_____

_____

_____

How has technology interfered with your interactions with your physician(s) and the medical system?

_____

_____

_____

_____

_____

November 13

DRINK LOTS OF WATER (PART-1)

"If there is magic on this planet, it is contained in water."
—**Loren Eiseley**

The third time I heard a patient say *"But doctor, water is so boring!"* after I had told them to increase their intake of water, I decided to put together this article to make water more *"interesting."* This is my puny effort to counteract the mind numbing campaign of soft drink giants, which spend millions on advertising to convince us that the only way to quench our thirst is to buy their products. So here are some of the common objections/questions in regards to drinking water with some suggestions to make water *"exciting"* again!

How much water should I drink in a given day?

There are several recommendations as to how much water, one should drink. 64 oz. seems to come up often. This is not written in stone as the body's needs may depend on the activity performed and also the efficiency of the kidneys which determine the salt and fluid load of the body. For example, a marathon runner may lose twice that amount at the end of a race and a patient on dialysis may actually need a fraction of that amount for adequate hydration.

My advice is to look at the color of the urine. If there is any yellowish tint to the urine, that is a good sign of dehydration. The urine should be clear and the colorless, *like water.* One word of caution though; if you are taking a multi-vitamin, it might give a yellowish hue to the urine because of the absorption and excretion of the B-vitamins. It is best to wait for six to eight hours after taking a multi-vitamin before checking the color of the urine.

DR. M. P. KHAN, MD/NMD

Why don't I feel thirsty?

A common misconception is that it should be hot to feel thirsty. Actually the body loses significant amounts of water in cold and dry environments due to loss from the skin from evaporation. Dry skin is a common sign and in the elderly can result in 'tenting' of the skin, as seen in the skin not returning to its natural state quickly after gently pulling up on the skin.

Also sometimes the signal of hunger and thirst are often mixed up in the brain. The next time you get a craving for cookies, drink a glass of water instead. Also two glasses of water before each meal is a good weight loss strategy.

Is tap water OK to drink?

In a previous article, we had discussed the problems with bottled water and the chemicals that leach into the water from the plastic it is stored in. If you are going to store water from your kitchen tap, use glass or stainless bottles. Yes, tap water is OK but because of the variability in the municipal water supply I suggest that you take some steps to make it more potable and to remove some of the more common chemicals that may be present.

November 14

DRINK LOTS OF WATER (PART-1)

*"Water does not resist. Water flows. When you plunge your
hand into it, all you feel is a caress. Water is not a solid
wall, it will not stop you. But water always goes where
it wants to go, and nothing in the end can stand against
it. Water is patient. Dripping water wears away a stone.
Remember that, my child. Remember you are half water. If
you can't go through an obstacle, go around it. Water does."*
—Margaret Atwood, 'The Penelopiad'

A good resource is the excellent go-to web site from ewg.org specifically

www.ewg.org/tap-water/home

*Which is searchable by zip code. Currently I have well water. When
I checked the water in my previous (Monroeville, PA) neck of the woods,
this was my water report:*

*TTHM (or total tri-halo methane products or the sum of four
disinfection products) in my zip code exceeded the health limit 9.8
ppb consistently and the legal limit 80 ppb once. A 9.8 ppb increases
estimated excess lifetime cancer risk of 1 in 1000,000.*

*HAA (or total haloacetic acid or the sum of five disinfection products)
was at a level of 0.07 ppb which was above the health limit but not above
the legal limit. Overall, the water quality was pretty good. But a simple
carbon filter can remove the TTHM and HAA pretty consistently.*

*If you have city water, chances are that you might perceive a
chlorinated taste*

*Squeeze a few drops of lemon juice or orange juice in the water.
Another strategy is to chill the water before drinking it. Some of the
newer tap filters now remove chlorine and add minerals to the water
which may help with the taste factor.*

*If you have not already subscribed to www.ewg.org now is the time
to do so. They have done a lot of the leg work for you and an excellent
resource for some very valuable information.*

DR. M. P. KHAN, MD/NMD

DRINK LOTS OF WATER (PART-2)

"Ever wonder about those people who spend $2 apiece on those little bottles of Evian water? Try spelling Evian backward."

—**George Carlin**

Below, I have modified guideline put out by EWG on tips to improve the quality of water that we drink. Remember that there was an ancestral time when we could drink water from a river or a pond without worrying about all these recommendations. Will we ever have the wisdom, once again, to reach that time when nature was pristine?

TIPS FOR SAFE DRINKING WATER:

Bottled Water: Drink filtered tap water instead.
You can read the bottle label, but you still won't know if the water is pure and natural, or just processed, polluted, packaged tap water. EWG found 38 contaminants in 10 popular brands. And it can cost you an average of $1500.00 per year if used exclusively. And there is also the environmental impact of all those plastic bottles!

Tap Water: Learn what's in it.
Tap water suppliers publish all their water quality tests. Bottled water companies don't. Read your annual tap water quality report. Look up your city's water in EWG's National Tap Water Atlas (www.ewg.org/tap-water). (Private well? Get it tested.) Also bottled water may be sitting on a shelf in some warehouse for months before consumption.

Filtered Tap Water: Drink it, cook with it.

- Choose a filter certified to remove contaminants found in your water: (www.ewg.org/tap-water/getwaterfilter) Effectiveness varies - read the fine print.
- Carbon filters (pitcher or tap-mounted) are affordable and reduce many common water contaminants, like lead and byproducts of the disinfection process used to treat municipal tap water. Change your water filters on time as per the manufacturer's recommendations. Old filters aren't safe – they harbor bacteria and let contaminants through.
- Install a reverse osmosis filter to remove contaminants that carbon filters can't eliminate. This process relies on a semi-permeable membrane that retains particles larger than water molecules. Reverse osmosis can remove many contaminants not removed by carbon, including arsenic, fluoride, hexavalent chromium, nitrates and perchlorate. Quality varies, both in terms of the membrane system itself and the carbon filter typically used with it. The filters use 3 times to 20 times more water than they produce. A reverse osmosis system can be purchased and installed by Sears or your local Home Depot for around $400.00 and costs around $90.00/yr. for filters that need replaced every six months or so. In the long run, it is cheaper than tap mounted carbon filters that may run around $360.00/yr.

On the Go: Carry water in safe containers.
Soft plastic bottles can leach a harmful plastics chemical called bisphenol A (BPA) into water. Carry stainless steel or glass bottles. Don't reuse bottled water bottles. The plastic can harbor bacteria and break down to release plastics chemicals. Also keep in mind that that the harder plastic bottles are not safe when reused repeatedly.

While Pregnant: Stay hydrated with safe water.
It's especially important for women to drink plenty of water during pregnancy. Follow all the tips above, and take your doctor's advice on

how much to drink. Read the previous article about how much water needs increase in pregnancy.

Infants: Use safe water for formula.
Use filtered tap water for your baby's formula. If your water is not fluoridated, you can use a carbon filter. If it is, use a reverse osmosis filter to remove the fluoride, because fluoridated water can damage an infant's developing teeth .Fluoridation of water is controversial and I generally do not recommend it although my dentist colleagues may differ. If you choose bottled water for your infant, make sure it's fluoride-free. Learn more at www.ewg.org/babysafe.

Breathe Easy: Use a whole house water filter.
Although the most expensive option, for extra protection, a whole house carbon filter will remove contaminants from steamy vapors you and your family might inhale while washing dishes or showering. These can be combined with a UV and ozone type filters to provide clean water for all your household needs.

Some Basic Approaches:
Boil water and then cool it. Growing up in India, this was the basic treatment that water was subjected to before use in cooking or for drinking. Also if you are camping, or in areas of natural disasters, there are UV wands available for treating small amounts of dirty water in emergency situations.

LETTER TO NERUDA (PART-1)

"But I love your feet
only because they walked
upon the earth and upon
the wind and upon the waters,
until they found me."

—Pablo Neruda

Pablo Neruda was born in July 12, 1904 and died of prostate cancer in September 23, 1973. It was the pen name and, later, legal name of the Chilean poet and politician, Neftalí Ricardo Reyes Basoalto.

In 1971 Neruda won the Nobel Prize for Literature. The above blurb was translated from Spanish into English and I am sure that there is something lost in the translation. Neruda always wrote in green ink as it was his personal color of hope. A staunch member of the Communist Party, he was exiled at one time and returned to Chile as a hero when Allende returned to power.

The movie **"I'l Postino"** inspired this letter and is a must see and also a great date movie. The poem that follows is my tribute to a poet *magnifico!* In the movie, during his exile Isle Santa Vista near Sicily, Neruda befriends the postman, Paolo who delivers his mail. When Paolo discovers that Neruda is a famous poet, he surreptiously uses his poems to woo his future wife Francesca, who believes that Paolo is the author of those romantic words. She ultimately falls in love with him (Paolo) and marries him.

In the movie, there was a letter that Paolo Alighieri wrote to Don Pablo Neruda after he left his exile from the island near Sicily He also wrote a poem for his beloved friend Neruda, and was going to read it at a large worker's rally. But the *Policia* violently broke up the crowd and in the ensuing struggle Paolo died. The poem and the letter were supposedly lost.

In my version of the movie which I would have preferred, he is badly hurt and survives. He mails this letter to Neruda along with the poem he was going to read. The letter and the poem is lost in the mail system because of an inadequate address. When Neruda finally receives this letter many years later, he is dying from cancer. The letter and the poem that follows is what Neruda reads on his death bed.

November 17

LETTER TO NERUDA (PART-1)

The letter:

From: Paolo Alighieri,
Isle Santa Vista .SICILY

To: Don Pablo Neruda
The World's Greatest Poet, CHILE

Dear Don Pablo,

It has been many years since you and Matilde left my beautiful island to return to Chile. I hope this letter finds you in good health and spirits! My son Pablo, who is your namesake, is now a handsome young man. Francesca, whom I once seduced with your words of romance and passion, still believes that I wrote them. But I feel that she jokes. You know how women are!

Each Anniversary of our marriage we gather in the company of good friends and when we are full of wine and laughter I have the honor of reading your beautiful words. For without them Pablo and Francesca would not have ever happened. Even you, Don Pablo, could not find the words to express the joys and sorrows that we have shared over the years.

I recently came across a book of some of your early poems. "Viente poemes de amor uno cancion desperado"(You were only 24 years old. when you wrote them) I read them sometimes to Francesca when Pablo has gone to bed. There is too much passion for little ears. When it came to women, you were the master. How could you have loved so many and been wounded by so many? For me, it took only one woman to unlock the passion?

"Body of a woman, white hills white thighs, you look like a world lying in surrender. You swallowed everything like distance. Like the sea, like time, In you everything sank."

DR. M. P. KHAN, MD/NMD

Don Pablo, I stole your words but unknowingly you also gave me a gift. You made me believe that in my soul, the spark of poetry was possible. I wrote this poem for you and it may be the only one I ever write. After all how much poetry can there be in the unschooled son of a fisherman?

You once scolded me for speaking your words. I told you that a poem belongs to the one who needs it. It is my humble hope that someday, you may need this poem.

Your friend always, Paolo Alighieri;

September 30, 1962

LETTER TO NERUDA (PART-2)

"And you will ask: why doesn't his poetry
speak of dreams and leaves
and the great volcanoes of his native land?

Come and see the blood in the streets.
Come and see the bloods in the streets.
Come and see the blood in the streets!"

"I'm Explaining a Few Things" (Explico Algunos Cosas) from *Tercera Residencia* (1947), *Selected Poems by Pablo Neruda*

This is the fictional poem that Paolo he wrote for Neruda and was enclosed with the letter. In case you are by now confused by now as to who actually wrote the poem and the letter, it is *moi*!

UNTIL I WASA POET
(For my friend Pablo Neruda)

Outside my window the sea-gods always murmur
The melancholy dirges of fishermen lost at sea.
And the winter storms scream with frothy despair
Of love that was, now drowned in the murky silence.
But on star-lit nights its song is like a lullaby
Seducing softly with words of endearment.
But until I was a poet I could not hear this.

In sleepless nights and waking dreams, as if drunk,
I wander through familiar forests and groves
Seeking love in the womb of a pregnant moon.
Even the cool winds swirling up the sea-cliffs
Cannot cool my desire, like fire in my loins

Or the wild longings of my ravenous heart.
But until I was a poet I could not feel this.

On my island, no raucous rooster, but songbirds herald the dawn,
Their ancestral melody gently greeting a newborn day.
Slowly I awaken to azure sky, azure sea, and answer the birds:
"Sing loud in great unbounded joy, for only this moment is certain".
I for one need no words, no metaphors, no heavenly chorus,
For I, Paolo, have now become this song, this poem!
But until I was a poet I could not speak this.

Paolo Alighieri / September 21 1926

Actually MK/2009

LETTER TO NERUDA (PART-2)

Books by Neruda:

*The Poetry of Pablo Neruda

*Twenty Love Poems and a Song of Despair

*The Essential Neruda: Selected Poems

Now that I have put you in the mood, think of someone you love or did love and write a romantic poem. Get as mushy as you want. This is your poem after all.

_____

_____

_____

_____

_____

_____

_____

_____

_____

_____

_____

_____

_____

November 20

THE PARABLE OF THE CROOKED TREE

"Trees sometimes grow crooked for their
own inner reasons."
—Chairman Moo

Karen had three magnolia trees planted in our front yard when we first moved into our house in Pittsburgh. This was almost ten years ago. The trio was planted at the same time by a professional nursery just so you know that it was not an amateur job.

Two of the three trees grew like trees should. Nice and straight as trees are wont to do. But the third tree decided to grow at a slight angle. Of course, being the compulsive Virgo, this was not tolerable.

Over the years I tried various strategies to straighten the tree. Once I lashed it to a vertical pole embedded into the ground. A few months later the pole was bent. Then I tried pushing it from one side with the same pole and this was unsuccessful. Then I tied part of the trunk to a rope and with the other end to a stake. Not only did that not work but I ruined my lawn mower blade when I accidentally caught it on that same stake.

I was running out of ideas. And then an epiphany! Maybe the tree in its own way was trying to tell me that imperfection is OK. It's what makes my yard more interesting. Everybody's yard has nice straight well behaved trees. But my yard has a crooked tree! Once I accepted the tree's logic, all my frustration at my feeble attempts vanished. I knew there was a parable in it somewhere. Who knew what destiny was in store for that tree? Maybe a strong hurricane would someday blow over my yard sparing only my wayward tree because it was crooked!

How often do we try to straighten our circumstances or change people because our inner judgment wants to conform them to our own value systems? And instead of accepting their unique imperfections and impossible dreams, we label them as weird or out there because it validates our own normalcy.

When I was a child I realized that I had a special gift. A gift confirmed several times by my teachers. It was writing. I had so many stories in my head. And I was a voracious reader. I found music in the sound of language; I reveled in its beauty. But growing up in India in the bosom of my family, I was promptly told that writing was not a respectable profession. I had to be a doctor!

It took me years to understand that there is music in medicine too. But for the first few years it was hell. It was like the love of my life had died and I had to settle for the arranged marriage. So intense was my passion. And slowly I reconciled my vocation and my avocation. This day book is a part of the process of fusion. And I can't help wonder at times if my crookedness was left alone, what would my life have been like?

DR. M. P. KHAN, MD/NMD

THE PARABLE OF THE CROOKED TREE

Are there any events or persons in your life that you would like to change because they do not conform to your values? What are the changes you would like to see?

_____

_____

_____

_____

_____

_____

_____

_____

What would your life be if you could totally accepted these changes?

_____

_____

_____

_____

_____

_____

_____

_____

How has <u>not</u> accepting these changes affected your life?

_____

_____

_____

_____

_____

_____

_____

_____

November 22

AN ENGAGING FRIDAY

*"We are all a little weird and life's a little weird, and when
we find someone whose weirdness is compatible with ours,
we join up with them and fall in mutual weirdness and
call it love."*

—Anon

Back in our Pittsburgh days, Karen and I were invited to an engagement ceremony on this day. To those of you who say "Huh! An engagement ceremony! What's that?" here's the explanation. We have mutual friends, one of German-Italian lineage and one of Indian (Asian) descent and they decided to have their engagement blessed by a Hindu priest at the local temple. An imposing structure, the temple is the hub of the spiritual life of Indians that reside in the tristate area. It was replete with chanting from the Vedas (ancient Hindu religious texts) and the symbolism of flowers, fruits and the exchange of clothes and the engagement rings celebrating their commitment to each other. A very happy occasion indeed, ending with brunch at a local restaurant.

Seeing their smiling faces and the mutual joy that they shared, took me back to a time when I first discovered love as a young man. The place was Bombay (or Mumbai as it is known today) and the time, almost a lifetime ago. 1972.

It was a year of sirens and blackouts. And crisp dark opaque paper taped over windows. From my balcony, I watched tracer fire streak like lightning across the night sky. India and Pakistan were at war over the Northern Province of Kashmir, as they ripped apart a land that was once the closest thing to the mythical Shangri-La. There was a lot of saber rattling and strident propaganda form both sides.

And then it was over!

It was a magical and celebratory time. From the pretty flower vendor who gave away garlands of mogra blossoms to the street urchins who

DR. M. P. KHAN, MD/NMD

swaggered around, singing the latest Bollywood songs, the specter of a long and bloody conflict was lifted. And around that time I fell in love. Again! I was twenty-two years old and romance was in the air. But we always remember our first love and mine was J.

'Mirror' was a poem inspired by that first stirring. J was a beautiful young woman who was part of our circle of friends. After school (Tenth Grade) we used to go to the same tuition class to do our homework. Over problems in math and physics, we fell in love in an awkward and shy way that first love usually is. And I remember kissing her on mid night one New Year's Day celebration near the harbor with all the ships blasting their sirens and their searchlights lighting up the night sky. But like most first loves, it was nascent. J moved away the following year and though we kept in touch, after a while we moved on with our own respective lives.

November 23

AN ENGAGING FRIDAY

<u>MIRROR:</u>

I saw her on V-day, dancing in the street,
Showering flowers on passersby with wild abandon,
War, already a distant memory; peace blossoming.
Rejoicing in sons and brothers returned,
Reclaiming, once again, their displaced humanity.

In mock street smart swagger, heard him singing,
Of glorious innocent youth, love lost and found.
Hopeful melodies of tomorrow dawning.
An impoverished child, soon fated to be a man,
Yet, on this day, I wished him joy.

Laughter tinkled from her softened lips,
From the forbidden depths of her inner soul.
Lovers on this day, her warmth, a part of me.
But soon, in our parting, laughter turned to tears.
Farewell has no words, only silence.

These were mirrored reflections of my soul.
Can I recognize the divine spark of her joy?
Grasp the reckless abandon of his melodies?
Understand the fleeting nature of grief and laughter,
And why love's bright beginning has an end.

MK/1972

DR. M. P. KHAN, MD/NMD

What was it like the first time you felt the stirrings of love?

_____

_____

_____

_____

_____

_____

_____

_____

_____

What was it like the next time around? How was it different?

_____

_____

_____

_____

_____

_____

_____

_____

_____

November 24

THE MIRACLE OF SPICE

"Once you get a spice in your home, you have it forever.
Women never throw out spices. The Egyptians were buried
with their spices. I know which one I'm taking with me
when I go."
— **Erma Bombeck**

The Wikipedia definition of a spice is *"A spice is a seed, fruit, root, bark, berry, bud or vegetable substance primarily used for flavoring, coloring or preserving food. Spices are distinguished from herbs, which are parts of leafy green plants used for flavoring or as a garnish."*

Growing up in India, I do not remember ever eating a meal which did not have some kind of spice as part of the recipe. What I did not realize then is that spices are an essential part of the Indian system of medicine known as 'Ayurveda' and I will discuss some of the more common spices and their uses from a medicinal viewpoint. DISCLAIMER! Most of the evidence of their use is based on over several millennia of a trial and error process and until very recently there were no formal double blinded RCT studies available.

Almost all spices have anti-bacterial properties and their use was initially in warmer climates to prevent spoilage of food. The earliest record of the use of spices in India is in the Rig Vedas recorded around 6000 BC. Spices were historically used by the Egyptians for embalming and a brisk trade route developed around 2000 BC. By 1000 BC, spices were part of most indigenous medical systems of the Middle East, China and India. Later in the Middle Ages, black pepper and cinnamon were worth their weight in gold and were used as a part of the dowry in marriage.

And were it not for Columbus trying to discover a shorter trade route to India, the New World may still be new. And coincidentally the first land fall he discovered is now named the West Indies in the mistaken

DR. M. P. KHAN, MD/NMD

assumption that he had actually discovered India! When he returned from the New World, he introduced to Europe, spices such as chili pepper, all spice and chocolate. ('Mole'; used in Mexican cooking as a spice!)

Today, 45% of all the world's production of spices is from India and is close to a billion dollar industry and has a staggering production of 500,000 tons annually. Indonesia is another power house.

On previous days we discussed turmeric, ginger and chocolate as well as fenugreek so we will discuss some of the lesser known spices in the days to follow. Most spices stay in a ground up form at room temperature for six months and in solid form (ground vs, whole nutmeg) for one to two years. One way to prolong shelf life is to store them in the freezer.

November 25

THE MIRACLE OF SPICE

*"I love the scents of winter! For me, it's all about the feeling
you get when you smell pumpkin spice, cinnamon, nutmeg,
gingerbread and spruce."*
—Taylor Swift

LIQUORICE (Glycyrrhiza glabra): Not to be confused with that twirly candy which is flavored with fake liquorice, this is a premier plant used in Traditional Chinese Medicine as well as Ayurveda practices. The root of the plant is dried and powdered. It is used primarily in western herbal tradition as an anti-acid agent by coating the stomach lining with mucus and thus helping in the healing of gastric ulcers. Glycyrrhizin tends to have an effect on the kidney and retains salt and water thus raising the blood pressure. A form of liquorice known as DGL or de-glycyrrhinated form is commercially available and is usually in the form of wafers that dissolve in the mouth.

It can also be used as a laxative and also for healing apthous oral ulcers. There are some studies pending its anti-cancer properties and can also be used topically as a paste in the treatment of corns. It also helps in restoring the adrenal glands. Also acts like cortisone in the treatment of muscular pains and in inflammatory conditions of the skin.

GARLIC (Allium sativum): A super-food as discussed previously, it has several medicinal purposes besides being an essential ingredient of Italian and Indian cooking. Garlic contains allicin which is a powerful anti-septic. One milligram of allicin is equivalent to fifteen Oxford units of Penicillin and with almost no resistance as compared to conventional antibiotics and has activity against over seventy species of bacteria. Garlic has been used historically in the treatment of pneumonia and diphtheria at a dose of 30-60 grams daily of a fresh preparation of garlic. Although garlic is available in a dried and processed form as supplements which

DR. M. P. KHAN, MD/NMD

claim to be odorless, I would recommend the real deal in the form of fresh garlic. Also chop up the garlic clove and let it sit for a few minutes. This activates the allicin and makes it more potent.

An infusion of garlic juice to three parts of distilled water can be used to clean wounds and a dressing of 15% garlic juice can be used to heal skin ulcers. It also has excellent anti-viral properties. I use three cloves of garlic plus an inch of ginger, both chopped finely and suspended in 2 Tbsp. of lemon juice, twice a day, when I have a cold with excellent results.

Other not so well known uses of garlic is in the treatment of high blood pressure, high cholesterol (slight) and as an anti-coagulant. It also improves symptoms of depression and asthma. Garlic also has powerful anti-carcinogen compounds but the research is still pending. It is also very useful in inflammatory conditions of the gut such as colitis and infectious diseases of the gut such as parasite infestations.

November 26

THE MIRACLE OF SPICE

*"I love Indian food. It's my favorite cuisine. I love the
mixture of spices and the subtle flavors. It's really erotic;
the spices are so sensuous."*

—Joe Perry

CLOVES (Syzyigium aromaticum) In spite of its almost tongue twister of a botanical name, it is one of the super stars of spices and comes from the French word '*clov*' or nail as it resembles a broad head nail in its natural form. Cloves are used as a cooking spice when mixed with chili powder, turmeric and cinnamon to make traditional Garam Masala and Curry Powder.

The active ingredient is found in clove oil which is a result of steam distillation of the clove buds, stem and leaves and yields the compound eugenol and eugenol acetate. This oil has anesthetic properties and is used widely in dentistry as a topical anesthetic especially if you have a painful cavity and cannot find a dentist handy to fix it. Soak a small cotton ball with clove oil and place directly on the cavity. Applied directly, it can also be used for numbing painful apthous (mouth) ulcers and is readily available over the counter in various commercial forms. A clove sautéed in a teaspoon of sesame oil and then 3-5 drops of the oil placed in the ear can relieve the pain of an ear infection

It can also be used in relieving flatulence and indigestion. An Ayurveda approach is to boil 6 cloves in an ounce of water, cool, separate the cloves, and ingest three times a day. It can also be used to control vomiting. Fry a teaspoon of cloves in a little olive oil on moderate heat for a minute or so, mix with teaspoon of honey and swallow.

BLACK PEPPER (Piper nirgum) is ubiquitous in almost every kitchen and was once known as 'King of Spices' and was a major player in the trade and commerce of medieval world powers. The active ingredient is chavicine and is useful in several home remedies.

DR. M. P. KHAN, MD/NMD

It is a useful folk remedy for the relieving the symptoms of a common cold. Boil half a teaspoon of ground pepper in a fourth of a cup of milk with a pinch of turmeric powder and consume three times a day for three days. Chewing three pepper corns and a pinch of caraway seeds is also helpful in relieving a cough.

A tablespoon of ground black pepper charred and mixed with two tablespoon of canola oil can be directly applied to a sprain or sore muscle and loosely covered with a bandage. It acts by dilating the superficial blood vessels and acting like a counter-irritant.

I cannot confirm this claim but four black pepper corns and four almonds chewed and followed with a glass of milk can be used as an aphrodisiac and in some cases of impotence.

November 27

I WILL TELL YOU A SECRET

*"Let mystery have its place in you; do not be always
turning up your whole soil with the ploughshare of self-
examination, but leave a little fallow corner in your heart
ready for any seed the winds may bring."*
—Henri Frederic Amiel

I wrote the poem that follows for my daughter, Amelia, as a graduation present. In June of 2010 she graduated from the University of Pennsylvania in Philly and is now a full-fledged veterinarian with the initials DVM after her name. I actually placed this poem in a frame when I presented it to her. As is so typical of heedless youth, she stored this in some obscure corner, probably filed under "Silly Stuff that Dads Give." I am once again putting this poem out in the Universe with the hope that someday she (and you, the reader) might appreciate its mystery!

SECRETS:

Did I tell you?
The futility of believing that ducks really swim in a row,
And spiders never quite weave tangled webs, only people,
Or that bees just pretend to be busy; it's the flowers they love,
And maybe life's greatest mystery lies inherent in its chaos.
Did I tell you?
In the humdrum of days, no two sunsets are the same,
And a cigar sometimes is just a cigar, not an epiphany.
Or that real beauty lies within, not in the eye of the beholder,
And if you are lucky, love can last a lifetime, never an eternity.

DR. M. P. KHAN, MD/NMD

Did I tell you?
You can kill them with kindness, never with compassion,
And a dog's bite if true, is better than a hundred false barks,
Or sorrows in that infamous box (Pandora) can be blessings,
And small acts of loving, sweeter memories than great leaps of faith.

MK 4/2010

I WILL TELL YOU A SECRET

Do you have a secret that made you succeed or fail (most of the time it is our failures that teach us our most valuable lessons) in your life's journey that you would like to share with others?

_____

_____

_____

_____

_____

_____

_____

_____

_____

_____

Are there any lines in the poem that resonate with your life? How?

_____

_____

_____

_____

_____

_____

_____

_____

_____

DR. M. P. KHAN, MD/NMD

November 29

TWO CASE STUDIES: THE
ENVIRONMENT

*Apples on the ground under an apple tree usually come
from the same tree.*
—**Chairman Moo**

If modern medicine has an Achilles Heel, it is the belief that for any data to be valid, it has to be subject to exhaustive double blinded control studies. And the interpretation of that data, tightly controlled by an obsessive demographer sitting in a darkened room as he spews out complicated mathematical formulas, ensures that the study is credible!

Though this is a tried and true scientific tool, there is the tendency to dismiss all other methods as invalid. After all, as the above quote implies, even though you did not actually see the apples fall, it is logical that the apples on the ground came from the same tree and that there is a causal relationship. It is highly unlikely that someone actually placed the apples under the tree. A recent International conference on the environment came to the same conclusion: *"When an activity raises threats of harm to human health or the environment, precautionary measures should be taken even if some cause and effect relationships have not been fully established scientifically."*

Which brings me to two case studies to demonstrate this point: *CASE STUDY: 1*

A 27 year old male presents with intermittent abdominal pain, generalized muscle aches, poor appetite and constipation. He also has non-specific headaches and difficulty concentrating at times. When he presents, he has been to a psychiatrist for his 'nerves' and a GI specialist for his "Irritable Bowel Syndrome" and has had an upper and lower endoscopies which are negative for any pathology.

He also has been to the Cleveland Clinic and has had an extensive lab work up for connective tissue disease and a cardiac workup with Cardiolite (nuclear) treadmill testing which are all inconclusive. In desperation, he is seen by a chiropractor who finds he has a slightly increased level of lead in the urine and is dismissed as an anomaly as there is no way he could be exposed to lead in his environment.

When he presents to me as a patient, I get an environment history on him. He is a flight instructor at a nearby airport where he spends up to ten hours a day, most days of the week. I order a heavy metal screen and find his level at 14(norm=10 and average levels in adults should be less than 2) and start him on DMSA. His symptoms almost immediately start improving.

I have him test his water and the paint in his apartment which test negative for lead. On researching the fuel used by piston aircraft engines, I find that it is still leaded and that the EPA has recommended that all individuals with exposure to those fumes be periodically be screened for lead levels.

The above is a good example of how an environment based history could be useful. Have your physician test you for heavy metals in your blood in any chronic disease states that cannot be explained by conventional medical testing.

November 30

TWO CASE STUDIES:
THE ENVIRONMENT

To know that even one life has breathed easier because you have lived, that is to have succeeded."
—Ralph Waldo Emerson

That last case study was not just a case, he was my son. Had I applied some of the principles discussed previously, I could have spared him some of the anguish and expense that he went through. The next case was an actual patient of mine and no relation! *CASE STUDY: 2*

A 53 year old male presents as a new patient to my practice. He is to get a bone marrow biopsy in a couple of days to diagnose a blood count disorder, and wants my opinion about it. He has had several blood tests and has seen his white cell count dropping over the last few months. He has been in good health until recently and has no significant family history of leukemia or lymphomas. He sometime complains that his feet get numb at times and he gets cramps. He attributes this to his job which involves a lot of walking. His kids are in good health.

He has been a postman for the last 20 years. His hobby is wood working which he has pursued for the last eleven years. He makes sculptures from lumber that he buys from the local hardware store. He has not worked in the past around any chemicals or fumes and is very careful about his diet which is mostly organic and vegetarian.

I am about ready to wrap up the visit, apologizing for the fact that I have no good explanation about his low white cell count. Since Karen is an artist, I ask him if he has any pictures of his sculptures. His face lights up and he promptly pulls out a small album from his pocket. They are pictures of some really exquisite large wood sculptures set in a wooded area.

I ask him, if being outside, they are safe from weather and insects. He advises me that after they are completed in his workshop, he sprays them with wood sealers and besides it is treated wood anyway. He replies that he wears a respirator when he sprays those chemicals. On further questioning, he moves the sculptures from his workshop to the outside setting to dry after the chemical treatment. When he carries them, the sculpture has direct contact with bare skin.

I have a real concern that he may have some kind of chemical poisoning from repeated exposure to insecticides used and absorbed by contact with his skin. I ask him to bring me the ingredients of the spray he uses and it is a common sealer with no significant toxicity.

The tipoff is the treated wood that he is using for his sculptures. It is pressurized and treated with arsenic to prevent insect damage. I order a 24 hr. urine for arsenic (urine better than blood as it is rapidly cleared) and find high levels of arsenic. This explains the neuropathy from the chronic exposure as well as the bone marrow suppression! I refer him to a toxicologist and advise him to use untreated wood in the future. He does not return for a follow up visit and he does not see the toxicologist I referred him to.

There are chemical toxins that can only be determined by testing the urine. Blood levels may not always be conclusive.

DR. M. P. KHAN, MD/NMD

DECEMBER

1-Dec	AND WE GO TO AN ART SHOW. 'Anti-Gravity.'
2-Dec	AND WE GO TO AN ART SHOW. 'The Three Sisters.'
3-Dec	AND WE GO TO AN ART SHOW. 'End of the Year Clean-up.'
4-Dec	AND WE GO TO AN ART SHOW. 'The Trinity.'
5-Dec	AND WE GO TO AN ART SHOW. 'Moroccan Fantasy.'
6-Dec	AND WE GO TO AN ART SHOW. Artistic ability, it's not funny.
7-Dec	TICK-TALK. (PT-1) Anyone for New England Lyme-onade?
8-Dec	TICK-TALK. (PT-1) Making a diagnosis.
9-Dec	TICK-TALK. (PT-2) And how about Post Lyme Syndrome?
10-Dec	TICK-TALK. (PT-2) Stages of Lyme disease.
11-Dec	TALES OF ENCHANTED LANDS. The American Southwest.
12-Dec	TALES OF ENCHANTED LANDS. And 'Santa Fe Dreams.'
13-Dec	MR. ARTHER IT IS. (PT-1) Some of the causes.
14-Dec	MR. ARTHER IT IS. (PT-1) Glucosamine and Weight Loss.
15-Dec	MR. ARTHER IT IS. (PT-2) Omega-3, D-3 and Mussels?
16-Dec	MR. ARTHER IT IS. (PT-3) Curcumin and Capsaicin.
17-Dec	MR. ARTHER IT IS. (PT-3) A Website and a Recipe.
18-Dec	THE WOLF WE FEED. Which animal will we feed?
19-Dec	THE WOLF WE FEED. The 'Wolf' I fed!
20-Dec	ASSORTED MEDICAL CHOCOLATES. Relapsing Depression and Brain Food.
21-Dec	ASSORTED MEDICAL CHOCOLATES. The Mediterranean Diet and HIIT.
22-Dec	ASSORTED MEDICAL CHOCOLATES. Vitamin D and Respiratory Infections.
23-Dec	ASSORTED MEDICAL CHOCOLATES. Vitamin D & C, Asthma & Red Meat
24-Dec	IT'S CHRISTMAS EVE. A Joy and a Sorrow.
25-Dec	IT'S CHRISTMAS DAY. Of 'Toy Trains in Sepia' and Forgiveness.
26-Dec	ONE MORE CUP OF COFFEE, PLEASE. Make mine Arabica.
27-Dec	ENTERING THE 'LUMINOSITY.' Our Journey is Ending.
28-Dec	ENTERING THE 'LUMINOSITY'. 'The Garden Gate.'
29-Dec	ENTERING THE 'LUMINOSITY'. 'The Arbor.'
30-Dec	ENTERING THE 'LUMINOSITY'. 'The Meadow.'
31-Dec	ENTERING THE 'LUMINOSITY'. 'The Garden Bench.'

DR. M. P. KHAN, MD/NMD

December 1

AND WE GO TO AN ART SHOW

"A picture is a poem without words."
—**Horace**

In June of 2015, Karen had an art show at the Welles Gallery in downtown Lenox. The poems that follow were specifically written for the show and reflects the verbal expression of the paintings. See if you can relate to the painting by first reading the poem and then viewing the reproduction of the painting.

ANTI-GRAVITY:

Out there, free from this firmament,
In another life, we will meet again.

Out there, we will be perfect luminous beings,
Floating together as heavenly objects.

Out there, like new stars in the night sky,
We will be a super nova, our own constellation.

MK 6/2015

DR. M. P. KHAN, MD/NMD

December 2

AND WE GO TO AN ART SHOW

"Drawing is the honesty of the art. There is no possibility of cheating. It is either good or bad."
—**Salvador Dali**

THE THREE SISTERS:

In the vast farms of the mid-west,
The combines roar from dawn to dusk.
Their hunger desecrating the graves of the ancient corn-gods
My forefathers once put to rest with long forgotten rituals.

I remember, once a shaman of the tribes of the Great Plains,
We were many people, we who hunted the buffalo herds
And played night games with the spirits of the wild ones,
Must now make simple offerings
Of
Husk dolls,
Dried flowers
And
Woven blankets.

MK 6/2015

DR. M. P. KHAN, MD/NMD

December 3

AND WE GO TO AN ART SHOW

"Color is my day-long obsession, joy and torment."
—Claude Monet

END OF THE YEAR CLEAN-UP:

They will come, like the inevitability,
Of a sunset which follows a sunrise,
Of the grave following the cradle.
They will come with measures and sterile precautions,
Sweeping the last breath, the last heartbeat,
Dissected into the dust heap of a forgotten life.

Only the shells remember the soft memories.
Once sheltered and nourished hopefully
In the stormy waters of youth and beauty,
Now, lost on silken sands of gold and amber,
Empty strewn monuments of spine and stripe,
They speak of promises un-kept.

MK 6/2015

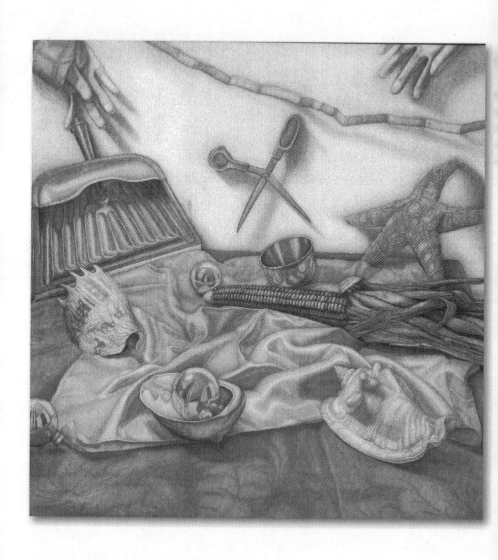

December 4

AND WE GO TO AN ART SHOW

*"The artist is a receptacle for emotions that come from all over
the place: from the sky, from the earth, from a scrap of paper,
from a passing shape, from a spider's web."*
—Pablo Picasso

THE TRINITY:

If you will invite the Father,
Why not the Mother?
*I am sure she could tell you a few risqué stories about Dad! Besides she has spent enough
time in the kitchen preparing this meal.*
All vegetarian dishes of course.
If you will invite the Son,
Why not the Daughter?
*Heard while Junior was finding Himself, she went on to Harvard and got a PhD in
Comparative Religious Studies.*
She would be an interesting dinner guest and provide a whole new slant on the conversation.
If you will invite the Holy Ghost,
Why not seraphim, and a host of Angels, fallen and otherwise?
The Buddha could say grace. And do not forget the Hindu Gods?
Shiva could dance afterwards and Brahma could create whole new worlds.
In fact, why don't we invite all six billion people on this planet?
And serve love as the main course
And peace for dessert?
This could be quite a party!!

MK 6/2015

DR. M. P. KHAN, MD/NMD

December 5

AND WE GO TO AN ART SHOW

*"To send light into the darkness of men's hearts - such is the
duty of the artist."*
—Robert Schumann

MORROCAN FANTASY:

Meet me in the bazaar at the designated hour,
When the muezzin calls to prayer and hope.

Amidst the dust and the flies,
I will show you my happy wares.
Flying silks from the gossamer wings of moths,
Metal lamps bright with the bio-luminescence of fire flies
Still dreaming of warm summer nights.
Carpets woven form the fuzz blossoms
Of the first dandelions of spring.

But if you do not buy, rest awhile!
I will serve you jasmine tea from flowers I tended through winter.
Feed you jeweled sweets resting in inlaid boxes
Of bone and mahogany and sing to you
Melodies of loss and longing.

So come meet me when the muezzin cries,
At the market place.

MK 6/2015

DR. M. P. KHAN, MD/NMD

December 6

AND WE GO TO AN ART SHOW

"Very few people possess true artistic ability. It is therefore both unseemly and unproductive to irritate the situation by making an effort. If you have a burning, restless urge to write or paint, simply eat something sweet and the feeling will pass."

—Fran Lebowitz

There may be some wisdom in the above quote. But seriously, if you feel the urge to express yourself creatively, by all means, do so.

What words do these paintings evoke in you? Write down below your first impressions. There is no right or wrong response. Just an exercise in art appreciation.

_____

_____

_____

_____

_____

_____

_____

_____

_____

_____

December 7

TICK-TALK (PART-1)

What used to be a hallmark if summer is now almost a year round problem if my patients are to be believed! I am seeing my share of patients presenting with small crawly things attached to them which on further investigation are deer ticks, a very common pest in Mass and also in Western Pa. I remember my very first patient that presented to my office several years ago which was eventually diagnosed to be Lyme disease. He had a sag of his facial features on one side also known as Bell's palsy, one of the neurological manifestations of Lyme. After an exhaustive workup and a referral to a neurologist, we confirmed his diagnosis and he was treated appropriately. He lived in the suburbs and his only contact with nature was a wood pile in his back yard. Later on he had irregular heartbeats consistent with the complications of advanced Lyme disease and is now well controlled with a pacemaker.

The full syndrome of Lyme disease was not recognized until an unusually large number of cases, were identified in southeastern Connecticut in 1975, in the town of Lyme. Originally thought to be a form of rheumatoid arthritis that affects younger populations, (JRA) the joint symptoms are similar to the arthritis seen in advanced Lyme disease. This was investigated by physicians David Snydman and Allen Steere of the Epidemic Intelligence Service.

Willy Burgdorfer, a researcher at the Rocky Mountain Biological Laboratory, when examining ticks for another disease condition, noticed unusual bacteria which were poorly stained, rather long, spring like and coiled (spirochetes). Burgdorfer confirmed his discovery by isolating from patients with Lyme disease, bacteria identical to those found in deer ticks. In June 1982 he published his findings in Science, and the bug was named *Borrelia burgdorferi* (Bb)in recognition of his discovery.

When I see those critters firmly attached to some body part, I recommend immediate removal. Some studies show that the longer (>24 hours) the tick is attached, the more likely is the transmission of Bb from the salivary glands of the tick. Although the exact removal of the tick is the

DR. M. P. KHAN, MD/NMD

stuff of folk legends, I recommend dousing the tick with rubbing alcohol. Then using tweezers as close to the mouth parts of the tick as possible, gently tug till it lets go. Another option is to use a tick removal tool that you can purchase from a pet store (yes, the same you would use on Fido). If you are an outdoors type, I recommend a full naked body scan after an outdoor activity in front of a mirror to see if you have picked up a tick. Insect repellants help but don't always work.

Although in an ideal world, antibiotics (doxycycline) are not recommended right after removal of a tick bite, I usually prescribe a prophylactic dose of 200mg once. A text book approach would be to wait till Lyme titers (blood tests) come back positive before treatment. This is one of the few instances where I am liberal with antibiotic therapy. The course is short and cuts down significantly on the anxiety levels as the patient waits for several days for the results.(which may be negative in the early stages.)

TICK-TALK (PART-1)

No diagnosis of Lyme disease should be made without a positive test for Lyme disease as the symptoms can mimic several diseases such as fibromyalgia and rheumatoid arthritis.

A two tier approach is recommended to make the diagnosis of Lyme disease. This approach uses a sensitive enzyme-linked immunosorbent assay (ELISA) followed by a Western blot. If the ELISA is positive or equivocal, then the same serum sample should be tested by Western blot (IgM and IgG) to confirm the ELISA. If the ELISA is negative, no further testing is needed. Also the test in the first few weeks of exposure may be negative and if the diagnosis is suspected, a repeat test 4-6 weeks later may be needed.

Although a target lesion or a ring like rash a few weeks later around the bite is diagnostic, (erythema migrans) it may not always be present in 10-15 % of cases and its absence should not exclude the diagnosis of Lyme disease. This sign is seen in the early stages of Lyme.

A good system of prevention is to spray clothing with a permethrin type of insect repellant and let the clothing dry completely before wearing. Also spray a eucalyptus oil based insect repellant (easily available; Burt's Bees) on exposed body parts before venturing out. After coming back from the outdoors, get naked in front of a mirror and follow with a hot head to toe shower. I am not a big fan of the more commercially available bug sprays.

December 9

TICK-TALK (PART-2)

The problem of blood testing is that once you are infected, even after adequate treatment with appropriate courses of anti-biotic therapy, the antibodies can persist indefinitely. What is useful is if the titers drop over a period of time and it is best to compare these numbers. Also reinfection can also occur in endemic areas.

There has been significant controversy in the past about the existence of Chronic Lyme Disease or "Post Lyme Syndrome" with death threats made to individuals who questioned the validity of the diagnosis. Connecticut is the only state that mandates that Insurance plans cover long term antibiotic treatment for the above syndrome.

The Infectious Diseases Society of America (IDSA) has proposed a definition of post-Lyme disease syndrome. *Criteria for this syndrome include a prior history of Lyme disease treated with an accepted regimen and resolution or stabilization of the objective manifestations of Lyme disease. In addition, the onset of subjective symptoms such as fatigue, widespread musculoskeletal pain, and complaints of cognitive difficulties must have occurred within six months of the diagnosis of Lyme disease and persist (continuously or relapsing) for at least six months after completion of treatment.*

The majority of patients improve within 6 months to a year. One way to confirm treatment success is the presence of DNA by a Polymerase Chain Reaction (PCR) test on the joint fluid or spinal fluid although that is not completely fool proof and can cause false positive test results. Because this disease mimics so many other diseases, it is tempting to assign all symptoms to the expression of Lyme and not even consider other disease states in the differential. Conversely Lyme should be considered in the differential in any chronic disease state keeping in mind that the antibodies persist indefinitely!

Patients with Lyme disease in endemic areas may also have other infections transmitted by ticks: *Anaplasma phagocytophilum,* which causes human granulocytic anaplasmosis (also called Ehrlichiosis), and *Babesia microti*. Infections with these bugs are usually asymptomatic except in the very young and old and individuals with their spleen surgically removed.

Although there was once a vaccine available to prevent Lyme, real world trials proved it to be ineffective. It is no longer available.

December 10

TICK-TALK (PART-2)

Lyme disease manifests in several stages with different signs and symptoms based on the stage the disease is in.

Early disease: Common early symptoms of Lyme are common to many viral type of illnesses but lung and upper airway symptoms such as cough and congestion are rare.

- *Fatigue*
- *Anorexia or Appetite loss*
- *Headache*
- *Neck stiffness*
- *Myalgias or Muscle pains*
- *Arthralgias –or Joint pains*
- *Regional lymph node swelling.*
- *Fever*
- *Erythema migrans (typical target lesion present in 80% of early infection but not always.*

Early disseminated: (Weeks to Months)Some of the neurological presentations as mentioned below of Lyme are seen earlier on when the bug has just spread through the body and can occur weeks to months after a tick bite.

- *Lymphocytic meningitis. (inflammation of the lining of the brain)*
- *Unilateral or bilateral cranial nerve palsies. (especially of the facial nerve as in the patient previously mentioned)*
- *Radiculopathy or irritation of the nerve root.*
- *Peripheral neuropathy or numbness and tingling in the feet and forearms.*

- *Mononeuropathy multiplex affecting the larger nerves.*
- *Cerebellar ataxia or balance and co-ordination problems.(rarely)*

Late disease: (Months to Years) Later on there may be some nonspecific problems such as difficulty remembering things along with generalized pain in the nerve root distribution. Hence the confusion with fibromyalgia which also can be triggered after a bout with Lyme but is not a disease presentation of Lyme disease.

Cardiac abnormalities include conduction defects that may need a pacemaker if the irregular heart rhythms cause symptoms. Sometime an abnormal enlargement of the heart is seen (cardiomyopathy) but this is rare.

Rarely, there can be chronic eye problems such as conjunctivitis.

As the disease progresses, in about 60% of patients, there is the classic finding of Lyme arthritis which primarily affects the knee joints. This can be a recurrent problem and responds well to common anti-inflammatory medications.

DR. M. P. KHAN, MD/NMD

TALES OF ENCHANTED LANDS

*"The wind whips through the canyons of the American
Southwest, and there is no one to hear it but us - a
reminder of the 40,000 generations of thinking men and
women who preceded us, about whom we know almost
nothing, upon whom our civilization is based."*

—Dr. Carl Sagan

One of the more memorable trips that Karen and I have taken in my
PA life, was one to Santa Fe; New Mexico. There was a medical meeting
that I was to attend. We had rented a room in a B&B nearby and used it
as our base as we travelled in our rental car. They call it "The Land of
Enchantment" on the license plate and it lived up to its name.

Every turn opened up vistas and landscapes as far as the eye could
see. Surrounded by the sometimes claustrophobic hills of Western PA,
this was a welcome change. Here the land was an open book, laid out in
all its honesty with an endless horizon.

Check out www.newmexico.gov for info on travel. And take a good
camera to capture the magic. This is a place that you must have on your
bucket list. Steeped in the ancient history of three cultures (American,
Spanish, and Anasazi Indian) which defined the American West and the
starting point of the Santa Fe Trail, it is also the place which gave birth to
the atomic age in a town called Los Alamos!

The poem that follows is actually a prose poem and was written jointly
on the airplane ride back to Pittsburgh. I think it captures what the wind
was trying to tell us.

And do not forget to bring back roasted Serrano peppers. Your palate
will thank you for their heat on cold December nights.

And for once, Sagan was wrong! Listen carefully and the wind will
whisper its secrets to you!

December 12

TALES OF ENCHANTED LANDS

SANTA FE DREAMS:

In the magic of the horizon, passages of aspen trees bloom gold in the ominous light of fall. The Sangria Christa Mountains grow nearer, larger than God herself. The briskly patterned hills, weave saffron, sage and adobe, in the undulating landscape. The pink desert willows blossoms fall along the arroyo. A cerulean sea forming overhead, etches light in glowing sheaths, fairy blue over the distance.

The surreal sweep of late afternoon, transforms desert into spirit lore. Dusk's brow approaches in awe before the subterfuge of night. The blackened raven's harsh song heralds the night and summons the warrior to his quest.

The distant mountains are a mythical earth mother, lying prostrate, her shape molds the horizon under a burnished moon naked in the forgiving sky. Resting in daylight, she awakes at night to greet him, her lucid memories embrace the sands of time.

The Lakota Wind- Warrior, resplendent in war paint, rides the phantom mustang. His ancient heart warmed by sunset fire, woos the night woman with ghostly coyote cries emanating from ancient sorrows.

Each night he merges with her beauty only to leave with the rising sun. Satiated, yet unborn, she sighs in forgotten farewell, awaiting his return in the counting grains of sand. She assembles her court; the coyote and the road runner, the magpie and the viper, they do her bidding under the sweltering sky

The warring wind, a fierce gale, commands brave spirits on snowcapped peaks. The Lakota, Hopi and the Anasazi. Their souls are summoned in the service of the Wind Warrior. A celebration of ancient glories, and battles won and lost. But all heed the shaman's call, carried on the wings of a gentle wind. As the evening shadows elongate, once again, they return silently to their burial grounds in the ancient hills.

The Wind-Warrior bides them farewell. The night beckons the return of dreams. Flowing in impossible hopes, he once again treads softly on the trail of sorrows.

MK/KK 9/2010

DR. M. P. KHAN, MD/NMD

December 13

MR. ARTHER, IT IS (PART-1)

"I don't deserve this award, but I have arthritis and I don't deserve that either."

—Jack Benny

The discussions that follow on osteoarthritis were contributed by Dr. Jessica Stevens DO, a third year resident in a local family practice program. She was spending time with me in my practice, as part of her teaching rotation and forwarded me an excellent monograph on complimentary approaches to the treatment of a very common and debilitating problem. It has been slightly modified based on my own experience. Sometimes the greatest reward of teaching is that we learn from our students!

Friday! A busy week and I am catching up on the inevitable paper work multiplying like so many rabbits on my desk. Still, the week ended with Mrs. Fields as my last patient and a bag of much appreciated cookies, still warm from the oven! This is how it went.

Hi Dr. Khan, make sure you share those cookies with your staff. They told me the last time you ate them all! I am having a problem with my hands. I used to be able to knit a scarf for my grandkids in a few days. Now I am lucky if I can do it in a week. They feel stiff and painful, especially when I wake up in the morning. It's very likely arthritis but do you have any magic herb or supplement that may help? I know from the internet that the prescription pills are very hard on the kidneys and the heart. They can also cause ulcers in the stomach!

You are in luck; Mrs. Fields. Let me introduce Dr. Jessica Stevens. She has some really good approaches to treat your problem using non pharmaceutical approaches. And I can't promise that I will share those cookies: just kidding.

Osteoarthritis (OA) affects millions of Americans, which suggests that billions of dollars are likely spent by those Americans seeking relief. OA was the reason behind the creation of aspirin in

the late 1800s by Bayer, in an effort to make the active ingredient of willow bark less destructive to the stomach. Since that time, many different pharmaceutical and non-pharmaceutical attempts to relieve this pain have been studied and touted; with no one remedy becoming a conclusive winner in this race to treat our patients. Many patients have pain that limits not just their daily activities, but also their livelihoods, and they will try most anything for even modest relief from symptoms.

OA is an overuse injury due to gradual deterioration of the cartilage and also known as Degenerative Joint Disease or DJD. Although it is also a normal process of aging, we see many younger patients from the physically active population manifesting symptoms that are due to a lifetime of heeding advice that purports cardiovascular exercise to help one remain healthy.

What better way to achieve optimal cardiovascular fitness levels than running, biking, tennis, etc.? All of these activities are hard on the joints. We must also consider our patients who were long-time athletes on a more extensive level of repetitive drills and long practice days, many of whom later settled into the above lifestyle.

We did discuss the value previously of turmeric in treating arthritis and I would recommend up to 1200 mg a day in divided doses (although up to 10,000 mg a day is considered a safe amount). I make it appoint to advise all my arthritis patients to give this amazing spice a trial. I have seen mostly positive results with this simple yet effective supplements with virtually no side effects. More on this later.

MR. ARTHER, IT IS (PART-1)

"My message is - keep moving. If you do, you'll keep arthritis at bay."
—Donna Mills

Many patients seek outside treatments for OA and they do so for many reasons that usually span across the realm of why people seek alternative treatments. Some find no relief from the current approved medicines. Others have side effects that make the medicine just as intolerable as the disease they are treating. Others would simply like to move towards a more natural option. One study suggested that only 15-20% of patients will continue to take an NSAID (Ibuprofen, Naproxen) one year after initiation due to the above. Below are some commonly used alternative approaches.

1) Glucosamine and chondroitin sulfate. Either separately or together, are two of the more frequently discussed options. They have been under study for some years now, with less than definitive advice, despite many trials. Glucosamine is a precursor to glycosamino glycan, which is one of the major building blocks of cartilage. Chondroitin sulfate is another building block of cartilage, and it is thought to enhance the efficacy of glucosamine. A literature review shows that some studies find efficacy, while others do not. Many of these studies are also flawed in length of study, standardization of dose, or other key aspects. A recent study examined the use of glucosamine, chondroitin sulfate, a combination of the two, celecoxib, or placebo demonstrated moderate benefit in the celecoxib and glucosamine monotherapy groups over placebo in a 2 year trial.

Glucosamine should be used at a dose of 1500 mg a day for 8-12 weeks to be effective. It does not affect the blood glucose levels despite its name. Individuals who are allergic to fish may have an allergic reaction.

2) *Weight Loss.* The ability to walk upright may have been a significant evolutionary advantage because it freed up our hands to use tools. But it also doubled the stress on our hips and knees, stress which would have been distributed to our elbow and shoulder joints. As a result; the act of walking places twice the body weight on our weight bearing joints and jogging or other high impact exercises around four times the body weight. So a two hundred pound man while walking bears 400 pounds of weight on his hip and knee joints with every step and an *amazing 800 pounds* with every step when jogging! Even a ten pound weight loss can make a significant difference in the symptom management of arthritis and weight loss is often overlooked as a treatment approach. And by the way a recent UK study showed that *hiking* was the best exercise for weight loss

December 15

MR. ARTHER, IT IS (PART-2)

The Doctor called Mrs. Cohen saying "Mrs. Cohen, your
check came back." Mrs. Cohen answered
"So did my arthritis!"
—Henny Youngman

3) *Omega 3 fish oil:* These fatty acids are a potent anti-inflammatory. Some data suggests they could have a role in decreasing the deterioration seen in OA. Despite clinical success seen in some patients, a recent literature review found that the studies available thus far were not conclusive enough to soundly recommend their exclusive use in the treatment of OA. As previously discussed, 8-12 grams of omega-3 may be very useful in relieving symptoms of Rheumatoid Arthritis or RA and studies in OA may need to be done using mega doses to see if they help. But it can't hurt (pun here).

4) *Vitamin D3*: This is another use of this vitamin that really is a hormone. It is presently being studied to determine its role in many pathologic processes, one of them being OA. We all know that vitamin D is needed for calcium absorption and the prevention of osteoporosis. It also works as a powerful anti-inflammatory, which can be helpful in our patients suffering from OA. A recent study published in the Journal of Clinical Rheumatology suggests that vitamin D can not only alleviate the pain associated with OA, but that it may also help to prevent OA. Doses taken by the patients studied were variable, but it appears that no patient was taking more than 400 IU/day. There are many sources that suggest varying doses from 2,000-10,000 IU/day to be more effective for treatment or prevention of many diseases. Another study that was somewhat smaller and followed patients for less time published in Arthritis and Rheumatism suggests similar findings. Dosage in the setting of OA is clearly an area that needs more study.

5) *Green-lipped mussel extract (Perna canaliculus)*: This is a supplement that has been gaining attention as of late as an OA treatment. GLM have a fatty acid composition not seen in other species. One of these fatty acids is glycosaminoglycan, which has been suggested as helpful in joint protection. A systematic review of several articles that showed modest improvement over placebo suggests that more vigorous studies need attempted, including a study to determine the optimal dose. Another concern for this supplement, like many supplements, is quality control. GLM are only found off the coast of New Zealand, which makes them more difficult to obtain than other types of shellfish. One study found that patients responded similarly to two different forms of GLM (lipid extract vs. stabilized mussel powder), but there are multiple forms available, and as we know, the difference in form can also mean a difference in price.

6) *Resveratrol*: This is another nutraceutical that has only recently been discovered and is being studied to determine if it has a role in many different disease processes, including OA. Found in large quantities in red wine, it appears to have a potent anti-inflammatory effect, which would lend it to treatment of OA. Trials are currently underway to determine just how effective resveratrol is for the treatment of OA, including which dose is most effective.

There are also several companies that have derived formulations, which are combinations of any number of the above supplements or others. One product that I recommend is Douglas Labs /Inflamend, one or two daily which is a blend of anti-inflammatory herbs specifically turmeric, boswellia and cat's claw (a plant and not from a kitty).

December 16

MR. ARTHER IT IS (PART-3)

"I knew it was going to be tough going when the menu
described the three levels of spiciness as 'Hot,' 'Way Hot'
and 'Legal Waiver Required.'"
                                                    —Al Apeno

The next time you visit an Indian restaurant and sample the cooking, you can be comforted in the fact that you are eating two key spices that can help arthritis (besides a variety of other ailments). The star in the recipe is curcumin or turmeric followed closely by capsaicin or the chili (cayenne) pepper. The other commonly used spices are garlic and ginger, the latter also an anti-inflammatory food.

7) *Curcumin:* A member of the ginger family, the root is harvested and dried. It is then ground to a powder form called turmeric which is used in cooking as well as in a variety of herbal remedies. Turmeric contains a wide variety of biologically active compounds called curcuminoids, and is believed to stimulate the production of bile. Because of this effect, it should not be used if you have gall stones or a bile duct obstruction.

One of the curcuminoids, *curcumin,* gives turmeric its typical yellow color and is the active component that has anti-inflammatory properties. Curcumin has been demonstrated to exhibit anti-inflammatory activity by changing the arachidonic acid pathway, a key acid responsible for the inflammation response as well as preventing aggregation of platelets (Coumadin users beware!). In rat studies, it was more effective than hydrocortisone in preventing inflammation,
A randomized, double-blind, crossover study, studied the effects of curcumin as compared to Butazolin, an NSAID, in 18 patients. All anti-inflammatory agents were discontinued four days prior to the study. Study goals included 1) duration of morning stiffness, 2) fatigue time, 8) time required to walk 25 ft., 4) grip strength of both hands, and 5)

overall general improvement and side effects. Both agents demonstrated significant subjective improvement in morning stiffness, walking time, and joint swelling with no side effects noted in the turmeric group. Butazolin on the other hand is no longer available because of toxicity on the kidneys with long term use which is a class effect of most NSAID drugs.

Dosing is advised at 400 mg three times a day as a standardized form (DL Turmeric Max-V) on an empty stomach for 8-12 weeks or better still, get a good Indian cook book and discover the sensual pleasure and the complex tastes of Indian cooking.(Recipe to follow).

9) *Capsaicin:* The active ingredient of the chili pepper plant, it is responsible for the burn and sometimes painful sensation on your tongue. It reacts with chemo receptors present in the skin, tongue and mucus membranes. The intensity is measured by Scoville Heat units, SHU, with bell peppers having a score of zero and the Indian chili, Naga jolokia, scored at over a million units (waiver needed).

It is approved by the FDA in the treatment of OA as an OTC topical application available in two strengths and it works by depleting the substance P, a neurotransmitter responsible for pain in arthritis sufferers. The topical form is also indicated for the treatment of post herpetic neuralgia. Caution: If you do use it topically, I would advise using disposable vinyl gloves that can be discarded after application so as to avoid accidental contact with eyes or lips; a potentially painful but reversible experience. Also start real slowly, with the lowest available strength once a day for a week and gradually increase it over the next three to four weeks to the recommended three times a day dosing. We will discuss the use of the health benefits of oral capsaicin another day.

MR. ARTHER IT IS (PART-3)

My advice to motivated patients who decide they would like to attempt their own "trial": keeping their own patient record. I suggest purchasing a pocket calendar to record a pain scale and activity level during the determined trial period. If they are exceptionally motivated, I would suggest recording this data two weeks prior to treatment and then repeat similar activity levels for a more balanced comparison of efficacy. If they are on a pharmaceutical based regiment, continue this calendar for a trial of weaning. While this method does allow for the possibility of patient bias, it also allows for a more organized record of effect, and can help a patient participate more in their treatment.

An excellent and credible resource for OA and its management is: www.arhritis.org

Hope you enjoy the recipe that follows. Tastes great and treats arthritis too!

<u>*Crock Pot Slow Cooker Lentils (Dal).*</u>

The recipe that follows is one of my favorite. It is loaded with soluble fiber and the spices we talked about. All the ingredients are readily available at your local Indian grocery store

3 cups dried yellow split lentils (washed thoroughly);

1 medium onion chopped;

1 medium tomato chopped;

1 tbsp. of prepared garlic ginger paste; (or mince 4 cloves garlic and 1 inch of ginger root)

1 or 2 Indian chilies, stems removed and chopped; 2 tsp turmeric powder;

1 tsp red chili powder; 1 tsp. cumin seeds;

1 tsp. salt;

And 12 cups water.

Place all of the above in a crock pot (slow cooker) or a pot and cook on low for 5 hours. Serve with Indian flat bread or rice. Make around 10-12 servings. Freeze the leftovers for another day.

DR. M. P. KHAN, MD/NMD

December 18

THE WOLF WE FEED

"One should see the world, and see himself as a scale with an equal balance of good and evil. When he does one good deed the scale is tipped to the good - he and the world is saved. When he does one evil deed the scale is tipped to the bad - he and the world is destroyed."

—Maimonides

Since antiquity and in almost every indigenous tradition worldwide, the wolf has had a special place in the mythology and culture of their lives. The Zoroastrians believed that the wolf was the agent of the Dark One: Ahriman. The Mongol people believe that they were descendants of offspring when a doe mated with a wolf. The Pawnee Indians associated the wolf with corn and was the first animal to experience death. The parable that follows is oft told and may be familiar. It is one of my favorite one.

Chief Lone Star decided that it was time to take his son, Moon Dancer on a spirit quest. They set out from their village one day in early spring. For forty days and night they wandered through the great wilderness, sometime living on nuts and berries and whatever small game they could hunt. On the fortieth day he told his son of the vision that he had.

"Son, in my vision I saw two wolves.

One was evil. He roamed the plains, indiscriminately killing sheep and other livestock. He did not take care of his fellow wolves and laughed at their attempts to live harmoniously in a pack. And if any of the younger wolves displeased him, he would kill them or drive them out of the pack.

The other wolf was the opposite. He would only kill a sheep only if he was really hungry. And then he would share his kill with the other wolves in the pack. He would only eat after the other younger wolves who could not hunt yet, had their fill. And he would protect the pack from any threats by fighting to the death if he had to."

The son listened quietly to his father.
Then the son asked:
"So which wolf was the stronger one?"
And the father replied:
"It is the one you feed the most!"

DR. M. P. KHAN, MD/NMD

December 19

THE WOLF WE FEED

"If time is not real, then the dividing line between this
world and eternity, between suffering and bliss, between
good and evil, is also an illusion."

—**Herman Hesse**

Every day we have a choice as to which wolf we want to feed.
Maybe that is the real meaning of free will. The result of that choice
is not in our control even though we may have the illusion of control.
That result is our fate or destiny. It's complicated.

The poem that follows is about the wolf I fed with love. Or lust. I
am not sure!

WOLF:

This is what love does,
Shredding the fabric of a
Carefully constructed existence.
It is the wolf, that in my ignorance
I thought was leashed and tamed.

This wolf, once again aware of its power,
Rips apart the crust of my temporal life.
And as I die to this world
Gifts me with sweet howl of redemption.

One stormy November night,
When I slept on clean sheets
In a room of harmonious color
And French period furniture,
His luminous gaze awakened my soul.

First soft, then a thunder of primal memories
That heralds the storm that must follow.
Suspended between living and dreaming
I awake, craving your arms and thighs,
Wet lips and small prayers.

Outside the room the wind sings,
And dancing trees weep their leaves
That smothers with gold, the frozen ground.
This is where I belong; open to the chill of winter,
Numbed by your absence.

A lover brings fire to the beloved
And only this heat will keep the wolf at bay.
Until then, the spring thaw and the summer sun,
The first birdsong, the new crocus; all of this beauty that I once knew
Will not be able to heal me of this sweet disease.

This pain, this longing, this insanity
Is the wolf's timeless wandering.

MK/2011

December 20

ASSORTED MEDICAL CHOCOLATES

Below are some medical bonbons from various areas of holistic medicine that you might enjoy. It's healthier than the real thing, unless the bonbons are 75% dark chocolate.

PREVENTING RELAPSE IN DEPRESSION: In a previous day (Dark Night of the Soul) we discussed about the financial and physical impact of depression. Equally important is the relapse rate of depression following an acute episode which in some studies can approach 80% and so the duration of treatment has gone from 9-12 months to two years. A recent study studied the efficacy of anti-depressant therapy with structured non pharmaceutical approaches such as mindfulness-based cognitive therapy (MBCT or also known as DBT or dialectic behavioral therapy) with 424 patients over a two year period in a group setting. The patients had to have a diagnosis of a major depressive episode MDD; in full or partial remission, three or more past episodes of MDD and currently taking an anti-depressant. The MBCT group had their anti-depressants tapered by their family physician.

At the end of the study, the relapse rate as per DSM-IV criteria was 44% in the MBCT group and 47% in the anti-depressant maintenance group; that is there was no significant statistical difference and MBCT was not more cost effective .An interesting outcome of the study was that MBCT patients who had reported child abuse had a lower rate of relapse than the anti-depressant group. The take home point of this study that non-pharmaceutical approaches are just as effective in preventing the relapse of depression. An alternative to consider for patients who wish to avoid the side effects of weight gain, diabetes and sexual dysfunction associated with pharmaceutical agents.

THE LARGE BRAIN DIET: If, by now, you have not heard of the Mediterranean diet, (just GOOGLE it) you are not living on this planet.

Its role in the prevention of cardiovascular disease and anti-inflammatory effect are well known benefits of the diet. What is less well known is the effect it has in reducing the incidence of Alzheimer's disease in equal age cohorts. But the studies in the past were discredited due to several variables. Now for the first time, using neuro-imaging techniques such as MRI measuring brain volumes of different structures of the brain, this can be finally validated.

2776 individuals age >65 years of age had a baseline cognitive studies and repeated every 18 months and a diagnosis was made of dementia during the course if they met dementia criteria based on DSM-III R. 769 individuals had MRI data available and their diet was monitored by appoint system with 9 points being the maximum for complete adherence to a Med Diet. At the end of the study the high scoring group (almost all of them had high fish intake) as compared to the low scoring group had a brain age (as measured by measuring brain volumes of different structures in the brain) *of five years more of relative brain volume.* Fish, greens and beans anyone? Or you could move to the Greek Isles. What is not known as to how long one has to maintain this diet to see this effect?

DR. M. P. KHAN, MD/NMD

December 21

ASSORTED MEDICAL CHOCOLATES

THE MEDITERRANEAN DIET POINT SYSTEM: Give yourself one point for every yes answer of the following components;

Vegetables 1; Legumes 1; Cereals 1 (Whole Grain); Fish 1 (Fatty and at least 100 grams a week);

Fruits and/or Nuts 1; High intake of Mono Unsaturated fats (Extra Virgin Olive Oil: EVOO) and low intake of Saturated fats 1;

Low intake of Red meat (no more than 1/week) 1; low intake of Dairy fats 1; Alcohol consumption of 1oz daily but no more than 3oz. Daily 1.

A perfect Mediterranean diet will have a maximum of 9 points!

HIGH INTENSITY INTERMITTENT TRAINING AND DM2: Type 2 Diabetes is not just a disorder of the endocrine system. Its primary impact is on the heart and diabetics have a very high risk of cardiovascular disease. Controlling the HbA1c is critical to prevent this problem in the future. Equally important is the role of diet and exercise.

There is some new data on the role of High-intensity intermittent training or HIIT. The previous recommendations on exercise were at least 150 minutes of continuous aerobic exercise a week. HIIT on the other hand involves brief intervals of vigorous activity followed by periods of low activity exercise or rest.

In a recent study by Cassidy et al in Diabetologia, 28 type 2 DM patients were randomized into two groups. Both groups continued their usual diabetic meds and dietary modifications. One group was to experience three HIT exercise sessions for 8 weeks. Each session consisted of five intervals of very hard cycling at a rate of 80 revolutions or at a scale of 16/20 on the perceived exertion scale lasting initially for 2 minutes and progressing finally to 3 minutes and 50 seconds. They were interspersed with a 5 minute warm up, a 3 minute cooldown and a 3 minute recovery period or a total of 11 minutes between the periods of intense exercise.

The variables were ventricular size by MRI measurements. Other variables were liver and visceral fat also by MRI and blood sugar control. At the end of the study, it was found that there was no significant difference in blood sugar control. However there was significant increase in ejection fraction and increase in the strength of contraction of the left ventricle. At the same time there was a decrease in the amount of visceral fat and liver fat (these are independent risk factors for heart disease) with some of them reversing values to normal range.

In summary, a HIIT has an important role in preventing cardiovascular disease and a session which lasts on an average of 60 minutes three times a week may be very beneficial in preventing the metabolic and cardiovascular complications of diabetes

December 22

ASSORTED MEDICAL CHOCOLATES

VITAMIN D AND INFECTIONS: As we wind down for the year and at least in the North East we can look forward to three more months of winter, it is fitting that we return to the benefits of Vitamin D. Just yesterday I received my influenza vaccine and I often get asked the question; "Doc, is there anything else I can do to prevent the flu?" and I give the usual advise of washing hands, getting adequate sleep and exercising regularly. But there is also a role for Vitamin D supplementation.

The effect of Vitamin D in prevention of infections was known as early as in the 1800s where the incidence of pneumonia and tuberculosis was seen more frequently in individuals suffering from rickets which later (1920s) was found to be associated with a Vitamin D deficiency. It was years later that the mechanism of this effect was finally understood.

One of the reasons, it has been posited, that there are an increase of viral and pneumococcal infections in the winter is a relative Vitamin deficiency as the sun sinks lower in the horizon and with a reduction in UV light needed for the skin to produce Vitamin D. Researchers did a complicated statistical analysis of 198 adults through the months of September to January in a double blinded study and found that individuals who had a level lower than 38 ng/ml were twice as prone to get viral Upper Respiratory Infections (URI). The greatest benefits seen in preventing infections was in individuals who had significantly low Vitamin D levels to begin with on baseline measurements. This also confirms my recommendations to have levels between 40-50 ng/ml so as to provide a safety zone. Also keep in mind that it takes 2-3 months of supplementation to reach a steady state in the serum.

The Mechanism of action is understood by the fact that the immune system has VDRs or Vitamin D Receptors. Although the exact effect on the immune system is too involved for today's topic, suffice to say Vitamin D has an effect on the innate and adaptive components of the immune system and in conclusion Vitamin D is a potent "immunomodulator" working by numerous mechanisms.

There are critics of the role of supplementation of Vitamin D especially in the medical community. This is specious considering that we prescribe drugs with far more serious side effects. Also a meta-analysis of 13 trials involving thousands of patients, there were only two cases of hypercalcemia which required a dose reduction or discontinuation of Vitamin D.

And I stand by my recommendation of 5000 IU daily come rain, snow or shine. I feel that we still have to discover the beneficial effects of this amazing vitamin (actually a hormone by definition) in the years to come!

DR. M. P. KHAN, MD/NMD

ASSORTED MEDICAL CHOCOLATES

VITAMIN D AND ASTHMA: Once again I cannot stop singing the praises of this very important supplement. If I was stranded on a desert island, this is one supplement I would want around. Of course if it was a tropical island with warm breezes and lots of sunshine, it would be a moot point. This information is from the VIDA trial by Castro et al, JAMA 2014, 311:2083-2091.

This trial was to understand the role of Vitamin D in patients with persistent asthma (almost daily episodes of asthma and also at night) who were not responding to inhaled and oral steroids. It was noted that these individuals had a consistently low level of Vitamin D (<30 ng/ml). This was a very well conducted trial over 28 weeks in 1068 patients. There was only a marginal difference in the treatment failures with 63 patients failing in the D3 arm and 83 in the placebo group. Although this study is not statistically significant when viewed at from a research viewpoint, I would definitely ensure that all my asthma patients using steroids have adequate Vitamin D levels. Also there is a genetic variation in the VDRs from individual to individual which can also confound the study. So supplement beyond levels needed to maintain bone health (>30 ng/ml) is my take home advise.

VITAMIN C AND YOUR HEART: Although the data on the role of Vitamin C in prevention of colds is not clear cut, it shines in improving endothelial function (cells that line the blood vessels) in patients with diabetes, heart failure, atherosclerotic heart disease and hypertension. This data was obtained from a meta-analysis (a process by which multiple studies are fed through a statistical grinder and the results reviewed) of 9685 studies.

2/3 of the studies showed improvement in endothelial function and 1/3 did not. Also it was seen that low dose Vitamin C did not lead to improved function and results were best seen at higher doses of 4000 mg daily. The mechanism of action was its action as an anti-oxidant and free radicals scavenger, as an enzyme cofactor and also as a vasodilator in maintaining nitrous oxide levels. It should be noted that it did not improve endothelial function in patients who were healthy or had isolated hypertension. Improving endothelial function is now the Holy Grail in cardiovascular medicine as the atherosclerotic process (think heart attack and stroke) starts at that level!

THAT JUICY STEAK AND CANCER: This connection with red meat and especially processed meats, has been all over the news recently. So before you order that ham for Xmas, you may want to switch to turkey as the main course of your celebratory meal. Red meat is defined as beef, veal, pork, lamb, and mutton,

A recent report in Lancet Onco in a study spanning 20 years and many countries and a review of 800 studies showed that for example, eating three pieces of bacon daily over a period of time would increase the risk of colorectal cancer by 18%. This risk also extends to pancreatic cancer and prostate cancer. My advice is to eat grass fed red meat products no more than 1-2/week if you think you can't absolutely do without it. Better to switch to poultry and fish!

December 24

ITS CHRISTMAS EVE

"As you prepare to celebrate Christmas, remind yourself that Life itself is a Celebration. Make each day a celebration!"

—Anon

It's that time of the year. One of my favorite holidays! In a broader sense it is a celebration for surviving the travails and trials of the year. Now we can take a deep breath and actually look forward to the incessant holiday themed music for the next few weeks before the end of this year and as the New Year begins with all its challenges. I am actually listening to Mannheim Steamroller's "Christmas Collection" album.

This year I decided to splurge a little and actually got on line and purchased a fake Xmas tree. I figured that if it lasts ten years, I would have saved ten real trees from the garbage heap. And then there is the risk for fire with real trees if not watered adequately. Anyway it is a facsimile of a Douglas fir and from a distance it is very convincing. I splurged some more and got jewel like Xmas ornaments (Made in China) and festooned with a silver ribbon from Michael's and a lighted star as a tree topper. I flood lit the whole tree from a distance. Anyway I am real proud of it. It's never too late to have a Happy Christmas or a Happy Childhood.

It was not always like that. Every Xmas when I was a child growing up India, I was painfully reminded of the fact that I was the only kid at the party who did not have a father. My parent were divorced when I was six months old; a distinct rarity in India of the early 50's. I would have given anything to be a part of a loving family with Mom and Dad and various members of an extended family gathered around the dining table partaking in some exotic holiday dish. Maybe this was a fantasy of perfection that we create in our minds to make up for what we feel we are lacking in our lives.

My absentee father would mail an occasional toy for Xmas. Once I remember getting a toy train. At six years of age, the engine was large enough that I could sit on it. Like most toys of that nature, it quickly fell apart and the wheels fell off. The poem that follows is about that Xmas and is part accusation and part forgiveness. In my mid-forties, I wrote him a letter forgiving him for how he had treated me and my mother. I never did get a response. It is a very personal poem and I have saved it towards the end as I feel by now that we are old friends and that we can trust each other to hold it sacred.

I am sure that at some time of your life, or even in present time that these Holy days have brought back sad and sometimes painful memories of loved ones who are not there anymore, or of those who failed to love you, or those who you failed to love in return. This is the time to honor your losses and petty grievances and let go. In forgiving them, I am sure that you will find your own peace of mind and maybe even grace!

DR. M. P. KHAN, MD/NMD

December 25

ITS CHRISTMAS DAY

"The 3 stages of man:
He believes in Santa Claus.
He doesn't believe in Santa Claus.
He is Santa Claus."

—**Rick Sutter**

TOY TRAINS IN SEPIA:

(I)
On a cold Wednesday morning in January,
A garbage truck frosted with winter salt,
Engine grumbling, barely paused near my mail box.
Its hydraulics devoured those boxes with a final crunch.
Shrouded wraith like in its exhaust, shifted gears,
Turned the corner and disappeared.

Three square boxes, their corners now frayed,
Held together by pieces of tape and string,
The Hindi script describing it original contents,
Illegible and faded with the passage of time,
Still held the aroma of spice and summer mangoes.

Boxes that now contained;
A yellow smoke stack and toy locomotive parts,
Assorted "O" gauge carriages, red with green stripes; wheels missing,
Various sundry sections of curved and straight tracks.
Junk bound for a landfill, detritus of a typical childhood or
Damning evidence of a crime, a trial, maybe a conviction in absentia! (Continued)

(II)

I used to call him Dad, the hero Flight Engineer; Air India.
In those dreams, together, we could ride the clouds at 35 thousand feet.
A 747 to exotic Singapore, fourteen hours overnight to Australia.
Now he's only Phil, with a hair dresser wife living in a Bombay suburb.
Phil, who, every few years interjected my existence with hope,
The prodigal father bearing gifts of empty promises and model trains.

First, just simple wooden ones with spindly wheels,
Then of enamel and tin driven by clockwork and springs,
And much later an Electric Lionel with whistles and fake steam
That whizzed by on complicated arrangements of tracks.

Trains that I deliberately dismantled into their elements,
Carefully stored them in square boxes believing,
Someday he would fix them.
That's what Dads do,
Real ones anyway!

(III)

I wrote him a letter at age 48 forgiving him (and maybe myself).
Much later, that cold January morning, I put those boxes out for the trash man.
Over the years I have tried to color my memories of Phil and those toy trains,
And never did understand, why they kept bleeding into sepia.

MK 3/2008

DR. M. P. KHAN, MD/NMD

December 26

ONE MORE CUP OF COFFEE, PLEASE.

*"It is inhumane, in my opinion to force people who have
a genuine medical need for coffee to wait in line behind
people who apparently view it as some kind of recreational
activity."*

—**Dave Barry**

One of Karen's goals is to be self-sufficient in trying to grow all our food. We have even looked into a Bio-shelter which uses passive solar heating to extend the growing season. There is one problem with that concept. There is no way we can grow the Coffea plant which yields coffee beans which are actually seeds of the berries of this plant. I cannot imagine starting my day without a brewed cup or two of coffee! Well fellow coffee aficionados, fret no more. There is good (data driven) news on the horizon. So here's a cuppa of Joe to you.

Interestingly, coffee was first used by the Sufis in the 15th century in shrines located in present day Yemen in Arabia. Hence the Arabica bean. Coffee is the second most consumed beverage on the planet after water and until recently there was conflicting advice as to the health benefits of coffee. Recent research has suggested potential health benefits in certain cancers, neuro-degenerative diseases and even diabetes. But it is still not clear as to which active ingredient in coffee (besides caffeine which is a stimulant, there is some speculation as to the effect of some compounds found in coffee) has the positive health effects as outlined below. So here is the good news.

1) All-cause mortality: A Meta-analysis of 23 studies showed that 4 cups (8 oz.) of regular coffee a day, showed the largest risk reduction of all-cause mortality as compared to a cohort of non-drinkers. What is not clear is if this effect would persist with decaf also. This was replicated in the Nurses' Health Study.

2) Cardiovascular Disease/Stroke: 3-4 cups of coffee is associated with a significantly lower risk of coronary artery disease, heart failure and stroke. This is probably due to Chlorgenic acid which is a major compound found in coffee and is anti-thrombotic and improves endothelial function.

3) Cancers: Reduced risk of almost all cancers but slightly increased risk of gastric cancer and a neutral effect on breast cancer. Chlorgenic acid is anti-carcinogenic but also could be anti-oxidant effect of Melanodin which is a flavonoid and is also anti-carcinogenic.

4) Neurodegenerative diseases: Reduced risk of Parkinson's and Alzheimer's disease. One mechanism is caffeine which can consolidate memory pathways and is a neuro-stimulant.

5) Fracture risk: Increased risk for women > 2/day especially with a diagnosis of osteoporosis. Reduced risk for men up to 8/cups a day.

6) Diabetes Type II: Reduced risk of onset of Type II DM because of Trigonelline which is hypoglycemic.

So do you need any more excuses to have a meaningful relationship with your favorite barista?

ENTERING THE LUMINOSITY

"Better to die one time than to die a thousand times.
(Suffering)"

—Yogananda

We are now nearing the end of our journey together. We have walked together on many paths. On some of these paths you may have enjoyed the view and some of the journey may not have appealed to you. But is that not a metaphor for life? The ups and downs are necessary. And sometimes the doorway that we wish to avoid is the one that we should actually open!

I am well aware that a book of this nature has never been attempted before. That this whole endeavor could be an exercise in futility, destined to fall flat on its face. After all I have made the presumption that by following the daily small bites of wisdom, knowledge and poetry that it will make you, the reader, a better human being. I hope in some small way I may have succeeded in this task; no not a task really but an expression of hope; for myself and for you too.

After all, we are works in progress. The great Yogi and spiritual teacher 'Yogananda' (check out his book "Autobiography of a Yogi" and the movie "Awake" now available on most streaming services like Netflix) stated in above book that human beings basically crave three things.

One: They would all like to be wealthy and prosperous so they can buy material things to make their life more comfortable. If done ethically, there is no problem with that endeavor. But money can come and go as unpredictably as the winds that blow over the ocean.

Two: We all want good health. What is the use of all the money in the bank if we are in poor health and the ravages of disease make it difficult to enjoy the wealth we possess? On the other hand we may not be wealthy but how much sweeter life is when we are in a state of good health and well-being? But this too is transient. The physical body follows the laws of entropy and as the expression goes "None of us are going to come out of this alive." At some point we will all feel the cold hand of age and illness upon us.

Three: As we grow older and hopefully wiser, we will realize that more important than wealth and good health is peace of mind. To be at peace with oneself is to be at peace with the world. But to attain this peace we will have to work at it. Unlike wealth, which can be given to us or attained by our efforts in the material world, there is no way to buy peace of mind. Yes, having a large bank account may give us a sense of comfort, but it will fluctuate with balance in the account. The same can be said of health as illness is inevitable! To be in an inner state of bliss at all times, no matter what life throws at us, is really the challenge of our times and the purpose of this day book.

"Luminosity" is the final three part poem that concludes this book. It is also a prayer and a blessing and an invitation to let the light in. It started as a word worm, I could not get this word "Luminosity" (like a tune that keeps playing) out of my head. I even wrote one version that started out as an Expresso bar and God was the Barista and served double Lattes (coffee again) if that was your destiny! Fortunately, I eventually scrapped that idea for a more spiritual one.

December 28

ENTERING THE LUMINOSITY

This poem was inspired by the view of the back yard from my home office window and is titled 'Luminosity'. It is actually a collection of four smaller poems. We were living in Monroeville at that time. Karen had created this garden complete with a gate leading up to a gate flanked by large urns. The central path led through an arbor to formally arranged beds planted with roses and assorted other flowering plants; a kind of a mini-Versailles. A small meadow at the lower end of the garden was topped off with a garden bench. Luminosity is a Meta physical record of a journey thought this garden. Welcome!

THE GARDEN GATE:

If you have traveled on this path of tears,
This is journey's end and
Your callused feet will lead you to the Garden Gate.
Come walk with me into this mystical place.
A few more steps, my friend.
It is your presence the Gardener awaits!
Enter the Luminosity.

What is your interpretation of this invitation? Is it death or birth? Does it cause you any apprehension?

_____

_____

_____

_____

_____

_____

December 29

ENTERING THE LUMINOSITY

The "Arbor" reflects the belief of our own perfection. A perfection that we have forgotten. We are truly born, winged angels, innocent in Eden. But we are unaware of this. Life, in this corporeal world rips off our wings, feather by feather and then, caught up in our pain and angst we have no memory of our divine connection and our true self.

THE ARBOR

In this arbor,
Look with the blessed eyes of childhood.
Gaze upwards, myriad hues of flowers consume vision itself,
Yet no sweet fragrances of the lilac or lavender emanates!
They are muted by your presence,
Awed by splendor they cannot match.

You, after all, were the Gardener's only blossom.

What is your interpretation of these lines? What do the words 'only blossom' mean to you?

What is the most blessed moment you remember of your childhood?

_____

_____

_____

_____

_____

DR. M. P. KHAN, MD/NMD

ENTERING THE LUMINOSITY

In the 'Meadow" we have the first glimmer of understanding the connection we have with all sentient beings, and this connection, as quantum physics tells us, is very real and is called 'entanglement.' We were never alone and the thread of life weaves its woof and warp through all beings into an amazing tapestry. To truly believe this is to be in grace, to synch with the rhythm of life, to flow and yet to be motionless in the river of the Universe. We must also honor the female energy as well as the male energy as we celebrate the dance of life.

THE MEADOW:

Travel on, barefoot across the meadow,
We may find the Gardener there.
As dusk descends, tread softly on the damp clover.
Feel the ground tremble with forgotten rhythms of the earth-mother.
Abandon yourself to her heartbeat, remember the womb.
We will celebrate her gifts by the neon flicker of fire-flies
And dance to the monotone songs of Cicadas.
Listen!
She asks surrender of your illusions of wisdom and fear.
And in return, she beckon the stars to kiss you.
The moon swells in the heavens to embrace you.

Was this not the grace you were always seeking?

Are you in touch with your opposite (male or female) energy? Are you comfortable with it?
Can you put aside your inhibitions and dance? How will you find grace?

_____
_____
_____
_____
_____
_____

ENTERING THE LUMINOSITY

The 'Garden Bench' is our final destination. We have awakened to our true nature, we have come home to our very being. Rejoice in the knowledge of a final awakening from the sleep of our false self. We were always 'Wingless Angels' and having found our wings, can once again fly to Eden. This is what our journey together was all about!

THE GARDEN BENCH

Sit for a while; life's sorrows may have wearied you.
But that journey is over, this one just beginning.
Fear not the shroud of silence, hear the music within.
It is the unwritten symphony that always slept in your soul;
The harmonics of Om, the Ten Thousand becoming One.
And as you awaken from this dream of existence,
Realize, in this Paradise you were already an angel!
My friend, you were the Garden and the Gardener.

Enter the Luminosity

MK/2010

What are your thoughts about our journey of transformation that lasted 366 days? Hope you had a great and productive time navigating this book which is more than a book to me. Maybe a friend. Maybe a finger pointing to the moon. What does the last line 'You were the Garden and the Gardener' mean to you?

_____
_____
_____
_____
_____
_____

DR. M. P. KHAN, MD/NMD

About the Author

MANDALA-365 is a daily workbook of self-transformation blending poetry, parables and practical suggestions for holistic healing. Its author, Mehernosh Khan MD/NMD, has distilled over three decades of an integrated-medicine practice; as a conventional physician, and also as a practitioner with a doctorate in naturopathic medicine. He lives and writes poetry in the Bliss-shires (actually the Berkshires, MA) with his artist/poet wife and two cats.

Printed in the United States
By Bookmasters